# THE TRANSFORMATION OF EUROPEAN PRIVATE LAW

This book emanates from a duo-colloquium which explored the Europeanisation of private law in the context of efforts to consolidate the consumer *acquis*, the Draft Common Frame of Reference, the appointment of an Expert Group on a Common Frame of Reference in the area of European contract law, the passage of the Consumer Rights Directive and the proposed Common European Sales Law. This book, with fully updated contributions, critically reflects on whether the process of Europeanisation, which has shaped private law in the EU Member States, has now reached a significant turning point in its development, a point of *punctuated equilibrium*. Written by a team of leading authors, the topics covered will be of concern in all European legal systems and beyond.

JAMES DEVENNEY is Professor of Commercial Law in the School of Law, University of Exeter.

MEL B. KENNY is Professor of Commercial Law at Leicester De Montfort Law School.

# THE TRANSFORMATION OF EUROPEAN PRIVATE LAW

## Harmonisation, Consolidation, Codification or Chaos?

Edited by
JAMES DEVENNEY
and
MEL B. KENNY

CAMBRIDGE
UNIVERSITY PRESS

**CAMBRIDGE**
**UNIVERSITY PRESS**

University Printing House, Cambridge CB2 8BS, United Kingdom

Published in the United States of America by Cambridge University Press, New York

Cambridge University Press is part of the University of Cambridge.

It furthers the University's mission by disseminating knowledge in the pursuit of education, learning and research at the highest international levels of excellence.

www.cambridge.org
Information on this title: www.cambridge.org/9781107038806



First published 2013

Printed in the United Kingdom by CPI Group Ltd, Croydon CR0 4YY

*A catalogue record for this publication is available from the British Library*

*Library of Congress Cataloguing in Publication data*
The transformation of European private law: harmonisation, consolidation, codification or chaos? / Edited by James Devenney and Mel B. Kenny.
pages cm
Includes index.
ISBN 978-1-107-03880-6 (Hardback)
1. Civil law–European Union countries. I. Devenney, James. II. Kenny, Mel B.
KJE995.T73 2013
346.4–dc23
2013011079

ISBN 978-1-107-03880-6 Hardback

CONTENTS

# FOREWORD

*The Queen of Hearts*
*She made some tarts,*
*All on a summer's day;*
*The Knave of Hearts*
*He stole those tarts,*
*And took them clean away.*
*The King of Hearts*
*Called for the tarts,*
*And beat the knave full sore;*
*The Knave of Hearts*
*Brought back the tarts,*
*And vowed he'd steal no more.*

(Lewis Caroll, *Alice in Wonderland*)

For the outside observer, European private law seems to be a conundrum of rather strange artefacts: PECL (Principles of European Contract Law), PEICL (Principles of European Insurance Law), PETL (Principles of European Tort Law), DCFR (Draft Common Frame of Reference), DCR (Directive on Consumer Rights), CESL (Common European Sales Law), maybe even ECC (European Civil Code) . . . The authors of this volume, coming from different European jurisdictions, try to put some clarity and order into this near-to Babylonian confusion while at the same time taking a closer, yet critical, look at several important yet rather controversial issues of the ongoing (truly) cross-border debate. These concern sources, subject matters, underlying rationalities and objectives, efficiency questions, relationships to different national and even non-European private laws, remedies and enforcement, and effects on legal education and training. Will European private law remain an 'irritant' in legal discourse, or allow legal innovations? This is the underlying question of all contributions even if they may come to different answers. In their conclusion, the editors give an overview of the rather complex testimonies collected in this volume of essays.

All contributions demonstrate that the 'Europeanisation' of national private laws is running at full speed, but also that a great number of intellectual 'blindspots' have arisen. So far, mostly contract law has been the object (some say the victim) of this movement, but there will and should be (or not?) spill-over effects to neighbouring areas like tort law, personal securities, even property regimes – one may not know where this 'incoming tide' is going to stop. Readers of this volume, which is the result of a conference organised by the editors, will probably not find simple answers but rich 'food for thought' for reaching their own conclusions on the central issues, paradigms and potential results of this truly European debate. Where is now the 'King of Hearts' calling back the national 'tarts' stolen by the (EU) 'Knave of Hearts', or will the 'Queen of Hearts' make truly 'European tarts' in the future?

*Professor Dr Dr hc Norbert Reich*

# ABBREVIATIONS

| | |
|---|---|
| ADR | alternative dispute resolution |
| B2B | business to business |
| B2C | business to consumer |
| C2C | consumer to consumer |
| CCCat | Catalan Consumer Code |
| CESL | Common European Sales Law |
| CISG | UN Convention on Contracts for the International Sale of Goods |
| CJEU | Court of Justice of the European Union |
| DCFR | Draft Common Frame of Reference |
| DCR | Directive on Consumer Rights |
| GPCCA | General Part of the Civil Code Act (Estonia) |
| IMD | Insurance Mediation Directive 2002/92/EC |
| ISD | Investment Services Directive 93/22/EC |
| LMADP | Law 15/2009 on Mediation in Private Law (Spain) |
| LOA | Law of Obligations (Estonia) |
| MiFiD | Markets in Financial Instruments Directive 2004/39/EC |
| PECL | Principles of European Contract Law |
| PEICL | Principles of European Insurance Contract Law |
| SGECC | Study Group on the European Civil Code |
| SME | small or medium-sized enterprise |
| TFEU | Treaty on the Functioning of the European Union |
| TRLGDCU | Royal Legislative Decree 1/2007 adopting the General Act for Protection of Consumers and Users (Spain) |
| UTCCR | Unfair Terms in Consumer Contracts Regulations 1999 (UK) |

# Introduction

JAMES DEVENNEY AND MEL B. KENNY

> I have come to the conclusion that as regards contract law, we need a new approach ... that on the one hand helps bring about the single market ... while on the other hand respects Europe's legal diversity and the principle of subsidiarity.[1]

This book emerges from a duo-colloquium – 'The Europeanisation of Private Law: Theory and Practice' – hosted by the Research Group on Credit, Debt and Consumer Protection at Leicester University, in association with the Institute of Commercial and Corporate Law at Durham University, in December 2010. That conference explored the Europeanisation of private law against the backdrop of a changing Europe and in the context of the (then) proposed Consumer Rights Directive, efforts to consolidate the consumer acquis,[2] the draft Common Frame of Reference,[3] the Commission's appointment of an Expert Group on a Common Frame of Reference in the area of European contract law,[4] and the Commission Green Paper on *Policy Options for Progress towards a European Contract Law for Consumers and Businesses*.[5] The issues explored by that conference are even more relevant today given, for example, the passage of the Consumer Rights Directive, the proposal for an optional Common European Sales Law and renewed debate on a European Civil Code. However, much work is yet to be done, as is highlighted by the early response of the Council of the European Union

[1] Commissioner Viviane Reding, *The Next Steps Towards a European Contract Law for Businesses and Consumers* (Leuven, 3 June 2011).

[2] On which see e.g., B. Heiderhoff and M. Kenny, 'The Commission's 2007 Green Paper on the Consumer Acquis: Deliberate Deliberation?' (2007) 32 *European Law Review* 740.

[3] C. von Bar and E. Clive, *Principles, Definitions and Model Rules of European Private Law: Draft Common Frame of Reference (DCFR)* (Oxford University Press, 2010).

[4] Commission Decision 2010/233/EU [2010] OJ L105/109.

[5] European Commission, *Green Paper from the Commission on Policy Options for Progress towards a European Contract Law for Consumers and Businesses*, COM(2010)348 final.

on Justice and Home Affairs to the proposal for an optional Common European Sales Law:[6]

> among the aspects of the proposal that require thorough discussion are the personal, material and territorial scope of the proposal, the complexity of linking the proposal with the different national legal systems, the details and consequences of choice of the instrument, the consequences of an invalid choice, the consumer protection rules relating to the choice and the reporting obligations of member states, including the envisaged online database of judgments.

Indeed, we may now be at a watershed moment in the Europeanisation of private law and this book, with fully updated contributions, critically reflects on whether the process of Europeanisation, which has shaped private law in the EU Member States, has now reached a critical turning point in its development, a point of *punctuated equilibrium*, with significant policy implications for EU law, national laws and the principle of subsidiarity.

The conference was the third in a series of events emanating from a project which was launched in 2008 with the generous support of Marie Curie research funds through the European Commission within the Seventh Framework Programme (FP7);[7] and we are indebted to Pascale Dupont, Chantal Huts and Laurent Correia, our former FP7 project officers. We are also grateful at an institutional and material level to the Institute of Corporate and Commercial Law at Durham and to the School of Law at the University of Leicester.

We are indebted to all those who submitted proposals, held papers, chaired sessions and made contributions to the conference and to this volume. In particular we are grateful to Mona Ahadi (Durham University), Prof. Tom Allen (Durham University), Prof. Cristina Amato (University of Brescia), Dr Jane Ball (Sheffield University), Prof. Hugh Beale (Warwick University), Prof. Immaculada Barral Viñals (Barcelona University), Prof. David Campbell (Leeds University), Prof. Olha O. Cherednychenko (Groningen University), Dr Jim Davies (Northampton University), Karen Fairweather (Queensland University), Dr Marine Friant-Perrot (Nantes University), Dr Amandine Garde (Liverpool University), Prof. Paula Giliker (University of Bristol), Dr Lorna Gillies (Leicester University), Ana Sofia Gomes (Lisbon), Mateusz Grochowski (Warsaw), Prof. Roger Halson (Leeds University), Prof. Axel Halfmeier (Leuphana University),

[6] PR CO 79. [7] Marie Curie Credit and Debt Project: FP7 ERG 223605.

Prof. Steve Hedley (UCC), Kieran Hosty (ICCL, Durham), Prof. Geraint Howells (Manchester University), Dr Monika Jagielska (Katowice University), Howard Johnson (Cardiff University), Sander Kärson (University of Tartu), Dr Cliona Kelly (Cardiff University), Ian Kilbey (De Montfort University), Prof. Irene Kull (Tartu University), Dr Dorota Leczykiewicz (Oxford University), Prof. Gerard McCormack (University of Leeds), Martin Morgan-Taylor (De Montfort University), Dr Adelaide Menezes Leitão (Lisbon), Ewa Marcisz (Warsaw), Dr Lucinda Miller (University College London), Zoe Ollerenshaw (Sheffield University), Dr Chiara Perfumi (University of Brescia), Prof. Norbert Reich (Bremen/Hamburg), Dr Séverine Saintier (Sheffield University), Dr Michael Schillig (Kings College London), Anna Natalia Schulz (Poznan), Prof. Peter Sparkes (Southampton University), Dr Warren Swain (Queensland University), Prof. Erika Szyszczak (Leicester University), Dr Sean Thomas (Leicester University), Dr Piotr Tereszkiewicz (Heidelberg University), Prof. Stefan Vogenauer (Oxford University), Prof. Stephen Waddams (Toronto University), Aneta Wiewiórowska (Ministry of Justice, Warsaw), Prof. Chris Willet (Essex University), Dr Paul Wragg (Leeds University) and Dr Qi Zhou (Leeds University).

As any conference and any project depends on the cooperation and dedication of many otherwise unsung members of the support staff, we would like to take the opportunity to thank the events staff at Leicester Law School for their patience and help. Crucial support has also been given by the highly dedicated staff at Cambridge University Press; in particular, we would like to thank Kim Hughes, Richard Woodham, Jonathan Ratcliffe, Samantha Richter, Helen Francis and Finola O'Sullivan for their ongoing support and efficient management of the production process. Editorial assistance to the project was enthusiastically delivered by Claire Devenney and Elizabeth Davison.

Since the organisation of this conference and the publication of this collection, we have both moved to new pastures: Mel to a Chair in Consumer and Commercial Law at De Montfort University; and James to a Chair in Commercial Law at the University of Exeter. Information on the ongoing work and forthcoming events under the project can be obtained from the editors.

This collection is dedicated to our parents.

1

# The Draft Common Frame of Reference in relation to English contract law

STEPHEN WADDAMS

## Introduction

On many points of contract law the Draft Common Frame of Reference (DCFR) invites comparison between English law and the legal systems based on Roman law. Such comparisons are by no means new. Comparison between the systems was familiar in the seventeenth century, as appears from the Preface, attributed to Sir Matthew Hale, to Rolle's *Abridgment* (1668).[1] Hale defended English law against other systems on the ground of the greater precision of the former:

> The Common-laws of *England* are more particular than other laws, and this, though it render them more numerous, less methodical, and takes up longer time for their study, yet it recompenseth with greater advantages, namely, it prevents arbitrariness in the Judge, and makes the law more certain ... It hath therefore always been the wisdome and happiness of the *English* Government, not to rest in Generals, but to prevent arbitrariness and uncertainty by particular Laws, fitted almost to all particular occasions.[2]

Critics of English law, Hale continued, objected to its lack of ordered classification, saying:

> that it wants *method*, order, and apt *distributions*, and this hath bred some prejudice against it, not only in men much addicted to subtil learning, but

Professor and Goodman/Schipper Chair, University of Toronto, Faculty of Law.

[1] Preface to Henry Rolle, Abridgement des plusieurs cases et resolutions del commmon ley, 2 vols. (1668), reprinted in [Francis Hargrave] *Collectanea Juridica, consisting of tracts relative to the law and constitution of England* (London, 1791), p. 263 ('Lord Hale's Preface to Rolle's Abridgement'); Alan Cromartie, *Sir Matthew Hale, 1606–1676* (Cambridge University Press, 1995), p. 119.

[2] Hale's Preface, p. 3 (emphasis in original).

> also in the Professors of the Civil Law, who think that Law much more methodicall and orderly than the Common-law.[3]

After a discussion of methods of resolving moral questions, Hale remarked, in defence of English law, 'yet it were a vain thing to conclude it is irrational, because not to be demonstrated or deduced by Syllogismes'.[4] Hale's extended treatment of the question shows that he thought a defence of English legal methods to be necessary.

The search for 'method, order, and apt distributions' was closely linked with the concept of principle. Towards the end of the eighteenth century Sir William Jones wrote, in his *Essay on Bailments*, that 'if LAW be a *science* and really deserve so sublime a name, it must be founded on principle, and claim an exalted rank in the empire of *reason*'.[5] In the nineteenth century the search for the principles of contract law intensified. Charles Addison wrote in the Preface to his treatise on contracts (1847) that English contract law was founded 'upon the broad and general principles of universal law' and that 'the law of contracts may justly indeed be said to be a universal law adapted to all times and races, and all places and circumstances, being founded upon those great and fundamental principles of right and wrong deduced from natural reason which are immutable and eternal'. He went on to compare English writings on contract law, to their disadvantage, with 'the elaborate and elegant works of Pothier'.[6]

Pothier had been extravagantly praised by Jones in his *Essay*, and was, for a time, treated almost as an authority on English law. In 1822 it was said by Best J (later Chief Justice of the Common Pleas) that:

> [t]he authority of Pothier is . . . as high as can be had, next to the decision of a Court of Justice in this country. It is extremely well known that he is a writer of acknowledged character; his writings have been constantly referred to by the Courts, and he is spoken of with great praise by Sir William Jones in his

[3] *Ibid.* p. 6. In his posthumously published *Analysis of the Law* (London, 1713), Hale pursued an attempt 'to reduce the laws of *England* at least into a tolerable *Method* or *Distribution*', Hale's Preface, p. 2 (emphasis in original).

[4] Hale's Preface, p. 7.

[5] W. Jones, *An Essay on the Law of Bailments* (London, 1781), p. 123 (emphasis in original). Every coherent subject of intellectual enquiry was supposed to have principles. See W. Paley's very influential *The Principles of Moral and Political Philosophy* (1885), Lord Kames (H. Home), *Principles of Equity* (1760), and many titles of eighteenth-century books on scientific and religious subjects.

[6] C. Addison, *A treatise on the law of contracts and rights and liabilities ex contractu* (W. Benning, London, 1847), Preface, pp. iv–v, vii.

> *Law of Bailments* and his writings are considered by that author equal, in point of luminous method, apposite examples, and a clear manly style, to the works of Littleton on the laws of this country.[7]

Many of the English nineteenth-century writers, including Pollock and Anson, made reference to civilian writings, especially to Pothier (1699–1772) and to the German jurist, Savigny (1779–1861). But the invocation of the names of Pothier and Savigny does not establish that Pollock and Anson were actually influenced by what they had written. Pollock indeed rejected Pothier's opinion on a point of contract formation (revocation of offers not known by the offeree to have been revoked) and Pollock's opinion on this point was expressly adopted by the English court in two separate cases in 1880.[8]

Pollock gradually distanced himself from Savigny's views on intention. In Pollock's first edition he had, in his second paragraph, assimilated 'agreement' with '*vertrag* as used by Savigny, whose analysis . . . we follow almost literally in this paragraph', quoting Savigny in the original German because 'a perfectly literal translation is not practicable'.[9] This is quite surprising, considering that these were the introductory words of a treatise on English law, written by an English writer in English for English readers, and because a sufficient knowledge of German language and culture to appreciate the subtle and untranslatable meaning that Savigny gave to *vertrag*, and to another word in Savigny's definition, *Willenserklaerung*, could scarcely have been assumed among most of Pollock's readers. In his ninth edition (1921), by contrast, Pollock omitted this reference to Savigny, and, referring to American writings, gave prominent approval to 'the modern tendency to look to "the realization of reasonable expectations" as the ground of just claims rather than an artificial equation of wills or intentions'. The express rejection here of what Pollock now called 'an artificial equation of wills and intentions', and the preference for a theory of reasonable expectations, indicates a marked departure from the view expressed in the first edition, and evidences Pollock's later recognition that the concept of intention could not, on its own, supply a complete explanation of contractual obligation.

On the influence of civil law more generally, he had written in his fifth edition (1889), that 'for my own part I have found myself, as time goes on, rather less than more disposed to make Romanistic elements bear up

7 *Cox* v. *Troy* (1822) 5 B & A 474, 480–1.
8 *Byrne & Co.* v. *Van Tienhoven* (1880) 5 CPD 344; *Stevenson* v. *McLean* (1880) 5 QBD 346.
9 F. Pollock, *Principles of Contract* (Stevens, London, 1876), p. 1 and 2 (notes).

any substantial part of the structure of the common law'.[10] There is a sense of loss in this comment ('for my own part . . . found myself . . . as time goes on'), for the attraction of the civil law lay in its close connection with a search for order, elegance, and a 'scientific' approach to the study of English law, ideas that could not be abandoned without a struggle.

It has been suggested from time to time by various comentators writing from different perspectives that the distinctions between English and continental law have been more apparent than real on several points, including the question of subjective intention and mistake in contract formation, and the primacy of specific performance, and these suggestions gain some support from the Draft Common Frame of Reference.[11] On other questions, including relief for mistake as to relevant facts, and relief for unfairness, the provisions of the DCFR may actually be closer to English law, including equity, as it stood before the Judicature Acts than is modern English law. On these points, the DCFR is of interest not only to comparative lawyers, or to those seeking immediate action on harmonisation, but also to those seeking to understand, from a historical perspective, the concept of principle in English contract law.

## Meaning of 'principle'

'Principle' has often been contrasted with 'policy', but in English law the two concepts have interacted with each other, because a proposition has not generally been recognised as a principle unless it has been perceived as establishing a rule that is judged likely to lead to acceptable results in the future. Approaching the matter from the other side, a rule adopted for overt policy reasons has usually, after its acceptance as a rule of English law, been itself called a 'principle'.[12]

The DCFR also casts doubt on the workability of a sharp distinction between principle and policy. In a paragraph headed 'Meaning of "principles"' the authors wrote that:

[10] F. Pollock, *Principles of Contract* (5th edn, Stevens, London, 1889), p. 698. See N. Duxbury, *Frederick Pollock and the English Juristic Tradition* (Oxford University Press, 2004), p. 194.

[11] C. von Bar *et al.* (eds.), *Principles, Definitions and Model Rules of European Private Law: Draft Common Frame of Reference*, Full Edition (Sellier, Munich, 2009).

[12] See S. Waddams, *Principle and Policy in Contract Law: Competing or Complementary Concepts?* (Cambridge University Press, 2011).

> the word is susceptible to different interpretations. It is sometimes used, in the present context, as a synonym for rules which do not have the force of law ... Alternatively, the word 'principles' might be reserved for those rules which are of a more general nature, such as those on freedom of contract or good faith. However, in the following paragraphs we explore a third meaning ...[13]

The document then discussed 'fundamental principles', mentioning that, in an earlier interim document no fewer than fifteen items had been listed as fundamental principles, including justice, freedom, protection of human rights, economic welfare, solidarity and social responsibility, establishing an area of freedom, security and justice, promotion of the internal market (of the European Union), protection of consumers and others in need of protection, preservation of cultural and linguistic plurality, rationality, legal certainty, predictability, efficiency, protection of reasonable reliance, and the proper allocation of responsibility for the creation of risks.[14] Any of these 'fundamental principles' could well have been described as policies.

This miscellaneous collection of objectives evidently seemed too varied and multifarious to be a satisfactory list of 'fundamental principles', and in the later version the document identified 'underlying principles', which were reduced to four (freedom, security, justice and efficiency).[15] The drafters go on to say that 'it is characteristic of principles such as those discussed that they conflict with each other'.[16] They also point out that 'the principles overlap', adding that 'many of the rules which are designed to ensure genuine freedom of contract can also be explained in terms of contractual justice'.[17] The drafters further seek to distinguish between 'underlying' principles (the four just mentioned) and 'overriding' principles 'of a high political nature', adding that 'the two categories overlap'.[18] These observations are not offered by way of criticism: they illustrate the inherent difficulty of attaching a single or simple meaning to the concept of principle, and of distinguishing it from policy. Any of the many objectives identified by the Draft Common Frame of Reference as principles might well be called policies.

13 DCFR, Introduction, para. 10, vol. 1, pp. 4–5.

14 *Ibid.* Introduction, paras. 11–12, vol. 1, p. 5, referring to Interim Outline Edition (2008).

15 *Ibid.* vol. 1, p. 37; Outline Edition, p. 60. 16 *Ibid.*

17 *Ibid.* Outline Edition, p. 61; Full Edition, vol. 1, p. 38.

18 *Ibid.*, Introduction, para. 16, p. 14 (Outline Edition) and vol. 1, p. 8 (Full Edition).

## Subjective intention in contract formation

Most of the nineteenth-century English treatises identified agreement, or consent, as the basis of contract law, suggesting that contractual obligation depended on the actual intention of the promisor. The phrase 'consensus ad idem' was in frequent use, and the expression 'will theory' has been so commonly used of nineteenth-century English law as almost to attain the status of received wisdom. But on many points nineteenth-century English law plainly did not require actual consent for the creation of contractual obligation. The question of revocation of offers not known to the offeree to have been revoked, on which Pollock differed from Pothier, has been mentioned. Agency law imposed contractual obligations on a principal for contracts purportedly made by an agent, even though the agent might be flatly defying express private instructions. More generally, the conduct and words of a promisor were construed objectively, not according to the promisor's private intention. In 1871, Blackburn J said, in a passage that has been quoted and relied on throughout the common law world, directly and indirectly, perhaps more than any other single passage in contract law, 'If, whatever a man's real intention may be, he so conducts himself that a reasonable man would believe that he was assenting to the terms proposed by the other party, and that other party upon that belief enters into the contract with him, the man thus conducting himself would be equally bound as if he had intended to agree to the other party's terms.'[19]

The underlying basis of this line of thinking was not intention, or mutual agreement, but protection of the promisee's expectation – that is to say, reasonable expectation of what promise had been made. It followed that a promisor might be bound by the promisee's reasonable understanding of what promise had been made, even though contrary to the actual intention of the promisor. The corollary was that if the promisee actually knew of the promisor's real intention, the promisee would have no reasonable expectation of holding the promisor to a different meaning.[20] This conclusion rests not on any subjective theory of contract formation, but on the limits of a theory based on protection of reasonable expectations (i.e., expectations of what promise had been made are protected, but only insofar as really held).

It is sometimes suggested that civil law differs from the common law on the question of subjective intention in contract formation, but on this point the DCFR provides that 'the intention of a party to enter into a binding legal relationship or bring about some other legal effect is to be

[19] *Smith* v. *Hughes* (1871) LR 6 QB 597, 607. [20] *Ibid.* 610 (Hannen J).

determined from the party's statements or conduct as they were reasonably understood by the other party'.[21] In the comment the drafters say that 'this represents the law in many (probably the majority) of Member States',[22] with reference to the statement of Blackburn J from *Smith* v. *Hughes*, quoted above, as representing English law on the point.[23] The present writer is not in a position to assess the accuracy of the DCFR comment on the law in civilian jurisdictions. The words 'many (probably the majority)' indicate that there was, in the minds of the drafters, some uncertainty on the matter. Nevertheless, the fact that the comment was made is of significance to a common law observer, as showing (at the very least) that it would be a mistake to suppose, without qualification, that civilian jurisdictions have adhered uniformly to a principle of subjective intent.

## Specific performance

Comparing common law and civilian systems, Anthony Ogus wrote, in an essay published in 1989, that:

> the latter [civilian systems] view the specific enforcement of agreements as a primary remedy, while the former [common law systems] accord it only secondary status, regarding it as appropriate only where the monetary equivalent of performance is 'inadequate'. At the same time, there is evidence that in practice the systems converge to some extent, that the types of contract which are specifically enforced in both systems share common characteristics.[24]

This view, which has been suggested also, more or less explicitly, by many other writers, common law and civilian, is to a considerable degree supported by the Draft Common Frame of Reference, which proposes the following rule:

> III 3:302: Non-monetary obligations
>
> (1) The creditor is entitled to enforce specific performance of an obligation other than one to pay money . . .
>
> (3) Specific performance cannot, however, be enforced where:
>
> (a) performance would be unlawful or impossible;
> (b) performance would be unreasonably burdensome or expensive; or

[21] DCFR, art. II 4:102. [22] *Ibid.* Comment B, and vol. 1, pp. 274–6 Notes 1–11.
[23] *Ibid.* vol. 1, pp. 275–6, Note 5.
[24] Anthony Ogus, 'Remedies 1: English Report' in D. Harris and D. Tallon (eds.), *Contract Law Today: Anglo-French Comparisons* (Clarendon Press, Oxford, 1989), p. 243.

(c) performance would be of such a personal character that it would be unreasonable to enforce it.

(4) The creditor loses the right to enforce specific performance if performance is not requested within a reasonable time after the creditor has become, or could reasonably be expected to have become, aware of the non-performance.

(5) The creditor cannot recover damages for loss or a stipulated payment for non-performance to the extent that the creditor has increased the loss or the amount of the payment by insisting unreasonably on specific performance in circumstances where the creditor could have made a reasonable substitute transaction without significant effort or expense.

The conceptual starting point here is the civilian idea of a right to performance, but the open-ended nature of the exceptions is likely often to lead to results very similar to those reached in practice (though with an opposite conceptual starting point) by English law.

The comment to this article, having noted the opposite conceptual starting points, which might well be called opposite principles, adds that 'there is reason to believe, however, that results in practice are rather similar under both theories'.[25] That an apparent right to specific performance in civilian systems may be restrained by concepts such as good faith or abuse of rights is suggested by another comment headed 'Limitation on abuse of remedy',[26] referring to 'good faith and fair dealing', and to unreasonable insistence by a creditor on specific performance. Even where, as in civilian systems, a right to performance is taken as the conceptual starting point, there are many instances, as the exceptions included in the Draft Common Frame of Reference show, which cannot be precisely defined or enumerated, where specific performance would be inappropriate, unjust and oppressive, particularly where enforced, as in Anglo-American systems, by the Draconian sanctions for contempt of court. A powerful reason for reluctance in granting a decree of specific performance has been that, if the promisee were entitled to specific performance in a case where the burden on the promisor greatly exceeded the benefit to the promisee of actual performance, the promisee would be in a position to extract from the promisor a sum of money approaching the value to the promisor of release, and possibly greatly exceeding the value to the promisee of actual performance, in other words to obtain what might be a very large transfer of wealth.[27]

[25] DCFR, Comment B, vol. 1, p. 829. [26] *Ibid.* Comment J, vol. 1, pp. 833–4.

[27] Lord Hoffmann in *Co-operative Insurance Society Ltd* v. *Argyll Stores (Holdings) Ltd* [1998] AC 1 (HL), 15.

Whatever terminology is used, it is a fair summary of the practical effect of English law to say that where a contract imposes a burden on the promisor that is disproportionate to the legitimate interest of the promisee in actual performance, specific performance will not be granted, and the promisee will be restricted to a money remedy. Other legal systems that accept specific performance as a conceptually prior remedy may achieve a similar result in practice in many cases by use of concepts such as good faith or abuse of rights. The Draft Common Frame of Reference, seeking to harmonise English law with continental systems, provides that 'specific performance cannot ... be enforced where ... performance would be unreasonably burdensome or expensive'.[28] This language, if not identical with English law, is readily compatible with English ways of thinking. As with the question of subjective intention, discussed above, the present writer is not in a position to assess the law in civilian jurisdictions. The wording of the DCFR comment ('there is reason to believe ... that results in practice are rather similar under both theories') indicates an element of uncertainty on the point. Nevertheless, the comment is significant as tending to exclude a facile supposition that specific performance is available as of right, without qualification, in all civilian jurisdictions.

## Mistake

If contractual obligation depended on consent, it would seem to follow that a material mistake on any matter that induced the consent would prevent the formation of a contract. It was by application of this principle that Pothier asserted that 'error is the greatest defect that can occur in a contract, for agreements can only be formed by the consent of the parties, and there can be no consent when the parties are in an error respecting the object of their agreement'. He did not hesitate to spell out the far-reaching consequences of this line of thinking: 'error annuls the agreement, not only when it affects the identity of the subject, but also when it affects that quality of the subject which the parties have principally in contemplation, and which makes the substance of it', adding, as an illustration, 'therefore if, with the intention of buying from you a pair of silver candlesticks, I buy a pair which are only plated, though you have no intention of deceiving me, being in equal error yourself, the agreement

[28] DCFR, art. III 3:302(3)(b).

will be void, because my error destroys my consent; for my intention was to buy a pair of silver candlesticks'.[29] Even where there was reasonable reliance by one party on the apparent consent of the other, as in the case of an artist commissioned to paint a picture by a person privately mistaken as to the artist's identity, Pothier thought that the mistaken party could not be liable on contractual principles, though he might be liable on a non-contractual principle: 'in this case I am obliged not by the agreement, which was void, and therefore could not produce any obligation; the reason of my obligation is the principle of equity which obliges me to indemnify the person whom I have imprudently led into an error'.[30]

Despite Pothier's very high reputation, this line of thinking could not be assimilated by nineteenth-century English law. The idea that any material mistake destroyed consent and made the contract void would have seemed too wide, because almost every case of a disadvantageous contract might be analysed as having been caused by a mistake. Notably in cases of mistake of quality of goods sold, as in Pothier's candlestick example, the English law was that the contract was enforceable, a result that might be explained (or perhaps merely restated) by saying that, in the absence of warranty or misrepresentation, the buyer takes the risk of the error; this rule of English law was often summarised by an expression in the Latin language, though not, it seems, reflective of Roman law (caveat emptor). Moreover, the idea that reliance might be protected, as in Pothier's painter example, by a non-contractual principle having the same result as though there were a contract but depending on principles of equity could not be assimilated to English legal thinking. It would have seemed convoluted and artificial to deny that there was a contract and then to create an equivalent obligation derived from a non-contractual source. And no such source was available in nineteenth-century English law: no tort liability existed in such a case, and English equity could not have imposed such an obligation (to pay money as compensation for loss caused by imprudence) as Pothier contemplated.[31]

[29] R.J. Pothier, *A Treatise on the Law of Obligations or Contracts* (W. Evans (trans.), London 1806), p. 12, 1, 1, III, 17, 18.

[30] *Ibid.* 1, 1, III, 19 (Evans, p. 13).

[31] Pothier made a somewhat similar suggestion in respect of the problem mentioned earlier of the uncommunicated withdrawal of an offer, proposing that, although there could be no contractual liability, there would be an equivalent non-contractual liability, again based on equity (*équité*). See S. Waddams, 'What *were* the Principles of Nineteenth-century Contract Law?' in A. Lewis. P. Brand and P. Mitchell (eds.), *Law in the City:*

Nevertheless, English equity did have a very important role in respect of contractual mistake: the court had a wide power to rescind an agreement for mistake. The existence of such a power was not doubted before the Judicature Acts. Though the existence of the power was not doubted, its limits were ill-defined. The power of the court to rescind a contract was, like all equitable remedies, 'discretionary', and the discretion would not be exercised in the absence of what seemed to the court to be sufficient reason. Where the agreement fairly allocated the risk to the mistaken party, the court would not intervene. But a large and accidental enrichment did present a strong case for rescission.[32]

After the Judicature Acts it might have been expected that the new court, uniting as it did the powers of the courts of law and equity, with equity to prevail in case of conflict, would exercise the power of the former court of equity to rescind contracts for mistake. However, despite the Judicature Acts, there was a reluctance by English writers and judges to recognise the full breadth of the equitable power to rescind for mistake. The main reason for this reluctance was probably that the limits of the equitable power had not been clearly defined,[33] and so recognition of the power, without the ability to state clear limits, appeared to jeopardise the stability and certainty of contracts. Another reason was that it appeared unnecessary, and therefore undesirable, to separate the concept of relief for mistake from that of contract formation: it seemed an attractive simplification to apply a single principle (consent) to both, and thereby to eliminate altogether the need for discussion of the old equitable jurisdiction. But looking at the question in terms of contract formation was wholly alien to the methods of thought of the old equity cases. Equity intervened in order to prevent an unconscionable result, but not because the contract was void. On the contrary, the contract was assumed to be valid at law, and this was precisely why the intervention of equity was both justified and required. The effect of merging the equitable and legal jurisdictions was, ironically, to suppress the former equitable powers to grant relief.

The collapse of the distinction between law and equity had other consequences. The concept of a contract that is not necessarily void, but that may be set aside by the judgment of the court for sufficient

*Proceedings of the Seventeenth British Legal History Conference, London, 2005* (Four Courts Press, Dublin, 2007), pp. 305, 307–8.

[32] See Waddams, *Principle and Policy in Contract Law*, n. 12 above, at pp. 123–47.

[33] See C. MacMillan, *Mistakes in Contract Law* (Hart, Oxford, 2010), p. 49.

reason (i.e., one that is voidable), admits the possibility of enforcement by the mistaken party if that party so chooses. It admits also the possibility of partial relief, or relief on terms, which the court can fashion in order to meet the justice of the particular case. And it admits the possibility of denying or restricting relief in order to protect third parties who may have relied on the validity of the contract. These important objects were familiar features of equity, but they tend to be lost if the only and decisive question is formulated in terms of whether the contract is 'void' for lack of consent. It is not necessary, and may well be undesirable in seeking to summarise the law applicable in the twenty-first century, to link these marks of flexibility with the history of equity. But for present purposes it should be noted that one of the hidden effects of the adoption of consent as the sole test of mistake in English law has had the effect of depriving the courts of important elements of flexibility that had existed in English law as it was (taking the two systems together) on the eve of the Judicature Acts. This loss of flexibility was not intended or authorised by the Judicature Acts and, partly because the former flexibility has not generally been recognised by modern courts or writers on English law, no serious justification of its removal has ever been developed.

George Palmer justly commented, 'in modern times English judges have sometimes remembered earlier English equity, but often it seems to be either forgotten or consciously discarded'.[34] In other jurisdictions a more flexible view has been preserved. The American *Second Restatement of Contracts* provides that 'a party bears the risk of mistake when . . . the risk is allocated to him by agreement of the parties . . . or . . . by the court on the ground that it is reasonable to do so'.[35] Canadian courts have accepted the survival of the equitable jurisdiction, with the consequence that the court may take account of such factors as the allocation of risk and the degree of enrichment.[36]

The Draft Common Frame of Reference provides for relief for fundamental mistake in certain circumstances unless the mistaken party had assumed the risk of the mistake.[37] The comment indicates that there is

[34] G. Palmer, *Mistake and Unjust Enrichment* (Ohio State University Press, Columbus, 1962), p. 14.

[35] American Law Institute, *Second Restatement of Contracts* (1972) s. 154.

[36] See *Miller Paving Ltd* v. *B. Gottardo Construction Ltd* (2007) 285 DLR (4th) 568 (Ont. CA), rejecting *Great Peace Shipping Ltd* v. *Tsavliris Salvage (International) Ltd (The Great Peace)* [2003] QB 679 (CA).

[37] DCFR, art. II 7:201(2)(b).

no uniformity among civil law systems, observing that 'there are substantial differences between the laws of the Member States in the way in which such cases are conceptualised and also in substantive outcomes'. The drafters add that the article 'does not purport to lay down rules which are "common principles" to be found in different laws, though it reflects what is found in many of them'.[38] Here, the drafters do not claim to detect even a semblance of uniformity among civilian systems, but they propose a rule that is very close to the old rule of English equity before the Judicature Acts, and much more flexible than the law as understood in the twentieth century.[39] Flexibility is maintained, and the link with unjust enrichment is emphasised, in the rules relating to benefits conferred under contracts set aside for mistake. Section II 7:212(2) provides that 'the question whether either party has a right to the return of whatever has been transferred or supplied under a contract which has been avoided under this Section, or a monetary equivalent, is regulated by the rules on unjustified enrichment'.

## Misrepresentation

One aspect of mistake that has given rise to immense difficulty in the common law is innocent misrepresentation. This must be considered as an aspect of mistake, because every case of a contract induced by misrepresentation is a case of mistake as to a material fact, with the added feature that the mistake has been induced (albeit innocently) by the words or conduct of the party seeking to enforce the contract. English equity permitted rescission for innocent misrepresentation, where rescission was practicable, even if the representor was entirely without fault, and even if the party seeking relief was careless in relying on the misrepresentation. Moreover, there was a presumption in favour of the party seeking relief that a material misrepresentation in fact induced the making of the contract. These features of equity were explained by Sir George Jessel MR in a case of 1881, and justified on the basis that it was inequitable for a person to seek to derive a profit from a statement that he *now* (i.e., at the time he stands before the court) admits to be false, even if he was free of fault when the statement was made originally.[40]

38 Ibid. Comment A, vol. 1, p. 457.

39 *Bell* v. *Lever Bros* [1932] AC 161 (HL); *Great Peace Shipping Ltd* v. *Tsavliris Salvage (International) Ltd (The Great Peace)*, n. 36 above.

40 *Redgrave* v. *Hurd* (1881) 20 Ch. D 1.

However, these advantages (from the point of view of the party seeking relief) were restricted by the fact that equity did not normally award money damages, and it was held that, at common law, damages were not available, even after the Judicature Acts, for innocent misrepresentation.[41] It may be accepted that an innocent misrepresentation does not in itself justify the imposition on the misrepresentor of any contractual or tortious obligation, and this is what was probably meant by the insistence, in the leading English case on the question, that the innocent misrepresentor was 'not liable in damages'.[42] But it does not follow from the absence of contractual or tortious liability that a monetary obligation is never appropriate. Where there is sufficient reason to rescind or set aside the contract in order to prevent unjust enrichment, but where it is impractical to forestall or reverse the transaction, it may be appropriate to require the party who has profited by the transaction to make a money payment in lieu of rescission in order to bring about an equivalent effect. Such a payment, probably not best described as 'damages', would not be measured by principles of compensation for breach of contract or for tort, but by the need to avoid or reverse an unjust enrichment.

The whole question of innocent misrepresentation, and its relation to money remedies, which has given so much trouble to the common law, is neatly resolved by the Draft Common Frame of Reference, which provides that 'a party may avoid a contract for mistake of fact or law existing when the contract was concluded if . . . the other party caused the mistake', and adds, in the provision already mentioned, that 'the question whether either party has a right to the return of whatever has been transferred or supplied under a contract which has been avoided under this section, or a monetary equivalent, is regulated by the rules on unjustified enrichment'.[43] Lord Moulton said, in very forceful language, that it was a principle that a person is not liable in damages for an innocent misrepresentation and, so important was this principle, that it was 'of the greatest importance' to maintain it 'in its full integrity' and 'no matter in what way or under what form the attack is made'.[44] But by looking at the matter from a different perspective, one principle is displaced by another. The relevant principle in the Draft Common Frame of Reference is neither that a misrepresention gives rise to an

[41] The law was modified by the Misprepresentation Act 1967, which, however, introduced its own complexities and anomalies.

[42] *Heilbut Symonds & Co.* v. *Buckleton* [1913] AC 30 (HL).

[43] DCFR, art. II 7: 212.

[44] *Heilbut Symonds*, n. 42 above, at p. 51.

obligation nor, on the other hand, that an innocent misrepresentor can never be required to pay money, but that *a person who causes a mistake should not profit from it.* The comment emphasises that the provision is not based on the concept of wrongdoing: 'even if the party giving the information reasonably believed it to be true, that party chose to give the information; and cannot complain if the recipient is allowed to avoid the contract provided that the resulting misapprehension was serious enough'.[45]

This comment is entirely consistent with the thinking of Jessel MR in the case just mentioned (*Redgrave* v. *Hurd*), and the allowance, in the DCFR, where appropriate, of a money award to give effect to the principle (i.e., the principle of preventing a person who has caused a mistake from profiting by it) is a step that English law might, with great advantage, have taken in 1875. The DCFR provision on this issue is indeed closer in spirit to English equity than is modern English law. The new court, in 1875, could well have asserted a power, in cases where actual rescission was impossible, to give a money remedy equivalent in effect to rescission. Unfortunately, the new court was too much concerned to minimise the equitable powers that it had inherited: while grudgingly accepting the power of rescission where actual rescission was possible, it adamantly refused to extend or supplement it with any sort of money award. Brett (Lord Esher), a judge with a common law background who succeeded Jessel as Master of the Rolls, was supposed to have said that 'Jessel MR had been sent to dragoon the Court of Appeal into substituting equity for Common Law, but that he [Esher] and his common law colleagues would not have it'.[46] Even though the actual occasion of this remark cannot be verified, the plausibility of the anecdote offers evidence of a spirit of rivalry between law and equity, and the equity bar had (unsuccessfully) resisted the Judicature Act in 1873 on the ground that common law judges would not be capable of understanding or applying equitable concepts.[47] Had the new court given any reasonably sympathetic attention to the reasons underlying the equitable power of rescission (i.e., avoidance of unjust enrichment) it would necessarily have concluded that it had ample power after 1875, in cases where actual rescission was impossible, to give a money remedy

[45] DCFR, Comment D, vol. 1, p. 459. *Redgrave* v. *Hurd* is mentioned in the DCFR at p. 464.

[46] A. Underhill, *Change and Decay* (Butterworth & Co, London, 1938), p. 87.

[47] *The Times*, 28 April 1873, 8f and 1 May 1873, 12d. See P. Polden, 'Mingling the Waters' (2002) 61 *CLJ* 575.

representing the economic equivalent of rescission – not common law damages for a contractual or tortious wrong, but an award calculated to prevent the maker of a false statement from profiting by it. It is little to the credit of English law that this opportunity was missed.

## Unfairness

Since the nineteenth century, writers on English contract law have emphasised the enforceability of contracts, and have tended to marginalise the instances in which contracts have been set aside for unfairness. The power of English courts to set aside contracts on grounds broadly relating to unfairness and inequality of exchange was, however, considerably wider than the extracts from the leading treatises suggest.[48] The court of equity commonly gave relief against forfeitures of all kinds, especially in relation to mortgages. Analogous relief was given against penal bonds, and later against penalty clauses generally. The English courts of equity relieved against transactions entered into by persons expecting to own property in the future. The typical case was of the 'expectant heir', and this phrase, together with the otherwise obsolete phrase 'catching bargain', is generally used to denote this branch of English law, but the jurisdiction was not restricted to heirs: it extended to every kind of case in which the borrower expected to become the owner of property in the future. Commonly, the substance of the transaction was a loan, but the transaction took the form of a sale of the expectancy or of the reversion. The court would set aside the transaction unless the purchaser proved that he had given full value.

Disadvantageous contractual transactions were set aside for 'undue influence'. This phrase covered a number of different circumstances. It might apply to an openly hostile relationship where one party threatens the other with adverse consequences if the agreement is not made. The courts of equity exercised a more general jurisdiction to set aside transactions that they regarded as very unfair. In 1888, summarising the cases, Kay J said:

> The result of the decisions is that where a purchase is made from a poor and ignorant man at a considerable undervalue, the vendor having no

[48] See S. Waddams, 'Protection of Weaker Parties in English Law' in M. Kenny, J. Devenney and L. Fox O'Mahony (eds.), *Unconscionability in European Private Financial Transactions: Protecting the Vulnerable* (Cambridge University Press, 2010), p. 26; Waddams, *Principle and Policy in Contract Law*, n. 12 above, at pp. 87–122.

> independent advice, a court of equity will set aside the transaction. This will be done even in the case of property in possession, and *a fortiori* if the interest be reversionary. The circumstances of poverty and ignorance of the vendor and absence of independent advice throw upon the purchaser, where the transaction is impeached, the onus of proving, in Lord Selborne's words, that the purchase was 'fair, just and reasonable'.[49]

There are several other techniques that have been used by English law to control potentially unfair contracts. One of these is the invalidation of disclaimer, or exemption clauses, a topic with a long and convoluted judicial and legislative history in the twentieth century. Another is the use of implied terms, which often have the effect of importing obligations of good faith, and of converting an apparently one-sided transaction into a more equal exchange. Another method is to find that insufficient consent has been given, in particular circumstances, to a burdensome contractual term. One twentieth-century judge said that 'we do not allow printed forms to be made a trap for the unwary'.[50]

The Draft Common Frame of Reference incorporates several of these concepts in its provision on unfair terms. An unfair term, which is 'not binding on the party who did not supply it', is defined differently according to whether the contracting parties are consumers or businesses. The definitions refer to 'transparency', 'significant disadvantage', 'good faith', 'fair dealing', and to whether terms are individually negotiated. A list is supplied of terms presumed to be unfair in consumer-business contracts.[51] The comments and notes to these articles show that this was a difficult and controversial question for the drafters.[52] Although no general duty of good faith has been adopted by English law, many of the concepts mentioned in the articles and comments are reflected also in English cases.

The DCFR also includes a general provision entitled 'unfair exploitation':

> II 7:207 Unfair exploitation
>
> (1) A party may avoid a contract if, at the time of the conclusion of the contract:
>
> (a) the party was dependent on or had a relationship of trust with the other party, was in economic distress or had urgent needs, was improvident, ignorant, inexperienced or lacking in bargaining skill; and

[49] *Fry* v. *Lane* (1888) 40 Ch. D 312, 322. Lord Selborne's words were from *Aylesford* v. *Morris* (1875) LR 8 Ch. App. 484, 491.

[50] *Neuchatel Asphalte Co. Ltd* v. *Barnett* [1957] 1 WLR 356, 360 (Denning LJ).

[51] DCFR, art. II 9:401–10.

[52] *Ibid.* vol. 1, pp. 628–67.

(b) the other party knew or could reasonably have been expected to have known this and, given the circumstances and purpose of the contract, exploited the first party's situation by taking an excessive benefit or grossly unfair advantage.

(2) Upon the request of the party entitled to avoidance, a court may, if it is appropriate, adapt the contract in order to bring it into accordance with what might have been agreed had the requirements of good faith and fair dealing been observed . . .

II 7:208 Third persons

(1) Where a person for whose acts a party is responsible or who with a party's assent is involved in the making of a contract:

(a) causes a mistake, or knows of or could reasonably be expected to know of a mistake; or
(b) is guilty of fraud, coercion, threats or unfair exploitation, remedies under this Section are available as if the behaviour or knowledge had been that of the party.

(2) Where a third person for whose acts a party is not responsible and who does not have the party's assent to be involved in the making of a contract is guilty of fraud, coercion, threats or unfair exploitation, remedies under this Section are available if the party knew or could reasonably be expected to have known of the relevant facts, or at the time of avoidance has not acted on the contract.

These provisions include many concepts familiar to English equity lawyers,[53] and suggest that it is no less important now than it was 250 years ago to avoid transactions that would 'ruin the distressed and unwary, and give unconscionable advantage to greedy and designing persons'.[54] The DCFR provisions are in many ways closer in spirit to eighteenth-century English equity than to the narrower and more formalistic view of contractual unfairness that prevailed in English law after the Judicature Acts and into the twentieth century.

## Conclusion

It will, no doubt, be a matter for debate among comparative lawyers to what extent the DCFR accurately represents the law of the various civilian jurisdictions mentioned there. Since the document deals with multiple jurisdictions, each with its own legal history, language and

[53] The English law on undue influence and unconscionability is referred to in Note 4.
[54] *Spurgeon* v. *Collier* (1758) 1 Eden 55, 59 (Sir R. Henley (Lord Northington)).

traditions, and since it extends to the whole of private law, it could hardly be expected that the law of every jurisdiction could be summarised in a single document in such a way as to command universal and unanimous approval. It will also be debatable to what extent the DCFR will be put to official or practical use, publicly or privately. But, whatever the outcome of these debates, the DCFR is, from the point of view of a reader interested in the history of English contract law, a valuable resource from several points of view. It is drafted in English, and therefore eliminates difficulties of translation and linguistic nuance that so often complicate legal comparisons. It discusses basic questions across multiple jurisdictions, indicating the different traditions among civilian jurisdictions, and comparing, as few studies do, all the civilian systems on each point both with each other and with English law. Moreover, it extends to the whole of contract law and beyond, so that it eliminates (or at least mitigates) another common difficulty of comparisons between legal systems, namely, the discussion by a writer of a particular question in isolation from other aspects of the same legal system that may affect the practical operation, within a particular system, of the writer's conclusions. Another valuable aspect of the DCFR is that it warns effectively against facile comparisons. Common law observers are sometimes tempted to draw over-generalised conclusions about the law in civilian systems, usually in support of arguments of their own as to how the common law should ideally develop, but these conclusions do not always withstand informed analysis of the actual operation in practice of various civilian systems.

2

# The Draft Common Frame of Reference and European contract law: moving from the 'academic' to the 'political'

PAULA GILIKER

The publication of the final version of the Draft Common Frame of Reference (DCFR)[1] in late 2009 marked the end of a major research project, funded by the European Commission,[2] to identify common principles, definitions and model rules of European contract law. In three major communications,[3] the Commission had considered the feasibility of an optional instrument of European contract law, in addition to improving the quality and coherence of the *acquis communautaire*, as a means of facilitating cross-border trade and increasing the protection of consumers contracting across national boundaries. The DCFR was swiftly followed by a major consultation exercise,[4] combined with expert revision of its contract law principles, resulting in the publication of a proposal for a Regulation on a Common European Sales Law (CESL)[5] in October 2011. The Commission stated its intention

Professor of Comparative Law, University of Bristol (UK).

[1] C. von Bar *et al.* (eds.), Principles, Definitions and Model Rules of European Private Law: Draft Common Frame of Reference, Full Edition (Sellier, Munich, 2009 and Oxford University Press, 2010).

[2] Funded as a 'Network of Excellence' under the European Commission's Sixth Framework Programme for Research and Technological Development, Priority 7 – FP6–2002-Citizens-3, Contract no. 513351.

[3] See Communication from the Commission on European Contract Law, COM(2001)398 final (11 July 2001); *A More Coherent European Contract Law: An Action Plan*, COM (2003)68 final; and *European Contract Law and the Revision of the Acquis: The Way Forward*, COM(2004)651 final.

[4] *Green Paper from the Commission on Policy Options for Progress towards a European Contract Law for Consumers and Businesses*, COM(2010)348 final (Brussels, 1 July 2010).

[5] Proposal for a Regulation of the European Parliament and of the Council on a Common European Sales Law, COM(2011)635 final (Brussels, 11 October 2011).

that the Regulation would be adopted in 2012, the twentieth anniversary year of the Single European Market.

This chapter will examine the process by which the academic proposal for a common frame of reference became a political proposal for a common European sales law and consider, in particular, whether adoption of the proposal for the CESL represents the victory or failure of the DCFR project. It will examine the reaction to the DCFR from both common and civil law Member States and critically assess the validity of these criticisms by means of a case study examining article 3:301 of Book II of the DCFR which establishes a duty to negotiate in accordance with good faith and fair dealing. This is chosen as a classic example of an area of law in which there is currently divergence at national level and where policy issues play a significant role, which any harmonising instrument must overcome. Finally, it will consider what future lies for the DCFR in the light of the Commission's current focus on the CESL, in what Vice-President of the Commission and EU Justice Commissioner, Viviane Reding, has described as the 'quantum leap towards a more European contract law'.[6]

## Draft Common Frame of Reference: an 'academic' proposal for legislative reform

The DCFR is an impressive document, consisting of ten books in six volumes with over 6,000 pages. It provides a highly structured, detailed and intricate framework for a new instrument of European private law, based on extensive comparative research by an international team of legal experts, and is undeniably a work of great scholarship to which over 150 scholars from various countries have contributed. It may clearly be said to represent the most comprehensive research project in this field. Even its critics have acknowledged that it is 'an immense achievement for the participating academic groups to have produced such a comprehensive body of rules in such a short time'.[7] A distinction is made, nevertheless, in the introduction to the DCFR between academic proposals for reform and the ultimate drafting of a political Common Frame of Reference (CFR): 'The "academic" frame of reference is not subject to

[6] Press Release IP/10/872, 'European Commission seeks contract law solutions to smooth Single Market for consumers and businesses' (1 July 2010).

[7] H. Eidenmüller *et al.*, 'The Common Frame of Reference for European Private Law: Policy Choices and Codification Problems' (2008) 28 *OJLS* 659, 706.

the constraints of the "political" frame of reference. While the DCFR is linked to the CFR, it is conceived as an independent text.'[8] From the very beginning, therefore, a line has been drawn between the work of European legal scholars, who expressly assert that the DCFR does not contain a single rule or definition or principle which has been approved or mandated by a politically legitimated body at European or national level,[9] and that of the Commission. The DCFR is not a mere facilitation of the Commission's strategy – it is a document to be discussed and debated. It would be naïve, however, not to identify an underlying ambition that the DCFR would provide a model for politicians to use: 'The DCFR presents a concrete text, hammered out in all its detail, to those who will be deciding questions relating to a CFR.'[10] The question therefore was how the Commission would use the DCFR and to what extent it would provide a draft for a future instrument of European contract law.

## Mixed reaction to the DCFR

The DCFR inevitably received both praise and criticism on its publication. In terms of its potential status as a model for a future instrument of European contract law, a number of reservations were expressed which will be examined below. Three main areas of criticism may be identified: scope (the DCFR covers the whole of private law, not simply contract law); drafting style (were the provisions sufficiently precise to be interpreted consistently across Member States?); and policy (to what extent do the provisions, for example, reflect the tensions between market individualism and consumer welfarism, inherent in any system of contract law?).[11]

### *Approaching private law 'as an organic entity or unit'*[12]

The decision of the DCFR to go beyond contract law (the remit set by the European Commission)[13] to cover most of private law including tort, unjustified enrichment, trusts and personal property, signified both a principled view that contract law could not be severed from other areas

[8] See DCFR, Introduction, para. 30. [9] See *ibid.* para. 5. [10] See *ibid.* para. 6.

[11] J. Adams and R. Brownsword, 'The Ideologies of Contract Law' (1987) 7 *LS* 205; T. Wilhelmsson, 'Varieties of Welfarism in European Contract Law' (2004) 10 *ELJ* 712.

[12] See DCFR, Introduction, para. 31.

[13] A fact acknowledged by the drafters in *ibid.* paras. 30–1.

of private law without difficulty, and an ambition to produce a model for a common European private law.[14] It is perhaps unsurprising that a research team headed by the Study Group on a European Civil Code (SGECC)[15] and the Research Group on the Existing EC Private Law (*Acquis* group)[16] would produce a work which reflected, to a certain extent, the results of work previously undertaken by these groups in proposing core principles of European private law, together with an 'elucidation' of the common structures emerging from the *acquis communautaire*. However, in approaching the law of obligations as a whole, the result was not a model for a European contract law but, *de facto*, a model for a traditional Civil Code extending to the essential parts of patrimonial law.[17] This was justified on the basis that the draft was a piece of academic research, not binding on the Commission, although the hope was evident that, 'If the content of the DCFR is convincing, it may contribute to a harmonious and informal Europeanisation of private law.'[18]

To produce a draft model code, in contrast to the Commission's astute decision in 2003 to abandon the unpopular terminology of a European Civil Code in favour of the less contentious 'Common Frame of Reference',[19] might be regarded as a controversial step. To those fearful of the prospect of a Euro-Code,[20] the DCFR was unlikely to allay their fears. The increased scope also delayed a project originally scheduled for 2007,[21] and the price of €798/£750 for the six volume set is likely to have restricted access to its provisions. In going beyond its remit, the final DCFR was not a model for an optional instrument of European contract law. Such a model would have to be extracted from the whole.

[14] The ten books of the DCFR are as follows: 'General principles' (Book 1), 'Contracts and other juridical acts' (Book II), 'Obligations and corresponding rights' (Book III), 'Specific contracts and the rights and obligations arising from them' (Book IV), 'Benevolent intervention in another's affairs' (Book V), 'Non-contractual liability arising out of damage caused to another' (tort law) (Book VI), 'Unjustified enrichment' (Book VII), 'Acquisition and loss of ownership of goods' (Book VIII), 'Proprietary security in movable assets' (Book IX) and 'Trusts' (Book X).

[15] See www.sgecc.net/. [16] See www.acquis-group.org/.

[17] See R. Zimmermann, 'The Present State of European Private Law' (2009) *Am. J Comp. L* 479, 480.

[18] See DCFR, Introduction, para. 8.

[19] For recognition of the tension between these concepts, see C. von Bar, 'A Common Frame of Reference for European Private Law: Academic Efforts and Political Realities' (2008) 12(1) *EJCL* (May), available at www.ejcl.org.

[20] See P. Legrand, 'Antivonbar' (2006) 1 *Journal of Comparative Law* 13.

[21] In fact only an Interim Outline DCFR was delivered to the European Commission on 28 December 2007.

### *Drafting style*

The style of the DCFR was therefore that of a Civil Code, notably one influenced by the German Civil Code (BGB). It further requires a familiarity with the systematic practice of cross-referencing used in the BGB, which is alien to a common law audience. As Legrand predicted, this triggered an inevitably hostile response from many common lawyers (particularly practitioners) unfamiliar with codified systems and traditionally sceptical of European intervention into national law.[22] To this may be added economic concerns from the English legal profession of the possible diminution of London's importance as a commercial and legal centre.[23] Solicitor Simon James speaks for much of the profession when he comments that 'it is hard to see why a multinational financial services business would opt to write its commercial derivatives contracts, its facility agreements or anything else by reference to a law whose uncertainties could only be resolved through the offices of the Court of Justice of the European Union which is a court that is not renowned for its speed, its commerciality or its predictability'.[24]

In February 2009, Simon Whittaker prepared an appraisal of the DCFR for the UK Ministry of Justice.[25] His views were also less than favourable, noting:

> the very considerable difficulties facing its authors: difficulties of methodology (in relation to the role of the *acquis* beyond its own provisions, the proper use of comparative law and 'best solutions'); difficulties of organisation and language (with the collaboration of so many scholars from different legal systems and traditions); difficulties of co-ordination . . . and difficulties of time and shifting purpose (the drafting of the DCFR itself taking place in a bare three years during which its purpose appeared to shift significantly).

22 P. Legrand, 'Against a European Civil Code' (1997) 60 *MLR* 44.

23 See S. Vogenauer and S. Weatherill, 'The European Community's Competence for a Comprehensive Harmonisation of Contract Law: an Empirical Analysis' (2005) 30 *ELRev.* 821, who note that by far the least enthusiastic responses to the proposal of new EU legislation in this field came from the United Kingdom. See also S. Vogenauer and S. Weatherill (eds.), *Harmonisation of European Contract Law: Implications for European Private Laws, Business and Legal Practice* (Hart, Oxford, 2006).

24 Clifford Chance LLP, March 2011, *European Contract Law: The Politics of Law* (March 2011). See also G. McMeel, 'The Proposal for a Common European Sales Law: Next Stop a European Contract Code?' (2012) 27 *BJIB and FL* 3.

25 *Draft Common Frame of Reference: An Assessment*, available at www.justice.gov.uk/publications/eu-contract-law-common-frame-reference.htm.

In a later article, Whittaker warned of the likely difficulties in applying the DCFR, concluding that 'Overall, therefore, in my view, the DCFR does not provide an appropriate basis for the CFR if this is to be used as an EC legal toolbox . . . what does appear is the extraordinarily open-textured nature of the propositions – be they values behind the law, or principles overriding or underlying the model rules'.[26] His Oxford colleague, John Cartwright, further highlighted the difficulties the DCFR would present to common lawyers in general:

> The proposal for a Common Frame of Reference (CFR) presents a challenge to every domestic legal system in Europe . . . the articulation of a possible framework of general principles and model rules . . . prompts each domestic system to reconsider its own principles and legal rules of (*inter alia*) the private law of contract . . . This is not to say that English law should fall in line with the CFR – not only because the style of drafting is alien to the English statutory draftsman . . . but also because there is no *a priori* reason to assume that the law of contract should be harmonised.[27]

Hugh Collins in his work, *The European Civil Code: The Way Forward*,[28] in contrast, favours a European Civil Code as a means of setting a framework of general principles promoting social justice across the European Union and contributing to the development of a common European identity, but this did not lead him to support the DCFR in its present form. Such views may be contrasted with the more favourable Scottish reaction. Laura McGregor, for example, noted that the DCFR represented an opportunity to develop Scots law in a manner that is consistent with the theoretical foundations of Scots law, permitting it to step away from the influence of English law which had left it under-theorised and diminished its civil law heritage.[29]

While common law disquiet might be predicted, perhaps more significant were the criticisms from leading civil law academics to whom the prospect of codification holds no innate fear. In a leading article published both in Germany and the United Kingdom, six senior German

[26] 'A Framework of Principle for European Contract Law?' (2009) 125 *LQR* 616, 647.
[27] 'The English Law of Contract: Time for Review?' (2009) 17 *ERPL* 155, 171–3.
[28] (Cambridge University Press, 2008), p. 123.
[29] L. Macgregor, *Report on the Draft Common Frame of Reference*, Report prepared for the Scottish Government (5 March 2009), available at www.scotland.gov.uk/Publications/2009/03/05095249/0.

scholars[30] highlighted a number of serious shortcomings relating to the DCFR, including unresolved or unconvincing policy decisions and ill-adjusted and inconsistent rules. Concern was again expressed at the abundance of general provisions and open-ended legal concepts. The writers accused the drafters of a massive erosion of private autonomy, shifting the content of the contract from the parties towards the law and the judiciary. They concluded that the DCFR did not constitute an appropriate basis for an optional code of European private law and that a thorough discussion of its normative foundations would be needed.

The response of the Common Core Group (also known as the Trento Group) is also of interest. This pan-European group was launched in 1995 to unearth the 'common core' of European private law and, in its evaluation of the DCFR, commented that:

> if the aim of the DCFR is to foster legal harmonization, this aim is particularly hard to reach by employing general clauses, because their meaning and scope cannot be defined *a priori*, and it is very likely that national interpreters will rely on the rules applied in their own system, which they know best, thereby reproducing at the European level the discrepancies that exist among national legal systems. On the other hand, general clauses fulfil a useful role, because their very vagueness allows flexibility to the system, which is consequently able to adjust to changing needs and different circumstances, a role that is as useful at the European level as in national laws. Yet, this objective can be attained only if the use of the margins of flexibility is kept under control by interpreters that share a common legal culture and working methods. As long as this element is missing in Europe (and this is clearly the case today), the risk of uncertainty and disparity is very high.[31]

A number of fundamental criticisms may be identified: the DCFR is too complex, abstract, uncertain and vague, leading to ambiguities and

[30] H. Eidenmüller *et al.*, 'The Common Frame of Reference for European Private Law' n. 7 above (previously published in (2008) *Juristenzeitung* 529 ff). See also N. Jansen and R. Zimmermann, 'A European Civil Code in All but Name: Discussing the Nature and Purposes of the Draft Common Frame of Reference' (2010) *CLJ* 98. For further criticism of the DCFR, see J. Basedow, 'Kodifikationrausch und kollidierende Konzepte – Notizen zu Marketbezug, Freiheit und System im Draft Common Frame of Reference' (2008) *ZEuP* 673.

[31] Common Core Evaluating Group, L. Antoniolli and F. Fiorentini (eds.), *A Factual Assessment of the Draft Common Frame of Reference* (Sellier, Munich, 2010), p. 255. This assessment has been carried out as part of the Joint Network of European Private Law Project (CoPECL), financed by the EU Commission, Contract No. 513351.

inconsistencies.[32] In view of such difficulties, the Common Core Group questioned how easy it would be to translate such a document accurately into the twenty-three languages of the European Union.

### *Policy*

The response of the German academics above also highlights the issue of policy.[33] Contract law is not value neutral and decisions must be made as to the extent to which party autonomy will be trumped by concerns for vulnerable parties and market failure. Modern contract law addresses not only the choices of the parties – consistent with the doctrine of freedom of contract – but also wider policy concerns, such as social justice.[34] The question remains on what policy basis a modern European contract law should be based.[35] The DCFR does not claim, however, to be politically neutral. The 'underlying' principles of freedom, security, justice and efficiency[36] outlined in the DCFR indicate that policy was far from ignored in its drafting. Two particular problems do, however, arise. First, the principles identified conflict. Anyone familiar with private law will appreciate the tensions which exist between principles such as freedom to act and the demands of justice which restrict freedom in order to protect contractual loyalty and cooperation, between advocating efficiency (that is, the freedom to avoid unnecessary impediments and costs) and promoting contractual security. The short commentaries on individual rules provide limited guidance. Secondly, such problems are exacerbated by the existence of 'overriding' principles of a high political nature: the protection of human rights, the promotion of solidarity and social responsibility, the preservation of cultural and linguistic diversity, the protection and promotion of welfare and the promotion of the internal market.[37] Again such principles will conflict.[38] Welfarism and social

[32] Note also the criticism found in the collection of essays edited by H.-W. Micklitz and F. Cafaggi, *European Private Law after the Common Frame of Reference* (Edward Elgar, Cheltenham, 2010).

[33] See M.W. Hesselink, 'The Politics of a European Civil Code' (2004) 10 *ELJ* 675; 'Common Frame of Reference and Social Justice' (2008) 4 *ERCL* 248.

[34] See, e.g., Study Group on Social Justice in European Private Law, 'Social Justice in European Contract Law: A Manifesto' (2004) 10 *ELJ* 653.

[35] See M.W. Hesselink, 'Five Political Ideas of European Contract Law' (2011) 7 *ERCL* 295.

[36] DCFR, Introduction, para. 15. [37] *Ibid.* Introduction, para. 16.

[38] The DCFR Introduction adds, unhelpfully, that freedom, security, justice and efficiency also have a role to play as overriding principles.

solidarity do not necessarily have any connection with promotion of the internal market, nor principles based on efficiency. Do we, in any event, have one notion of 'welfarism' capable of being stated in a single set of principles, or differing notions dependent on national public opinion and socio-economic norms?[39] Many have also questioned how a 'harmonised' form of law ensures the preservation of cultural and linguistic *diversity*: national law being, to a certain extent, part of and reflecting our national cultural norms.[40] The drafters recognised that this principle would conflict with principles of solidarity, the protection and promotion of welfare and, most fundamentally, the promotion of the internal market.[41] Their reaction, however, suggests that this 'overriding' principle will have limited impact. Diversity, we are told, is respected by ensuring the participation on an equal footing of lawyers from all European legal cultures in the preparation of the DCFR and by the attempt to reflect, as far as possible, all legal systems of the EU Member States in the Notes. Linguistic diversity is respected by ensuring that the DCFR is translated into as many European languages as possible.[42] Such limited recognition of cultural and linguistic diversity is perhaps unsurprising in a harmonisation project, but it demonstrates the political compromises implicit in balancing conflicting principles. In setting out model rules, the drafters of the DCFR made their own policy choices, but it remained for the legislator to determine the ultimate validity (and political acceptability) of the choices made.

This section has illustrated both the strengths and weaknesses of the DCFR. It provides a valuable academic resource, capable, as John Cartwright has noted, of making its readers reappraise their own legal system and is thus likely to influence future academics and possibly legislators and practitioners. In areas of law where no overall European consensus exists, it also provides a basis for discussion and a draft framework for any future harmonisation of law. The next section will assess these strengths and weaknesses not in the abstract, but in terms of a case study focusing on an area of law which has been traditionally viewed as an obstacle to harmonisation: precontractual liability arising

39 T. Wilhelmsson, 'Varieties of Welfarism in European Contract Law' (2004) 10 *ELJ* 712.

40 See R. Sefton-Green, 'Cultural Diversity and the Idea of a European Civil Code' in M.W. Hesselink, *The Politics of a European Civil Code* (Kluwer Law International, The Hague, 2006); T. Wilhelmsson, E. Paunio and A. Pohjolaienen (eds.), *Private Law and the Many Cultures of Europe* (Kluwer Law International, The Hague, 2007).

41 DCFR, Introduction, para. 19. 42 *Ibid.*

from negotiations contrary to good faith. Former UK Supreme Court judge Lord Steyn, commenting in 1997, noted that 'In the new *jus commune* of Europe there is a general principle that parties must negotiate in good faith . . . But English lawyers remain resolutely hostile to any incorporation of good faith principles into English law. The hostility is not usually bred from any great familiarity with the way in which the principle works in other systems. But it is intense.'[43] To what extent has the DCFR been able to bridge this divide?

## Case study: DCFR Book II, article 3:301 (liability for negotiations contrary to good faith and fair dealing)

Precontractual liability provides an interesting vantage point to survey the ability of the DCFR to reconcile conflicting national traditions and provide a common European principle of liability. This section, with reference to the diverse legal traditions of the common law, Romanistic and Germanic legal families, will seek to analyse how the DCFR addressed the different approaches to good faith in bargaining found across European Member States.[44]

The Draft Common Frame of Reference in Books II ('Contracts and other juridical acts')[45] and III ('Obligations and corresponding rights') follows essentially the life cycle of a contract from precontractual duties to remedies for non-performance. The treatment of precontractual liability in Chapter 3 of Book II ('Marketing and precontractual duties') has two aims: to improve the existing *acquis communautaire* imposing precontractual informational duties on parties[46] and, more generally, to

[43] J. Steyn, 'Contract Law: Fulfilling the Reasonable Expectations of Honest Men' (1997) 113 *LQR* 433, 438.

[44] For a recent survey, see J. Cartwright and M. Hesselink (eds.), *Precontractual Liability in European Private Law* (Cambridge University Press, 2009).

[45] This term, invented by the drafters of the German Civil Code, is problematic in itself in that it is meaningless to a common law audience and potentially confusing to French lawyers familiar with the term '*acte juridique*' from which it is conceptually distinct: see R. Sefton-Green, 'Sense and Sensibilities: The DCFR and the Preservation of Cultural and Linguistic Plurality' (2008) 4 *ERCL* 281, 291–2.

[46] This is consistent with the Commission's view that consumer protection may be achieved in part by better informed consumers. Chapter 3, section 1 thus sets out duties of disclosure in relation to goods, other assets and services (arts. II 3:101–3:108) and remedies for breach of information duties (II 3:109). Many provisions generalise existing EU consumer contract law provisions dealing with precontractual information duties and reflect the work of the *Acquis* Group in this area: see e.g., Directive 90/314 on package travel, package holidays and package tours [1990] OJ L158/59 and Directive 2008/122 on

draw out general model rules of precontractual liability. Whilst this may give rise to uneasy questions as to the extent to which consumer protection provisions can (and should) be generalised to business to business (B2B) contracts and why the general statement of the duty to negotiate in accordance with good faith and fair dealing (II 3:301) is placed *after* detailed duties to inform (II 3:101–3:109) and to prevent input errors and acknowledge receipt (II 3:201–3:202),[47] one point is clear: precontractual good faith is regarded as an essential principle of European contract law.

This contrasts, of course, with the current position in European private law where a clear divergence exists between common and civil law.[48] There is, however, also no single civil law approach: *culpa in contrahendo* in German law is not the same, in origin or theory, as the remedies based on fault/delictual responsibility found in other civilian jurisdictions.

Put simply, the following approaches may be identified in the common law, Romanistic and Germanic legal systems.

*Common law*: Rejects any general principle of negotiation in good faith as 'inherently repugnant to the adversarial position of the parties when involved in negotiations'.[49] Nevertheless, some precontractual liability does arise from existing doctrines such as misrepresentation and undue influence. As Lord Justice Bingham stated in *Interfoto Picture Library Ltd* v. *Stilletto Visual Programmes Ltd*,[50] English law has, characteristically, committed itself to no such overriding principle, but has favoured piecemeal solutions in response to demonstrated problems of unfairness.

*Romanistic model* (France, Belgium, etc.): Generally no specific provisions, but abusive negotiating behaviour may give rise to fault-based liability for wrongful breaking off of negotiations.[51]

the protection of consumers in respect of certain aspects of timeshare, long-term holiday product, resale and exchange contracts [2009] OJ L33/10. See T. Wilhelmsson and C. Twigg-Flesner, 'Pre-contractual Information Duties in the *Acquis Communautaire*' (2006) 2 *ERCL* 441.

[47] See B. Fagès, 'Pre-contractual Duties in the Draft Common Frame of Reference: What Relevance for the Negotiation of Commercial Contracts?' (2008) 4 *ERCL* 304.

[48] See P. Giliker, *Precontractual Liability in English and French Law* (Kluwer, The Hague, 2002); R. Zimmermann and S. Whittaker, *Good Faith in European Contract Law (The Common Core of European Private Law)* (Cambridge University Press, 2000); H. Collins, 'Good Faith in European Contract Law' (1994) 14 *OJLS* 229.

[49] *Walford* v. *Miles* [1992] AC 128, 138, per Lord Ackner. [50] [1989] QB 433, 439.

[51] See e.g., France: art. 1382 of the Civil Code, Cass. com. 20 March 1972, Bull. civ. 1972, IV, no. 93; JCP éd G 1973, II, 17543, note J. Schmidt; and J. Ghestin, 'La responsabilité

*Germanic model* (Germany, Austria, etc.): The doctrine of *culpa in contrahendo* imposes mutual obligations on parties who negotiate with one another and was recently inserted into the German Civil Code (s.311(2) BGB in the 2001 German reform of the law of obligations (*Schuldrechtsreform*)).[52] A duty arises, therefore, not to break off negotiations arbitrarily, but also where, in the legitimate expectation that an agreement will be concluded, one party allows another to exercise influence over its rights and legal interests to its detriment.[53]

The above picture indicates fundamental differences between common law and civil law systems. There is, as conceded by Hugh Beale (one of the drafters of the DCFR),[54] a positive resistance still to notions of good faith in English law which expects less cooperation between negotiating parties.[55] Beale attributes this to the type of cases which create precedents (mainly commercial), but also to the common law preference for party autonomy with law merely setting the outer limit of permissible behaviour. Divergence also exists how conceptually to classify precontractual liability as either contractual or tortious liability,[56] and, of course, in interpreting the standard by which good faith in negotiations should be adjudged.

Chapter 3 of Book II of the DCFR, therefore, faced the challenge of finding a common form of precontractual good faith, capable of consistent application across all Member States.

délictuelle pour rupture abusive des pourparlers' JCP éd. G 2007, I, 155. Specific provision does, however, exist in the Italian Civil Code: art. 1337.

52 'An obligation with duties under s.241(2) also comes into existence by: (1) the commencement of contract negotiations; (2) the initiation of a contract where one party, with regard to a potential contractual relationship, gives the other party the possibility of affecting his rights, legal interests and other interests, or entrusts these to him; or (3) similar business contacts' (all translations of the BGB are taken from Ministry of Justice website, www.gesetze-im-internet.de/englisch_bgb/).

53 Damages may be awarded under s.280(1) BGB: '(1) If the obligor breaches a duty arising from the obligation, the obligee may demand damages for the damage caused thereby. This does not apply if the obligor is not responsible for the breach of duty.'

54 'The Impact of the Decisions of the European Courts on English Contract Law: The Limits of Voluntary Harmonization' (2010) 18 *ERPL* 501, 516, although he argues that English lawyers have no legitimate reason to object to good faith when used as 'an expansion joint' to develop new principles or 'excluder' to prevent parties benefiting from bad behaviour, and their hostility is, in reality, to its use as a policing power.

55 See, generally, Cartwright and Hesselink, *Precontractual Liability*, n. 44 above, at p. 461.

56 J. Dietrich, 'Classifying Precontractual Liability: A Comparative Analysis' (2001) 21 *LS* 153.

Article 3:301 provides:

> Negotiations contrary to good faith and fair dealing[57]
>
> (1) A person is free to negotiate and is not liable for failure to reach an agreement.
>
> (2) A person who is engaged in negotiations has a duty to negotiate in accordance with good faith and fair dealing and not to break off negotiations contrary to good faith and fair dealing. This duty may not be excluded or limited by contract.
>
> (3) A person who is in breach of the duty is liable for any loss caused to the other party by the breach.
>
> (4) It is contrary to good faith and fair dealing, in particular, for a person to enter into or continue negotiations with no real intention of reaching an agreement with the other party.

While paragraph (1) is unlikely to prove controversial even to a common lawyer – a basic statement of freedom of contract – the remaining paragraphs immediately restrict this freedom. The act of engaging in negotiations imposes a duty to negotiate in good faith and, most importantly, not to break off negotiations contrary to good faith and fair dealing. 'Good faith and fair dealing' are defined at I 1:103 as referring to

> a standard of conduct characterised by honesty, openness and consideration for the interests of the other party to the transaction or relationship in question. It is, in particular, contrary to good faith and fair dealing for a party to act inconsistently with that party's prior statements or conduct when the other party has reasonably relied on them to that other party's detriment.

In addition to this specific example (to the common lawyer resembling the doctrine of estoppel, to the civilian the principle *venire contra factum proprium*)[58] may be added the specific concern of 3:301(4): it is contrary to good faith and fair dealing for a person to enter into or continue negotiations with no real intention of reaching agreement with the other party. The remedy will be damages based on reliance loss (which may,

[57] See also art. II 3:302: 'Breach of confidentiality'. Fagès, 'Pre-contractual Duties', n. 47 above, comments that the title ('Negotiations contrary to good faith and dealing') immediately places freedom of negotiation in a negative context.

[58] 'No one may set himself in contradiction to his own previous conduct' (in German, '*Zuwiderhandlung gegen das eigene frühere Verhalten*'). On this basis there is a general principle in the DCFR that a person who has induced another to incur a change of position on the faith of an act should not be allowed to exercise rights inconsistent with the resultant state of affairs: Comments to art. I 1:103 at 90.

however, extend to loss of opportunities), but not specific performance or expectation loss per se.[59]

Apart from these specific examples (and one might wonder how often parties will enter into negotiations with *no* real intention of reaching agreement), we are left with a test of negotiating in accordance with the values of good faith and fair dealing, i.e., honesty, openness and consideration for the interests of the other party. One might legitimately ask how we identify more precisely such open-textured standards. 'Honesty' is said to have its 'normal' meaning, whilst 'openness' denotes an element of transparency in a person's conduct.[60] In contrast, consideration of others will depend on the circumstances, including the nature of the contract. It is not a requirement to prefer the other, but one should exercise a basic level of consideration and not act out of pure malice.[61] The commentary to II 3:301 divides liability into two categories: entering negotiations contrary to good faith and fair dealing (the ubiquitous 'no intention to contract' example) and continuing or breaking off negotiations contrary to good faith and fair dealing. The examples for the second category include carrying on with negotiations having clearly decided not to contract, and breaking off negotiations having used information provided by the other party to obtain a lower bid from a third party. Despite such guidelines, there is clearly considerable room for debate how these requirements will operate in practice.

One might question to what extent it is possible, apart from these few examples, to generalise a standard of contracting behaviour to be applied consistently across Member States. The duty appears substantive and not merely procedural, requiring 'objective' good faith, but a number of questions remain, such as the extent to which the identity of the negotiation parties would be relevant and how the courts would identify the normal risks of the contracting process.[62] Consider, for example, the differing concerns which may be raised in commercial and consumer contracts. To what extent should the courts take account of the particular vulnerability of the parties (e.g., consumers/small businesses contracting with large commercial concerns) or the superior economic or market knowledge of the other? Further, is it necessary to have actual or foreseeable knowledge of the other's degree of commitment? Whilst the guidance is helpful in highlighting clear examples of bad faith, courts

[59] DCFR, p. 248. [60] Comments, Book 1, article 1:103, p. 89. [61] *Ibid.*

[62] Consider, e.g., the controversial English case of *Regalian Properties Plc* v. *London Docklands Development Corp.* [1995] 1 WLR 212.

ultimately will have to judge what amounts to 'negotiating according to good faith and fair dealing', for example in the common situation where one party complains that it has incurred costs believing it will be awarded a contract, but finds that the other negotiating party has decided to place its order elsewhere: surely a clear risk in any competitive tendering process. In the absence of pan-European agreement as to what we mean by 'good faith and fair dealing' in precontractual negotiations[63] and the lack of a precise guide in the notes to the DCFR how to identify the underlying principles and values, it is difficult to see how consistent application of article 3:301 would be achieved, particularly in the English courts unfamiliar with a general application of precontractual good faith reasoning. Will 'good faith', as Teubner predicted, become a 'legal irritant' leading to new divergences or can a common understanding be achieved permitting it to fit into a European culture of good contracting?[64] The evidence to date worryingly seems to support Teubner's view.

This case study leads to a number of conclusions. Harmonisation raises questions of policy, interpretation and coherency of principle. To be successful, there must be a willingness to tackle the tensions existing between national and European legal rules and to accept the need to compromise in the interests of a common European position. Smits has questioned whether, in the absence of a common understanding of the meaning of specific rules of European contract law, it is simply too early to draft principles of European contract law and whether energy would be better placed in building up a common European legal tradition through teaching and legal scholarship.[65] Harmonisation requires a readiness to move towards a united position on key policy choices and it may be disputed whether the European Union is yet at this stage. The DCFR by itself cannot address these political issues. It represents an academic model with its own policy choices. Reinhard Zimmermann has warned, nevertheless, that if it is taken by the Commission, not as an important contribution to an ongoing debate, but as a reference text, there is a danger that further necessary debate may be stultified.[66] This, as will be seen, has not occurred. The reaction of the European Commission

[63] See generally R. Zimmermann and S. Whittaker (eds.), *Good Faith in European Contract Law* (Cambridge University Press, 2000), esp. ch.1 and pp. 675–84.

[64] G. Teubner, 'Legal Irritants: Good Faith in British Law or How Unifying Law Ends up in New Divergences' (1998) 61 *MLR* 11.

[65] J.M. Smits, 'The Draft Common Frame of Reference, Methodological Nationalism and the Way Forward' (2008) 4 *ERCL* 270.

[66] Zimmermann, 'The Present State of European Private Law', n. 17 above, at 491.

to the DCFR has been to reassert a focus on European contract law, more precisely on contracts for the sale of goods, digital content and related contracts, and emphasise the need for a more user-friendly and straightforward instrument.

## Moving from the academic to the political: the Green Paper, the Expert Group Feasibility Study and the proposal for a Regulation on a Common European Sales Law

On 3 March 2010, the European Commission indicated that, under the Europe 2020 strategy, one means of driving forward economic recovery would be to work on harmonised solutions for consumer contracts, and make progress towards an optional European contract law.[67] On 26 April 2010, the Commission set up an expert group to assist it in making further progress on the development of a possible future European contract law instrument.[68] The Expert Group, composed of specialists from different legal traditions with outstanding competence in the area of contract law, was asked to conduct a feasibility exercise on a draft instrument of European contract law. The feasibility study went hand in hand with a Green Paper, launched on 1 July 2010, seeking contributions from all citizens and stakeholders in Member States on the policy options for progress towards a European contract law for consumers and businesses.[69] In engaging in a large-scale consultation exercise, the Commission made it clear that, from its own perspective, a common European contract law would maximise the benefits of the internal market and increase cross-border trade, giving consumers a high level of consumer protection and rendering it easier and cheaper for businesses, particularly small and medium-sized enterprises (SMEs), to contract with parties from other Member States.[70] In addition, the Commission surveyed business and consumers through Eurobarometer,

[67] Press Release, IP/10/225, 'The European Parliament gave its backing to the idea of an optional European Contract Law in a resolution on 25 November 2009: P7_TA-PROV (2009)0090' (3 March 2010).

[68] Commission Decision 2010/233/EU of 26 April 2010 setting up the Expert Group on a Common Frame of Reference in the area of European contract law [2010] OJ L105/109.

[69] COM(2010)348 final.

[70] *Citizens' Summary: Public Consultation – EU Contract Law for Consumers and Businesses* (2010), available at http://ec.europa.eu/justice_home/news/summary/docs/contract_law_en.pdf.

the SME Panel and the European Business Test Surveys. An Impact Assessment Report was also prepared.

The Green Paper resulted in 320 responses from a wide range of stakeholders. The Feasibility Study was delivered in April 2011 and consisted of a text of 189 articles covering issues central to contract law.[71] The Impact Assessment of October 2011 indicated that an optional Common European Sales Law would best meet the overall policy objective of supporting the economic activity in the internal market by improving the conditions of cross-border trade by reducing the barriers caused by differences in contract law between Member States.[72] The Commission, as stated earlier, chose to proceed with a draft Regulation on a Common European Sales Law (CESL).

This section will consider the future role of the Draft Common Frame of Reference in the light of such developments. The reaction of the Commission, in engaging the Expert Group to redraft its contract proposals in a more 'user-friendly' way, may be seen to endorse some of the criticisms outlined above. The Group was instructed (a) to select those parts of the DCFR which were of direct or indirect relevance to contract law; and (b) to restructure, revise and supplement the selected contents of the DCFR, taking also into consideration other research work conducted in this area, as well as the Union *acquis* within, ideally, 150 articles.[73] The Commission's investment in continuous consultation, through the Green Paper, commissioned surveys, but also the stakeholder expert group, workshops, meetings with the European Consumers' Organisation (BEUC) and the European Consumer Consultative Group, again indicates recognition of the need to go beyond academic analysis and involve all interested parties in legal development. Most significantly, in restricting the scope of the CESL to contracts for the sale of goods and digital content, the CESL is but a pale shadow of the six volumes of the DCFR.

[71] See http://ec.europa.eu/justice/contract/files/feasibility_study_final.pdf. The consultation on the Feasibility Study was opened on 3 May and closed on 1 July 2011. The Commission received 106 contributions: see http://ec.europa.eu/justice/contract/expert-group/index_en.htm.

[72] SEC(2011)1166 final (Brussels, 11 October 2011).

[73] See art. 2 of Commission Decision 2010/233/EU [2010] OJ L105/109; Synthesis of the First Expert Group's Meeting on 21 May 2010, p. 1. Summaries of the contents of Expert Group's meetings are available at http://ec.europa.eu/justice/policies/consumer/policies_consumer_intro_en.htm.

What role does this leave for the DCFR? It will be argued that there are a number of possible uses for the DCFR: some legitimate, some not. It will be submitted that the DCFR is best used as a valuable resource for legal education and academic argument. In contrast, if used as a source of soft law by legislators at a national or European level, the difficulties in terms of interpretation, consistency and coherency outlined above are likely to arise. In the absence of an arbiter, the brief notes and comments within the DCFR are unlikely to provide sufficient guidance for it to operate as a source of law.

### *A source for legal science, research and education*

The Introduction to the DCFR lists the possible uses of the DCFR as three-fold: a model for a political CFR, a contribution to legal science, research and education, and a source of inspiration for courts and legislators.[74] The first goal has to a limited extent been met by the publication of the CESL. The second would also appear to be fulfilled by the very act of publication in 2009 of a text which brings together both summaries of national laws and a draft framework for a future European Civil Code written by leading academics in the field of European private law. In view of increased interest in this topic, and indeed the foundation of the European Law Institute in Paris in June 2011,[75] the DCFR provides a useful resource and, it is hoped, the basis for future work and development. Martijn Hesselink has rightly commented that no other project has attempted such a comprehensive survey of European private law nor is likely to appear in the near future due to the extent of the work involved.[76] The DCFR facilitates access to the law of other Member States and provides a first port of call for a comparative overview on questions of EU private law. On this basis, the DCFR does appear to be successful in achieving its stated goal of furnishing a new foundation for European private law which will increase mutual understanding and promote collective deliberation on private law issues, even if, with time, its survey of current law is likely become dated and its provisions overtaken by events.

[74] DCFR, Introduction, paras. 6–8.

[75] Described by Justice Commissioner Reding as 'an important milestone in building an EU-wide area of law, rights and justice': Press Release IP/11/666, 'European Commission welcomes foundation of the European Law Institute' (1 June 2011).

[76] 'The CFR as a Source of European Private Law' (2009) 83 *Tul. L Rev.* 919, 927.

### *DCFR as a source of law*

It is more controversial, however, whether the DCFR may, despite the introduction of the CESL, succeed in acting as a source of soft law. Two arguments may be made. First, the CESL itself, which owes its origins and some of its contents to the DCFR, will require interpretation by the courts. Indeed, many of the members of the Expert Group were also involved in drafting the DCFR.[77] The draft Regulation is brief and lacks the detailed commentary and notes of the DCFR, raising the question of how difficulties in interpretation will be resolved without expensive and time-consuming resort to the Court of Justice of the European Union (CJEU). In case of doubt, therefore, the DCFR may provide a means of resolving such difficulties, simply by virtue of having discussed many of the relevant issues in question in more depth. Nevertheless, the CESL and the DCFR are not identical, even in their contractual provisions. The Expert Group was instructed to look not only at the DCFR, but at other relevant sources, such as the United Nations Convention on Contracts for the International Sale of Goods ('CISG'), and the responses to the Green Paper consultation exercise.[78] The DCFR will not, and cannot, therefore, offer a complete and accurate point of reference to the CESL. It may offer some guidance, but cannot be regarded as an official source of law.

The second argument is more ambitious. The CESL is limited in scope and will therefore only provide a basis for a European contract law relating to the sale of goods and digital content (and related contracts). In applying EU law more generally, the DCFR may provide both national courts and the CJEU itself with a source of law whose origin is purely 'European'. Commentators have noted, for example, reference to the predecessor to the DCFR, the Principles of European Contract Law (PECL), by the Advocate-General of the CJEU,[79] and, indeed, the DCFR itself has been referred to on a number of occasions by Advocate-General Trstenjak.[80] PECL has further been used by national courts, such as the

[77] See Press Release IP/10/595, 'European Commission convenes legal expert group to seek solutions on contract law' (21 May 2010).

[78] Green Paper, n. 4 above, at p. 4.

[79] See e.g., C-412/06 *Hamilton* v. *Volksbank Filder eG* [2008] ECR I-2383, para. 24 n. 8 per AG Maduro.

[80] See C-227/08 *Martin Martin* v. *EDP Editores SL* [2010] 2 CMLR 27; C-215/08 *E. Friz GmbH* v. *Von der Heyden* [2010] 3 CMLR 23 and C-445/06 *Danske Slagterier* v. *Bundesrepublik Deutschland* [2009] 3 CMLR 10.

Spanish Tribunal Supremo and its lower courts,[81] as a driver for change and as an authoritative reference text in the process of modernising law.[82] The Scottish Law Commission, for example, has commenced a review of Scottish contract law in the light of the publication of the DCFR.[83] It cannot be denied, therefore, that some law-makers have found PECL and the DCFR useful in developing European and domestic private law.

It must be questioned, however, to what extent an academic proposal, without any political legitimacy, subject to considerable criticism and notably rejected by the European Commission in favour of a more user-friendly version focusing on cross-border sale of goods contracts, should influence EU courts. A useful perspective may be found in the treatment of PECL by the English Supreme Court. The Court, as a whole, has drawn a line between using this text as a source of academic argument and treating it as a statement of law. Lord Hope, for example, in *Director General of Fair Trading* v. *First National Bank Plc*[84] (concerning the interpretation of the Unfair Contract Terms Directive 93/13/EEC) found PECL to be a helpful indicator of differences between the legal systems of Member States. Further, Lord Hoffmann in *Chartbrook Ltd* v. *Persimmon Homes Ltd*[85] was able to rely on PECL to identify alternative means of approaching a difficult point of law. This suggests a role for the DCFR as a tool for legal inspiration rather than a point of reference in interpretation of existing law.

It is likely, therefore, that the DCFR will be of interest to legislators, judges and law reform bodies as an academic source to assist in legal reform and in developing European principles, but that its influence will

[81] C. Vendrell Cervantes, 'The Application of the Principles of European Contract Law by Spanish Courts' (2008) *ZEuP* 534. See also D. Busch, 'The Principles of European Contract Law before the Supreme Court of Netherlands' (2008) *ZEuP* 549.

[82] N. Jansen, *The Making of Legal Authority* (Oxford University Press, 2010), p. 62. PECL has also served as one of the main sources for the Estonian Law of Obligations Act: P. Varul, 'Performance and Remedies for Non-performance: Comparative Analysis of the PECL and DCFR' (2008) *Juridica International* 104.

[83] See Scot Law Com. No. 220 (2010), para. 2.16 and the 2012 discussion paper on formation of contract (Discussion Paper No. 154, March 2012). The Commission described the DCFR as 'an instrument to provide an important area of Scots law with a systematic health check'.

[84] [2001] UKHL 52; [2002] 1 AC 481, para. 45. Lord Steyn, in contrast, found the commentary to PECL helpful in interpreting the Directive: at para. 36.

[85] [2009] UKHL 38; [2009] 1 AC 1101, para. 39: PECL considered in addition to the Unidroit Principles of International Commercial Contracts and an academic article.

wane over time. It will have to compete with new sources of inspiration, such as the publication of new volumes of section-specific model principles and the ongoing work of academics in the field of European private law. Nevertheless, as a text covering most of European private law, it remains a valuable resource for lawyers and the judiciary alike.

## Conclusion

Reinhard Zimmermann has argued that the key difficulty with the DCFR arises from the fact that an academic exercise of drafting principles of European contract law has been transformed into a political project.[86] I would agree. This is not to diminish the significance of the DCFR in terms of increasing awareness of European private law, nor to criticise the scholarship which has been undertaken in this enterprise, but to recognise that the long-term impact of the DCFR is likely to be limited by the fact that the European Commission, at least, has moved on and is focused now on the proposed Common European Sales Law as its future instrument of European contract law. My example of precontractual liability also casts interesting light on the relationship between the CESL and the DCFR. As discussed earlier, article II 3:301 of the DCFR states a general principle of precontractual good faith, raising difficulties of consistent interpretation and policy conflict. Such a provision is noticeably absent from the CESL, despite surviving the early stages of the Expert Group study.[87] The CESL confines itself to a non-excludable 'general principle' that each party has a duty to act in accordance with good faith and fair dealing,[88] as defined in the Regulation itself at article 2(b), which all parties, we are told, need to observe in their dealings and which should guide the extent to which parties have to cooperate. The section on precontractual duties in Part II of Annex 1 is now explicitly entitled 'Chapter 2: Precontractual information' and omits any general duty to negotiate in good faith. Further, article 11 of the draft Regulation confines the remedies provided by the CESL to circumstances where a contract was actually concluded, thereby excluding from its scope cases where one party breaks off negotiations in bad faith and

86 Zimmermann, 'The Present State of European Private Law', n. 17 above, at 493.

87 Synthesis of the Second Expert Group's Meeting on 24 June 2010, p. 4.

88 CESL, Annex 1, art. 2. Breach of this duty may preclude the party in breach from exercising or relying on a right, remedy or defence which that party would otherwise have, or may make the party liable for any loss thereby caused to the other party.

contracts with another. This case study highlights the independence of the CESL from previous proposals for harmonised principles of European contract law. Clear differences exist between the DCFR and the CESL in terms of ambition and scope. The CESL is an autonomous instrument which will develop its own legal rules,[89] and may indeed find it helpful to seek guidance from the application of other model contract rules such as CISG. This does not prevent the DCFR being an important point of reference in the *debate* over contractual liability, but indicates the limits of its ability to act as a source of law.

The legacy of the DCFR will, therefore, lie in its impact on the future development of European private law. As Lucinda Miller has noted, the DCFR illustrates that 'there is a real possibility for academic private law collaboration across Europe, and that common ideas about the notion of private law can evolve'.[90] Its strength lies in its scholarship, informing both scholars and law-makers of the current state of European private law and presenting future options for development.[91] As such, the DCFR is to be welcomed and will continue to justify its place in the libraries of the universities and Supreme Courts of all European Member States for many years to come.

[89] See CESL, art. 4.1: 'The Common European Sales Law is to be interpreted autonomously and in accordance with its objectives and the principles underlying it'.

[90] L. Miller, *The Emergence of EU Contract Law* (Oxford University Press, 2012), pp. 204–5. See also Smits, 'The Draft Common Frame of Reference', n. 65 above, at 281: 'Europeanisation should start with the emergence of a common European legal tradition, for which teaching and legal scholarship are far more important than the drafting of specific rules. Such teaching and scholarship should indeed focus on finding common *arguments* in European jurisdictions, thus allowing for a competition of legal ideas.'

[91] See Lord Mance, 'The Common Frame of Reference' (2010) *ZEuP* 457.

# 3

# The Europeanisation of contract law and the role of comparative law: the case of the Directive on Consumer Rights

CRISTINA AMATO

## The harmonisation process: the confused paths and goals of European institutions

### *Introduction*

It is well known among private law scholars that several separate official and private attempts to harmonise European contract law currently exist.[1] The former initiatives include EU Directives, Regulations, action plans and Green Papers; examples of the latter include the Lando Commission, the *Acquis* Group and the Expert Group, which the Commission recently appointed to assist in drafting a concise and range-restricted optional instrument (Regulation for a Common European Sales Law, CESL).[2]

Associate Professor of Comparative Law, University of Brescia (Italy).

[1] For a complete account of the different projects and roles played by courts, public and academic projects in laying the groundwork of European private law, see E. Hondius, 'Fifteen Years of European Private Law' (2009) 2 *Opinio Juris in Comparatione*, Paper 5; V. Roppo, 'Prospettive del diritto contrattuale europeo. Dal contratto del consumatore al contratto asimetrico?' (2009) 2 *Corriere giuridico* 267.

[2] The Expert Group on European Contract Law was appointed by the European Commission (Decision 2010/233, 26 April 2010) to set out a Proposal for a European Sales Contract 'of whatever legal form or nature'. On 11 October 2011, the European Commission delivered the Proposal for a Regulation of the European Parliament and of the Council on a Common European Sales Law (CESL), COM(2011)635 final, based on the 'feasibility study' issued by the Expert Group on 19 August 2011. The CESL is applicable to B2B and B2C contracts; the material scope of application covers sales contracts and service contracts associated with sales and digital contracts: C. Castronovo, 'L'utopia della codificazione europea e l'oscura realpolitik di Bruxelles. Dal DCFR alla Proposta di Regolamento di un diritto comune europeo della vendita' (2011) 4 *Europa e diritto privato* 837; H. W. Micklitz and N. Reich, *The Commission Proposal for a 'Regulation on a Common European Sales Law (CESL)': Too Broad or Not Broad Enough?*, EUI Working Papers

It is not possible to provide an exhaustive and coherent list of the relevant documents concerning European contract law, depending on whether or not we include the consumer's *acquis*. Most importantly, it is not clear whether the consumer *acquis* may be considered as the core of a European contract law, with the idea that such could lead to a codified European law of contract consisting of a general part and specific rules devoted to unbalanced transactions; or whether it is more convenient to ignore the bulk of the *acquis* (whether dealing with business to business (B2B) or business to consumer (B2C) contracts) located in official documents and consider them as a separate set of rules, making way for private documents dealing with general contract law and special contracts only, as embodied in the Draft Common Frame of Reference (DCFR), published in 2008 and then set aside in favour of the shorter and range-restricted optional instrument, the CESL.[3] Keeping this chaotic background in mind, the present chapter will concentrate on the attempts to revise the consumer *acquis*, making an effort to highlight the final goals that these attempts aim at, as well as the quality of their rules. This will be done using a comparative method of analysis.

It is difficult to understand why the revision efforts have been fragmented, instead of aiming for a single, coherent re-statement of contract law, as initially planned by the European Commission in its 2003 Action Plan.[4] The project of adopting a *single* legal act amending and/or filling in the gaps of the previous consumer contract law seems to have been set aside without providing an adequate explanation. Recently

(European University Press, 2012); W.M. Hesselink, *How to Opt into the Common European Sales Law? Brief Comments on the Commission's Proposal for a Regulation*, Centre for the Study of European Contract Law Working Paper Series no. 2011-15, available at http://ssrn.com/abstract=1950107; *The Case for a Common European Sales Law in an Age of Rising Nationalism*, Centre for the Study of European Contract Law Working Paper Series no. 2012-01, available at http://ssrn.com/abstract=1998174; G. Low, *A Numbers Game: The Legal Basis for an Optional Istrument in European Contract Law*, available at http://ssrn.com/abstract=1991070. See also numerous contributions in (2011) 6 *European Review of Private Law*.

3 P. Brulez, 'From the Academic DCFR to a Political CFR, Trier, 18–19 March 2010' (2010) 5 *ERPL* 1041.

4 COM(2003)68 final. See *Green Paper on the Review of the Consumer Acquis*, COM(2006) 744 final (8 February 2007), concerning the review of eight Directives on consumer acquis: Directive 85/577/EEC (contracts concluded away from business premises); Directive 90/314/EEC (on package travel, package holidays and package tours); Directive 93/13/EEC (on unfair terms in consumer contracts); Directive 94/47/EC (on timesharing); Directive 97/7/EC (on distance contracts); Directive 98/6 (on the indication of the prices of products offered to consumers); Directive 98/27 (on injunctions); Directive 99/44/EC (on consumer sales and guarantees).

the European Parliament and the Council have passed two new Directives, one on consumer credit (2008/48/EC) and another on time-sharing (2008/122/EC). Eventually, apart from the above-mentioned revisions, four Directives[5] have been variously redrafted and amended by the European Commission in the Directive on Consumer Rights (DCR).[6] According to the Commission's Directorate-General Justice, the DCR should become part of the optional instrument, provided that the full harmonisation option is maintained. The CESL has introduced separate special rules governing B2C contracts, thus rendering the present legislative offer in the area of consumer law even richer. Here we begin with questions that still need to be answered: first, why does the DCR not include the *entire acquis* on consumer protection from the outset, for example, consumer credit contracts, timesharing, travel packages, and so forth? Secondly, should the CESL be considered as a second legal order for cross-border transactions, which does not replace national consumer law, but runs parallel to it, and what would the relationship be between the CESL and the DCR? Thirdly, what is the relationship between the CESL and the UN Convention on Contracts for the International Sale of Goods (CISG) 1980? Should the latter be considered as superseded by the former,[7] at least in B2B contracts?[8] Fourthly, how can an 'optional' instrument be associated with a consumer legal area that is of a mandatory nature? The CESL seems to create even more legal uncertainty.[9]

To sum up, it seems that, notwithstanding the official statements, the European institutions are pursuing at least two different strategies: one of elaborating an *optional* instrument; and one of reviewing the consumer *acquis* 'for the promotion of a real consumer internal market striking

5 Directive 85/577/EEC (on contracts negotiated away from business premises); Directive 97/7/EC (on distance contracts) have been amended, while Directive 93/13/EEC (on unfair terms in consumer contracts) and Directive 1999/44/EC (on consumer sales and guarantees) have been repealed.

6 Directive 2011/83/EU of 25 October 2011. The 'non-link' of the Proposal for a DCR, COM (2008)614/3, with the DCFR is highlighted by E. Hondius, 'The Proposal for a European Directive on Consumer Rights: A Step Forward' (2010) *ERPL* 115; M.E. Storme, 'Consumer Rights Proposal and Draft CFR' (2010) *ERPL* 1.

7 N. Kornet, *The Common European Sales Law and the CISG: Complicating or Simplifying the Legal Environment*?, Maastricht European Private Law Institute Working Paper 2012/4, available at http://ssrn.com/abstract=2012310, arguing that, rather than simplifying the legal environment, the CESL might render it even more complex.

8 Although according to art. 7(1), the scope of application of CESL is limited to B2B contracts as defined by art. 7 (2).

9 As promptly underlined by two resolutions of the UK Parliament, Council Doc. 18547/11, 14 December 2011 and of the German Parliament, 30 November 2011.

the right balance between a high level of consumer protection and the competitiveness of enterprises, while ensuring respect for the principle of subsidiarity'.[10] The present chapter will focus on the main contents of the DCR, through a comparative perspective. However, before dealing in depth with the Directive, a preliminary issue must be faced, that is, the choice between a minimum or maximum level of harmonisation.

### *In defence of a 'full targeted harmonisation'*

Choosing minimum rather than maximum harmonisation[11] implies the adoption of a normative approach. In other words, within the parameters of the subsidiarity and proportionality principles, the European Union's intervention must be qualified as necessary in order to provide adequate and equivalent levels of consumer protection. On the other hand, one could argue whether consumer law must necessarily remain an exclusively European concern, or whether consumer protection may be shared between Member State and EU jurisdiction (as happens in the United States), without compromising the effectiveness of the protective rules.[12] In truth, a preference for a protective policy designed at a European rather than a national level was expressed years ago,[13] and although it could be properly challenged, such a (political) choice has apparently been accepted by Member State law-makers, courts and legal scholars. It seems to view the harmonisation process brought about at a legislative level as a help to the existence of Europe.

Thus, for thirty years the European-level law-maker has encroached upon the Member States' legislative competence as regards certain contracts, and consumer contracts in particular. This encroachment necessarily raises the question of the extent to which we are willing to accept the EU institutions' intrusion into spheres of national private law, or the legal question of whether maximum harmonisation will solve the problems caused by minimum harmonisation.

One of the most striking rules of the DCR is the option in favour of full harmonisation, stated in article 4. As striking as it may appear, it may be

[10] Recital 4 DCR.

[11] The problem was raised in the Green Paper, n. 4 above, on stakeholder responses.

[12] J. Smits, 'Full Harmonization or Consumer Law? A Critique of the Draft Directive on Consumer Rights' (2010) 1 *European Review of Private Law* 11; C. Pongibò, 'Some Thoughts on the Methodological Approach to EC Consumer Law Reform' (2009) 21 *Loyola Consumer Law Revue* 367.

[13] On the EU consumer contract harmonisation debate, see C. Amato, *Per un diritto europeo dei contratti con I consumatori* (Milan, 2003), p. 27 ff.

argued that a (very) high level of protection, and one that does not stifle European competitiveness, would require full harmonisation. With this said, however, problems due to the different levels of protection provided (or permitted) to date by the different Member States and connected to the principle of subsidiarity may still arise.[14] In turn, *minimum* harmonisation would certainly permit the survival (and even strengthening) of national peculiarities, allowing a theoretical race of protection to the top. However, the country of origin principle, if applied to the consumer, would either hinder the growth of a fully integrated internal market (the costs, especially for small and medium-sized enterprises (SMEs), would remain high) or encourage the hardening of market players' attitudes and practices in the preparation of general contract rules. In both cases, the outcome would be inconsistent with the aims of harmonisation. On the other hand, full harmonisation implies a more politically difficult set of choices, and could be criticised for freezing the level of protection (either at too high or too low a level) and for frustrating national cultural legal identities.[15]

Clearly, alternatives might better serve the aims of reducing internal market barriers in a legal environment characterised by a high level of consumer protection. For instance, minimum harmonisation, coupled with a very highly protective optional instrument developed by co-regulation with market players, could provide a constructive competitive tension between both the Member States and market players in order to identify the best available set of rules suitable for a given type of transaction/market/set of stakeholder interests. Minimum sufficient harmonisation would reduce consumer worries in cross-border transactions, while the optional instrument would offer incentives to balance out the costs of a higher level of protection and the benefits of a less fragmented market.

In short, the goal of full harmonisation would not necessarily lead to a 'race to the bottom', but may lead to a 'race to the top', provided that the issues which are 'not completely harmonised' are clarified. In order to simplify and clarify the *acquis*, without annoying those Member States which have already chosen a higher level of consumer protection, it is necessary to identify the issues to be included in the full harmonisation programme, and also outline those which could be left to Member State

[14] Smits, 'Full Harmonization or Consumer Law?', n. 12 above, at 12.

[15] Contra: E. Hondius, 'Fifteen Years of European Private Law' (2009) 2 *Opinio Juris in Comparatione*, Paper 5, 5.

discretion under the mutual recognition clause. One criterion could be to include in the full harmonisation programme all the issues linked to the subjective and objective scope of the horizontal instrument (i.e., consumer/professional definitions, the types of contracts and their purposes). A second criterion could be the identification of rules which by their 'neutrality' would not offend any single Member State, but at the same time could not significantly differ from one state to the next, without creating an incomprehensible disparity among consumers of different nationalities (e.g., the notification of the lack of conformity). This is in fact what a 'targeted full harmonisation' should consist of. This concept was first suggested in the Working Document issued by the European Parliament and followed up in the consolidated version of the Proposal issued on 9 June 2010, after comments from the European Parliament.[16] It seemed to be the 'way out', or the correct compromise between full and minimum harmonisation policies,[17] but it has now been completely modified by article 4 DCR, in which 'targeted full harmonisation' was rejected in favour of a maximum harmonisation policy. So, according to the 'new' article 4: 'Member States shall not maintain or introduce, in their national law, provisions diverging from those laid down in this Directive, including more or less stringent provisions to ensure a different level of consumer protection, unless otherwise provided for in this Directive'.

As will be argued in this chapter, a comparative approach involves the contextualisation of the rules and their selection according to two fundamental considerations: the maintenance of flexibility to correct the EU rules, and the ease of adapting them to the national systems.[18] Both arguments involve, therefore, the application of the comparative approach to test the

[16] Amended text of art. 4 of the Proposal: '1. Save as otherwise provided by this Directive, Member States may not maintain or introduce, in their national law, provisions diverging from those laid down in this Directive, including more or less stringent provisions to ensure a different level of consumer protection. *Member States shall forward the text of diverging provisions of national law to the Commission*' (emphasis added).

[17] In the Working Document, 3 March 2010 (rapporteur A. Schwab): 'While most Committee Members acknowledge that the legal fragmentation issue must be tackled, the general view is that the full harmonisation approach proposed by the European Commission is in fact not feasible at this stage given the nature and the scope of the Proposal. In accordance with the European Parliament's Resolution on the review of the consumer acquis ... Committee Members prefer a *targeted full harmonisation* approach, limited ... to specific aspects of certain contracts, whilst maintaining high levels of consumer protection' (emphasis added).

[18] V. Mak, 'Review of the Consumer Acquis: Towards Maximum Harmonization?' (2009) *ERPL* 58; 'Full Harmonisation in European Private Law: A Two-Track Concept' (2012) 1 *ERPL* 213; Smits, 'Full Harmonization or Consumer Law', n. 12 above, at 8, questioning both the European consumer policy and the full harmonisation principle.

main set of DCR rules.[19] In order to render this test more effective, references to the former DCR Proposal of 24 March 2011 will be made.[20] The choice for a maximum harmonisation set out in article 4, as well as the general framework of the DCR, are therefore seriously questioned.

## Directive on Consumer Rights and the effects of full targeted harmonisation from a comparative perspective

### *Strucure of the Directive on Consumer Rights*

The DCR has largely betrayed the original aim of the 2011 Proposal, as it repeals two previous Consumer Directives, leaving almost untouched the other two Directives. As for its contents, it mainly deals with information requirements, the right of withdrawal, formal requirements and delivery (Chapters II and III). Distance and off-premises contracts have a separate discipline than the other contracts to which the DCR applies; while special applications of the general regime are prescribed in article 17 to contracts for the unlimited supply of water, gas or electricity, and to district heating or the supply of digital content not supplied on a tangible medium. Lastly, only a few provisions (Chapter IV) are devoted to 'other rights', concerning delivery, passing of risk, communication by telephone and payments. In truth, the structure of the DCR is complicated, the framework confusing and the contents excessively detailed – failings which a comparative approach could have addressed.

### *Definitions of 'consumer', 'professional' and 'consumer contracts' and their possible extension*

With regard to the definition of 'consumer', the DCR contains a definition that matches the traditional strict definition and interpretation provided, respectively, by the previous Consumer Directives and by the

[19] Pongibò, 'Some Thoughts on the Methodological Approach to EC Consumer Law Reform', n. 12 above, at 359–61, who argues that comparative private law arguments should be linked to new modes of governance, thus building bridges between private and public law following a 'hybrid method'.

[20] The first draft of the Proposal for a Directive on Consumer Rights was presented on 10 Ocotber 2008, COM(2008)614/3. For a critical review, see K. Lilleholt, 'Notes on the Proposal for a New Directive on Consumer Rights' (2009) *ERPL* 335; M. Loos, 'Consumer Sales Law in the Proposal for a Consumer Rights Directive' (2010) *ERPL* 15. For a defence of the Proposal, see E. Hondius, 'The Proposal for a European Directive on Consumer Rights: A Step Forward' (2010) *ERPL* 103.

Court of Justice of the European Union (CJEU):[21] thus, according to article 2(1) DCR '"consumer" means any *natural* person who, in contracts covered by this Directive, is acting for *purposes which are outside his trade, business, craft or profession*'.[22] Yet arguably, no substantive grounds would justify the categorical distinctions adopted in certain Consumer Directives.[23] Notwithstanding its coherence with the previous *acquis*, this definition does not take into account the European debate questioning such a strict definition, and therefore raises issues concerning the relationship between 'intellectual' professionals and their clients/patients, as well as the exclusion of legal persons, non-profit organisations in particular SMEs and any person acting for purposes to some extent mixed with his/her trade, craft or profession.[24]

As regards the first issue, of the definition of 'consumer' and 'professional', comparative analysis shows that a 'consumer' may also include a client or a patient, as happens in France.[25] Although at the outset the word 'professional' employed in the *acquis* would not distinguish between 'intellectual' professionals and commercial traders, at this stage the *acquis* seems to separate *traders* (this is the preferred DCR definition in article 2(2)) from intellectual services. This is certainly true of hospital-based medical care. This kind of relationship was excluded from the scope of Directive 2006/123/EU on internal market services. Although the DCR also includes contracts dealing with both goods and services in the broad definitions of 'sales' and 'service' contracts (articles 2(3)–(6), 3(3)(b)), and excludes contracts for healthcare services provided by health professionals to patients under Directive 2011/24/EU, it does not clearly exclude *other* intellectual services.

As regards the second issue, the exclusion of legal persons, SMEs and mixed purpose contracts, a comparative approach has highlighted the non-harmonised application of the *acquis* in the Member States, and the need for a broader discussion. Spain, for example, has extended the

[21] C-464/01 *Gruber* v. *Bay Wa AG* [2005] ECR I-439.

[22] Emphasis added. This narrow definition has also been adopted by the CESL in art. (2)(f).

[23] M. W. Hesselink, 'Towards a Sharp Distinction between B2B and B2C Contracts: On Consumer, Commercial and General Contract Law after the Consumer Rights Directive' (2010) *ERPL* 57.

[24] In particular in *Gruber*, n. 21 above.

[25] For a French/Italian comparison as regards the relationship between professionals and clients, see C. Perfumi, 'Disciplina consumeristica e contratto di spedalità' (2010) 10 *Obbligazioni e Contratti* 685.

definition of consumer to legal persons, and in Germany the recent BGB reform (Book II on (Obligations)) has extended certain specific rules (especially those dealing with unfair contract terms) to B2B contracts. In the United Kingdom, there is a debate within the Law Commission on the potential extension of such definition to SMEs. One of the most controversial issues is, in fact, the extension of the revised provisions on unfair terms in contracts to businesses with nine or fewer staff.[26] Having regard to the objective scope of consumer contracts, the DCFR contains a broader notion, including transactions 'primarily for purposes which are not related to his or her trade, business or profession'. To solve the ambiguity pertaining to the adverb 'primarily', an express indication could be given on the basis of the competence and of the distinction (already adopted in some Member States) between 'acts of the profession' and 'acts relative to the profession', in order to include the latter in the scope of consumer protection. This could provide a solution to the complex question of 'mixed use' contracts, permitting one to identify the borderline between 'consumer acts' and professional ones based on the prevailing purpose. The aim of this extension would be to include mixed purpose contracts as consumer contracts.[27] This issue is particularly important having in mind the contractual position of digital services consumers, to which the DCR also applies,[28] where it is sometimes impossible to distinguish 'mixed' acts from 'acts outside the trade'; and where each 'consumer' may act as professional.

This said, the scope of consumer and professional definitions should be widened to all contracting parties, either natural or legal persons, acting within an 'asymmetric contract' (including SMEs, corporate bodies acting for non-profit/not-for-profit purposes, such as foundations, associations, committees and consortiums). In this way, it should be

[26] Law Commission Report (2005) and Draft Bill (2005), following-up the *Unfair Terms in Contracts: A Joint Consultation Paper* (2002), where those consulted were asked whether or not they agreed to treat 'all businesses alike in being able to benefit from the protection, allowing the courts to take into account the size of the business, and whether it makes transactions of the kind in question regularly or only occasionally, in assessing the fairness of the terms complained of'.

[27] This corresponding to the 'reality of social and economic life, in which mixed situations are increasingly frequent': M. E. Storme, 'Editorial: Consumer Rights Proposal and the Draft CFR' (2010) *ERPL* 2.

[28] Recital 19. A special protection will be granted to these kinds of transactions, as their economic importance is increasing in relation to the spreading of new and innovative 'mass technologies': the CESL applies to digital service contracts, but as yet it is still a Proposal.

possible to provide a clearer, more coherent definition of the 'weaker' contractual party, considering that the scope of consumer protection aims at assessing contractual equilibrium in the light of the asymmetric power operating on the marketplace. Based on a broader notion of 'asymmetry', the notion of a consumer contract should include a restricted category of B2B contracts, a category of 'unbalanced' contracts.[29] This category may be inferred by considering a set of rules issued by EU law-makers and addressed not only to consumers (as narrowly defined by the *acquis*), but also to a business 'which for some reason is the weak party and therefore needs legal protection'.[30] This is particularly evident in supply of services contracts in which the weakness of the party is related to the fact that the recipient is subject to the supplier's control over the elements which constitute the characteristic performance of the contract.[31] We can find an initial clear-cut example of this trend in Directive 2000/31/EC, applying to persons that 'for professional ends and otherwise' use an information technology service. In addition, the Directive on distance marketing of consumer financial services[32] seems to leave open the possibility for Member States to extend the scope of the Directive to 'non-profit organisations and persons making use of financial services in order to become entrepreneurs' (recital 29), that is, investors being in essentially the same position as that of an ordinary consumer. By the same token, the Markets in Financial Instruments Directive[33] (MiFID)[34] should be addressed to retail clients that are not necessarily consumers – the subjective characterisation of the investor based on his/her level of investing sophistication. The consumer purchasing financial services may be in a weak contractual position, both as regards his/her access to information and actual freedom of choice. To sum up, consumer law legislation should

[29] C. Amato, *Per un diritto europeo dei contratti con i consumatori* (Milan, 2003), ch. IX.

[30] V. Roppo, 'From Consumer Contracts to Asymmetric Contracts' (2009) *ERCL* 339. This category includes small or micro-businesses; business parties which economically/legally depend on the other party or that are exposed to financial risks (for example, the risk of late payment) vis-à-vis the other party. The Feasibility Study seems to have adopted this view, so far as it extends some protective rules to B2B contracts (Part III, ss. 3–5).

[31] *Ibid.* 315.

[32] Directive 2002/65/EC, art. 2d: 'consumer means any natural person who, in distance contracts covered by this Directive, is acting for purposes which are outside his trade, business or profession'.

[33] Directive 2004/39/EC on markets in financial instruments.

[34] The MiFID is now under review: Proposal for a Directive on Market Financial Instruments, repealing Directive 2004/39/EC, COM(2011)656 final.

review investor protection at the EU level, by including this definition in consumer protection legislation, and by simplifying remedies and access to justice through the establishment of a hierarchy of remedies.[35] On the contrary, according to article 3(3)(d) DCR,[36] financial services contracts are excluded from the scope of the Directive.[37]

The number of EU Directives regulating unbalanced business contracts is increasing due to the special attention being paid to the crucial role of SMEs in the internal market. Directives on commercial agents (1986/653/EC) and on late payments in commercial transactions (2000/35/EC) aim to regulate the weaker position of business parties that may be economically or legally dependent on the other party, or exposed to a financial risk in relation to the other party. Similarly, the Rome I Regulation (593/2008) considers situations in which 'contracts (are) concluded with parties regarded as being weaker', stating that 'those parties should be protected by conflict of law rules that are more favourable to their interests than the general rules' (recital 23). This is, for example, the case not only in consumer contracts, but also in franchise and distribution agreements. It thus aims at understanding and interpreting the scope of consumer protection in a more effective 'real life' sense, with the goal of assessing the contractual equilibrium in light of the asymmetric power held by market players. The present DCR does contain a recital (13) allowing Member States to extend the application of consumer rights to legal or natural persons who are not consumers within the strict meaning of the DCR, but this extension is delegated to Member States' discretion. This is a clear example of undesired effects of the exceptions to maximum harmonisation, leading to non-harmonisation and uncertainty – the scope of application of a protective law should not be left to Member State discretion, on the contrary, it

[35] C. Amato and C. Perfumi, 'Financial Investors as Consumers: Recent Italian Legislation from a European Perspective' in M. Kenny and J. Devenney (eds.), *European Consumer Protection: Theory and Practice* (Cambridge University Press, 2012), p. 279 ff.

[36] Directive 2011/83/EU.

[37] The reason is clarified in recital 32 of Directive 2011/83/EU: 'Union legislation, *inter alia*, relating to consumer financial services, package travel and timeshare contains *numerous rules on consumer protection*. For this reason, this Directive should not apply to contracts in those areas. With regard to financial services, Member States should be encouraged to draw inspiration from existing Union legislation in that area when legislating in areas not regulated at Union level, in such a way that a level playing field for all consumers and all contracts relating to financial services is ensured' (emphasis added).

should represent the outcome of comparative debate and aim at reaching a shared and broader definition of the 'consumer'.

### *Consumer rights and unfair contract terms: the grey and black lists*

As regards unfair terms, the most important novelty introduced pursuant to the 2011 Proposal was the 'black list' of terms which are considered unfair in all circumstances (proposal, article 34 and Annex II). That novelty was the product of a comparative study; most Member States had already provided a list of terms considered unfair in all circumstances. This is the case in Italy (article 36 Consumer Code), France (article R132 Code de la Consommation) and Germany.[38] In the United Kingdom, the Law Commission has also recommended the adoption of a double list in the *Unfair Terms in Contracts Report* (2005), paras. 3.41–3.47. For instance, some of the terms considered unfair in all circumstances as listed in Annex II of the Proposal have already been deemed as such in France,[39] and in both Italy and France.[40] Nevertheless, the terms contained in Annex II were more restrictive and less protective than the lists provided by France and Italy.[41] This raised the broader question of the risks of full harmonisation in the special case of unfair terms. As highlighted by the European Parliament's Committee on the Internal Market and Consumer Protection, at this stage the black and grey lists should not be (fully) harmonised (Working Document,

[38] AGB-Gesetz, 19 December 1976, as modified by Law of 19 July 1996, and now introduced into the BGB pursuant to the Gesetz zur Modernisierung des Schuldrechts, 26 November 2001 (in force from January 2002): s. 309 in particular contains the 'schwarze Liste', where certain clauses are considered as ineffective *juris et de jure* and despite any contrary judicial advice (*Klauselverboten ohne wertungsmöglichkeit*). D. Vanni, *Clausole abusive nel diritto tedesco e spagnolo* (December 2007), available at www.ratioiuris.it.

[39] This is the case of special kinds of limitations on a trader's liability related to entire agreement clauses: see Annex II, (b): 'limiting the trader's obligation to respect commitments undertaken by his agents or making his commitments *subject to compliance with a particular formal requirement*' (emphasis added). Article R132-1 French Consumer Code, n. 2, reads: 'Restreindre l'obligation pour le professionnel de respecter les engagements pris par ses préposés ou ses mandataires'. The French provision is wider and therefore more protective, as it does not restrict the scope of the unfair term to formal requirements.

[40] This is the case of terms excluding or limiting the trader's liability in case of death or physical injury of the consumer.

[41] The so-called 'surprise clauses' (listed in the French and Italian Consumer Codes) have been excluded from the black list in Annex II. It is worth noting that in the Feasibility Study, surprising terms are listed among the unfair terms in B2B transactions.

3 March 2010), to prevent the deletion of terms (or a strict construction of them) from the lists provided for at a national level.

Similarly, in amending the Proposal the Council and the Parliament have completely removed article 34 (that is, the mandatory black list), and have added article 8a to Directive 93/13/EC, according to which Member States are free to keep or adopt lists of terms, and to define them as unfair in all the circumstances (article 32 DCR).[42] However, this is subject to the proviso that such national provisions must be notified to the Commission, which will make that information public in an accessible way. As argued above, a 'targeted full harmonisation' together with a correct use of comparative law would have reached the same goal, but without introducing the dangerous Commission-based control over the Member States' legislative prerogatives.

### *Sales contracts and associated guarantees*

The amendments the DCR made to Directive 99/44/EC consisted in allowing Member States to adopt more stringent provisions as regards the limitation period, second-hand goods, and the non-binding nature of contractual agreements concluded with the seller before the lack of conformity is brought to the seller's attention. As in the amendments to Directive 93/13/EC, this is subject to the proviso that such national provisions must be notified to the Commission, which will make that information public (article 33 DCR). I shall deal briefly with the interpretation and assessment of the first amendment concerning the limitation period, before addressing how two new rules introduced by the DCR, on the time of delivery and passing of risk, have *de facto* also amended Directive 99/44/EC, as they indirectly affect the regime of contractual remedies in the sale of goods.

#### Limitation period

The original Proposal in 2008 had limited the seller's liability to a two-year period from the time when the risk has passed, that is, the time of delivery (article 28(1)). However, some Member States had already provided for a longer liability period. In the Netherlands and in Finland, for example, the trader's liability period depends on the

[42] Article 32 DCR amends Directive 93/13 (inserting art. 8a): Member States are now allowed to introduce their own provisions extending the unfairness assessment to individually negotiated contract terms.

expected life-span of the product (to be assessed by the judge on a case-by-case basis). In Belgium, France and Luxembourg, traders can be held liable if a hidden (major) defect is discovered by the consumer *after* the initial period of two years (subject to a limitation period, rather short in France, longer in Belgium) and provided that *the consumer* can prove that the defect in question already existed at the time of delivery (in this case, there is no reversal of the burden of proof). In Italy, the period of a seller's liability is set at two years from delivery. However, by adding the two months for notice of defects, consumers have up to twenty-six months to take action. In other words, the provision set forth in article 28(1) of the Proposal would have seriously diminished consumers' acquired rights in most Member States. Moreover, article 28(4) of the original Proposal mandated a duty of notice for consumers to inform traders of the lack of conformity within two months of the date on which the lack of conformity was detected. And in fact, the period of notice suggested in article 5(2) of Directive 99/44 was considered by most Member States as a needless restriction of the consumer's rights. Therefore, only six states introduced this period of notice: Denmark, Finland, Italy, the Netherlands, Slovenia and Spain. Most of them chose the two month period. The Netherlands implementation imposed a 'reasonable time' upon consumers, while Slovenia went even further, pressurising consumers to inform traders of the lack of conformity 'as soon as possible'.

A better use of the comparative approach has highlighted the legal debate in the Member States, thus showing that imposing a strict time limit on consumers in the case of remedies cannot be considered a preferred 'better rule' to fully harmonise national laws. Although the resulting regime on time limits should be a welcome revision, once again the broad discretion left to Member States is striking. As argued above, Member States' legislative options reveal a range of strategies which could be adopted at EU level, that is, a longer limitation period, coupled with a reversal of the burden of proof and the abrogation of the duty of notice. In this case it should be evident that 'targeted full harmonisation', supported by a comparative approach, might have provided the 'better rule'.

## Time of delivery

Article 18(1) concerns the time for delivery and gives traders a maximum of thirty days from the conclusion of the contract to deliver by transferring the material possession of the goods. This can be considered as a 'neutral' provision in itself, meant to speed up the delivery process (that otherwise might create obstacles to the market, especially in relation to distance sales, out of premises sales or e-commerce sales) without affecting the trader's interests (recital 51). At the same time, this rule affects the recourse to national contractual remedies, such as granting the trader an additional time for delivery, enforcing the performance of the contract, witholding payment, seeking damages or terminating the contract. Therefore, the subsequent paragraphs of article 18 contain the discipline to be applied should the trader fail to fulfil his obligation to deliver the goods within the time limit set out in para. 1 (or agreed upon with the trader). In particular, the consumer must give the trader a reasonable additional period of time to make the delivery, after the expiry of which he will be entitled to terminate the contract should the trader fail to deliver the goods within that additional period of time.[43] This rule does not apply when the trader has unequivocally refused to deliver the goods, or where the delivery period is essential as such, or where the consumer informs the trader that delivery on a specified date is essential. In truth, such a discipline is not 'neutral' in itself, as it implies the acceptance of a general principle, the preservation of the contract, not necessarily shared by all Member States. It also implies a preference for the performance of the contract in lieu of damages, a choice that may not entirely convince common lawyers.

On the other hand, the issue of the hierarchy of remedies in case of lack of conformity has not been confronted by the DCR. It is well known that Directive 99/44/EC listed four different remedies in favour of consumers: (i) to have the goods repaired or (ii) replaced, at the traders' choice, free of charge (performing remedies); (iii) to make an appropriate reduction in price; or (iv) to rescind the contract, if the performance remedies are impossible or disproportionate, or if the seller has not completed the remedy within a reasonable time or with significant inconvenience to the consumer. The most controversial result of this provision is the so-called 'hierarchy' of remedies. There is no choice for consumers, but rather a strictly normative tool-box decided on by law-makers, giving some minimum choice to traders. Evidence of the doubtful quality of these provisions is provided by national implementation of such, as well as the solutions provided by the DCFR and the

[43] The same regime for the time of delivery and termination for late delivery can be found in CESL, arts. 95 and 115.

CESL.[44] As regards national implementation, suffice it to say that five Member States did not fully accept this hierarchy: Poland, Germany, Greece, Lithuania and Slovenia. The United Kingdom and Ireland have adapted the new regime of remedies introduced by the Sale of Goods Act 1979. In particular, the rejection of goods is suspended for a reasonable time until the goods have either been repaired or replaced *at the consumer's choice*. In the Italian Consumer Code, implementing Directive 99/44/EC, the consumer may ask to have the goods repaired or replaced, at his/her choice. Moreover, Italian regulations offer a new set of rules, outside of the strict hierarchy, and provide a free choice to consumer, should the trader offer different remedies to the consumer (article 130 Consumer Code). As regards the DCFR (article III 3:101(1)) and the CESL (article 106), a creditor may resort to *any* of the available remedies; moreover, remedies may be accumulated if not incompatible. Even in international commercial sales, the solution provided by the CISG is fairer for the purchaser: he/she can choose among the remedies, first giving the seller a chance to remedy non-performance at his own expense without unreasonable delay or inconvenience (article 48(1)).

Against this background, the original Proposal (article 26) had suggested a paragraph modifying the previous rules on remedies. The new provision would have allowed Member States to adopt or maintain national laws giving consumers the right to terminate the contract (after a short period within which the trader might cure his performance), or the free choice among the remedies listed in article 26. This provision took into account the European debate over the undesirable 'hierarchy of remedies', but it simply disappeared from the final DCR text.

## Passing of risks

Article 20 DCR has introduced a rule passing to the consumer the risks of loss or damages to the goods only when he/she has acquired the physical possession of the goods. It is well known that Directive 99/44/EC did not take any position on the issue of the passing of risks, on the assumption that this was too difficult a task to be dealt with at EU level, as it would have encroached upon an area of private law which was intimately

[44] On the issue of the remedies available to the buyer in case of breach of the seller's obligation in the CESL, see C. Amato, 'Les moyens d'action en cas d'inexécution des obligations contractuelles' in O. Deshayes (ed.), *Le droit commun de la vente. Examen de la proposition de règlement du 11 octobre 2011* (Société de Législation Comparée, Paris, 2012), p. 177.

related to the law of property and to commercial law. After several years, the Council and the European Parliament have changed their position. Article 20 of the DCR clearly postpones the passing of risk related to supervening events. This choice has been adopted on the assumption that delivery itself is a risky moment, and that risk should be placed on traders, not on consumers.[45] This new rule has had a substantial impact on Italian contract and commercial law, as the general rule in the Italian Civil Code (article 1376 as specified by article 1465 (1))), derived from the French Code Napoléon, provides that risk of loss and damage passes together with the passing of title (at the very moment when consent is exchanged). Notwithstanding the importance of the rules on the passing of title and risk within national systems, the adoption of this rule may not be characterised as the introduction of a 'legal irritant'. In my opinion, the passing of risk can be defined as a 'neutral' rule, certainly deriving from specific national history, but not necessarily linked to general principles seriously impacting the system itself. In fact, this is exactly the case. The severance of the passing of risk from the passing of property does not upset the relevant property or commercial rules, it simply provides a protective shield to a contractual party presumed to be the weaker party. The same would not have been true had the rules on the passing of property been changed. As the comparative approach highlights, consensual systems as opposed to traditional delivery systems adopting the conveyance rules, are based on profoundly divergent technicalities rooted in the legal past, which cannot be changed with a simple rule contained in a Directive.

Evidence for this argument is provided by the Sale and Supply of Goods to Consumers Regulations 2002 (SI 2002/3045), implementing Directive 99/44/EC in the United Kingdom. Regulation 4 added subsection (4) to section 20 of the Sale of Goods Act 1979 which places the risk[46] on the seller until delivery of goods to the consumer.[47] In other

45 Unless the consumer has commissioned the delivery to a carrier, in which case the risk will pass to the consumer on delivery of the goods to the carrier: see art. 20.

46 Though the law is not clear on this issue, the risk seems to relate to perishable and damaged goods.

47 As specified in s.32(4) of the Sale of Goods Act 1979, delivery of goods to a carrier is not deemed to be a delivery for transmission of title: 'In a case where the buyer deals as consumer or, in Scotland, where there is a consumer contract in which the buyer is a consumer, subsections (1) to (3) above must be ignored, but if in pursuance of a contract of sale the seller is authorised or required to send the goods to the buyer, delivery of the goods to the carrier is not delivery of the goods to the buyer'.

words, the Regulations achieved the solution (now adopted by the DCR) by implementing Directive 99/44/EC, thus improving consumer protection without either misinterpreting the Directive or conflicting with the national legal system. By applying the comparative method, that is, by analysing the different national implementations of Directive 99/44/EC in search of a 'harmonising rule' that may be easily transplanted into different legal systems, article 20 DCR thus appears to be both a modest and a highly effective provision.

## Final remarks

Following this rapid and limited review of some of the DCR's provisions, it is clear that the correct use of comparative methodology is essential if we are to avoid the making of 'bad law'. 'Bad law' results where a detailed comparative study has not previously been carried out to clearly identify the main objectives of European legislation, the historical background of specific provisions, and their effectiveness in each national system. Such a comparative survey should also take into account the role of the courts in evaluating the effects of rules. Through recourse to this cautious methodology, it is possible to achieve that which has been called 'targeted full harmonisation', resulting neither in a race to the bottom, nor in the creation of dangerous 'legal irritants'. The present version of the DCR, though informed by a comparative approach, still suffers in two main critical respects: the legislative technique is poor and the political choice made in favour of maximum harmonisation, coupled with some discretionary powers left to the Member States, leads to the undesirable effects of uncertainty and partial harmonisation. It is time for the European institutions to stop and think seriously about the goals they wish to achieve, if a competitive tool-box is to be created.

4

# The private law dimension to the 'state of the Union': (D)CFR/CESL initiatives and the Europeanisation of private law

JAMES DEVENNEY AND MEL B. KENNY

## Context of consolidation: ever closer Union?

The intervention of EU secondary law in national legal systems has led to the emergence of an unstable, 'wildly unsystematic' body of 'Europeanised' private law:[1] a body in which 'vertical' EU secondary law combines unevenly with divergent national transpositions and judicial interpretations.[2] Historically, this instability strengthened the case for further legislative intervention notwithstanding that the elaboration of a single *ius commune*[3] would require Treaty revision.[4] Yet the body of law which emerged was functional rather than systematic.[5] Indeed, initially, it was envisaged that EC law would erode national private law through a process of negative integration,[6] and subsequent re-regulation under Articles 94 and 95 EC (now 115 and 114

Mel B. Kenny, Chair in Consumer and Commercial Law, Leicester De Montfort Law School.
James Devenney, Chair in Commercial Law, Exeter Law School.

1 See generally, M. Kenny, 'Options between Legislative Intervention and Judicial Collaboration: Improving the Effectiveness and Coherence of EU Law?' (2012) 63 *NILQ* 435; R. Brownsword, H.-W. Micklitz, L. Niglia and S. Weatherill (eds.), *The Foundations of European Private Law* (Hart, Oxford, 2012); termed 'wildly unsystematic' by S. Weatherill, 'The Consumer Rights Directive: How and Why a Quest for "Coherence" has (Largely) Failed' (2012) 49 *CMLRev.* 1279, 1280.

2 See C. Twigg-Flesner, ''Good-Bye Harmonisation by Directives, Hello Cross-Border Only Regulation?' A Way Forward for EU Consumer Contract Law' (2011) *ERCL* 235.

3 C. von Bar, 'From Principles to Codification: Prospects for European Private Law' (2002) 8 *Colum. J Eur. L* 379; O. Lando, 'Does the European Union Need a Civil Code' (2003) *RIW* 1.

4 S. Weatherill, 'Why Object to the Harmonisation of Private Law by the EC?' (2004) 12 *ERPL* 636.

5 N. Reich, 'A Common Frame of Reference (CFR): Ghost or Host for Integration?' (2006) 24 *Wis. Int'l L J* 425.

6 W. Sauter, 'The Economic Constitution of the EU' (1998) 4 *Colum. J Eur. L* 27; N. Reich, 'Europe's Economic Constitution, or: A New Look at Keck' (1999) *OJLS* 337.

TFEU).[7] Moreover, outside the ambit of Europeanisation, national laws continued to apply and national demarcations, *inter alia*, between contract and tort, contract and property held their divergent validities. Against this background, the case for consolidation appears vital. Indeed, the prize of a European Civil Code, just as the introduction of a common currency, reinforces the functionalism at the heart of the European project.

## Fragmentation and polycentricity

Yet despite decades of EU legislative intervention, 'uniform' legal solutions were rare: EU Regulations failed to unify the law due to legislative horse-trades, while EU Directives established transposition frameworks, which allowed for measures of upward derogation.[8] Different European Commission approaches to drafting and national transpositions generated further inconsistencies. Simultaneously, *lex mercatoria* contracting and arbitration were becoming more common, meaning that *polycentricity* came to dominate in cross-border trade with a variety of non-national sources – EU law, *lex mercatoria*, UN Convention on Contracts for the International Sale of Goods (CISG) rules, UNIDROIT Principles or the 1980 EC Rome Convention – becoming important sources of private law. Unsurprisingly, calls for codification became popular and initiatives aimed at simplifying and improving the regulatory framework emerged.[9] Yet, simultaneously, 'spontaneous' harmonisation was also becoming more common, eroding the case for codification,[10] fuelling the perception that consolidation could fuel fragmentation and that, indeed, functionalism itself was inherently and dangerously inflexible.

[7] N. Reich, 'Economic Law, Consumer Interests and EU Integration' in H.-W. Micklitz *et al.* (eds.), *Understanding EU Consumer Law* (Intersentia, Antwerp, 2009), pp. 30–7.

[8] Via minimum harmonisation: Art. 114(4) TFEU. See further Arts. 193 and 169(5) TFEU. See also, e.g., *Green Paper on the Review of the Consumer Acquis*, COM(2006)744 final, p. 6, where it is stated: 'The existing EU consumer protection rules are fragmented basically in two ways. Firstly, the current Directives allow Member States to adopt more stringent rules in their national laws (minimum harmonisation) and many Member States have made use of this possibility in order to ensure a higher level of consumer protection.'

[9] *European Governance: A White Paper*, COM(2001)428 final [2001] OJ C287/1; *SLIM Initiative (Simpler Legislation for the Internal Market)*, COM(1996)204 final; *Review of SLIM*, COM(2000)104 final; *Simplifying and Improving the Regulatory Environment*, COM(2001)726 final.

[10] A.I. Ogus, 'Competition between National Legal Systems: A Contribution of Economic Analysis to Comparative Law' (1999) *ICLQ* 405; N. Reich, 'Competition of Legal Orders: A New Paradigm of EC Law?' (1992) 29 *CMLRev.* 861.

## Coherence of EU law

The rationale for consolidation is connected to ensuring the effectiveness and coherence of EU law, the framework for which relies on the forms of action,[11] the effects of EU law[12] and the doctrine of state liability – a combination which, in theory, produced coherence:

> [T]he Treaty has established a complete system of legal remedies and procedures designed to ensure judicial review of the legality of acts of the institutions . . . where natural or legal persons cannot . . . directly challenge (EU) measures . . . they are able . . . either indirectly to plead the invalidity of such acts . . . or to . . . ask [national courts] . . . to make a reference.[13]

Yet, inevitably, the importance attached to Article 267 TFEU as the main form of enforcement action meant that the coherence of EU law has always been qualified by reliance on ad hoc litigation and the variation in national legal remedies and procedures. Furthermore, the characteristics of EU law reinforced the basic 'incompleteness' of EU law: subsidiarity; national discretion; attributed competences;[14] the margins of direct and individual concern (Article 263 TFEU) and state liability;[15] and Commission discretion under Article 258 TFEU.

Yet can one go further and argue that precisely the chimerical quality of EU law exists for a number of important reasons: the polycontextual nature of legal doctrine across the European Union and subsidiarity in particular. EU law in this interplay requires not a 'one size fits all' functionalism but discretion, margins of appreciation *and* incompleteness; and this, not least, to accommodate the instability of the judicial policy of the Court of Justice of the European Union (CJEU). Moreover,

[11] Direct actions (Arts. 258 and 259 TFEU); judicial review (Art. 263 TFEU); preliminary references (Art. 267 TFEU); actions for non-contractual institutional liability (Art. 340 TFEU).

[12] P. Craig and G. de Búrca, EU Law (4th edn, Oxford University Press, 2008), pp. 279–300.

[13] C-50/00 P *Unión de Pequeños Agricultores* v. *Council (UPA)* [2002] ECR I-6677, para. 40.

[14] Articles 2(5), 169 and 114 TFEU.

[15] C-224/01 *Köbler* [2003] ECR I-10239; C-173/03 *Traghetti del Mediterraneo* [2006] ECR I-5177. D. Nassimpian, '. . . And We Keep on Meeting: De-fragmenting State Liability' (2007) 32 *ELRev.* 819; B. Beutler, 'State Liability for Breaches of Community Law by National Courts: Is the Requirement of a Manifest Infringement of the Applicable Law an Insurmountable Obstacle?' (2009) 46 *CMLRev.* 773; S. Drake, 'State Liability under Community Law for Judicial Error: A False Dawn for the Effective Protection of the Individual's Community Rights' (2004) *IJEL* 34; P.J. Wattel, '*Köbler, CILFIT* and *Welthgrove*: We Can't Go on Meeting Like This' (2004) 41 *CMLRev.* 177, 178–9: 'if a national highest Court wants to avoid the real risk of making its government liable, it had better ask for a preliminary ruling . . . in . . . every case involving a question of EC law'.

if our focus is pragmatically recalibrated to ensuring a high standard of protection in cross-border consumer contract, the ambit for coherence is reduced away from a 'grand design' of a Civil Code. Set against an uncertain rationale, we turn to map the evolution of the (Draft) Common Frame of Reference ((D)CFR) and Common European Sales Law (CESL).

## Developing the (D)CFR/CESL initiative

The 2001 Communication[16] drew attention to the uneven operation of EC contract law and encouraged debate on four options: non-intervention; the introduction of non-binding principles (based on Lando Commission or UNIDROIT); the improvement of existing instruments; and, finally, introduction of (an) (optional) new legal instrument(s). Predictably, the 2003 Action Plan[17] rejected non-intervention and distilled three areas for further elaboration. First, the role of the Common Frame of Reference (CFR) in strengthening the *acquis:* tackling divergent transpositions, providing guidance on interpretation[18] and identifying priorities in overhauling fundamental concepts[19] and areas requiring special treatment.[20] Secondly, debate was encouraged on the utility of EC-wide standard contract terms and conditions.[21] Finally, the Action Plan invited consideration of (a) new optional instrument(s).[22]

The 2004 Communication elaborated a possible Principles of European Contract Law (PECL)-based CFR structure.[23] Meanwhile Annex II set out the parameters for the optional instrument. The proposals can be summarised as follows:

[16] Communication on European Contract Law, COM(2001)398 final, [2001] OJ C255/1.

[17] Communication on a More Coherent Contract Law: An Action Plan, COM(2003)68 final [2003] OJ C63/1; D. Staudenmayer, 'The Commission Action Plan on European Contract Law' (2003) 2 *ERPL* 113.

[18] C-168/00 *Simone Leitner* v. *TUI Deutschland GmbH & Co. KG* [2002] ECR I-2631.

[19] 2003 Action Plan, n. 17 above, paras. 33, 34, 35–6, 32: conclusion and validity of contracts, non-performance and unjust enrichment, representation of foreign companies, formal demands and the exclusion or limitation of liability.

[20] *Ibid.* paras. 30–1, 47–8, 41–2, 43, 49–50 and 67: financial and insurance services, transfer and reservation of title, cabotage transport, factoring, consumer protection and tort law.

[21] *Ibid.* paras. 81–8.

[22] *Ibid.* paras. 89–97.

[23] Communication on European Contract Law and the Revision of the *Acquis*: The Way Forward, COM(2004)651 final (11 October 2004), Annex I, 14–16.

- The CFR was of central importance[24] and aimed at improving the *acquis* through uniform definitions.[25] In surveying the *acquis*,[26] the Communication stressed the need to address differences derived from the patchwork of EU law and from national measures of upward derogation, as well as areas in which sector-specific solutions were required.[27]
- EC-wide standard terms and conditions: a platform for the exchange of information on terms and conditions to simplify cross-border trade.[28]
- The optional instrument: the 2004 Communication advocated a single, horizontal optional instrument.

That this 'non-code' was to be developed by the Study Group on the European Civil Code (SGECC) confirms a central paradox of this initiative.[29]

The 2007 Green Paper marked a further consultation[30] presenting a collection of thirty-one questions, for many of which there could only be one correct answer, and appeared to define a more modest field of vision: narrowing the objectives to measures in consumer law; deprioritising work on a CFR and optional instrument; and promoting a 'mixed approach' to consumer law,[31] involving a Framework Directive on EC consumer contract law and a revision of the EC consumer *acquis*.

24 *Ibid.* 2–5 (functions and legal nature); 9–13 (preparation and elaboration); 14–16 (structure).

25 *Ibid.* section 2.1.1 at 3; section 3.1.3.

26 *Ibid.* 3–4: desirability of codification given interplay of Consumer Directives: Directive 85/577/EC on doorstep selling [1985] OJ L372/31; Directive 90/314/EC on package travel [1990] OJ L158/159; Directive 94/47/EC on timeshares [1994] OJ L280/83; Directive 97/7/EC on distance selling [1997] OJ L144/19; Directive 98/6/EC on consumer protection in the indication of the prices of products [1998] OJ L80/27; Directive 98/27/EC on injunctions for the protection of consumer interests [1998] OJ L166/51; and Directive 1999/44/EC on certain aspects of the sale of consumer goods and associated services [1999] OJ L171/12.

27 2004 Communication, n. 23 above, at 9: insurance contracts, contracts of sale and services, clauses relating to the retention and transfer of title and late payments.

28 *Ibid.* 6–8.

29 For a critical view see K. Riedl, 'The Work of the Lando-Commission from an Alternative Viewpoint' (2000) 8 *ERPL* 71. See also Trento Group on the Common Core of European Contract, www.jus.unitn.it/elsg; Society of European Contract Law (SECOLA), www.secola.org; European Research Group on Existing EC Private Law (*Acquis* Group), www.acquisgroup. org; European Private Law Forum, www.iue.it.

30 *Green Paper on the Consumer Acquis*, COM(2006)744 final (8 February 2007). Following European Commission, *First Annual Progress Report on Contract Law and Acquis Review*, COM(2005)456 final (2005).

31 *Ibid.* Option II, point 4.2: the mixed approach at 8–9.

The 2007 Green Paper was nevertheless controversial. Aside from continuing legal base objections and the countervailing commitment to minimum harmonisation contained in the legal base of Article 169(2)(b) TFEU (ex 153(3)(b) EC),[32] the redefinition of the relationship between EU and national consumer law was contentious,[33] as was the contradiction of the Rome I Regulation (593/2008/EC)[34] which had adopted a standard of minimum protection and expressly excluded mutual recognition for contract law.[35]

Nevertheless, one of the most significant initiatives in the search for more coherence in European private law was the preparation and publication of Principles, Definitions and Model Rules of European Private Law: Draft Common Frame of Reference (DCFR).[36] The ambition of the Draft Common Frame of Reference was immediately striking:[37] consisting of ten 'books' and six volumes, including provisions relating to: general contract law (Books II and III); specific types of contracts such as personal security (Book IV, Part G) and sales contracts (Book IV, Part A); unjust enrichment (Book VII); non-contractual obligations (Book VI); and trusts (Book X). Yet what was the purpose of the DCFR? Was it intended as an EU Civil Code blueprint or a glorified 'tool-box'?[38] This intrigue was encouraged by the European Commission's 2010 Green Paper[39] in which a number of options for the future of EU contract law were set out:

32 C-376/98 *Germany (Tobacco Advertising)* [2000] ECR I-8419, para. 84; C-210/03 *R.* v. *Secretary of State for Health (Swedish Match)* [2000] ECR I-11893, paras. 26, 30–2, 34 and 68. Weatherill, 'Why Object to the Harmonisation of Private Law', n. 4 above, at 646. See also S. Weatherill, 'The Limits of Legislative Harmonisation 10 years after Tobacco Advertising: How the Court's Case Law has Become a Drafting Guide' (2011) *German Law Review* 827.

33 Embrace the small business, the professional, entrepreneur and intermediary: Green Paper 2007, n. 30 above, at para. 4.2, Question B2, Option 2, pp.16–17.

34 Regulation (EC) 593/2008 of the European Parliament and Council of 17 June 2008 on the law applicable to contractual obligations (Rome I) [2008] OJ L176/1.

35 Reich, 'Economic Law', n. 7 above, at 58–9.

36 See C. von Bar and E. Clive, *Principles, Definitions and Model Rules of European Private Law: Draft Common Frame of Reference* (Oxford University Press, 2010) (DCFR).

37 'The perspective is thoroughly European and … [m]odel rules, with comments and notes, bring together rules derived largely from the legal systems of the Member States and the overarching Community law': *ibid.* p. 1.

38 See S. Vogenauer, 'Common Frame of Reference and UNIDROIT Principles of International Commercial Contracts: Coexistence, Competition, or Overkill of Soft Law?' (2010) 6 *ERCL* 143.

39 *Green Paper on Policy Options for Progress towards a European Contract Law for Consumers and Businesses*, COM(2010)348 final (2010).

- a Directive on European contract law (Option 5);
- a Regulation establishing a European contract law (Option 6);
- a Regulation establishing a Civil Code (Option 7);
- a Common Recommendation on European contract law (Option 3);
- a Regulation establishing an optional instrument (Option 4).

However, it soon became clear that an 'optional instrument' was the most likely, and politically acceptable, option.[40] The essential idea of an optional instrument was outlined as follows:

> A Regulation could set up an optional instrument, which would be conceived as a 'second Regime' in each Member State ... providing parties with an option between two regimes of domestic contract law. It would insert into the national laws of the 27 Member States a comprehensive ... self-standing set of contract law rules which could be chosen by the parties ... It would provide parties, primarily those wishing to operate in the internal market, with an alternative set of rules. The instrument could be applicable in cross-border contracts only, or in both cross-border and domestic contracts.[41]

Moreover, it transpired that the scope of a legislative CFR would be much narrower than the DCFR, and would probably only relate to sales and some services contracts.[42] Yet, beyond these indications, there was initially uncertainty on a number of issues, including the scope of the instrument; the extent to which it would cover both business to business (B2B) contracts and business to consumer (B2C) contracts;[43] and whether the instrument would be limited to cross-border transactions. Indeed, Reich advocated not a Regulation but a soft law instrument limited to B2C relations within the framework of the EU conflicts regime.[44]

[40] J. Devenney and M. Kenny, 'Unfair Terms and the Draft Common Frame of Reference: The Role of Non-Legislative Harmonisation and Administrative Co-Operation?' in J. Devenney and M. Kenny, *European Consumer Protection: Theory and Practice* (Cambridge University Press, 2012).

[41] Green Paper 2010, n. 39 above.

[42] Vogenauer, 'Common Frame of Reference', n. 38 above.

[43] See N. Reich, 'EU Strategies in Finding the Optimal Consumer Law Instrument' (2012) 8 *ERCL* 1, but contrast with, *inter alia*, C. Herrestahl, 'Ein Europäisches Vertragsrecht als Optionales Instrument' (2011) *EuZW* 7 (advocacy of optional instrument including B2B and B2C, second rather than twenty-eighth regime), contrasted with a contract law limited to B2C: K. Tonner, 'Das Grünbuch der Kommission zum Europäischen Vertragsrecht für Verbraucher und Unternehmer' (2010) *EuZW* 767.

[44] Reich, 'EU Strategies', n. 43 above, at 13–29, advocating a soft law instrument in consumer sales and limited to transactions on the Internet between business and consumers. See Regulation 593/2008.

Uncertainty continued with the appointment of an Expert Group in 2010,[45] its task being to 'conduct a feasibility study on a draft instrument of European contract law whatever its legal form or nature'. Subsequently, in June 2011, Commissioner Reding gave her support to the idea of an optional instrument.[46] Yet a number of issues remained to be resolved.[47] Then, in August 2011, a draft was produced containing provisions of 'general' contract law (see Parts II, III and VI); provisions on parties' obligations and remedies to a sales contract or a contract for the supply of digital content (Part IV); and provisions on parties' obligations and remedies to a related service contract (Part V).[48]

Rather than the more modest proposal of a European Consumer Contract Law Regulation (ECCLR),[49] a full Proposal for an (optional) Regulation on a Common European Sales Law (CESL) was subsequently published on 11 October 2011,[50] adopting a similar structure to the August 2011 draft. Article 3 of the Proposal states that:

> The parties may agree that the CESL governs their cross-border contracts for the sale of goods, for the supply of digital content and for the provision of related services within the territorial, material and personal scope as set out in Articles 4 to 7.

[45] Commission Decision 2010/233/EU, [2010] OJ L105/109.

[46] Commissioner Viviane Reding, *The Next Steps Towards a European Contract Law for Businesses and Consumers* (Leuven, 3 June 2011): 'as regards contract law, we need a new approach ... that on the one hand helps bring about the single market ...while on the other hand respects Europe's legal diversity and the principle of subsidiarity. For me, this can be achieved by proposing a legal instrument on European Contract Law that is voluntary and optional, that can be chosen by businesses and consumers and then serves as basis for their transactions, that does not replace existing national contract law, but that would exist alongside it'; available at http://europa.eu/rapid/pressReleasesAction.do?reference=SPEECH/11/411&format=HTML&aged=0&language=EN&guiLanguage=en.

[47] *Ibid.* 'We are still discussing the details of how this optional instrument should look like ... But one thing is clear: Nobody will be forced to use the optional instrument ... Only those who choose the instrument will be able to contract under it. Those who do not want to use it will continue to contract under national laws ... the optional instrument will only become a success if many businesses and consumers will find it attractive to make use of it for their transactions.'

[48] Available at http://ec.europa.eu/justice/contract/index_en.htm.

[49] Reich, 'Economic Law', n. 7 above, at 59–60.

[50] Available at http://ec.europa.eu/justice/contract/files/common_sales_law/regulation_sales_law_en.pdf.

Article 7 of the Proposal states:

> The CESL may be used only if the seller of goods or the supplier of digital content is a trader. Where all the parties to a contract are traders, the Common European Sales Law may be used if at least one of those parties is a small or medium-sized enterprise (SME).

Yet, significantly, it was proposed that Member States could extend use of the CESL:

> A Member State may decide to make the CESL available for:
>
> (a) contracts where the habitual residence of the traders or, in the case of a contract between a trader and a consumer, the habitual residence of the trader, the address indicated by the consumer, the delivery address for goods and the billing address, are located in that Member State; and/or
>
> (b) contracts where all the parties are traders but none of them is an SME within the meaning of Article 7(2).[51]

## Critical reflections on the (proposed) CESL

The proposed CESL has already stimulated much debate, a debate which is likely to intensify and include issues related to the drafting of the CESL,[52] the assumptions underpinning the optional instrument,[53] and the methodology adopted in the instruments, not least the continuing

[51] Proposed art. 13.

[52] Prior to publication of the proposed CESL, the Department for Business, Skills and Innovation and Ministry of Justice asked the Law Commission and the Scottish Law Commission to advise the UK Government on the optional instrument; see www.scotlawcom.gov.uk/law-reform-projects/contract-law-in-light-of-the-draft-common-frame-of-reference-dcf/. Shortly after the publication of the proposed CESL, the Law Commissions published their advice: *An Optional Common European Sales Law: Advantages and Problems Advice to the UK Government* (November 2011), available at www.justice.gov.uk/lawcommission/docs/Common_European_Sales_Law_Advice.pdf. The advice expressed their doubts about the proposal: 'Distance selling needs its own clear rules, designed around automated processes. The CESL is based on more general contract law principles and we think that it would benefit from greater focus on distance sales. More could be done to clarify when the contract is formed; the effect of a change of circumstances; and unfair terms protection. Provisions on the transfer of property could also usefully be inserted' (*ibid.* s. 14).

[53] In their advice, the Law Commissions were not convinced of the merits of pursuing a CESL in relation to commercial contracting (*ibid.* s.51). They were, however, more supportive of a CESL for some consumer sales (s.51): 'We think efforts would be better spent on developing a European code for consumer sales over the internet, where there is stronger evidence that the current variety of contract laws inhibits the single market.'

issue of competence, legal base, proportionality and subsidiarity considerations. Here, four further challenges for the CESL are discussed: (i) fragmentation; (ii) ensuring consistency of interpretation; (iii) differences in application; and (iv) the enforcement of consumer protection provisions.

### *A new fragmentation – shifting fault-lines?*

Arguably, the proposed CESL would also result in fragmentation, albeit that the fault-lines may have shifted. More specifically, the CESL does not cover all aspects of the sales relationship:

> All the matters . . . that are not addressed . . . are governed by the pre-existing rules of the national law . . . under Regulations (EC) No. 593/2008 and (EC) No. 864/2007 or any other relevant conflict of law rule. These issues include legal personality, the invalidity of a contract arising from lack of capacity, illegality . . . the language of the contract, matters of non-discrimination, representation, plurality of debtors and creditors, change of parties . . . set-off and merger, property law including the transfer of ownership, intellectual property law and the law of torts.[54]

Additionally, there is the question of the interaction between the CESL and (non-harmonised) areas of law outside the CESL. Here, we are reminded of our work on the protection of non-professional sureties.[55] Surety transactions are an interesting case study for any harmonisation agenda as such contracts are polycontextual in nature, transcending traditional legal boundaries and involving aspects of suretyship law; contract law; consumer law; family law; insolvency law; constitutional law; and property law. The crucial point is that, whilst most Member States have attempted to increase surety protection, there is significant diversity in the means used.[56] In particular, surety protection in individual states involves different complex orchestrations of these legal fields, concepts and mechanisms.[57] This may mean that tinkering with one

[54] Proposed recital 27.

[55] M. Kenny and J. Devenney, 'The Fallacy of the Common Core: Polycontextualism in Surety Protection – a Hard Case in Harmonisation Discourse' in M. Andenæs and C. Andersen (eds.), *The Theory and Practice of Harmonisation* (Edward Elgar Publishing, 2012).

[56] See A. Colombi Ciacchi, 'Non-legislative Harmonisation of Private Law under the European Constitution: The Case of Unfair Suretyships' (2005) 13 *ERPL* 297.

[57] See J. Devenney and M. Kenny, 'Unfair Terms, Surety Transactions and European Harmonisation: A Crucible of Europeanised Private Law?' (2009) *Conveyancer and Property Lawyer* 295.

of these elements may have very different consequences in different Member States.[58] Similarly, harmonising strands of the sales relationship may sometimes have different consequences in different Member States.

### *Challenge of ensuring consistency of interpretation*

One of the core advantages of an optional instrument set out in the 2010 Green Paper was that:

> Consistent reference to a single body of rules would remove the necessity for judges and legal practitioners to investigate in certain cases foreign laws, which is currently the case under conflict-of-law rules. This could not only reduce costs for businesses, but also alleviate the administrative load on the judicial system.[59]

The key challenge relates to ensuring both consistency of interpretation in the Member States and an appropriately 'European' approach to the interpretation of any CESL when, under existing EU private law, there has already been unevenness in interpretation across the European Union.[60] Indeed, even within the same Member State there has been some unevenness of interpretation. For example, one is reminded of the debate in England and Wales on the question of whether or not the Unfair Terms Directive (93/13/EC) applies to non-professional suretyships;[61] the difficulty with applying the relevant Unfair Terms in Consumer Contracts Regulations (UTCCR) 1999 (SI 1999/2083)[62] to such transactions being that it is the non-professional surety *who supplies the service*, whereas the creditor, as beneficiary, will usually be acting in the course of business.[63] Nevertheless, support for the view that the

[58] See Kenny and Devenney, 'The Fallacy of the Common Core', n. 55 above.

[59] COM(2010)348 final. Green Paper 2010, n. 39 above.

[60] See Devenney and Kenny, 'Unfair Terms, Surety Transactions and European Harmonisation', n. 57 above.

[61] See J. Devenney, 'Gordian Knots in Europeanised Private Law: Unfair Terms, Bank Charges and Political Compromises' (2011) 62 *NILQ* 33; G. McCormack, 'Protection of Surety Guarantors in England: Prophylactics and Procedure' in A. Colombi Ciacchi (ed.), *Protection of Non-Professional Sureties in Europe: Formal and Substantive Disparity* (Nomos, Baden-Baden, 2007), pp. 172–3.

[62] Unfair Terms in Consumer Contract Regulations 1999 (SI 1999/2083), transposing the Unfair Terms Directive in England and Wales.

[63] J. O'Donovan and J. Phillips, *The Modern Contract of Guarantee* (Sweet & Maxwell, London, 2003), p. 223.

Unfair Terms Directive applies to suretyships can be found in *Dietzinger*, a case involving the applicability of Directive 85/577/EC to suretyships, the CJEU stating:

> it is apparent from the wording of Article 1 of Directive 85/577/EEC and from the ancillary nature of guarantees that the Directive covers only a guarantee ancillary to a contract whereby, in the context of 'doorstep selling', a consumer assumes obligations towards the trader with a view to obtaining goods or services from him. Furthermore, since the Directive is designed to protect only consumers, a guarantee comes within the scope of the Directive only where, in accordance with the first indent of Article 2, the guarantor has entered into a commitment for a purpose which can be regarded as unconnected with his trade or profession.[64]

In reaching this conclusion, the CJEU noted that nothing in the Doorstep Selling Directive required that 'the person concluding the contract under which goods or services are to be supplied be the person to whom they are supplied'[65] and that suretyships are merely ancillary to the main contract.[66] Moreover, in *Kufner*,[67] Field J, relying heavily on *Dietzinger*, held that suretyships are not excluded from the scope of the UTCCR 1999.[68] By contrast, in *Bank of Scotland* v. *Singh*,[69] Judge Kershaw QC held that the UTCCR 1999 did not apply to suretyships, a view subsequently described as 'compelling'[70] and 'convincing'.[71]

## *Divergences in application*

Yet, even where rules are being interpreted consistently, the application of those rules may vary as a result of local conditions. This was partially

[64] C-45/96 *Dietzinger* [1998] ECR I-1199, para. 20. See generally, M. Kenny, 'Standing Surety in Europe: Common Core or Tower of Babel' (2007) *MLR* 175, 180. Although cf. C-208/98 *Berliner Kindl Brauerei AG* v. *Andreas Siepert* [2000] ECR 1–1741, paras. 25–6 where the CJEU, in considering the Consumer Credit Directive 87/102/EC, noted: 'the scope of the Directive cannot be widened to cover contracts of guarantee solely on the ground that such agreements are ancillary to the principal agreement whose performance they underwrite, since there is no support for such an interpretation in the wording of the Directive ... or in its scheme and aims'.

[65] *Ibid.* para. 19. [66] *Ibid.* para. 18. [67] [2008] EWHC 2319 (Comm).

[68] *Barclays Bank* v. *Kufner* [2008] EWHC 2319, para. 28.

[69] QBD, unreported, 17 June 2005.

[70] *Manches LLP* v. *Carl Freer* [2006] EWHC 991, para. 25 per Judge Philip Price QC.

[71] *Williamson* v. *Governor of the Bank of Scotland* [2006] EWHC 1289, para. 46 per George Bompas QC, sitting as a Deputy Judge.

recognised in *Freiburger Kommunalbauten*,[72] where the CJEU noted that it 'may interpret general criteria used by the Community legislation in order to define the concept of unfair terms. However, it should not rule on the application of these general criteria to a particular term'.[73] More specifically, this issue can be illustrated by the impact of 'background rules' on the unfairness test under the Unfair Terms Directive:

> the application of the same general criterion in two Member States may give rise to very different decisions, as a result of the divergences between the rules of substantive law that apply to different contracts. Hence harmonisation under the Directive is more apparent than real.[74]

For example, in *UK Housing Alliance (North West) Ltd* v. *Francis*,[75] the (non-harmonised) protection that could be offered by courts in possession proceedings contributed to a finding that a term in a sale and lease-back arrangement was not unfair under the UTCCR 1999.

An allied point is that national social, cultural and economic norms may affect the application of some of the tests under any optional instrument. Again, this may be illustrated by reference to UTCCR 1999, reg. 5(1) which provides:

> A contractual term which has not been individually negotiated shall be regarded as unfair if, contrary to the requirement of good faith, it causes a significant imbalance in the parties' rights and obligations arising under the contract, to the detriment of the consumer.

Clearly pivotal to reg. 5 is the conceptualisation of 'good faith'.[76] This was an issue addressed in *DGFT* v. *First National Bank plc*,[77] where Lord Bingham stated: 'Good faith in this context is not an artificial or technical concept; nor, since Lord Mansfield was its champion, is it a concept wholly unfamiliar to British lawyers. It looks to good standards of commercial morality and practice.'[78] The key point is that

[72] C-237/02 *Freiburger Kommunalbauten* v. *Hofstetter* [2004] ECR-I 3403.
[73] *Ibid.* para. 22.
[74] *Report on Directive 93/13/EEC on Unfair Terms in Consumer Contracts*, COM(2000)248 final) (2000), p. 30.
[75] [2010] EWCA Civ 117.
[76] M. Kenny, J. Devenney and L. Fox O'Mahony, 'Conceptualising Unconscionability in Europe in the Kaleidoscope of Private and Public Law' in M. Kenny, J. Devenney and L. Fox O'Mahony, *Unconscionability in European Private Financial Transactions: Protecting the Vulnerable* (Cambridge University Press, 2010) 377.
[77] [2002] UKHL 52. [78] *Ibid.* para. 17.

such a test is inevitably loaded with social, cultural and economic norms and there are differences in such norms across the European Union.[79]

### *Effective enforcement of consumer protection provisions*

Commissioner Reding has noted that: 'The right balance between business and consumer interests is . . . key to the success of the optional instrument'.[80] By contrast, the Expert Group's Feasibility Study stated: 'the Commission tasked the Expert Group with drafting contract law rules which would afford consumers a high level of protection in business-to-consumer contracts'.[81] Thus, to encourage consumers to use the optional instrument, the level of consumer protection needs to be high. If so, further reflection on the enforcement of consumer protection provisions in any optional instrument needs to be undertaken, in particular, consideration of the role of collective proceedings in the regulation of unfair terms, and that consumers often lack the information, resources and/or inclination to challenge 'unfair' standard terms in the courts.[82]

## Conclusions

The responses emerging from the DCFR and CESL initiatives threaten disproportionate legislative intervention where much more circumspect steps respecting the established consumer *acquis* and the pre-existing conflicts framework may have been more appropriate. While reform needs to be more targeted to ensure that a genuine twenty-eighth regime is available to consumers in cross-border constellations, the (D)CFR/CESL initiative(s) go well beyond this brief and threaten, in fact, a competing rather than a purely opt-in regime which would lead to further legal fragmentation. The suspicion must be that the proposals do more than assemble a tool-box, but rather prepare for a fragmentation

[79] P. O'Callaghan, 'Protection from Unfair Suretyships in Ireland' in A. Colombi Ciacchi (ed.), *Protection of Non-Professional Sureties in Europe: Formal and Substantive Disparity* (Nomos, Baden-Baden, 2007).

[80] Reding, *The Next Steps Towards a European Contract Law*, n. 46 above.

[81] See http://ec.europa.eu/justice/policies/consumer/docs/explanatory_note_results_feasibility_study_05_2011_en.pdf at p. 6.

[82] H. Beale, 'Legislative Control of Fairness: The Directive on Unfair Terms in Consumer Contracts' in J. Beatson and D. Friedmann (eds.), *Good Faith and Fault in Contract Law* (Clarendon Press, Oxford, 1995).

out of which a broader exercise and further measures of consolidation can emerge. Again, the initiative(s) seem result-oriented, with the European Commission at pains to obscure the true scale of the proposals: just as the DCFR extended well into private law, the proposed CESL extends well into broad areas of general contract law. Such initiatives, to the extent that a new category of 'opt-in consumer law' would drive further fragmentation between purely domestic and Europeanised private law, would ultimately serve as a stalking horse for further legislative intervention. In terms of policy development, the way events have conspired to support the introduction of a CESL is sobering. Once again, attention centres on top-down legislative intervention. The danger of such policy development is clear with, once again, pragmatism being subverted by functionalism.

5

# European contract law: how to exclude land?

PETER SPARKES

## Land and the Draft Common Frame of Reference

The debate about European contract law assumes that it is feasible to bring together national contract laws whilst partitioning off property law, leaving national land laws unaffected. Publication of the Draft Common Frame of Reference (DCFR) provides a starting point for the discussion since it lays down Principles, Definitions and Model Rules for the new European private law,[1] the ambition being a Civil Code for Europe.[2] This chapter assesses whether this partition has been achieved satisfactorily by the current work and questions whether it is ever achievable. The intention is to debate the technical adequacy of the DCFR as presented to operate as a Frame of Reference for the entire European Union, recognising that the eventual 'political' document will be much narrower and that the United Kingdom will opt out anyway.

A large potential interface exists between the rules of the Common Frame of Reference as drafted and real property in two particular aspects:

(a) the application of the DCFR to juridical acts as well as contracts; and
(b) a material scope extending beyond contract to include non-contractual rights and obligations and related property matters.[3]

This wide field is cut down by a land exclusion which appears, superficially, to be much too narrow in scope. The very first article provides that the rules:

Professor of Property Law, University of Southampton.

[1] C. Von Bar and E. Clive, *Principles, Definitions and Model Rules of European Private Law: Draft Common Frame of Reference* (Oxford University Press, 2010) (DCFR).

[2] N. Jansen and R. Zimmermann, 'European Civil Code in All But Name' (2010) *CLJ* 98; S. Whittaker, *Draft Common Frame of Reference: An Assessment* (Ministry of Justice, London, 2008), para. 13; H. Eidenmuller *et al.*, 'Common Frame of Reference for European Private Law: Policy Choices and Codification Problems' (2008) 28(4) *OJLS* 659, 668; S. Whittaker, 'A Framework of Principle for European Contract Law?' (2009) 125 *LQR* 616, 645.

[3] DCFR, art. I 1:101(1).

> are not intended to be used ... except where otherwise provided, in relation to: ... (f) the ownership of, or rights in security over, immovable property.[4]

This is (dare one presume to say?) much narrower than the drafters intended. Read literally it leaves a contract to sell land within the Common Frame of Reference, so the balance of the definition between things and rights in things does not appear quite right. It is tricky to achieve the right balance since movables are in, including both contracts to sell goods and property in goods.

## Things immovable

### *Human action test*

A market requires agreement on commoditarisation, a shared perception of which things should be the subject of ownership and barter.[5] Professors Von Bar and Drobnig found that there was substantive agreement across Europe about the nature of property, though with differences of terminology and of detail.[6] Most divergence was identified in relation to incorporeals, which do not count as property in Germany and Greece, reflecting the line drawn by Gaius and Justinian, whereas elsewhere property is allowed in intangibles. Land is, of course, an object of property everywhere across the continent.[7]

The scope of European contract law turns on the exclusion from the Common Frame of Reference of what is described as immovable property,[8] and is defined to mean:

> land and anything so attached to land as not to be subject to change of place by usual human action.[9]

Property commonly means a right in a thing, but this definition focuses on the physical thing, a plot of land, trees growing in the ground and a building; in terms of English law this is land itself

[4] DCFR, Principles, para. 38, I 1:101(2)(f). Further restrictions appear in later Books: art. 101(3).

[5] J. Basedow, 'Common Contract Law for the Common Market' (1996) 33 *Common Market Law Review* 1169, 1180.

[6] C. Von Bar and U. Drobnig, *Interaction of Contract Law and Tort and Property Law in Europe: A Comparative Study* (Sellier, Munich, 2004), para. 467.

[7] P.B.H. Birks and G. McLeod, *Justinian's Institutes* (Duckworth, London, 1987), p. 22.

[8] DCFR, art. I 1:108(1).

[9] DCFR, Annex ('immovable property').

without the statutory extension to embrace also rights.[10] Civilian lawyers distrust 'land' as the description of a category of property, because many states have special rules for ground that is covered with water (is a river immovable?) not to mention the potential confusion with the term for a German region (Land), but above all because of the need to include rights in land. Hence the preference for the word 'immovable', understood to mean an ownership right rather than a physical parcel of land. The test of movability/immovability is really suitable for things and much less apt for rights since these can always move. The object of property, a particular house, may be fixed in relation to its neighbours, and although the entire street is hurtling together through space the concept of movability is readily understandable in relation to a thing: 'immovable' is a close match for 'land' but the fit is not perfect and is not close enough to obviate the need for conflicts rules to cope with cases where one system treats a thing as immovable which another system allows to move.[11]

Land must include the airspace using the cursed *cujus est solum* rule,[12] limited nowadays to the level of reasonable human exploitation;[13] flying a balloon low over a French field should remain a French delict.

One wonders whether the test proposed is subtle enough to comprehend all thirty or so EU fixtures rules, or the fifty or so rules of the greater Europe. English law has three categories, chattels, fixtures and things forming part of the land.[14] The latter includes, for example, a shack not physically attached to the land of the Gower peninsular but resting on concrete blocks, but constructed over the years in such a way that it would collapse if any attempt were made to move it. Though not attached to the land this might well fall within the DCFR definition as 'land' itself – that it could not move under usual human action. In England, the test of fixture has moved on from the degree of fixing to take much more account of the purpose of fixing; a thing fixed to become

[10] Law of Property Act 1925, s.205(1)(ix).

[11] *Dicey and Morris, Conflict of Laws* (Lord Collins (ed.), 14th edn, Sweet & Maxwell, London, 2006), ch. 22.

[12] *Cujus est solum, ejus est usque ad coelum et ad inferos* (= whoever owns the soil, it is theirs up to Heaven and down to Hell). The phrase is attributed to Accursius, author of the *Great Gloss* at Bologna in 1230, and was introduced into the common law by William Blackstone's Commentaries.

[13] Bernstein v. Skyviews and General Ltd [1978] QB 479, per Griffiths J.

[14] *Elitestone Ltd* v. *Morris* [1997] 1 WLR. 687, 691, per Lord Lloyd.

immovable might be part of the land included in a sale but be removable by a tenant at the end of a lease and an item attached to the same degree might be detachable if it was put up for enjoyment but part of the land if it was put up for some functional reason.[15]

Again, the proposed text hardly begins to do justice to the subtleties of the French law of immovables.[16] Immovables by nature are determined according to the degree of attachment to the ground, which might fit well with the European draft but raises the issue of how the Morris' shack might have fared in France. However, there is also a category of immovables by destination, things placed on land for service or exploitation of the land. In *Tiersonnier*, a farmer stocked his holding with eighty cattle, sixty being the appropriate quantity for the particular farm, so sixty were immovable and twenty movable;[17] it is not quite clear how from looking at them in the field one could tell one kind of kine from the other kine.[18] The Napoleonic rural economy also envisaged rabbits, beehives and vats used in beer making.[19] So far as fruit and produce is concerned, it seems clear that the transformation from national land to European produce occurs at the moment of harvest, with scope neither for anticipation[20] nor delay: an English tenant who loses the lease of his holding can re-enter to reap his harvest under the preserved right to emblements,[21] but a European tenant will not be able to do this. Nor is there any differentiation between rightful and wrongful picking, either of which could Europeanise the apples in an orchard by converting them from land to goods.[22]

European contract law requires a simple invariable rule, but such a rule will not fit with all national property systems. So, in an area in

15 *Leigh* v. *Taylor* [1902] AC 157 (HL).

16 French Civil Code, art. 517 ff; J. Bell, S. Boyron and S. Whitaker, *Introduction to French Law* (2nd edn, Oxford University Press, 2008), pp. 272–3.

17 *Tiersonnier*, Requêt 19 October 1938, D.H. 1938.613; Bell, Boyron and Whitaker, *Introduction to French Law*, n. 16 above, at p. 273.

18 Animals are defined to be goods: DCFR, Annex ('goods').

19 French Civil Code, art. 524.

20 As it happens, French law also takes the moment of harvest, though there is provision for crops and trees to become movables when earmarked for felling; the point is that European property systems may vary on this point.

21 C. Harpum, S. Bridge and M. Dixon, *Megarry and Wade's Modern Law of Real Property* (7th edn, Sweet & Maxwell, London, 2008), para. 3–105.

22 The rules on acquisition of property in goods do not apply when a thing is detached from land: DCFR, art. VIII 1:201.

which thirty or more property systems are more or less aligned, the conclusion must be that the simple definition of immovable property requires small but essential changes to all Civil Codes in Europe; and in England it would require tinkering with the Law of Property Act 1925 definition of land.[23] Otherwise a contract could relate to movable property so as to fall within the European Common Frame of Reference and at one and the same time relate to land so as to require formality.[24] It will be very awkward to unpick all the national rules, even in an area such as fixtures where the broad shape of the various laws is already aligned.

No problem arises where the European DCFR and the local law treat the item the same way, but insistence on autonomous definitions[25] gives rise to the unfortunate possibility that something might be treated as land by the Common Frame of Reference so as to be excluded from European contract law, and yet be treated as a movable by the local law, say the French Civil Code, resulting in a vacuum in which no law applies to it at all. A more pragmatic solution would reverse and apply the law of the site to determine what is land.[26] Autonomous interpretation is a sensible general principle but less so at the interface of the code with national systems. However, there may exist a national system in which immovables are defined in terms of rights and there is no discrete category of immovable things as such.

### *Land as an excluded category*

The structure of the common law of property would not be greatly harmed by a Europeanisation of contract/obligation which excluded land. That is not to say that it would be welcomed, but is merely to say that it would be technically feasible to implement a contract law excluding land. Little statutory surgery would be involved. A separation between land and not-land is made right at the beginning of property law, a feudal legacy not yet erased, a consequence of recognising ownership of land through the medium of an estate. A lease of a flat or a shop is quite distinct from hiring a car, mortgages are distinct from credit secured on movables, and neighbour obligations such as easements and

[23] Law of Property Act 1925, s.205(1)(ix).
[24] In England under the Law of Property (Miscellaneous Provisions) Act 1989, s.2.
[25] DCFR, art. I 1:102(1).
[26] P. Sparkes, *European Land Law* (Hart, Oxford, 2007), para. 3.07.

covenants are recognised between landowners but not between neighbouring yachts in a marina.

Almost all of the Law of Property Act 1925 deals with land law, despite its name, and the process of separation of movables would only require minor changes: the rule about the legal assignment of things in action to be moved elsewhere,[27] a few other provisions to be transferred to the legislation governing trusts,[28] and it might improve the coherence of the law to split the limitation regime. Land law, conveyancing and registration, land charges and landlord and tenant are already distinct. In fact, the common law would be improved if the currently underdeveloped law of personal property had to be set out *de novo*.[29]

Civilian Codes would suffer far more damage from a partition between land and movables. Personal obligations are clearly separated from property, but the property part of the Code always includes generic rules intertwined with rules applying specifically to immovables and to movables. Ownership of movables could only be moved to a European code by leaving in place a parallel national code for land in an horrifically messy form. This can readily be seen from a glance at the indexes to Book 2 ('Property and different types of ownership') of the French Civil Code or to Book 3 ('Law of property') of the German Civil Code (Bürgerliches Gesetzbuch).

If property in land was left in a mangled form, obligations would have to be cut in half to exclude contracts to sell movables (now Europeanised) leaving contracts to sell immovables in the truncated Civil Code. Separate obligations would arise from a nuisance to a greenhouse bolted to a concrete base and nuisance to a greenhouse resting on its base. It would then be logical to recodify what was left into a Land Code, either national or covering a number of states with comparable property systems. At least the public/private divide ensures that all public controls on land ownership are kept out of the European remit, so national land codes might emerge, despite the uncomfortable echoes of Soviet-style economic planning.

In short, a split between land and other property would be fairly friendly to the common law but would require a great deal of structural

[27] Law of Property Act 1925, s.136.

[28] Law of Property Act 1925, Parts VII (perpetuities and accumulations), X (wills).

[29] At least in legislation; for texts see e.g., M.G. Bridge, *Personal Property Law* (3rd edn, Clarendon, Oxford, 2002).

reorganisation of civilian Codes and would result in a large duplication of legislative overhead. For this reason, a simple land exclusion is unlikely.

## Movables

The Draft Common Frame of Reference intrudes deeply into the property law affecting movables.[30] It is not the purpose of this chapter to address the adequacy or shortcomings of the Books covering these subjects, but merely to demonstrate the wide-ranging nature of the proposed codification, and the overwhelming necessity for a watertight land exclusion.

Goods are corporeal movables, and the category of movables also includes incorporeals but excludes immovables.[31] This sense is quite distinct from the '*biens*' protected at Strasbourg.[32] Contracts affecting movables are covered, both general contracts and specifics such as sale and hire.

The inner core is a general law covering:

> definition, pre-contract, formation, withdrawal, representations, grounds of invalidity, interpretation, contents and effects, performance, remedies, non-performance, plurality of parties, change of parties, set off and merger and prescription.[33]

This draft may not sit well with English contracts affecting movables, but it is not the purpose of this chapter to explore areas of divergence which have already provoked so much debate. Since contracts live and die in a short time-frame it is easier to change contract law than substantive property law, and substantive property rights in movables have a shorter shelf-life than corresponding rights in land, making movables the more promising subject of harmonisation.

A second layer includes obligations, a broad category including restitution, tort/delict, unjustified enrichment and beneficial intervention in another's affairs.[34] This is straying rather beyond the strict needs of the

[30] DCFR, Books VIII, IX; S. Van Erp '(D)CFR, Consumer Acquis, Property Law and Euromortgage' (2007) 11(4) *European Journal of Comparative Law Internet* 1.

[31] DCFR, Annex ('corporeal', 'goods', 'movables', 'property').

[32] This means things in a much wider sense, including tangibles, intangibles and claims.

[33] *Green Paper on Policy Options for Progress Towards European Contract Law for Consumers and Businesses*, COM(2010)348 final, para. 4.3.1.

[34] *Ibid.* paras. 4.3.2, 4.3.4.

common market in goods; it is as if the European Union has suddenly decided to take over Asia, and is quietly pondering Africa as well, and risks exceeding European competence.

Still wider are the special contracts,[35] the nominate contracts familiar in Civil Codes, a territory previously uncharted by comparative law.[36] One or two might, if not artificially restricted, affect land, notably:

Book IV.A sales;
Book IV.B leases; and
Book IV.H donations.

So it is recognised that it is necessary to exclude land, an exclusion carried out in a belt and braces way. Each of these three topics is inherently limited to (movable) goods,[37] and land is then excluded (again) from the Books covering sales of goods and donations.[38] Yet even an exclusion in this comprehensive form could easily be broken in future by an expansionist Commission simply by the addition of new Books with further species of special contracts.

Finally, two Books set out substantive property law for goods:[39]

Book VIII acquisition of ownership of goods;
Book IX proprietary security in movable assets.[40]

The most immediate intersection between contract law and property law is where goods are sold with a reservation of title.[41] Civilian systems generally provide for title to goods to pass on their delivery to the buyer and once goods are in the buyer's possession an action for the price is personal in nature and must be pursued in contract. Common law systems allow the seller to reserve title until the goods are paid for, opening the way to a proprietary claim to recover the goods in the event of non-payment and providing strong protection against the insolvency of the buyer, and few continental Codes take the same line. Although a

[35] *Ibid.* para. 4.3.3. [36] Eidenmuller, 'Policy Choices', n. 2 above, at 663–4.
[37] DCFR, arts. IV A 1:101(1); IV B 1:101(1), (5); IV H 1:101(1), (5); this is also true of acquisition of title, VIII 1:101(1), and proprietary security, IX 1:101.
[38] DCFR, IV A 1:101(1); IV F 1:101(1)(b); IV H 1:103(2).
[39] Green Paper 2010, n. 33 above, para. 4.3.2; B. Akkermans, 'Concurrence of Ownership and Limited Property Rights' (2010) 18(2) *ERPL* 259, 281 ff.
[40] H. Drobnig, 'Security Rights in Movables', ch. 40 in A. Hartkamp *et al.*, *Towards a European Civil Code* (3rd edn, Kluwer, The Hague, 2004).
[41] Von Bar and Drobnig, (Interaction), n. 6 above, para. 501.

European contract code needs to deal with reservation of title,[42] this is a matter of commercial law and a marginal topic for land lawyers.

Overall in relation to property in goods, the foray behind national lines is limited, because, as Faber points out,[43] it relies on national registers, and the national registration could turn much of the European structure upside down.[44] In each case there is a solid land exclusion, achieved in each case by limiting the scope to goods.[45]

The division between a European property law for movables and national schemes for land obviously gives rise to a problem of legislative duplication. Some points may well conflict with existing national property law. Examples are the definition of formalities[46] and the provision that no form is required for contracts and other juridical acts;[47] clearly the latter would not be suitable for land, and mixed contracts will need to be severed.[48] Other eye-catching details are the rules for the service of notice,[49] already complex without another level of detail, and rules for imputed knowledge.[50] It will be very confusing if Europe uses the word 'notice' to describe the process of giving notice of an assignment that has been completed, rather than observing the normal English usage, the duty on a buyer to enquire for discoverable interests before buying. Specific performance would become a general remedy, albeit with some bars,[51] a major extension of English law for goods,[52] and with important ramifications in land law. The rules on contractual assignment would also be very awkward if applied to land: a European contract would be assignable even if it says it is not.[53]

The proposals for a property law for movables will surely fall on the issue of competence.[54] If there is a single market in goods, it seems logical

[42] Interaction between contract and property law causes significant practical problems: G. Betlem and E. Hondius, 'European Private Law after the Treaty of Amsterdam' (2001) 9 *ERPL* 3, 9.

[43] W. Faber, 'Book VIII of the DCFR: Overview of Content and Methodology' (2010) 14(3) *Edinburgh Law Review* 499, 500.

[44] DCFR, art. VIII 1:102. [45] DCFR, arts. VIII 1:101(1); IX 1:101.

[46] DCFR, arts. I 1.106, 1.107. [47] DCFR, art. II 1.106. [48] DCFR, art. II 1.107.

[49] DCFR, art. I 1:109. [50] DCFR, art. II 1.105.

[51] G. de Vries, 'Right to Specific Performance: Is there a Divergence Between Civil and Common Law Systems and has it been Bridged in the DCFR?' (2009) 17(4) *ERPL* 581; M. Van Kogelenberg 'Right to Enforced Performance of Non-monetary Obligations' (2009) 17(4) *ERPL* 599.

[52] DCFR, art. III 3:302.

[53] DCFR, art. III 5:108(1); Whittaker, *Assessment, above* n. 2 above, App. IV; Eidenmuller, 'Policy Choices', n. 2 above, at 687.

[54] Article 345 TFEU (ex Art. 295 EC); Sparkes, *European Land Law*, n. 26 above, para. 3.18.

to stop at the edge of contracts to sell movables where the guiding principles are freedom of contract and just results, and to leave aside property where the scope for party autonomy is limited and the core aims are security and certainty.[55]

## Consumption of land

Purchasers of land could, potentially, be consumers within the ambit of EU law. Physical land is rooted in the territorial jurisdiction of one Member State, but investment in land can move across borders and thus falls within the remit of the internal market.[56] Some aspects of the European consumer *acquis* do indeed apply in full to land purchasers, most notably the prohibition on unfair commercial dealings[57] and the controls regulating unfair terms in contracts.[58] In these areas, the main concern is to ensure that the final version of the Common Frame of Reference should mesh properly with EU legislation, which is far from the case with the present draft, but proper alignment should not be too tricky.[59] In other areas the land exclusion is not an issue because immovable property is entirely removed from the European remit, for example, in relation to consumer credit secured on land.[60]

There remains a tricky area in which a balance has to be drawn between pure land sales left to national legislators and other transactions with land that are within the European net. The balancing act is needed when products are marketed and contracts negotiated away from the business premises of a trader; consumer protection in this area originally differentiated 'distance selling' over the Internet and off-premises selling, on the 'doorstep' or elsewhere, but these are now rolled up into a single Consumer Rights Directive,[61] which continues to offer rights to information and to withdraw from transactions. The interface between consumers entitled to these protections and the land exclusion is reset. This

[55] DCFR, Principles, para. 36, art. I 1:102(3)(c); J. Basedow, 'Freedom of Contract in EU' (2008) 16(6) *ERPL* 901; G. Alpa, 'Party Autonomy and Freedom of Contract Today' (2010) 21(2) *European Business Law Review* 119.

[56] Sparkes, *European Land Law*, n. 26 above, paras. 1.32, 3.18.

[57] Unfair Commercial Practices Directive 2005/29/EC [2005] OJ L149/22; Sparkes, *European Land Law*, n. 26 above, para. 5.40.

[58] Unfair Contract Terms Directive 93/13/EEC [1993] OJ L195/29.

[59] DCFR, art. II 9:401.

[60] Credit Agreements for Consumers Directive 2008/48/EC [2008] OJ L133/66.

[61] Directive 2011/83/EU [2011] OJ L304/64.

gives rise to a subsidiary question about the transition from the previous regime,[62] and the more important issue of how to draw the line with what may loosely be termed 'holiday' arrangements, ones which are particularly likely to be negotiated over the Internet.

Straightforward house sales are of the consumer to consumer (C2C) pattern, and so outside the business to consumer (B2C) pattern of consumer transactions. These lie beyond the aspiration of the European Commission to regulate. However, the exclusion goes wider to exclude any contract for the sale or transfer of rights in immovable property.[63] Buyers of homes do not need protection beyond ensuring that they receive professional advice about their purchase, a matter left to national law. Surely, however, there is no one in greater need of protection than a person buying a home in another Member State? The author's view is that such contracts should attract European information and withdrawal rights, unless and until the buyer has appointed a professional advisor. The Consumer Rights Directive also removes European protection from land transactions which fit the B2C pattern where new build property is acquired direct from the developer, and also from contracts for the construction and substantial conversion of premises.[64] Home improvement, a big business, is, of course, very much within the marketing controls.

Rental is a puzzle. The old legislation brought rental within the controls on Internet selling by the roundabout route of excluding land but de-excepting rental,[65] and the DCFR was designed to mesh with this.[66] However, the enacted version of the Consumer Rights Directive makes an unexplained volte face to exclude rental of accommodation for residential purposes and all aspects of social housing.[67] The Common Frame of Reference will need corresponding amendment. The self-reliant tourist renting a holiday home for a fortnight's self-catering in a sunnier climate is now to be treated as a purchaser of land, outside the shield of European consumer law, and so required either to fend for himself or to employ a notary to read over the contract. Such a holiday maker is only

[62] The new regime will apply full harmonisation to contracts formed on and after 13 June 2014; the old rules with minimal harmonisation are covered in Sparkes, *European Land Law*, n. 26 above, para. 5.16.

[63] Consumer Rights Directive, art. 3(3)(e); DCFR, art. II 5:201(2)(c).

[64] Consumer Rights Directive, art. 3(3)(f); DCFR, art. II 5:201(2)(c).

[65] Distance Selling Directive 97/7/EC [1997] OJ L144/19, art. 3(2)9a); contrast the exclusion of rental in Contracts Negotiated Away from Business Premises Directive 85/577/EC [1985] OJ L372/31, art. 3(1).

[66] DCFR, art. II 5:201. [67] Consumer Rights Directive, art. 3(3)(a), (f).

one step removed from a hotel guest, a package tourist, or a person 'investing' in a timeshare unit, all of whom are favoured by the European consumer rules.

So the pre-existing patchy and incoherent protection has been altered but not improved. There is still no logical connection between the need by a consumer for protection and the provision of protection. In short, the revision of the *acquis* does not fill the land lawyer with confidence.

## Rights

Most states include in their legislation an extended meaning of land (or immovables) covering physical land and things annexed, but also covering estates in land and limited property rights.[68] This saves a lot of legislative duplication since, for example, a formality rule established for a contract to sell land applies, without more, to a contract for a mortgage or to create an easement of land. The DCFR operates in reverse. The rules are not intended for use in relation to 'the ownership of, or rights in security over, immovable property'.[69] It starts with the tangible thing (immovable property) which is then limited so that the only rights outside the DCFR are ownership and security rights. As a consequence of the (apparently unintentional) omission of limited proprietary rights,[70] they are, it seems, within the DCFR.

### *Ownership*

Ownership is defined to be the most comprehensive right that a person can have over property; it should confer exclusive rights of use, enjoyment, modification and destruction, the power of disposition and the right of recovery of the property.[71] This definition was undoubtedly conceived in the context of movable property and is used as the basis for the rules on the acquisition and loss of ownership of goods.[72] Their ephemeral nature and their ability to get lost make multiple layers of ownership unsatisfactory. Land is more complex, with many forms of ownership possible, but only outright ownership falls within the definition. Another problem is the radically different starting positions of the

[68] Law of Property Act 1925, s.205(1)(ix).

[69] DCFR, Principles, para. 38, art. I 1:101(2)(f). This is subject to further restrictions in later Books: art. 101(3).

[70] DCFR, Annex ('limited proprietary right').

[71] DCFR, Annex ('ownership'), art. VIII 1:202.

[72] DCFR, art. VIII 1:101(1).

common law and civilian systems. Civilian systems identify an outright ownership but then allow it to be encumbered with certain large subtractions, emphyteusis, superficie and usufruct – rights that almost negate the core of ownership. Eigentum or *propriété* constitute ownership but emphyteusis or superficie or usufruct do not on this view; indeed the definition of ownership seems literally to exclude Eigentum or *propriété* burdened by a usufruct or long real lease. The common law starts from the holding of estates which may be partial ownership of a particular parcel of land, but English law then selects from the range of common law estates the most extensive – the fee simple absolute in possession – as the absolute ownership right, now dignified with a unique legal status.[73] The end result of these two journeys is strikingly similar. European ownership equates to the absolute ownership of goods and hence to the English freehold or commonhold. It seems to exclude leaseholds, however long, and (more arguably) the encumbered freehold.[74] Ownership is well understood and the definition needs tweaking to make it correspond to that understanding.

### *Limited proprietary rights*

A security right is a limited property right in an asset which entitles the secured creditor to preferential satisfaction of the secured right from the encumbered asset.[75] This seems to deal adequately with the mortgage, the legal charge, the hypothec and the *Grundschuld*.

Rights other than ownership are defined to be 'limited proprietary rights', a concept which includes security rights, but also rights to use, rights to acquire and trust related rights.[76] The land exclusion (ownership and security over land) leaves open the general contract rules and the rules on contractual obligations (respectively, Books II and III of the DCFR), for the other limited rights, namely, rights to use, to acquire and trust related rights. This is unintended. It arises because positive provision is made for property in goods (Book VIII) and for security rights in goods (Book IX) and the intention was to exclude land from these Books, even though land was inherently excluded. What was required was a comprehensive land exclusion covering all rights (or at least all real rights) in land.[77]

[73] Law of Property Act 1925, s.1(1)(a).
[74] A freeholder subject to a mortgage does not have exclusive rights, e.g., of destruction.
[75] DCFR, Annex ('security right in a movable asset'), art. IX 1:102(1).
[76] DCFR, Annex ('limited proprietary rights'). [77] DCFR, art. I 1:101(2)(f).

Ownership of land is very often fragmented, all systems being functionally similar despite the conceptual variation covering in England estate theory, in France dismemberment and in Germanic systems a charge on the ownership of another.[78] A life estate is rather like a usufruct, but the point is better made by focusing on the long leasehold. In England, this is the only way to buy a flat (given the practical failure of the commonhold scheme). In civilian systems flats are bought in absolute ownership through condominium or *copropriété*. However, emphyteusis or superficie constitutes ownership subject to a rent, particular systems recognising one or the other or both. These are ownership rights in practice bought, sold, registered and mortgaged in the same way, even if civilian systems adhere to the theory that they are limited rights in the land of another, just like servitudes and usufruct.

Long leases apart, there is a major division in approach to short leases, that is to rack rental. English law sees them as one more type of estate. Civilian law sees hire as a single concept, whether it relates to a house or a car, and sees hiring as a matter of obligation rather than partial ownership. Rules are included in the DCFR for leases of goods,[79] with no corresponding Book for rental of homes. How could a single code cover all the security regimes of the European Union? Yet it seems that general contract rules could nevertheless apply to determine when a contract for rental has been formed: a rental is a matter of personal obligation within the scope of Books I and III and not an excluded real right in land. Leases require a custom drawn line. Even if short-term rack renting is treated as land, there is undeniably an extreme at which a contract is personal in nature even if it gives the right to use land – a letting of a hotel room or short-term holiday letting. In England, the line is drawn between leases and licences by exclusive possession,[80] but the line is drawn in different places in different jurisdictions and the line also varies between the various conflicts rules.[81] Contracts to use land have to be sifted according to function and a line drawn in each specific context.

[78] B. Akkermans, *Principle of Numerus Clausus in European Property Law* (Intersentia, Antwerp, 2008), pp. 116, 191, 343.

[79] DCFR, Book IV B.

[80] *Street* v. *Mountford* [1985] AC 809 (HL); *Antoniades* v. *Villiers* [1990] 1 AC 417 (HL).

[81] Sparkes, *European Land Law*, n. 26 above, ch. 10. For example, the Rome I Regulation selects a site-based rule for land contracts which relate to 'a right in rem in immovable property or a tenancy of immovable property': Regulation (EC) 593/2008 [2008] OJ L177/6, art. 4(1)(f).

### *Real rights in civilian Europe*

Between its original six members, Europe was a civilian club, and so it was logical to structure European law around the basic assumptions of Roman law. Brussels I Regulation jurisdiction over actions[82] is posited on the distinction between real and personal actions:

> A right in personam can only be claimed against a particular person. A right in rem on the other hand is available against the whole world. The most important legal consequence flowing from the nature of a right in rem is that its owner is entitled to demand that the thing in which it exists be given up by anyone not enjoying a prior right.[83]

This reflected the architecture of civilian Civil Codes. Property equates to real rights whereas the personal rights reflect obligations – general contract, specifics, delict and unjust enrichment. Europeanisation at its simplest would exclude rights *in rem* but harmonise and recodify rights *in personam*, according to the degree of Napoleonic ambition either stopping at the end of contractual obligation or extending to all forms of civil obligation. A clean cut could be made in most Civil Codes.

In France we find a *numerus clausus* of real rights including *propriété*, long lease (superficie and emphyteusis), usufruct, servitudes and security (*hypothèque*).[84] The German *numerus* similarly embraces Eigentum, long lease (hereditary building right), real servitudes, usufruct, pre-emptions, real charges and security (*Hypothec* and *Grundschuld*).[85] This shared heritage derives from the centrality of classification by actions to the Roman scheme, made axiomatic by Justinian[86] through the *Institutes*, a structure borrowed from Gaius.[87] This work was crafted around the fundamental divide between property enforceable in things and obligations relating to things but enforceable against individuals, that is between, on the one hand, the vindication of ownership and similar

[82] Regulation (EC) 44/2001 on jurisdiction and the enforcement of judgments in civil and commercial matters [2001] OJ L12/1.

[83] *Schlosser Report* [1979] OJ C59/71, 120–1, para. 166. The Report considers the accession of Spain and Portugal to the former Brussels Convention but it reflects a system developed between the original members before the accession of the United Kingdom.

[84] French Civil Code, Book 2, Titles II–IV and Book 3, Title XVIII; long leases are covered by the Construction and Rural Codes.

[85] Bürgerliches Gesetzbuch, Book 3, ss. III–VIII.

[86] Justinian *Institutes*, 1.2.12; J.B. Moyle, *Institutes of Justinian* (5th edn, Clarendon, Oxford, 1933), p. 6.

[87] Gaius *Institutes* 1.1.8; W.M. Gordon and O.F. Robinson, *Institutes of Gaius* (Duckworth, London, 1988), p. 23.

actions *in rem* and, on the other, actions *in personam*. Such a division at the top of hierarchy of actions created an equivalent division of the substantive law,[88] which was refined into a substantive classification of rights by the post glossators.[89] The Napoleonic Code was informed by the real/personal divide, though the Third Book on 'Different modes of acquiring property' is a pragmatic mixture of property and obligation. Fanatical devotion to the separation of the law of property and the law of obligations, the *Trennungsprinzip*, was developed by Pandektenrecht, which was then carried forward into the Bürgerliches Gesetzbuch (German Civil Code, BGB). Civil law was, and should be, divided into fully independent parts,[90] separated rigidly between the personal (obligation, *Schuldrecht*, particularly contract, *Vertrag*) and property (*Sachenrecht*). The abstraction principle separates the obligation to pass title from the actual transfer.

That the real/personal divide has not been adopted by the codifiers remains a notable fact calling for explanation. It seems that the desire to avoid a repetition of the Allgemeiner Teil (the General Part) of the Bürgerliches Gesetzbuch forms a unifying feature across much of Europe,[91] though this creates scepticism about the project among German academics.[92] The cut may not be clean in civilian law, but it would cause horrendous damage to the structure of the common law.

Removal of the personal category would leave an untidy category of property, partly because of the winding and indistinct border between real and personal rights.[93] The *numerus clausus* of property rights often leaves parties unable to achieve their aspirations for property rights forbidden by their code, and forced to stitch together a patchwork of real and personal obligations into a single do-it-yourself property right.[94] Pieces of a patchwork like this cannot be unstitched; it would be messy to

[88] E. Metzger, 'Actions' ch. 6 in E. Metzger, *Companion to Justinian's Institutes* (Duckworth, London, 1998) p. 217; H.F. Jolowicz and B. Nicholas, *Historical Introduction to the Study of Roman Law* (Cambridge University Press, 1972), pp. 211, 268–70.

[89] G. Samuel, 'English Private Law in the Context of the Codes' in M. Van Hoeke and F. Ost, *Harmonisation of European Private Law* (Hart, Oxford, 2000), p. 50.

[90] Akkermans, *Numerus Clausus*, n. 78 above, at p. 244.

[91] C. Von Bar, 'Launch of the DCFR' (2008) XIV *Juridical International* 4, 6; A. Vacquer, 'Farewell to Windschied' (2009) 17(4) *ERPL* 487; Whittaker, *Assessment*, n. 2 above, at p. 84.

[92] See the articles cited by E. Hondius, 'England and the European Civil Code' (2009) 17(2) *ERPL*. 85 n. 1.

[93] K.G.C. Reid, 'Obligations and Property: Exploring the Border' (1997) 227 *Acta Juridica* 225, 233.

[94] Akkermans, *Numerus Clausus*, n. 78 above, at pp. 400–2.

leave parts of a single obligation governed by different laws. Further, the real/personal divide often allows a choice of remedies for a single situation; for example, where a landlord seeks to recover land from a tenant at the expiration of the lease, the action being either a contractual action to enforce the obligation to return it or a proprietary vindication.[95] The real/personal divide breaks down completely when land subject to a rental is sold, since, illogically, the lease is often treated as quasi-real and so allowed to bind a purchaser.[96] Hence, a neat conjunction of action, right and proprietary force proves to be illusory.

For all these reasons it would be unsatisfactory to have real and personal obligations affecting land enforced under different legal orders, and the *in rem/in personam* division has rarely been chosen by European legislators.

## *Common law*

A cut removing personal rights to a European Civil Code would cause horrendous damage to the structure of the common law, which is simply incompatible with a real/personal divide,[97] even without the Hohfeld extremism.[98] Real actions suffered procedural obsolescence at an early date[99] meaning that the enforcement of a real right did not require an action *in rem*.[100] Vindication is not available, especially in relation to chattels[101] and ownership is always protected *in personam*,[102] and at the level of enforcement all proprietary rights are personal.[103] The common law evolved around a category of property rights, rights enforceable or

[95] E. Levy, *West Roman Vulgar Law: Law of Property* (American Philosophical Society, Philadelphia, PA, 1951), p. 228 ff.

[96] BGB, art. 571.

[97] J. Austin, *Lectures on Jurisprudence* (5th edn, R. Campbell (ed.), John Murray, London, 1912), vol. 2, lectures XLV–XLVIII, XLIX–LVII.

[98] W.N. Hohfeld, *Fundamental Legal Conceptions* (Yale University Press, New Haven, CT, 1964); T.E. Merrill and H.E. Smith, 'Property/Contract Interface' (2001) 101 *Columbia Law Review* 773, 782.

[99] W.W. Buckland and A. McNair, *Roman Law and Common Law* (2nd edn, F.H. Lawson (ed.), Cambridge University Press, 1952), pp. 66–7.

[100] F.W. Maitland, *Forms of Action at Common Law* (Cambridge University Press, 1936), pp. 73–8.

[101] P.B.H. Birks, *Classification of Obligations* (Clarendon, Oxford, 1997), pp. 10–11.

[102] B. Nicholas, *Introduction to Roman Law* (Clarendon, Oxford, 1962), p. 99.

[103] J.H. Dalhuisen, 'Moving From a Closed to an Open System of Proprietary Rights' (2001) 5 *Edinburgh Law Review* 273, 281.

potentially enforceable against a purchaser, a category that does not precisely match civilian real rights.

This is especially so because English land law relies on the interplay between legal rights that are virtually real and equitable rights that are (often) overreachable, and in any case are neither fully real nor fully personal. Civilians tend to emphasise the personal characteristic of equitable rights because civilian trusts operate *in personam*. This is in defiance of the common law categorisation of equitable rights which 'follow' legal rights, are fully proprietary and approach full reality. An English property law with no real rights has proved a challenge to the Brussels I Regulation jurisdiction regime,[104] which assigns exclusive jurisdiction, short lettings apart, to the courts of the state in which the land is situated 'in proceedings which have as their object rights in rem in immovable property or tenancies or immovable property'. This allows *in personam* actions to be taken away from the site of the land. This was indeed what happened in *Webb* v. *Webb* when an English resulting trust of a holiday flat situated in Antibes on the Cote d'Azur was enforced in the English Chancery Division,[105] the absurd effect being to negate the apparent gift conferred contrary to the French law of the site. Trust law should not override foreign property systems in this way. '*In rem*' rights are not a reliable way of differentiating genuine rights in land (e.g., long leasehold) from trivial rights (e.g., overnight hotel booking) in English law, since the property obligational divide is not drawn at the same place as in civilian systems.

### *Trusts*

Book X deals with trusts at length, a full 116 articles. This combines the English fiduciary obligation with the civilian perception of a trust as essentially contractual in nature. The proposal presents no threat to English pre-eminence in commercial fund management, since the crux is the recognition of beneficial interests with proprietary character.[106]

### *Personal rights*

Property rights often include overlapping contractual and proprietary rights, for example, the mortgage consists of a loan agreement and an

[104] Brussels I Regulation (44/2001); Sparkes, *European Land Law*, n. 26 above, para. 4.22.

[105] [1994] ECR I-1717, ECJ

[106] DCFR, Book X; A. Braun, 'Trusts in the Draft Common Frame of Reference: The "Best Solution" for Europe?' (2011) *CLJ* 327.

agreement to use land as security for repayment of the loan. This is replicated throughout, for example, the tenant's duty to vacate enforceable in contract and the landlord's proprietary right to repossess and an easement constitutes a contract with the immediate neighbour and a proprietary duty to future neighbours, rights which separate when the burdened land is sold. Europeanisation of the personal obligations may cause rights to diverge when they ought to fit together.

Very often owners of property are constrained by the *numerus clausus* of property rights which limits property rights to pre-formulated varieties. The consequence is that rights in land on the continent may be made up of a close admixture of real and personal contractual rights, the whole designed to replicate a property interest recognised in the more flexible common law system.[107] Europeanisation of the *in personam* element will create a bizarre mix of EU personal and national real right. The result will be much like land of mixed tenure before 1926, part freehold/part leasehold, where the title would be rent asunder on the death of the owner. There is no clean borderline between property and contract because parties utilise freedom of contract to modify property rights in ways that cannot be done directly.[108]

## Juridical acts

'Contract' is a term that has seeded itself promiscuously across Europe, and although there is a similarity of core meaning it cannot be assumed that all European usage confirms to the pure strain of the common law contract, certainly not at the level of detail. Shades of meaning are a potential problem when seeking to harmonise contract laws across Europe.[109]

Consider a standard bilateral[110] contract with consideration provided on both sides, the contract of the commercial lawyer. This would include a straightforward sale where a seller agrees to transfer ownership in a house at a given price to a buyer who promises to pay the price on completion; this is a contract in English law. A similar document would

[107] Akkermans, *Numerus Clausus*, n. 78 above, at pp. 308 ff.

[108] Admittedly the abstraction principle reduces duplication but it does not eliminate it.

[109] The definition of contract was identified as a problem by Prof. Vogenauer in evidence to the House of Lords; *European Contract Law, the Draft Common Frame of Reference* (House of Lords EU Committee, 12th Report, 2008–9 session, HL Paper 95), para. 27.

[110] The same applies to a multilateral contract with more than two parties.

be used in Germany but translated usually as a 'pre-contract' since the transfer of title is accomplished by a 'real agreement' (*dinglicher Vertrag*).[111] Similarly, in France the practice is to use a pre-contract which is not strictly binding, so it seems inevitable that the final document, a '*contrat*', should translate into English as a contract.[112]

'Contract' is merely an example of a wider concept of 'juridical act', by reference to which the scope of the Common Frame is set. A juridical act may be unilateral, and hence non-contractual but binding even without acceptance.[113] It is much wider than just a unilateral contract of English law, including a wide range of unilateral acts, such as a transfer of legal title, a deed of grant of an easement or a deed of gift. If a donor promises to give his house to a donee, English lawyers use the lack of consideration to deny contractual validity and decline to perfect a gift lacking full formality. A civilian system would see the same arrangement as a contract, given the valid *causa* of intention to give or of family obligation.[114] This wide remit is reduced by land exclusion, though donations of goods are included. Curiously, however, Book IVH covers *contracts* for the donation of goods[115] – and since a contract is defined to be a bilateral act,[116] it seems not to include the unilateral act of gift itself. It is surely odd to Europeanise the arrangement to give but to leave the actual gift of a movable to national law.

The application of the Draft Common Frame of Reference to non-contractual bilateral 'acts' might include a conveyance or transfer or the French *acte authentique* used to complete a transaction.[117] Again, this very wide scope is reduced by the land exclusion, which rules out the Europeanisation of a straightforward land transfer and which ought to (but does not) also exclude a deed of grant of an easement. The DCFR creates an unintended and patchy effect on substantive land law.

[111] E.J. Schuster, *Principles of German Civil Law* (Clarendon, Oxford, 1901), para. 309.

[112] H. Dyson, *French Property and Inheritance Law* (Oxford University Press, 2003), chs. 3, 4, 5.

[113] DCFR, art. II 1:103(2).

[114] French Civil Code, art. 931; Bell, Boyron and Whittaker, *Introduction to French Law*, n. 16 above, at p. 317.

[115] DCFR, art. IVH 1:103(2); the same terminological ambiguity arises in relation to a contract for proprietary security over goods in Book IX.

[116] DCFR, Annex ('Contract').

[117] The two are difficult to disentangle in causal systems where a defect in the contract affects the passing of property: Van Erp, '(D)CFR, Consumer Aquis, Property Law and Euromortgage', n. 30 above, at 2; Eidenmuller, 'Policy Choices', n. 2 above, at 687–90.

## Contracts for sale of land

Were the Common Frame of Reference to be narrowed so as to be confined to cross-border transactions,[118] this would ground it more firmly in the logic of the internal market and also neutralise its likely effect on land. However, as drawn it applies to transactions within a single EU state and might apply to 'domestic' transactions with land.

A special contract is provided for sales of goods, its scope excluding land,[119] and there is no corresponding set of rules for the sale of land. True, there is also a special Book covering construction contracts.[120] However, it seems reasonable to deduce that the intention was to exclude a contract for the sale of land from the DCFR completely.

If so, it is surely unfortunate that the basic rules on contracts and contractual liability in Books II and III might apply to a sale of land. Civilian Codes would have a single basic law of contract, including, for example, rules of offer and acceptance, supplemented by rules for special nominate contracts. It would be almost equally awkward either (1) to include land without a special sale of land contract, or (2) to exclude land from the basic contract provisions and thus require two separate Codes operating in parallel. What would suit civilians would be very awkward for common lawyers who might form a land contract under the European Code inconsistent with the conveyancing rules and Standard Conditions of Sale. On balance, it seems better to exclude land contracts which are distinguished by the need for written formality or notarisation and by the practice of entering into a contract before conveyance. The DCFR general Books on contract rules and contractual obligations (respectively, Books II and III) apply with the exception of contracts affecting the 'ownership of ... immovable property'.[121] When land is intended to be excluded from the Book covering the sale of goods (Book IVA) the equivalent exclusion is for 'immovable property and all rights in immovable property'.[122] Comparison of these two exclusions suggests that sales of land are within the general contract rules, even if the contracts relate to ownership or security interests. The DCFR falls well short of providing a watertight and logically satisfying exemption.

[118] Commission Decision 2010/233/EU on setting up the Expert Group on a Common Frame of Reference in the Area of European Contract Law; Green Paper 2010, n. 33 above, para. 4.2.2.

[119] DCFR, art. IVA 1:101(1). [120] DCFR, art. IVC. [121] DCFR, art. I 1:101(2)(f).

[122] DCFR, art. IVA 1:101(3); the exclusion for donations is similar: IVH 1:103(2).

## Conclusion

This chapter has considered the exclusion of land from the draft European Contract/Civil Code proposed in the Draft Common Frame of Reference, which would undoubtedly cover the law of property in movables. From this small snapshot the only possible conclusion is that the technical quality of the work is not good enough to form the basis for legislation. A new draft must provide a much more rigorous land exclusion, and only then would it be possible to answer the question whether civil law can be separated between property and obligation in a way that works for both civilian and common law systems. This question is likely to remain unanswered now that the United Kingdom has opted out of the proposal. The Frame of Reference that emerges may be 'Common' only within the confines of civilian assumptions.

6

# Harmonisation and its discontents: a transaction costs critique of a European contract law

ROGER HALSON AND DAVID CAMPBELL

> The fiction of frictionlessness and/or invok[ing] transaction cost considerations selectively . . . easily leads to extreme and untenable 'solutions'.
>
> Oliver Williamson[1]

## Introduction

In furtherance of the Europe 2020 strategy,[2] the European Commission is currently seeking to encourage 'economic recovery' by tackling perceived 'bottlenecks' in the internal market.[3] A European law of contract is seen as key to this project, the latest development being the Commission's proposal for a Common European Sales Law (CESL)[4] which transacting parties may select to govern cross-border contracts for the sale of goods, the supply of digital content, and some related services. A European Contract Law initiative has been working towards some such objective for three decades.[5] As long ago as 1999, the Council and the Parliament

Leeds University, School of Law.

1 O. Williamson, *Economic Organisation* (Wheatsheaf Books, Brighton 1986), p. 259.

2 Communication from the Commission on Europe 2020, COM(2010)2020 final, (3 March 2010), p. 21.

3 'Contract law: Commission considers way forward', Press Release, 31 January 2011, MEMO/11/55.

4 European Commission, *Proposal for a Regulation on a Common European Sales Law*, COM(2011)635 final (11 October 2011). On the implementation of the Law by means of a Regulation, see the accompanying Explanatory Memorandum, COM(2011)0284, (11 October 2011), p. 10.

5 We date the process from November 1982, when the 'Lando' Commission, comprised of leading contract law specialists from different European jurisdictions, was established. The resulting *Principles of European Contract Law* were published in 3 volumes between 1995 and 2003: I–II *Principles of European Contract Law* (O. Lando and H. Beale (eds.), Kluwer Law International, The Hague, 2000) and III *Principles of European Contract Law*

urged the harmonisation of particular aspects of Member States' civil laws.[6] However, the pace with which harmonisation has been pursued has very noticeably, and in our view improperly, quickened over the past decade. Following its 2001 Communication[7] and the 2003 Action Plan[8] that led to the draft Common Frame of Reference (CFR),[9] the Commission's 2010 Green Paper on a European Contract Law sets out the entire range of policy options the Commission believed were open for implementation of the CFR.[10] The particular interest of the Green Paper is that it is the most comprehensive and theoretically unified review of those options ever produced by an EU body.

This chapter challenges the theory of and the evidence for the argument around which the Green Paper is organised: that the legal transaction costs of cross-border commerce within the single market will be minimised, and so productive trade maximised, to the extent that European law of contract is fully harmonised. This chapter argues that there is almost no merit to this key underpinning of the most ambitious attempt to refashion the contract law of Europe ever made.

The Green Paper identifies the problem it is claimed that a harmonised law will solve in this way: '[d]ivergences between national contract laws' constitute 'barriers' to 'the smooth functioning of the internal market',[11] and so '[a]n instrument of European Contract Law should respond to the problems of diverging contract laws'[12] in order 'to ease cross-border transactions' in a way which will allow 'citizens [to] take full advantage of the internal market'.[13] These barriers are caused because 'differences between national contract laws may entail additional transaction costs and legal uncertainty for businesses and lead to a lack of consumer confidence in the internal market'.[14] The same

(O Lando *et al.* (eds.), Kluwer Law International, The Hague, 2000). Professor Lando himself traces the process back to 1974: I–II *Principles of European Contract Law*, p. xi.

6 The European Council meeting in Tampere in 1999 called for further study of the possibility of a harmonised European civil law. See Tampere European Council, Presidency Conclusions 15–16 October 1999, VII 'Greater Convergence in Civil Law', available at www.europarl.europa.eu/summits/tam_en.htm.

7 Communication from the Commission on European Contract Law, COM(2001)398 final (11 July 2001).

8 Communication from the Commission, on A More Coherent European Contract Law: An Action Plan, COM(2003)68 final (12 February 2003).

9 C. von Bar and E. Clive, *Principles, Definitions and Model Rules of European Private Law: Draft Common Frame of Reference* (Oxford University Press, 2010) (DCFR).

10 *Green Paper on Policy Options for Progress Towards a European Contract Law for Consumers and Businesses*, COM(2010)348 final (1 July 2010).

11 *Ibid.* para. 3. 12 *Ibid.* para. 4. 13 *Ibid.* para. 1. 14 *Ibid.*

claim is repeated in the Explanatory Memorandum to the CESL: '[d]ifferences in contract law between Member States hinder … cross-border trade … Additional transaction costs compared to domestic trade usually occur for traders'.[15] It is now being asserted that these transaction costs are retarding economic recovery in Europe and that an 'instrument of European Contract Law could help the EU to meet its economic goals and recover from the economic crisis'.[16] This bold claim is supported by Project Europe 2030, a report to the European Council by a group focusing upon recovery from the current economic crisis.[17]

This transaction cost argument for harmonisation of European contract law is purportedly an economic one based on improving market efficiency.[18] But the concept of the transaction cost is gravely misused here in just the ways that the most important contributor to the formulation of the concept, Ronald Coase, has repeatedly counselled against. Indeed, this particular transaction cost argument is so weak that it amounts to no more than a sort of tautology. It can be thought to work only if one has a prior political commitment to the harmonisation of the contract laws of the EU members. Without such a prior commitment, the argument has no weight at all.

## Haste and its customary consequences

If one assumes a fully harmonised contract law which, in effect, makes the EU a completely unified single contract jurisdiction, then the transaction costs of cross-border exchange which arise when '[t]he internal market is built on a multitude of contracts governed by different national contract laws'[19] *must* be eliminated by this unification, and the benefits of internal trade maximised so far as the elimination of these costs can do this. When the Green Paper generally speaks of providing 'a common European Contract Law which could be applied and interpreted uniformly in all the Member States',[20] it has this optimal solution in

[15] Explanatory Memorandum, n. 4 above, at p. 2.
[16] Green Paper 2010, n. 10 above, para. 4.1 (options 6 and 7).
[17] Reflection Group on the Future of the European Union 2020, *Project Europe 2030: Challenges and Opportunities* (2010), p. 41, available at www.reflectiongroup.eu/2010/05/08/project-europe-2030-challenges-and-opportunities/.
[18] B. Lurger, 'The Common Frame of Reference/Optional Code and the Various Understandings of Social Justice in Europe' in *Private Law and the Many Cultures of Europe* (T. Wilhelmmson *et al.* (eds.), Kluwer Law International, The Hague, 2007), pp. 177, 187.
[19] Green Paper 2010, n. 10 above, para. 1. [20] *Ibid.* para. 3.2.

mind, and this sort of thinking has been implicit in all talk – going back at least to the Tampere European Council's commitment to a 'genuine European Area of Justice'[21] and now part of the Europe 2020 economic strategy[22] – of the 'completion or perfection of the Internal Market' as 'one of the central themes' of the Contract Law initiative.[23]

But, of course, this optimal solution is not remotely a possibility. In saying this, it is not meant to refer to the limits to the European Union's competence to pursue harmonisation of national contract laws.[24] This pursuit so clearly raises questions of subsidiarity and proportionality[25] that it is, to say the least, surprising that the Green Paper does not engage in any sustained way with the problems its proposals raise in EU law. The failure to do this might, of course, result in challenges to any instrument enacted, via motions for preliminary rulings in the Court of Justice of the European Union (CJEU) or by '*ultra vires*' challenges in national courts with constitutional jurisdiction.[26] The downplaying of perhaps the two core formal principles of EU jurisprudence that is implicit in the extraordinarily ambitious project of codifying all the Member States' national laws of contract is so serious as to call into question the actual strength of the European Union's stated basic commitment to diversity.[27]

Though the essentially 'surreptitious' character of the harmonisation process is perforce the subject of this chapter,[28] we do not intend to dwell on the detail of the political technique used to extend the necessary competence, especially the creative 'soft law' interpretation of what is possible within the current framework, in order to turn what its drafters initially insisted was an academic draft CFR into the political reality of a CFR.[29] We merely note that understanding this detail is the real key to

[21] Tampere European Council, Presidency Conclusions, n. 6 above, at para. 28.

[22] See http://ec.europa.eu/europe2020/tools/improving/index_en.htm.

[23] D. Wallis, 'European Contract Law: The Way Forward, Political Context, Parliament's Preoccupations and Processes' (2006) 7 *ERA (Europäische Rechtsakademie) Forum* 8.

[24] J. W. Rutgers, 'The Rule of Reason and Private Law, or the Limits to Harmonisation' in *The Rule of Reason* (A. Schrauwen (ed.), Europa Law Publishing, Groningen, 2005), p. 187.

[25] Green Paper 2010, n. 10 above, para. 4.1 (options 6 and 7).

[26] M. W. Hesselink, *An Optional Instrument on EU Contract Law: Could it Increase Legal Certainty and Foster Cross-border Trade?*, Working Paper No. 2010/06 (Centre for the Study of European Contract Law, University of Amsterdam, 2010), para. 3.3.

[27] These issues are given no weight by Prof. Lando: O. Lando, 'Can Europe Build Unity of Civil Law whilst Respecting Diversity?' (2006) *Europa e diritto Privato* 1.

[28] K. P. Berger, 'The Principles of European Contract Law and the Concept of the "Creeping Codification" of Law' (2001) 9 *European Rev. Private Law* 21.

[29] C. von Bar *et al.* (eds.), *Principles, Definitions and Model Rules of European Private Law: Draft Common Frame of Reference* (Outline Edition) (Sellier, Munich 2009), p. 7.

understanding the actual history and prospects of the Contract Law initiative.[30] However, some things might be said specifically of the manifestly gathering pace of the harmonisation process after the Green Paper was issued, and its inevitably adverse effect upon the quality of the evidence mustered in support of the proposals under consideration.

In the Stockholm Programme for 2010–14 announced in December 2009, the European Council reaffirmed that the CFR would be of a non-binding nature, merely furnishing a 'set of fundamental principles, definitions and model rules to be used by the lawmakers at Union level to ensure greater coherence and quality in the lawmaking process'.[31] In effect, this is option 2 set out in the Green Paper, where it is described as an 'An Official "toolbox" for the legislator'. At the close of the seven-month formal consultation on the Green Paper, 320 responses had been received. German nationals and organisations made over ninety submissions, more than twice as many as that of the next national cohort, the United Kingdom. In April 2011, just two months after the end of the consultation, the European Parliament's Legal Affairs Committee had come to support something rather different than a mere tool-box: a European Contract Law instrument intended to encourage cross-border trade.[32] Concurrently with the Green Paper consultation, a Group of Experts established by the European Commission was also tasked with producing a study of the feasibility of 'a potential European contract law instrument', a 'self-standing and comprehensive text covering most aspects of a contractual relationship'.[33] This was delivered on 3 May 2011 and feedback was invited to be made within the following two months.

[30] M. Kenny, 'The 2004 Communication on European Contract Law: Those Magnificent Men in their Unifying Machines' (2007) 30 *European L. Rev.* 724. The ultimate background to this process is the tendency wisely described by the late Prof. Farnsworth: '[i]t is only a small step from the search for a "common core" to agendas of contract law harmonization and unification': Allan Farnsworth, 'Comparative Contract Law' in *The Oxford Handbook of Comparative Law* (M. Reiman and R. Zimmerman (eds.), Oxford University Press, 2006), pp. 899, 903.

[31] European Council Notice, 'The Stockholm Programme: An Open and Secure Europe Serving and Protecting Citizens' [2010] OJ C115/01 at para. 3.4.2. See further Bar Council of England and Wales, Response to the European Commission Consultation on Contract Law, (31 January 2011) para. 92.

[32] D. Wallis, rapporteur, report adopted 12 April 2011 (INI/20111/2013).

[33] 'A European Contract Law for Consumers and Businesses: Publication of the Results of the Feasibility Study carried out by the Expert Group on European Contract Law for Stakeholders' and Legal Practitioners, Feedback' (3 May 2011), available at ec.europa/justice/contract/files/feasibility-studyen.pdf.

This unfeasibly short,[34] and for the northern hemisphere also unseasonal, period for comment, combined with the evident preference for concurrent, rather than consecutive, procedures, conveys the impression of hurried travel towards a predetermined destination. Both business and professional bodies responding to the Green Paper emphasised the difficulty in contributing to a debate when parallel processes are in action and short timescales are imposed. Typical comments from UK respondents were that a 'sounding board' is not effective 'if you can only comment on the content without having an overview of the total picture',[35] and that the opportunities for engagement were 'being needlessly, and damagingly truncated'.[36] As is discussed below, UK legal practitioners have a greater engagement with cross-border trade than any of their continental counterparts, and surely weight should be given to the cogent and extensive evidence submitted by their representative bodies that the process of consultation followed was 'fundamentally flawed',[37] being characterised by 'a lack of practitioner input (both in general and from common law jurisdictions)'.[38]

Predictably, a similar problem has occurred with the CESL. The Law Commission for England and Wales and the Scottish Law Commission were asked by the UK Government to advise on the potential advantages and disadvantages of the CESL. In order 'to promote discussion and debate'[39] of 'a complex document ... which is not always easy to understand',[40] given that the proposed legislation was already tabled, the Commissions elected to publish their document within a month, with the inevitable effect that there were major omissions. The Commissions were forced to concentrate on sales contracts and note simply that they had 'not had time to consider the supply of digital content'.[41]

[34] The Commission would appear to have unrealistic expectations here. The seven-month consultation on the Green Paper was described as 'longer than usual to ensure as wide as possible participation in the policy discussion': Press Release, n. 3 above.

[35] EuroCommerce, Response to the European Commission Consultation on a Green Paper on Policy Options for Progress towards a European Contract Law for Consumers and Businesses (27 January 2011), p. 1. See further COMBAR Response to EU Green Paper on Policy Options for Progress towards a European Contract Law for Consumers and Businesses, sec. V.

[36] Bar Council of England and Wales, Response, n. 31 above, para. 10.

[37] *Ibid.* para. 91.

[38] Law Society, Response to Commission Green Paper on Policy Options for Progress Towards a European Contract Law for Consumers and Businesses (January 2011), para. 9.

[39] Law Commission and Scottish Law Commission, *An Optional European Common Sales Law: Advantages and Problems, Advice to the UK Government* (November 2011), para. S2.

[40] *Ibid.* [41] *Ibid.* para. S3. The document is still 123 pages long(!)

We have spoken already about what appears to be a hurried journey towards a known objective. Our views about this appear to be reinforced by the European Commission's use of the past tense to describe their aspiration that: 'this chapter will explain the contents of the proposed Regulation and highlight the policy choices *which have been made*'.[42]

## Transaction cost argument

When we say that what we have called the optimal solution to the transaction cost problem set out in the Green Paper is not possible we mean that, for so long as the European Union is not itself an actually unified jurisdiction, it is theoretically impossible that there can be a fully harmonised law, whether of contract or of anything else. We do not believe ourselves to be doing anything original,[43] or indeed to be doing more than pointing out the obvious, when we say that residual national divergences in the implementation, interpretation and application of even a purported completely uniform law must remain,[44] and even were the CFR[45] substantively perfect (which surely it goes without saying it is not),[46] it must inevitably fragment and unravel to a great extent as it is made into law and then applied. In essence, to the extent it is carried out, purportedly uniform implementation must implant a hybrid of

42 *Ibid.* para. S3 (emphasis added).

43 P. Legrand, 'European Legal Systems are Not Converging' (1996) 45 *International and Comparative Law Quarterly* 52; P. Legrand, 'Against a European Civil Code' (1997) 60 *Modern Law Review* 44; and P. Legrand, 'Codification and the Politics of Exclusion: A Challenge for Comparativists,' (1998) 31 *UC Davis L Rev.* 799.

44 This point is captured nicely by S. Whittaker, 'The Proposed "Common European Sales Law": Legal Framework and the Agreement of the Parties' (2012) 75 *Modern Law Review* 578, 588. So the Regulation would not create a '28th contract law regime' for all Europe but rather at least 27 identical '2nd national contract law regimes' in each Member State. See also J. Smits, 'A Principled Approach to European Contract Law?' (2000) 7 *Maastricht Journal of European and Comparative Law* 221.

45 Or the CESL. The Law Commission and Scottish Law Commission, n. 39 above, seem to us to give a balanced evaluation.

46 We entirely agree with the point that has repeatedly been made (e.g. G. Wagner, 'The Economics of Harmonisation: The Case of Contract Law' (2002) 39 *Common Market Law Review* 995, 999–1013) that it is wrong to regard legal diversity only negatively because such diversity creates *prima facie* valuable regulatory competition which a uniform law extinguishes, and we would add that putting all the European Union's 27 contract eggs in one basket in this way might enormously increase the risk of harm and cost caused by a single ill-judged law. We are putting these points to one side in order to conduct our argument on the basis of accepting the transaction cost argument in principle.

transnational and national law within the national jurisdictions which could greatly unsettle the national law.[47]

It is conceptually misleading to believe that harmonisation will incur 'set-up costs' that will settle down.[48] There will, of course, be such costs,[49] though those proposing harmonisation sometimes neglect to account for them, and in certain contexts they may settle down after sufficient time has elapsed to allow a reasonably consistent jurisprudence to emerge from the litigation and appeal of disputes. But the crucial point is that, in the context of the persistent national differences within the European Union, any settling down will always be marginal. It is only because the Contract Law initiative typically has focused on an implausibly formal conception of the law, saying very little about both the ineradicable national linguistic and cultural influences on the constitution of substantive law and about the extremely difficult procedural issues that certainly will arise, that the goal of uniformity can apparently be maintained.

The Green Paper points to the US Uniform Commercial Code (UCC) as an example of productive unification,[50] but surely this is a most inappropriate and misleading example.[51] Let us put it aside that the process which has led to the CFR can hardly be compared to the largely

[47] J. Basedow, 'Codification of Private Law in the European Union: The Making of a Hybrid' (2001) 9 *European Review of Private Law* 35.

[48] Hesselink, *An Optional Instrument*, n. 26 above: 'the costs of introducing an optional instrument are likely to be modest'. No evidence is offered to support this assertion. It might be that Hesselink is proceeding on the basis of an overly narrow definition of set-up costs. For a critique of the CESL which focuses upon the private international law consequences and costs of its implementation, see Whittaker, 'The Proposed "Common European Sales law"', n. 44 above, at 604: 'The technical legal framework by which the Proposal seeks to give effect to the CESL could hardly be more complex'.

[49] This experience of the Netherlands, which enacted a new Civil Code in 1992, is instructive in this respect: M.W. Hesselink, 'The Ideal of Codification and the Dynamics of Europeanisation: The Dutch Experience' in *The Harmonisation of European Contract Law* (S. Vogenauer and S. Weatherill (eds.), Hart, Oxford, 2006), p. 39.

[50] Green Paper 2010, n. 10 above, at pp. 8–9.

[51] T. Weir, 'Divergent Legal Systems in a Single Member State' (1998) *Zeitschrift für Europäisches Privatrecht* 564, 565: 'the outstanding example of a common market with no common law continues to be the United States'. The late Mr Weir, one of the United Kingdom's most distinguished comparative lawyers, made this observation in the course of a analysis of the relationship between the legal systems of England and Wales and Scotland in which he raised numerous points to the effect that: '[t]hose who propose a code of contract for multilingual Europe, and *a fortiori* those who propose a code of private law, ought to pay some heed to the fact that two bodies pledged to [law] reform [the Law Commission and the Scottish Law Commission] cannot agree on a contract code for Britain'. We are grateful to Prof. MacQueen for drawing this to our attention.

transparent and very time-consuming process of drafting and redrafting the UCC, carried out by private institutions which could work only by securing consent.[52] Let us also put it aside that even the UCC process has run into the gravest difficulties over the proposed redrafting of article 2.[53] It is more relevant here that, not only are the US deliberations over unification models of openness by comparison to what is going in the European Union, but that, notwithstanding this, approximately half of the Commissioners on Uniform State Laws' proposals have not been adopted by any US state, and many of those proposals that are regarded as most successful have been adopted by less than half of the states.[54] Most importantly, the Green Paper's admiring reference to the achievement of the UCC does not address the fact that the UCC works because it represents a systematised common law regime. One is, as so often, left in doubt whether the European Commission intends to mislead or is simply ignorant, when one realises that the only US state with a civilian tradition, Louisiana, has never adopted the article of by far the greatest relevance to the CFR, article 2 on sales(!) The Green Paper refers to this situation by saying that the UCC 'has been adopted by all but one of the 50 states'.[55]

It is a valid criticism of the CFR that it is arguably redundant for businesses engaged in cross-border commerce as, not only is there the usual choice of law options open to those businesses, but they may also, of course, use the UN Convention on Contracts for the International Sale of Goods (CISG) or the UNIDROIT Principles.[56]

52 W. Twining, *Karl Llewellyn and the Realist Movement* (Weidenfeld and Nicolson, London, 1985), ch. 11. The Green Paper 2010, n. 10 above, at p. 8, describes the National Conference of the Commissioners on Uniform State Laws and the American Law Institute as 'quasi-public bodies'.

53 R. E. Speidel, 'Revising UCC Article 2: A View from the Trenches' (2001) 52 *Hastings L J* 607.

54 For a well argued comparison with the UCC, see Law Society, Response, n. 38 above, paras. 75–80.

55 Green Paper 2010, n. 10 above, at p. 9.

56 S. Vogenauer, 'Common Frame of Reference and UNIDROIT Principles of International Commercial Contracts: Coexistence, Competition, or Overkill of Soft Law?' (2010) 6 *European Rev. Contract Law* 143. Professor McKendrick goes so far as to say that the creation of a European law displays a failure 'to go a stage further and advocate harmonisation at a global level': McKendrick, 'The State We are In' in Vogenauer and Weatherill., *The Harmonisation of European Contract Law*, n. 49 above, at pp. 5, 29. His discussion of the issues is commendably that of, as it were, a disengaged academic and does not engage with the issues of making sure the European law is not ignored in the way that the international laws have been.

When considering whether to implement the CFR as another 'optional instrument',[57] the Green Paper, in addition to unfavourably comparing choice of law rules to a fully harmonised system,[58] says that the use of 'optional regimes'[59] may be criticised because it means that 'businesses do not have the option of a common European Contract Law which could be applied and interpreted uniformly in all the Member States'.[60] This carries the ridiculous implication, which nevertheless is central to the Green Paper, that under full harmonisation, uniformity of legislation and ultimate adjudication of disputes by the CJEU 'could replace the diversity of national laws with a uniform European set of rules [which] would remove legal fragmentation in the field of contract law and lead to ... uniform application and interpretation'.[61]

One might have thought that, rather than maintain that full harmonisation can produce this theoretically optimal but practically fanciful solution,[62] those contributing to the Contract Law initiative, other than outright politicians, would prefer to talk in much more measured ways of, in essence, degrees of convergence based on an instrument which currently displays undeniable flaws,[63] and of 'the harmonisation of the general contract law within the European Union' as 'a longer-term

57 Green Paper 2010, n. 10 above, para. 4.1 (options 3b and 4). The Green Paper believes that, if the optional instrument is implemented by a Regulation rather than a Recommendation by the Commission, it could deal with the divergence of mandatory rules of e.g. consumer law in a superior way to the purely voluntary CISG or UNIDROIT. It is a microcosm of our argument here that, although the Contract Law initiative has long been aware that the fate of opt-in instruments has typically been that they are ignored (e.g. there is not a known single instance in English law of a party opting in to the ULIS rules despite legislative encouragement to do so under the Uniform Law of Sales Act 1967, s. 1 (3): Action Plan, n. 8 above, para. 4.4.5), the response to this has typically been, not to take this as evidence that another optional instrument is not needed, but that any such instrument brought in should be optional only in a (highly) qualified sense.

58 Green Paper 2010, n. 10 above, para. 4.1 (option 4). 59 *Ibid.* 60 *Ibid.* para. 3.2.

61 *Ibid.* para. 4.1 (option 6).

62 Or that a coherent 'multi-level' (or whatever synonym is used) system of contract law may be established. S. Grundmann, 'The Optional European Code on the Basis of the Acquis Communitaire: Starting Point and Trends' (2004) 10 *European Law Journal* 698, 708–10.

63 Professor Whittaker's report commissioned by the Ministry of Justice is something of an object lesson in speaking to its audience in a nuanced way which, by virtue of this, secures agreement from that audience with the strong harmonisation which always had been maintained: S. Whittaker, *The Draft Common Frame of Reference: An Assessment* (2008), available at www.justice.gov.uk/publications/eu-contract-law-common-frame-reference.htm.

objective'.[64] But if harmonisation cannot possibly realise the theoretically optimal elimination of national differences, what economic advantage can it realise? The principal point this chapter seeks to make is that no sensible answer to this has emerged or can emerge from the Contract Law initiative because the concept of the optimal solution plays an essential and indispensable part in the transaction cost argument on which the initiative rests. The optimal solution is impossible, but without the concept of it, the economic case for a European code simply falls.

## Evidence for the transaction cost argument

The costs central to the transaction cost argument have been described at various lengths in various contributions to the Contract Law initiative, but the brief statements about them in the Green Paper capture the essential idea:[65]

> [d]ivergences in contract law rules may require businesses to adapt their contractual terms . . . national laws are rarely available in other European languages, which imply [*sic*] that market actors need to take advice from a lawyer who knows the laws of the legal system that they are proposing to choose . . . Businesses wishing to engage in . . . cross-border trade may face high legal costs when their contracts are subject to foreign . . . law. In extreme cases, some businesses may even refuse to sell across borders and thus potential consumers of that company may be locked in their national markets and be deprived of the enhanced choice and lower prices offered by the internal market.[66]

It is our view that, though the transaction cost argument claims to be supported by empirical data, this vital claim is the least well investigated and substantiated part of the argument for harmonisation.[67] Despite the

[64] I–II *Principles of European Contract Law*, n. 5 above, at p. xxiv. It is obvious that there is some considerable divergence between the editors of these *Principles*. Professor Beale would seem to rather repent of this statement of the *Principles*' purpose and continues to endorse only the most minimal idea of a European Code (see text accompanying n. 108 below) in a way we think simply fails to reflect the teleology of the Contract Law initiative. Professor Lando has, in contrast, always had a firm, vanguard commitment to that teleology: Lando, 'Can Europe Build Unity', n. 27 above, at 8.

[65] Green Paper 2010, n. 10 above, at paras 1, 3.1.

[66] Similar assertions are made in the Opinion of the European Economic and Social Committee on the Green Paper from the Commission on Policy Options for Progress Towards a European Contract Law for Consumers and Businesses, COM(2010)348 final, para. 4.2.

[67] Our evaluation of this evidence should be contrasted with the earlier evaluation of some it in S. Vogenauer and S. Weatherill, 'The European Union's Competence to Pursue the

efforts of the European Commission, utilising its great resources, to marshal this evidence, commentators who have directly addressed the problem of the corrigibility of the empirical evidence for the transaction cost argument have usually concluded that it is 'slender' and 'would clearly not withstand scrutiny'.[68] As if to demonstrate this inadequacy, the evidence the Green Paper itself seeks to put forward[69] (some of the opinions invited in the consultation which followed the 2001 Communication;[70] two Eurobarometer surveys;[71] a survey conducted in 2005 by Clifford Chance, the City of London law firm;[72] and an observation derived from sectoral Commission work on e-commerce)[73] is opaque,[74] partial, lacks methodological rigour, and, even if accepted, is overall highly equivocal. All variants of the transaction cost argument are subject to the same basic criticism: that transaction costs are not proven but asserted to justify a conclusion preferred for other, implicit reasons.

It is exceedingly unsatisfactory that the single statistic the Green Paper itself cites in support of the transaction cost argument is that 'for 61% of cross-border e-commerce offers, consumers were not able to place an order mainly because businesses refused to serve the consumer's country', surely with the implication in this context that this is related to divergences between national laws. However, the research from which this statistic is derived provides no information about the relevance of such divergences and, indeed, gives other reasons for this situation.[75]

Harmonisation of Contract Law: An Empirical Contribution to the Debate' in Vogenauer and Weatherill, *The Harmonisation of European Contract Law*, n. 49 above, at p. 105.

68 C. Twigg-Flesner, *The Europeanisation of Contract Law* (Routledge-Cavendish, London, 2008), p. 31. See generally *The Need for a European Contract Law: Empirical and Legal Perspectives* (J. Smits (ed.), Europa Law Publishing, Groningen, 2005), especially the final chapter and summary by the editor.

69 Green Paper 2010, n. 10 above, paras. 3.3.1.

70 The views of these contributors, elevated to the status of 'stakeholders' whether they wanted a stake or not, are available at http://ec.europa.eu/consumers/rights/stakeholders_en.htm and digested in an Annex to the 2003 *Action Plan*, n. 8 above.

71 DG SANCO, *Special EUROBAROMETER* 298 (2008) (in the Green Paper this is given as *Special EUROBAROMETER* 292 (2008)) and DG SANCO, *Flash EUROBAROMETER* 278 (2009).

72 Clifford Chance LLP, *Survey on European Contract Law*, (2005).

73 Communication from the Commission on Cross-Border Business to Consumer e-Commerce in the EU, COM(2009)557 (22 October 2009), para. 13. The research was commissioned from the YouGov polling organisation by DG SANCO: YouGov Psychonomics, *Mystery Shopping Evaluation of Cross-border e-commerce in the EU* (2009), para. 5.

74 As is the Opinion of the European Economic and Social Committee on the Green Paper, n. 66 above, where statistical support is not referenced, see e.g., paras. 4.1 and 4.3.

75 Communication from the Commission, n. 73 above, para. 13.

In a Eurobarometer poll that asked EU citizens who hypothetically had purchased goods abroad what principles they would prefer a dispute to be settled under, 57 per cent expressed a preference for harmonised EU law.[76] But, on the other hand, none of the 181 responses to the 2001 Communication, including associations representing small and medium-sized enterprises,[77] expressed dissatisfaction with a sectoral approach to specific problems of cross-border trade or thought it should be abandoned in favour of a general harmonisation approach.[78] The Green Paper itself suggests, without reference to supporting evidence, that 'consumers and businesses from small Member States might be particularly disadvantaged'.[79] Eurobarometer evidence would in fact seem to contradict, rather than support, this view. A 2008 survey found that cross-border trade exceeded domestic transactions only in the small states of Luxembourg, Malta and Cyprus, and further that Luxembourg, Denmark and Malta recorded the highest figures for cross-border distance purchases at, respectively, 45, 25 and 25 per cent.[80]

It is interesting that the latest manifestation of the European Contract Law initiative, the CESL, is itself prefaced[81] by a highly selective reference to two more recent Eurobarometer surveys,[82] in which traders were said to rank the difficulty of ascertaining the applicable provisions of foreign

[76] 54 per cent in the United Kingdom. Interestingly, the United Kingdom recorded the highest percentage, 23 per cent, who expressed a preference for the national law of their contractual partner.

[77] Despite this, as it is hard to argue with a straight face that the EU consumers, other than an elite, are much interested in solving the legal problems of cross-border trade, or that large companies cannot sort out their solutions, and that public assistance of either this elite of consumers or this elite of businesses with their legal expenses is defensible, small and medium-sized enterprises feature prominently in the transaction cost argument. Numerous subsequent consultations of small and medium-sized business organisations by EU bodies have produced results more favourable for the Contract Law initiative: e.g. *SME Panel Survey on the Impacts of a European Contract Law* (February 2011), available at http://ec.europa.eu/justice/policies/consumer/docs/report_sme_panel_survey_feb_2011_en.pdf. This reports the results of a consultation conducted in November and December 2010 by the Enterprise Europe Network, a Commission agency which offers support to small and medium-sized businesses:, available at www.enterprise-europe-network.ec.europa.eu/index_en.htm.

[78] *Action Plan*, n. 8 above, para. 14.

[79] Green Paper 2010, n. 10 above, at p. 1.

[80] *Special EUROBAROMETER* 298, n. 71 above.

[81] Explanatory Memorandum to the Common European Sales Law, COM(2011)0284 (11 October 2011), p. 3.

[82] *Special EUROBAROMETER* 320 (2011), p. 15 on European contract law in B2B transactions and *Special EUROBAROMETER* 321 (2011), p. 19 on European contract law in consumer transactions. For an earlier critique of policy prescriptions derived from

contract law as the first and third most significant obstacles to cross-border trade in, respectively, business to consumer (B2C) transactions and business to business (B2B) transactions. However, closer inspection of the survey reveals that only 9 per cent of the businesses polled replied that 'contract law obstacles' had a major impact on their cross-border trade with consumers, compared to 68 per cent who said they were never deterred and 23 per cent who reported that they were 'not very often' deterred.[83] The corresponding figures for B2B transactions provide even weaker support for a European Contract Law as only 7 per cent of businesses replied that 'contract law obstacles' were a major impediment to cross-border trade, whilst 69 per cent were 'never' and 24 per cent 'not very often' deterred.[84] The Law Commission's advice to the UK Government on an optional European sales law gives careful consideration to these surveys and concludes that 'it is important not to overstate the problem'.[85]

As we have mentioned, the Green Paper also refers to the Clifford Chance survey, in which 66 per cent of the 175 businesses in eight EU countries which responded were of the view that there are obstacles to cross-border trade in the European Union. However, there was a huge divergence between nationals as to whether the European Union had reduced such obstacles in the past. In Hungary 88 per cent, but in the United Kingdom only 34 per cent, of those interviewed thought that it had. Over 80 per cent of respondents believed that an EU Contract Law might help for the future, but *only* if that law is optional. The Green Paper's brief reference to the results of the Clifford Chance survey does not reveal the larger picture. Interviewees were invited to rate a number of factors, including variations between legal systems, which might impede cross-border trade. Tax was, in fact, the highest rated factor, but, of course, this would not be affected at all by the options considered in the Green Paper. As will be argued, the marginal value of addressing a single impediment to trade when others, such as differential tax regimes, language barriers and cultural differences are endemic and enduring,[86] is entirely questionable.

EUROBAROMETER surveys, see T. Wilhelmson 'The Abuse of the "Confident Consumer" as a Justification for EC Consumer Law' (2004) 27 *J Consumer Policy* 317, 324–8.

83 *Ibid.* 84 *Ibid.*

85 Law Commission and Scottish Law Commission, *An Optional European Common Sales Law*, n. 39 above, para. 2.76 examining B2C contracts. See also para. 6.27 with regard to B2B contracts.

86 Bar Council of England and Wales, Response, n. 36 above, paras. 70–5.

Two other surveys have revealed further complexities. In 2010, the Law Society of England and Wales interviewed senior personnel from 602 law firms.[87] This survey confirmed the results of an earlier Cap Gemini survey commissioned by the Lord Chancellor's Department[88] which had emphasised the primary importance of legal certainty to contracting parties.[89] Though harmonisation claims perhaps its fundamental background justification to be the 'certainty' to be obtained through civilian, code-based jurisprudence, it is clear that the very notion of certainty is itself uncertain, for it is important to note that the Anglo-American common law, and standard terms based on it, are the law of choice in international trade, and the principal reason given for this by its users is that law's certainty(!) In the Clifford Chance survey, 83 per cent of respondents said that it was important to be able to choose the governing law, and English law was recorded as the most frequently utilised system at 26 per cent. This was confirmed by a survey conducted by the Oxford Institute of European and Comparative Law and the Oxford Centre for Socio-Legal Studies which found that almost 60 per cent of respondents said that English law was the most utilised regime in cross-border contracting.[90] A further recent survey by Queen Mary College, University of London, examined the applicable systems of law when the dispute was to be settled by arbitration. English law was the most popular at 40 per cent, followed by New York law at 17 per cent, Swiss law at 8 per cent and French law at 6 per cent.[91] The preference for common law jurisdiction is said to be a result of its practical nature, market orientation and superior problem-solving ability.[92]

87 Law Society, *Firms' Cross-border Work, Survey* (December 2010).

88 Cap Gemini Ernst and Young, *Commercial Court Feasibility Study* (2001).

89 The Law Society Survey, n. 87 above, emphasised the importance of both 'legal certainty' and 'familiarity with the legal system of contracting parties', whereas the Cap Gemini Report, n. 88 above, found that enforceability and predictability of decision-making was twice as important as familiarity with the applicable legal regime.

90 Oxford Institute of European and Comparative Law and the Oxford Centre for Socio-Legal Studies, *Civil Justice Systems in Europe: Implications for Choice of Forum and Choice of Contract Law* (2008).

91 School of International Arbitration, Queen Mary, University of London, *International Arbitration Survey 2010: Choices in International Arbitration*, available at http://choices.whitecase.com/. This and the Oxford Survey, n. 90 above, are examined in Law Society, Response, n. 38 above, paras. 54–5.

92 V. Gessner, 'Globalisation and Legal Certainty' in *Emerging Legal Certainty: Empirical Studies on the Globalisation of Law* (V. Gessner and A. Cem Budak (eds.), Dartmouth Publishing, 1998).

It is instructive at this point to consider the latest *Doing Business* survey by the World Bank.[93] This survey ranks countries by reference to the ease of doing business in them, determined by evidence about nine areas of business activity: starting a business, dealing with construction permits, registering property, getting credit, protecting investors, paying taxes, trading across borders, enforcing contracts and closing a business. A notable feature here is that the top five aggregate ranking positions are taken by common law based systems: Singapore, Hong Kong, New Zealand, the United Kingdom and the United States. The next five positions are taken by Nordic (Denmark and Norway), common law (Australia and Ireland) and mixed common and civil law (Canada) systems. The major civil law systems do not score highly in these tables: Germany ranks 22nd, after Estonia and Thailand, and France 26th, after Lithuania and Latvia. The clear preference for common law based systems would seem to be at odds with assertions that trade would be facilitated by the greater use of a contract code that would more fully reflect civilian rather than common law principles.

Though it is indeed our provisional belief, we are not arguing that the common law generally provides a superior framework for the law of contract than the civilian systems, including the essentially German position articulated in the CFR and now the CESL.[94] Any such argument raises fundamental issues about, *inter alia*, the relationship between legal institutions and economic performance that are of the greatest complexity and cannot be sensibly claimed to be resolved in the discussion of the CFR.[95] We are arguing that the evidence marshalled by the Contract Law initiative for the transaction cost argument is ambivalent, and that the interpretation it most readily bears is overall satisfaction with the existing position. That evidence can be read as support for the argument for harmonisation only on the basis of a most strained interpretation. All this reflects the fact that, prior to the Contract Law initiative, there was no significant market or political demand for harmonisation even from those engaged in cross-border commerce, and the evidence of such a

[93] International Finance Corporation and the World Bank, *Doing Business 2011: Making a Difference for Entrepreneurs* (2010), available at www.doingbusiness.org/reports/global-reports/doing-business-2011/.

[94] O. Lando, 'The Structure and Legal Values of the Common Frame of Reference (CFR)' (2007) 3 *European Rev. Contract Law* 240. See further Law Commission and Scottish Law Commission, *An Optional European Common Sales Law*, n. 39 above, paras. 7.57–7.93.

[95] They have been pursued in relation to the codification project by Prof. Legrand: P. Legrand, 'Are Civilians Educable?' (1998) 18 *Legal Studies* 216.

demand put forward in the Green Paper is that the evidence that there is such a demand is essentially, as it were, self-referential. All such evidence is the result of solicitations of opinions about hypothetical situations made under the Contract Law initiative itself, or of other, related efforts by the European Commission, or sometimes other EU bodies, since the 2001 Communication.

### Evidence that is ignored

The way responses to the consultation under the 2001 Communication have been interpreted is very telling.[96] As we have mentioned, the 2003 Action Plan concluded that none of the responses expressed dissatisfaction with a sectoral approach. This is how this was dealt with by the Commission in its 2004 Communication on the *acquis*:

> The Action Plan concluded, *inter alia*, that at this stage there were no indications that the sectoral approach followed thus far leads to problems or that it should be abandoned. It was nevertheless considered appropriate to examine whether non-sector-specific measures such as an optional instrument may be required to solve problems in the area of European contract law. The Commission intends to continue this process in parallel with the work on developing the CFR and taking into account the comments received so far from stakeholders about their preferences for the parameters of any such instrument, if the need for it were to arise.[97]

The consequence of proceeding down the line 'nevertheless considered appropriate', for reasons which are not set out but about which it is possible to speculate, is that the revealed preferences of the citizens of the European Union who are supposed to benefit from harmonisation are ignored, despite all the rhetoric about consultation.[98] The first of the four policy options set out in the 2001 Communication was to take 'no EC action',[99] and therefore '[t]o leave the solution of any identified problems

96 M. Kenny, 'Constructing a European Civil Code: Quis Custodiet Ipsos Custodes' (2006) 12 *Columbia Journal of European Law* 775.

97 Communication from the Commission on the European Contract Law and the Revision of the Acquis: The Way Forward, COM(2004)651 final (11 October 2004), para. 2.3.

98 *Action Plan*, n. 8 above, para. 89 tells us that, during the consultation invited by the 2001 Communication, 'there were calls to continue reflections on the opportuneness of non-sector-specific measures in the area of European contract law', but does not tell us by who, though one can guess and find one's guess confirmed by reading the responses.

99 Communication from the Commission, n. 2 above, paras. 49–51.

to the market'.[100] Of those who participated in the consultation under the Communication, '[o]nly a small minority' favoured this option,[101] and almost no weight has been given to it in the subsequent course of the Contract Law initiative. Significantly, this option just dropped out of the Action Plan[102] and is long forgotten in the Green Paper. But surely the significance of the response to this option is being misunderstood. Those who contributed to the consultation preponderantly were academics committed to harmonisation[103] who, as so often in transnational law, identified their 'own best intentions with society's best interests'.[104] To imply that the majority of contributors to the consultation represent the views of the majority of the citizens of the European Union, as the initiative largely has done, is ridiculous.

The main result of the Contract Law initiative's concentration on responses to questions about hypothetical states of affairs which its own efforts have produced is that the main source of evidence about the actual views of the citizens who supposedly are to benefit from harmonisation is almost entirely disregarded. This is the evidence of preferences revealed by the choices made on the existing market. Of course, these choices are constrained by transaction costs. But to acknowledge this does not give one scope simply to ignore those choices, though this is what the initiative, committing gross errors of policy formulation, has done.

It is wrong to believe, as the initiative evidently believes, that the unsurprising, indeed inevitable, fact that the existing market is affected by transaction costs means that the market has 'failed' and that the preferences revealed on that market should therefore be ignored. If this was so, then all preferences revealed on all markets should be ignored, because all markets fail in this way. Positive transaction costs may be

100 *Ibid.* Executive Summary. 101 *Action Plan*, n. 8 above, para. 7.

102 'Editorial Comments: European Contract Law: Quo Vadis?' (2005) 42 Common Market Law Review 1, 2.

103 *Action Plan*, n. 8 above, at p. 55.

104 P. B. Stephan, 'The Futility of Unification and Harmonisation in International Commercial Law' 39 (1999) *Virginia J International Law* 743, 796. See also the influence of Bourdieu's sociological theories which emphasise the fact that transnational elite lawyers might champion legal globalisation as a result of conviction or self-interest: Y. Dezalay and B. Garth, *Dealing in Virtue, International Commercial Arbitration and the Construction of a Transnational Legal Order* (University of Chicago Press, 1996), p. 343. For a historical survey of legal professional self-interest in relation to codification in the United States, see the magisterial G. A. Weiss, 'The Enchantment of Codification in the Common Law World' (2000) 25 *Yale J International Law* 435, 502–9.

identified in any empirical market, which therefore can never conform to the conditions for general equilibrium and optimal welfare. To say that the presence of these costs constitutes market failure is absurd. The concept of market failure as it is normally understood is far too wide and extends a general power to identify any market, not as inevitably imperfect, as all are, but as having failed in such a way as to justify intervention. The very looseness of the identification of market failure extends a discretion to focus on a particular cause of failure for reasons which cannot be traced to the analysis of the market and typically remain implicit.

The transaction cost argument for harmonisation is a clear example of the common mistake of selectively identifying a particular cost, in this case legal divergence, in order to argue for its removal, ignoring the evidence of the existing market that, in overall context, and in consciousness of resource implications, choosing not to sustain the cost of harmonisation may be entirely rational and optimal. To make one's economic choices locally or, when engaging in cross-border commerce, which was not entirely unknown within the European Union prior to the initiative, to deal with its problems by means other than pursuit of harmonisation, are the 'options' chosen by the citizens who are supposed to benefit from a European Contract Law, and in this case these choices are the best evidence of the real preferences of those citizens.

The 'barriers' to the operation of the internal market other than legal divergence, including fundamental ones such as language and culture, the preference to inspect goods and the cost of travelling to do so, transport costs, confidence in relationships with local suppliers, especially in the event of necessity of a remedy, etc., can and do make preferences to obtain goods principally locally entirely rational in the case of the great majority of exchanges by both consumers[105] and businesses, and this would mean that, in respect of these exchanges, the pursuit of legal harmonisation is a pointless expense. The adoption of lower cost methods of dealing with the legal issues of cross-border trade as these

[105] The findings of the European Consumers' Network, recently cited by the Law Commission and the Scottish Law Commission in *An Optional European Common Sales Law*, n. 39 above, para. 2.80, are that consumers' major concerns about cross-border purchases are the risk of fraud (62%), how to resolve problems if they occur (59%) and issues around delivery (49%). Furthermore, the Commissions go on to say, *ibid.* para. 2.81, that these are more problems of perception than reality. When consumers have actually engaged in such transactions they report that these concerns are very substantially reduced.

arise by those who do wish to engage in such trade (though these methods, such as obtaining advice over conflicts of law, are always depicted in the Contract Law initiative as costs to be eliminated),[106] would also appear to be generally entirely rational. They avoid the perceived greater expense of pursuing harmonisation by those engaging in such trade.[107]

How can it be that the, at best, slender evidence of a need for general harmonisation under the Contract Law initiative may be thought to carry greater weight than the existing empirical evidence that the alternative means of dealing with the legal issues of cross-border trade are found to be satisfactory? The whole idea of public intervention is based on the belief that market evidence of this sort does not reflect the existence of an optimal situation and so a welfare improvement may be possible. This is indeed so. But the crucial word is 'may'. Whilst we can conceive of cautious cases for sectoral intervention being made, perhaps particularly for digital content,[108] and whilst certain parts of EU consumer law (but,

[106] This chapter will not go into this matter, for it raises issues of a theoretical profundity which it is not really appropriate to discuss here, but the transaction cost argument for codification exemplifies the tendency to describe facilitative institutions, such as the existing principles of conflict of law, as costs, which makes much transaction cost analysis incoherent: D. Campbell, 'On What is Valuable in Law and Economics' (1996) 8 *Otago L Rev.* 489, 505–6.

[107] Wagner, 'The Economics of Harmonisation', n. 46 above, at 1013–18.

[108] Though the Green Paper is essentially an argument for a purportedly fully harmonised contract law, it rather inconsistently does hold out the possibility of 'an instrument tailor-made for the online world' (Green Paper 2010, n. 10 above, para. 4.2.2), and this seems to us a suggestion worth considering. The idea of the 'blue button', by which consumers making Internet purchases could click on an on-screen EU flag to indicate their preference for the sale to be subject to European contract law (H. Schulte-Nolke, 'EC Law on the Formation of Contract: From the Common Frame of Reference to the "Blue Button"' (2007) 3 *European Rev. Contract Law* 332), seems to us to have merit, as does the suggestion that by this means businesses would effect a saving in transaction costs sufficient to persuade them to accept higher levels of consumer protection: H. Beale, 'The Future of the Common Frame of Reference' (2007) 3 *European Rev. Contract Law* 257.

There is, of course, a considerable irony here as, although under art. 1(1) the CESL will apply to cross-border 'supply of digital content', the Law Commission and the Scottish Law Commission were forced to omit any discussion of this in order to ensure its timely publication: Law Commission and Scottish Law Commission, *An Optional European Common Sales Law*, n. 39 above, at para. S3. Nevertheless, the Commissions have commented that, rather than pursue a general sales law, 'efforts would be better spent on developing a European Code for consumer sales over the internet where there is stronger evidence that the current variety of contract laws inhibit the single market': *ibid.* para. S.51.

tellingly, not all) are good evidence that such intervention can produce a superior level of welfare,[109] the claim that intervention at the extremely ambitious level of generally harmonising the laws of contract of the EU Member States will maximise welfare has simply not been made out.

Just because a transaction cost exists does not mean that steps should be taken to eliminate it. Those steps should be taken only when there is a net welfare improvement to be obtained from the elimination. A step taken towards a goal, such as a 'level playing field' for competition, will not be a welfare improvement if that step involves costs greater than its benefits.[110] What market choices typically bring home to those making them is that benefits have costs. This may well not be the case when a political case for an intervention, which naturally focuses on benefits, is made. The Contract Law initiative has typically not asked questions about the cost of harmonisation as a solution to the problems of cross-border commerce but has presented it entirely as a matter of the benefits of an optimal solution to the problems of divergence.[111]

It is important to see how the concept of the optimal, uniform solution does its work. If one is asked whether one would prefer to maintain the undeniable current transaction costs of divergence or to have a fully harmonised system which eliminates those costs, then, of course, it would be perverse not to say that one prefers the fully harmonised system.[112] The choice is between the empirical world with its defects and the theoretically optimal unified solution. But, as this optimal solution cannot be achieved, the evidence cited in the Green Paper, putting aside its shortcomings in its own terms, is irrelevant. It is evidence about a choice that is not available. The actual choice available is between the divergent systems and a code which itself will in many ways be defective by contrast to the optimal solution. It therefore simply is not the case that 'the implementation of a European Code leads, inevitably, to a reduction

[109] O. Gerstenberg and C. F. Sabel, *Regulating Private Law: The CJEU's Framework Jurisprudence* (unpublished paper on file with the authors).

[110] R. Van den Bergh, 'Forced Harmonisation of Contract Law in Europe: Not to be Continued' in *An Academic Green Paper on European Contract Law* (S. Grundmann and J. Stuyck (eds.), Kluwer Law International, The Hague, 2002), pp. 249, 253–5.

[111] M. Kenny, 'The 2003 Action Plan on European Contract Law: Is the Commission Running Wild' (2003) 28 *European Law Rev.* 538, 545–6.

[112] To these costs could be added the costs of ensuring a consistent and frictionless interface between the instrument codifying the law of contract and the national based areas of contiguous law such as tort, property and restitution law.

in transaction costs'.[113] If this implementation produced the optimal solution of an actually uniform European law of contract, this argument would apply, but the actual choice will be between alternatives both of which have costs.

The Contract Law initiative has failed to produce any substantial evidence about the preferences of the citizens who are supposed to benefit from harmonisation in respect of the actually relevant choice between defective and costly harmonisation and the existing state of legal divergence.[114] Though this failure no doubt follows from the basic misunderstanding of the nature of the choice actually available, it nevertheless is providential, for such evidence is not obtainable.[115] The choice between a costless, optimal solution and the existing market is obvious in itself and easy to formulate for the purposes of consultation. The choice between an intendedly general, uniform and costless but inevitably partial, uneven, complicated and costly 'solution' and the existing situation is extremely hard. The least one can say is that any attempt to assess whether any claimed savings in transaction costs will be greater than the inevitable increases caused by harmonisation would have to be immensely more sophisticated than the transaction cost argument that

[113] D. Kallweit, 'Towards a European Contract Law: For a Prosperous Future of International Trade' (2004) 35 *Wellington Law Rev.* 269, 283. A similar easy reliance upon assertion is perhaps apparent in some of the English language discussions that preceded the Uniform Contract Act in China, e.g. P. Jiang, '*Drafting the Uniform Contract Law in China*' (1996) 10 *Columbia J Asian Law* 245, 246: 'China's market economic policy is the driving force behind the drafting of the UCL [Uniform Contract Law]. A contract law that is applicable to all areas will better serve the homogeneous market prescribed by the policy'.

[114] HL EU Committee, 12th Report (2008–9), *European Contract Law: The Draft Common Frame of Reference*, HL Paper 95, paras. 40, 83–4.

[115] This makes the EU Committee's own insistence, *ibid.* para. 85, that an impact assessment should precede 'any form of mandatory harmonisation', though commendable in its intent, pointless or worse, for we have no doubt that, if the political necessity arose, such an assessment could be undertaken, with predictable results. The necessity for such an assessment was pointed out to the Commission at least as early as the response to consultation under its 2003 Communication Action Plan, n. 8 above, para. 4.4.2. This distance between the evidence base of the Green Paper and what Prof. Schwartze, one of the contributors to the Contract Law initiative who has looked the problems of data collection in the face, thinks should be done, is immense: A. Schwartze, 'Design for an Empirical Data Investigation into the Impact of Existing Contract Law Harmonisation under the White Paper of 1985' in Grundmann and Stuyck, *Academic Green Paper*, n. 110 above, at p. 59. Though we are anxious not to put words in his mouth, our point that the really relevant data is not obtainable seems to us to be effectively conceded by Prof. Schwartze.

has been articulated so far. But, in our opinion, reflection on the extent and complexity of the issues which would be encountered by private contracting parties throughout the European Union caused by adoption of a generally harmonised law leads one to conclude that these are simply too complicated to be at all plausibly modelled from the centralised perspective of an intervening public authority. Once one acknowledges what is involved in it, assessment of the welfare outcomes of harmonisation of all the national contract laws of the European Union is simply too great an informational and computational challenge for any intervening public authority which seeks legitimately to implement a rational policy.

The inevitable consequence of this is the questionable nature of the evidence about the demand for harmonisation which has been discussed. The right questions cannot be asked, much less answered. This cannot be remedied by reference to the very substantial literature discussing various doctrinal alternatives produced by the consultation of experts committed to the Contract Law initiative, though this is, of course, what typically has been done in the course of producing the *Principles of European Contract Law* and the draft CFR. These experts are not really the citizens who are to benefit from harmonisation, though they will indeed be the ones who principally do obtain 'a significant non-financial utility, such as that derived from increased prestige'[116] from it. When such experts claim to point to 'practical problems' of divergence that require full harmonisation, they are laying claim to a knowledge of the general empirical operation of contract law that is not available for any national legal system in the world;[117] and to make it for all of the European Union is, *a fortiori*, quite without foundation.

[116] A. I. Ogus, 'Competition between National Legal Systems: A Contribution of Economic Analysis to Comparative Law' (1999) 48 *International and Comparative Law Quarterly* 405, 416.

[117] Stewart Macaulay reached the age of 80 in 2011. Perhaps it is as well to seek to learn from the greatest empirical researcher into contracting who has ever lived: S. Macaulay, 'Contracts, New Legal Realism and Improving the Navigation of the Yellow Submarine' (2006) 80 *Tulane Law Rev.* 1161, 1165: 'We need an accurate empirically informed picture of how law is working on the ground if we are to assess whether it actually promotes efficiency. Overlooking the way the law in action may distort the consequences of various rules is bad enough when we are focused on American problems. The distortion is likely much worse when we advocate rules to be applied in international transactions or in nations with very different constellations of legal institutions and cultures'.

## Teleology of the Green Paper

What the welfare effects of the Contract Law initiative will be will, of course, depend upon its end product. The Green Paper sets out the range of options. The way in which these options are presented is highly revealing. The view of the CFR as a tool-box without necessary legal effects from which private parties can select as they wish is, as it were, the minimal result.[118] As it seems to contemplate leaving adoption of the harmonised law entirely optional, the tool-box view can be defended as imposing the least cost on private parties were it adopted.[119] The principal question about it would be whether the construction of the tool-box was a wise use of public funds, a question that is not asked in the general atmosphere of congratulation about the academic merits of the CFR, but this is a question not relevant to our concerns here.

However, having served its purpose as the thin end of the wedge, we do not, despite persistent authoritative opinion to the contrary, think the tool-box is now anything other than a distraction. Not only has it been very effectively demonstrated that the CFR has been (rightly, indeed inevitably in our view) drafted in a way that powerfully works against cherry-picking from it,[120] and not only would widespread use of the tool-box by European and national legislators and other governmental bodies committed to harmonisation (centrally including the Commission itself) undermine the idea of its remaining optional for private parties,[121] but the entire direction of the harmonisation argument made quite explicit in the Green Paper has been towards much more maximal implementation. The Green Paper criticises all variants of the tool-box idea because they 'would not provide immediate, tangible internal market benefits since it will not remove divergences in law [and] could

[118] Green Paper 2010, n. 10 above, para. 4.1 (options 1 and 2).

[119] Beale, 'The Future of the CFR', n. 108 above, at 268–9. For an example of similar reasoning about the optional instrument which must have seemed like a good idea at the time see D. Staudenmayer, 'European Contract Law: What Does It Mean and What Does It Not Mean?' in Vogenauer and Weatherill, *The Harmonisation of European Contract Law*, n. 49 above, at p. 235.

[120] R. Schulze, 'The Academic Draft of the CFR and the EC Contract Law' in *Common Frame of Reference and the Existing EC Contract Law* (R. Schulze (ed.), Sellier, Munich 2008), pp. 3, 14.

[121] This is made quite explicit in European Parliament Committee on Legal Affairs, *Draft Report on Policy Options for Progress Towards a European Contract Law for Consumers and Businesses* 2011/2013(INI), para. 3.

not ensure a convergent application and interpretation of European Union contract law by the courts'.[122]

The Green Paper applies essentially the same criticism it made of the tool-box to all other variants of implementation, ordered according to the EU legislative mechanisms necessary to give effect to their increasing degrees of harmonisation, which fall short of a mandatory uniform code. Even a Directive on European contract law which 'could harmonise national contract law on the basis of minimum common standards' 'would not necessarily lead to uniform implementation and interpretation of the rules [and] might not be able to deliver the necessary legal certainty and businesses would thus continue to incur compliance costs'.[123]

Nothing, it seems, will do, save a Regulation establishing a European Contract Law (and, one step further, a European Civil Code covering other types of obligations),[124] which could include mandatory rules as deemed necessary and so 'could replace the diversity of national laws with a uniform set of rules'.[125] The undeniable teleological logic, if it may be put this way, of the Green Paper inexorably follows from the postulation of the optimal solution to the transaction cost problem, for everything that falls short of this is, by definition, inadequate, and so can be criticised as leaving a market failure. That the optimal solution is, as we have already argued, absurd becomes irrelevant in a way which should be understood.

When addressing the possible scope of the implementation of a European Contract Law, it becomes clear to what extent the Green Paper is prepared to press the transaction cost argument. Whilst an 'instrument covering cross-border contracts only' would be 'capable of resolving the problems of conflict of laws [and] could make an important contribution to the smooth functioning of the internal market', the existence of 'two sets of terms – one for cross-border and one for domestic contracts' obviously is not the optimal solution. The Green Paper therefore argues that 'an instrument covering both cross-border and domestic contracts could represent a further incentive for businesses to expand across borders, as they would be able to use one single set of terms and one single economic policy'.[126] In a sense, the transaction cost argument has become incidental. The whole problem of cross-border commerce was merely the starting point for a project which must ultimately aim at

[122] Green Paper 2010, n. 10 above, para. 4.1 (option 2b). [123] *Ibid.* para. 4.1 (option 5).
[124] *Ibid.* para. 4.1. (option 7). [125] *Ibid.* para. 4.1 (option 6). [126] *Ibid.* para. 4.2.2.

producing a purportedly uniform European Contract Law, for only this optimal, if illusory, solution to the transaction cost problem can ground any argument for general harmonisation.

One is grateful for this clarity of statement of intention in an area of policy formulation that has been and continues to be dogged by quite the opposite, for it allows us to assess the mischief that will eventually be caused by the contract law initiative as it approximates to its goal.[127] The European Contract Law will create within national jurisdictions the transaction costs of legal complexity that it is meant to eliminate between those jurisdictions. Even insofar as the harmonised law will allow parties to opt out of its provisions, it will generate the costs of understanding when ouster is necessary and of the means of accomplishing it, but insofar as that law is mandatory, its costs will increase. At an impressionistic level, we cannot but conceive that these costs will be immense.

## Implicit foundation of the transaction cost argument

The transaction cost argument for harmonisation commits the errors identified by Ronald Coase as characteristic of the typical economic argument for public intervention.[128] In that argument, it is pointed out that the existing market is deficient because of the existence of

[127] Save for the purposes of making an incidental point, we will ignore the mischief which pursuit of increasing harmonisation threatens to consumer law which itself gives rise to considerable political difficulty and complicates the Green Paper's review of possible options. One is speculating, but it does seem to us to be highly likely that the main pressure for whatever call for weak harmonisation there ever was, was, in a sense, generated by the European Union because the amount of inconsistent mandatory consumer law presented a genuine problem: G. Howells, 'European Consumer Law: The Minimal and Maximal Harmonisation Debate and Pro-independent Consumer Law Competence' in Grundmann and Stuyck, *Academic Green Paper*, n. 110 above, at p. 73. But, although it gained strength from earlier being in large part a sort of tidying up of the consumer *acquis* which disavowed full harmonisation (Communication from the Commission, n. 97 above, para. 2.3), the Contract Law initiative was bound eventually to run into the contradiction between full harmonisation and ineradicable (on plausible political assumptions) divergences in the levels of consumer protection that are possible in different Member States: T. Wilhelmsson, 'International Lex Mercatoria and Local Consumer Law: An Impossible Combination' (2003) 8 *Uniform L Rev*. 141.

[128] The clearest single statement of Coase's views is R. H. Coase, 'Social Cost and Public Policy' in *Exploring the Frontiers of Administration* (G.A. Edwards (ed.), Bureau of Research, Faculty of Administrative Studies, York University, Toronto, 1970), p. 33. An attempt to ascertain those views from *The Problem of Social Cost* must approach this seminal work through Coase's own comments on it in the collection of his essays in

transaction costs, in this case the transaction costs imposed on the internal market by divergences between national contract laws. This argument is indisputably true. But for it to carry, as it unproblematically has carried for the Contract Law initiative, the implication that the existence of these transaction costs is enough to justify public intervention, is, we are afraid, a major mistake in policy formulation. Intervention is warranted only if the result of the intervention is a superior level of welfare than that produced by the existing situation. In the transaction cost argument for general harmonisation, the conclusion is reached that intervention is warranted, but only because it is thought that the intervention will produce (at no specified cost) a theoretically optimal uniform law which eliminates the relevant transaction costs. And, of course, replacing the defective real world of transaction costs with a utopia in which they do not exist does produce, at least in the minds of those who believe such things, a major welfare improvement.

Maintaining this absurd position, the Contract Law initiative has done little or nothing to estimate the level of welfare which will be produced by the real world pursuit of harmonisation, which will require a contrast between the transaction costs of the existing market and the transaction costs of the imperfectly unified market which is bound to be the actual result of that pursuit. We are of the opinion that the relevant evidence about the results of attempts to create a general European Contract Law is far too difficult to be obtainable by a public body operating from the perspective of centralised intervention. The shabbiness of the evidence the Contract Law initiative has marshalled in its support is the result of this difficulty. The overwhelming evidence is that harmonisation is unwanted by those it is supposed to benefit, and in this case this is the best available evidence.

Though the Green Paper restates the purportedly economic case for harmonisation, the crucial feature of that case is that it is not fundamentally economic at all. It is a sort of tautology. If one has a prior commitment to the political aspiration of the European Union, then even full harmonisation can seem plausible and arguments such as the transaction cost argument can then be marshalled for it.[129] Though, on any

which it is reprinted: R.H. Coase, *The Firm, the Market and the Law* (University of Chicago Press, 1986), pp. 1–31, 157–86.

[129] T. Wilhelmsson, 'The Design of an Optional (Re)statement of European Contract Law: Real Life Instead of Dead Concepts' in Grundmann and Stuyck, *Academic Green Paper*, n. 110 above, at p. 353.

reasonable assumptions about the facts of national diversity, the idea that there can be a fully harmonised contract law is absurd, that idea may nevertheless be posited as a goal. The purportedly rational economic argument about transaction costs may then be made, but it is a façade for a far more visceral prior commitment to EU unification.

If one has this prior commitment to harmonisation, one has the attitude that can make harmonisation seem to approximate to the optimal solution. Without this prior commitment, the economic case for harmonisation is exposed as worthless and falls, and the emerging irony of the European Contract Law can now be seen. On any but the most minimalist of views of the way that Law will be used, views which in our opinion are now irrelevant, it must exacerbate within national boundaries the very transaction costs of legal complexity which it is supposed to eliminate.

## Collins and citizenship

By demonstrating the worthlessness of the purportedly economic case for harmonisation, we have attempted to expose the prior political assumptions that are essential to that case but which normally remain implicit. However, it might be valuable to conclude by making reference to an explicit statement of this part of the case. Professor Collins' argument for a European Code[130] registers many of the criticisms of the transaction cost argument (with which he is, in any case, out of sympathy as he is really interested, not in an economic case as such, but in fairness under the European social model) which we have sought to make, though in our opinion he very much underestimates the impact of those criticisms.[131] However this is, Professor Collins therefore does not rest his argument for harmonisation on the transaction cost argument or on an

[130] H. Collins, *The European Civil Code* (Cambridge University Press, 2008).

[131] In a 2010 paper, Prof. Collins seems to be using the implementation of the Unfair Commercial Practices Directive (2005/29/EC) to bolster an embattled belief in the general efficacy of EU institutions: H. Collins, 'Harmonisation by Example: European Laws Against Unfair Commercial Practices' (2010) 73 *Modern Law Rev.* 89. In essence, in an area of vexed disagreement even amongst those broadly committed to the harmonisation agenda (see n. 127 above), Prof. Collins approves the 'much more aggressive approach towards harmonisation of national laws' he argues is taken by the Directive (*ibid.* 118). But this approval surely runs into the problem about the plausibility of full harmonisation which Collins himself previously acknowledged. On this occasion, Collins says that: '[u]ltimately, given the divergences in national legal traditions and practices, complete uniformity seems an unlikely outcome' (*ibid.*). The use of

economic case at all. Having registered the weakness of that argument, he goes on to make an outright political argument for codification of the civil law as part of, in essence, building a European identity. Explicitly maintaining the political commitment we have argued others hold implicitly, Professor Collins does not need the transaction cost argument:

> The need for a European Civil Code derives from the need to facilitate the construction of a European civil society, in which national boundaries appear less significant as social and economic ties cross these artificial borders in increasingly dense networks ... the case for developing common principles of private law in Europe need not be tied to the question of whether or not these uniform rules are needed to reduce barriers to cross-border trade. Instead, it becomes possible to imagine how common principles of private law might contribute more broadly to the aims of the European Union to secure peace, prosperity and respect for human rights.[132]

Professor Collins' explicitness is part of his highly commendable, long-standing commitment to ensuring that codification is achieved by legitimate, not surreptitious, means.[133] We do not find his vanguard political project attractive, but we applaud the honesty of his expression of it. However, we cannot but believe that he is being somewhat naïve here. Why are others who share his commitment to a European code insistent on the transaction cost argument despite its feebleness? We feel it churlish not to join in the common pastime of putting our words into the mouths of the citizens of the European Union who the Contract Law initiative believes will benefit from harmonisation and so let us ask what those citizens would say if they were asked to disrupt or abandon their national contract laws, at likely very great cost, in order to forge a European identity? We believe, and we believe those committed to the Contract Law initiative believe, that an overwhelming majority would say 'no thanks', and whilst we believe they would be wise to do so, we can see that this failure to subjugate their private interests (and their commitment to national diversity and their suspicion of a major intervention of this nature) to the great project of overcoming the 'artificial borders' of

the term 'unlikely' is not an adequate acknowledgement of the magnitude of the problem in line with Collins' previous statements.

132 Collins, *European Civil Code*, n. 130 above, paras. 7.89–90.

133 See e.g., H. Collins, 'Transaction Costs and Subsidiarity in European Contract Law, in Grundmann and Stuyck, *Academic Green Paper*, n. 110 above, at p. 269 and Study Group on Social Justice in European Private Law, 'Social Justice in European Contract Law: A Manifesto' (2004) 10 *European Law J* 653.

the nation states may be felt disappointing by those who rise to this aspiration. The function of the transaction cost argument is to deal with the inconvenient preferences held by those who are supposedly to benefit from the European Contract Law by getting the ball rolling with a purportedly economic argument that nullifies those preferences. And just as the transaction cost argument needs a prior commitment to harmonisation to seem plausible, commitment to the forging of a European identity needs the transaction cost argument to turn that commitment from the anti-democratic political aspiration of a vanguard to something that appears to be in the economic interests of the common citizens of the European Union, who therefore can be claimed to want it. Surreptitiousness is not an unfortunate characteristic of the Contract Law initiative; it is its necessary form.

It is, we repeat, highly commendable of Professor Collins to argue against a 'technocratic approach' which he feels seeks to establish the code he desires by illegitimate means. But he does not see that this approach is essential to the codification project, nor that the problem with it is not that it is economic, but that its economics are nonsense, for sensible economics, based on the best evidence of real preferences, very strongly counsel against codification. Professor Collins is to be strongly distinguished from those pursuing full harmonisation by surreptitious means. But whilst they have their fantasy of an actually uniform law as an optimal solution to the transaction cost problem, Professor Collins has his own fantasy of a European Contract Law initiative which is open in its overriding political commitment to the generation of a European identity when that initiative cannot possibly take this form.

## Conclusion

Perhaps the message of this examination of the purported economic argument for a European Contract Law is that, to those involved in the contract law initiative, there is simply no need really to prove the claimed economic advantages of the Law because the necessity and mandate for it are inevitable corollaries of membership of the European Union and its concomitant commitment to the single market. Let us conclude by making our own position clear. We have sought to focus on theoretical issues of policy formation and to put to one side the underlying issue of how legitimate a policy-making process one can in general sensibly expect the EU institutions, particularly the European Commission, to follow, though the generation and selective invocation of congenial evidence in support of a predetermined agenda is entirely consistent with common Commission practice. That the European Union can promote so incredibly ambitious a project as harmonising the contract laws of all the Member States itself raises a serious question about the wisdom of extending the effective competence presently enjoyed by the European Union. That it can do so in so ill-argued a fashion, generating an inevitably highly costly policy, is so worrying as to further call the legitimacy of so defective a set of institutions into question.

In conclusion, we give the final words to the official responses of the French Government and the House of Lords' European Union Committee to the Contract Law initiative:

> pour la délégation française il semble que la Commission procède essentiellement par voie d'affirmations mais ne produit aucun résultat d'enquêtes pour soutenir les postulats qui constituent les fondements de son raisonnement.[134]

And:

> There is still little hard evidence on the fundamental question whether and how far differences in substantive law are a source of extensive problems which require addressing at the European level or whether and how far a common framework of contract law in the EU would bring net benefits, which would justify the expenditure of time, effort and money in developing it and the transactional costs for users of adaption to a new product ... But even in relation to the suggestion that an optional instrument might be prepared, there appears to be no real idea whether and how far this would be welcomed, worthwhile and feasible.[135]

This chapter provides empirical and theoretical support for this gratifying, if rare, agreement between guardians of the two dominant legal traditions of Europe.

[134] Translated by the Law Commission as: 'for the French delegation, it seems the Commission is essentially proceeding by way of affirmations without producing any empirical evidence to support the assumptions underpinning its argument': Law Commission and Scottish Law Commission, n. 39 above, para. 1.29.

[135] HL EU Committee, 12th Report, n. 114 above, para. 83.

# 7

# Theory and practice of constructing a common contract law terminology

CHIARA PERFUMI

## Impact of multilingualism on the contract

Multilingualism constitutes a 'fundamental EU principle'[1] aiming to uphold democracy, transparency and the right to knowledge.[2] It involves the promotion and the valuing of linguistic diversity at European level in order to foster the respect of national identities. From this principle derives the corollary according to which each language has official *status* and enjoys the same dignity in the EU legal order. It implies, on the one hand, that each citizen can address EU institutions in his or her own language and, on the other, that legislation must be made available in every official language.[3]

Each version, additionally, is authentic and must therefore be considered in order to determine the wording of EU law[4] that enjoys an autonomous meaning.[5] In doing so, the European legislator uses a peculiar terminology and legal concepts that do not necessarily have the same meaning in EU law and in the law of the various Member States[6] but, at

Research Assistant, Brescia University, Faculty of Law.

1 EU Charter on Fundamental Rights, Art. 22.

2 B. Pozzo, 'Multilinguismo, Terminologie giuridiche e problemi di armonizzazione del diritto privato europeo', in V. Jacometti and B. Pozzo, *Le politiche linguistiche delle Istituzioni comunitarie dopo l'allargamento* (Milan, 2006), p. 3.

3 A. Gambaro, 'A proposito del plurilinguismo legislativo europeo', (2004) *Rivista Trimestrale di Diritto e Procedura Civile* 287. Communication of the Commission, on Multilingualism: an asset for Europe and a shared commitment, COM(2008)566 final; European Parliament Resolution of 24 March 2009 on Multilingualism: an asset for Europe and a shared commitment, 2008/2225(INI).

4 C-283/81 *CILFIT* v. *Ministry of Health* [1892] ECR 3415, para. 18; C-152/01 *Kyocera Europe GmbH* v. *Hauptzollamt Krefeld* [2003] ECR I-13821, para. 32.

5 Original proposal for a unique authentic version: T. Shilling, 'Beyond Multilingualism: On Different Approaches to the Handling of Diverging Language Versions of a Community Law' (2010) *ELJ* 47.

6 *CILFIT*, n. 4 above, para. 19.

the same time, it necessarily implies the terminological background proper to the institutions' working language, leaving sophisticated terminological issues out of consideration.

Transposed into the contractual context, multilingualism can become a concrete obstacle for parties on two levels: as a matter of fact, it affects each single contract in relation to the choice of its language, as well as the language of the applicable contract law. Diversity, first of all, has an effect on the party's choice of the language regime of the contract. Nevertheless, this issue has either been ignored[7] (until the most recent Consumer Directives),[8] or has been left to Member States,[9] giving rise to different levels of consumer protection.[10] However, a clear convergence is detectable in the Directive on Consumer Rights[11] (DCR) as well as in the Proposal for a Common European Sales Law[12] (CESL), as both leave the

[7] Older Directives do not mention the language issue (Directives 85/577/EC, 90/314/EC). Directive 93/13/EC requires that certain terms be written 'in plain intelligible language' without supplying further clarification.

[8] Directive 94/47/EC, art. 4 provides that the contract should be drawn up 'in the language or one of the languages of the Member State in which the purchaser is resident or in the language or one of the languages of the Member State of which he is national which shall be an official language or official languages of the Community, at the purchaser's option. The Member State in which the purchaser is resident may, however, require that the contract be drawn up in all cases in at least its language or languages which must be an official language or official languages of the Community, and . . . the vendor provides the purchaser with a certified translation of the contract in the language or one of the languages of the Member State in which the immovable property is situated which shall be an official language or official languages of the Community'. These principles were recalled in Directive 2008/122/EC (recital 10 and art. 4(3)). A more neutral approach is adopted where only the contractual choice of language regime is provided (Directives 2002/65/EC, art. 3 and 2000/31/EC, art. 10). Directive 2008/48/EC contains provisions on the language regime in Annex II, Impact of Multilingualism on Businesses: 'Languages mean business. Companies work better with languages. Recommendations from the Business Forum for Multilingualism established by the European Commission', available at http://ec.europa.eu/education/languages/pdf/davignon_en.pdf.

[9] This is the case in Directive 99/44/EC, art. 6(4). The same approach is adopted in Directive 97/7/EC, recital 8.

[10] See generally the debate on the broad scope of art. 2 of the French Loi no. 94–665 of 4 August 1994. A.-M. Leroyer, 'Langue française', *JCL Concurrence-Consommation*, n. 872. Critical approach to the issue: R. Libchaber, 'Retour sur le droit de la langue française' (2001) *RTD Civ.* 709 and S. Feuillerat, 'Emploi de la langue française: information des consommateurs et loyauté des transactions' (1997) 12 *Rev. Conc. Consom.* 41; S. Bertolaso, 'L'utilisation de la langue française: protection réelle ou illusoire du consommateur ?', *PA*, 19 February 1997, 17.

[11] Directive 2011/83/EU of 25 October 2011 on consumer rights.

[12] Proposal for a Regulation on a Common European Sales Law, COM(2011)635 final, (11 October 2011), recital 27, p. 20.

rules on language determination to national law which has to be applied under the relevant conflict of law rule. Equally, national laws are, in any case, rarely available in other European languages.

These circumstances require market participants to obtain professional advice on the laws of the given legal system in which they propose to conclude a contract.[13] Nevertheless, even in areas in which the European Union has implemented a harmonised regime, important dissimilarities still remain at the national level, such that a mere translation does not suffice to grant a common understanding of legal concepts and terms enrooted in Member States' legal traditions. If, therefore, the elaboration of common rules related to certain aspects of contract law could, whether optional or not, be desirable they do not automatically solve the obstacles hinted at by multilingualism in the EU context. Moreover, these issues are strictly related to the inner quality of the terminology used by the European legislator[14] as well as to the process of translation in all the official languages.[15]

## Need for a common terminology

It is currently acknowledged that the existing private law *acquis* is essentially unsystematic in several respects,[16] creating what has been defined as an 'odd batch'[17] of rules expressed with a puzzling terminology. Indeed, whilst national private law aims to regulate the relationships between individuals in the light of general principles arising from a

[13] Only sophisticated parties can afford the expert legal advice that is needed for making an informed choice of law: M.W. Hesselink, *CFR and Social Justice, A Short Study for the European Parliament on the Values Underlying the Draft Common Frame of Reference for European Private Law: What Roles for Fairness and Social Justice?*, Centre for the Study of European Contract Law, Working Paper Series No. 2008/08 (2008), p. 10; L. Linnainmaa, *EU Contract Law as a Tool for Facilitating Cross-border Transactions: A Point of View from Industry*, p. 6, available at www.europarl.europa.eu/webnp/cms/lang/en/pid/1483.

[14] Institutional initiatives towards a better quality of legislation: Declaration no. 39 on the quality of drafting of Community legislation [1997], OJ C340/139; Interinstitutional Agreement on Common Guidelines for the Quality of Drafting of Community Legislation, 22 December 1998 [1999] OJ C73/1; Interinstitutional Agreement on better law-making, 16 December 2003 [2003] OJ C321 1; Council Decision 2937/937/EU of 1 December 2009 [2009] OJ L325/35), esp. art. 22. To ensure uniformity and accessibility, the Publications Office has issued the Interinstitutional Style Guide, available at www.publications.europa.eu/code.

[15] V. Heutger, 'A More Coherent European Wide Legal Language' (2004) 8(2) *European Integration Online Papers* 1.

[16] M.W. Hesselink, 'The Common Frame of Reference as a Source of European Private Law' (2009) 3 *Tul. L Rev.* 946.

[17] R. Zimmermann, 'The Present State of European Private Law' (2009) 7 *Am. J Comp. L* 485.

given constitutional legal order, the legislation enacted by the European institution has been merely instrumental to the completion of the internal market.[18]

The language there used sticks to the specific matters covered by EU polices and does not aspire to a general conceptualisation. Only some definitions have been inferred in the case law from the specific wording of a given provision to a more general extent at European level.[19]

Thus, the European legislator has mainly engendered a peculiar terminology that often deviates from the original meaning of the working language and refers to non-technical wording whose interpretation has been entrusted to the Court of Justice of the European Union (CJEU). In doing so, the Court combines the linguistic argument, considering the semantic and syntactical features of texts in comparison with the authentic language versions,[20] and the teleological one.[21] The latter implies that EU law must be placed in its context and interpreted in the light of the provisions of Community law as a whole having regard to its objectives and to the state of evolution at the date on which the provision in question is to be applied.[22] It is currently hoped that such a *pointilliste* and technocratic approach can be overcome in favour of a values-oriented harmonisation through the constitutional interpretation of EU private law in the light of the Charter of Fundamental Rights.[23] As we will see, this would be a ground-breaking argument aimed at broadening the narrow notion of consumer.

[18] Contrast with the approach promoted in Study Group on Social Justice in European Private Law, 'Social Justice in European Contract Law: A Manifesto' (2004) *ELJ* 654.

[19] AG Tizzano in C-168/00 *Simone Leitner* v. *TUI Deutschland GmbH* [2002] ECR I-2631, clarifying the autonomous 'European meaning' of the notion of damage; P. Rott, 'What is the Role of the ECJ in EC Private Law? A Comment on the ECJ Judgments in *Océano Grupo, Freiburger Kommunalbauten, Leitner and Veedfald*' (2005) 1(1) *HanseLR* 6; P. Mengozzi, 'Il risarcimento del danno morale da vacanza rovinata dopo la sentenza della Corte di giustizia CE del 12 marzo 2002' (2003) *Contratto e impresa / Europa* 589.

[20] This argument is linked to semantic and syntactical features of legal language as well as to comparison of authentic language versions: E. Paunio and S. Lindros-Hinheimo, 'Taking Language Seriously: An Analysis of Linguistic Reasoning and its Implications in EU Law' (2010) *ELJ* 400.

[21] M. Poiares Maduro, *Interpreting European Law: Judicial Adjudication in a Context of Constitutional Pluralism*, p. 6, available at SSRN http://dx.doi.org/10.2139/ssrn.1134503.

[22] *CILFIT*, n. 4 above, para. 20.

[23] A. Colombi Ciacchi, 'The Constitutionalisation of European Contract Law' (2006) *ERCL* 180. See also C. Mak, *Europe-building through Private Law: Lessons from Constitutional Theory*, Centre for the Study of European Contract Law Working Paper Series No. 2012–02, available at SSRN: http://ssrn.com/abstract=2023141.

Notwithstanding, the appreciation of legal concepts contained in EU law is frustrated by the lack of a shared uniform terminology as it is not the expression of a common legal tradition but rather consists in the formalisation of a political compromise according to EU competences and in the light of subsidiarity. Multilingualism, on its part, increases legal uncertainty because of inevitable discrepancies generated by the multiplication of official languages[24] and it has often led to a 'simplified, or naïve attitude' towards translation.[25] In striking the balance between unity and diversity, a common terminology should express at the same time a shared European culture and the respect of diversity in language, culture and traditions. In order to achieve this objective, it could be wiser to fix some 'prototypes'[26] standardising the main key concepts enshrined in the legal order.[27] Alongside the EU legislator, national and European courts, as well as comparatists, should play a major role in building a truly European legal culture through a constructive dialogue leading to a common and shared terminology.[28]

Indeed, many of the academic contributions to the European debate on the future of European contract law have enriched and influenced the construction of a European legal culture over the last two decades[29] and may be found under the auspices of the European Law Institute that has recently been created for better law-making in Europe and the enhancement of European legal integration.[30] On this premise, the building of a common terminology does not imply (at least, not immediately) a radical choice on the most suitable instrument dealing with European private law but rather concerns the emergence of a common legal culture.

[24] Multilingualism adding to problems of 'inter-lingual' uncertainty: Paunio and Lindros-Hinheimo, 'Taking Language Seriously', n. 20 above, at p 408.

[25] G. Ajani and M. Ebers, 'Introduction' in G. Ajani and M. Ebers (eds.), *Uniform Terminology for European Private Law* (Nomos, Baden-Baden, 2005), pp. 13–14.

[26] A. Tenenbaum, 'Droit européen des contrats: mythe ou réalité? L'enjeu et les difficultés d'une terminologie commune' (2009) *RIDC* 181. See O. Moréteau, 'Le prototype, clé de l'interprétation uniforme: la standardisation des notions floues en droit du commerce international' in R. Sacco (ed.), *L'interprétation des textes juridiques rédigés dans plus d'une langue* (Paris, 2002), p. 183.

[27] A. Gentili, 'I concetti nel diritto private europeo' (2010) *RDC* 761. The author recalls the relevance in European private law of the theory of Scarpelli, according to which legal concepts have a 'core meaning' that does not depend on the discretion of each legislator.

[28] Process conducted with lawyer-linguists: O. Moréteau, 'Les frontières de la langue et du droit: vers une méthodologie de la traduction juridique' (2009) *RIDC* 695.

[29] M. Bussani, 'Faut-il se passer du common law (européen)? Réflexions sur un code civil continental dans le droit mondialisé' (2010) *RIDC* 8.

[30] See www.europeanlawinstitute.eu.

## Emergence of a European legal terminology

The 2003 Action Plan considered the elaboration of a Common Frame of Reference (CFR) as an important step towards the improvement of the contract law *acquis*, providing for best solutions in terms of common terminology and rules. The preparation of a first draft of the CFR (Draft Common Frame of Reference, DCFR) was delegated to a group of researchers[31] and the European Commission intended it to serve as a tool-box for reviewing existing legislation through 'a clear and coherent structure' and 'a plain and clear wording'.[32]

Though the Commission undertook different and parallel initiatives, these lacked coordination. For example, in 2007, it issued a Green Paper[33] on the review of the consumer *acquis* and presented a Proposal for a Consumer Rights Directive in 2008 without reflecting on the results of the DCFR group.[34] The Proposal, in fact, did not even refer to the set of definitions proposed in the DCFR and adopted a different drafting style, thus frustrating the very function of the academic contribution. The inconsistency was evident for those terms whose definition was clearly divergent[35] whilst analogous definitions were expressed with different terms.[36] Finally, some expressions were clearly contradictory.[37]

[31] *Principles, Definitions and Model Rules of European Private Law: Draft Common Frame of Reference* (DCFR) (Outline Edition, Sellier, Munich, 2009), p. 17: the DCFR is mainly based on a revision of the Principles of European Contract Law (PECL) and the *acquis* principles.

[32] To fulfil this commitment, drafters consider that 'being designed for the Europe of the 21st century, it should be expressed in gender neutral terms. It should be as simple as is consistent with the need to convey accurately the intended meaning': DCFR, p. 29. Important initiatives have been promoted within the CoPECL group on terminology: B. Fauvarque-Cosson and D. Mazeaud (eds.), *Projet de Cadre commun de référence: Terminologie contractuelle commune* (Paris, 2008). See Tenenbaum, 'Droit européen des contrats: mythe ou réalité?', n. 26 above, at 177. Critics have noted that DCFR provisions 'are not definite enough for a court to tell how they should be applied. Nor do they provide solutions to specific legal problems that can be adopted piecemeal': L. Antoniolli, F. Fiorentini and J. Gordley, 'A Case-based Assessment of the Draft Common Frame of Reference' (2010) 58 *Am. J Comp. L* 357.

[33] *Green Paper on the Review of the Consumer Acquis*, COM(2006)744 final (8 February 2007).

[34] DCFR, p. 37.

[35] As to 'durable medium', see n. 49 below. Similarly with the definition of the 'producer'. Examples in Zimmermann, 'The Present State of European Private Law', n. 17 above, at 488.

[36] As we shall see, the term 'trader' seems now to be generally agreed.

[37] For example, the expressions 'rescission' and 'material possession' discussed in K. Lilleholt, 'Notes on the Proposal for a New Directive on Consumer Rights' (2009) *ERPL* 342.

Negotiations between the EU institutions for the adoption of this text have thus been quite slow and complicated. In reviewing the Proposal, the European Parliament reporter, Andreas Schwab, recalled that it was essential 'to ensure an appropriate level of consistency between the Proposal, the Common Frame of Reference and the remainder of the consumer *acquis*'[38] but the ultimate reaction to what looked 'very much like disregard of the DCFR in preparing the new Consumer Directive' has not been that effective.[39]

Contextually, the Commission set up an Expert Group for the elaboration of a user-friendly instrument of European contract law, published on 3 May 2011.[40] The text was mainly based on the DCFR[41] but the final version deviated in more than one respect from it, such as in the core definition of contract. The DCR was adopted on 25 October 2011. The new Directive applies to any contract concluded between a trader and a consumer and adopts a 'maximum harmonisation' approach.[42] Accordingly, definitions listed in article 2 could represent an embryonic common terminology in contract law. Their effective quality, as well as their authoritative nature as a uniform linguistic model of reference for European contract law, can already be noted in comparison with the Proposal for a Common European Sales Law.

The CESL Regulation should in fact introduce a parallel list of definitions pertaining to an optional instrument on contract law available to parties as a second regime alternative to national law.[43] Based on Article 114 TFEU, it aims to harmonise national laws through regulatory competition providing a uniform law directly applicable and available to qualified parties.[44] The CESL thus constitutes an autonomous set of rules

[38] Working paper, available at www.europarl.europa.eu/meetdocs/2009_2014/documents/imco/dt/807/807372/807372en.pdf.

[39] See Lilleholt, 'Notes on the Proposal', n. 37 above. Both terms were maintained as such in the European Parliament amended version but were eliminated from the actual DRC text.

[40] Feasibility Study, available at http://ec.europa.eu/justice/contract/files/feasibility_study_final.pdf. The Commission subsequently began a consultation (COM(2010)348 final), containing an explicit disclaimer that the terminology utilised had been taken from the DCFR, even if this choice was 'only indicative and it does not pre-empt either the structure or the terminology of the instrument'.

[41] Feasibility Study, p. 5.

[42] *Ibid.* recital 8.

[43] The CESL is applicable to cross-border transactions covering both B2C and B2B contracts involving SMEs. See H.-W. Micklitz and N. Reich, *The Commission Proposal for a Regulation on a Common European Sales Law (CESL): Too Broad or Not Broad Enough?*, EUI Working Paper LAW 2012/04, ISSN 1725-6739.

[44] The CESL is based on the same voluntary-basis technique as the CISG.

that should be interpreted and applied as such by the CJEU as well as by national courts,[45] whose relevant decisions will be collected in a European database to improve accessibility.[46]

Therefore, a cross-analysis of the original English version of both documents with the DCFR could highlight the institutional establishment of converging definitions (if any) and lead to a first assessment of the state of the art of the construction of a common terminology.

If such covergence is found, consolidated definitions could be inferred to a more general extent through the dynamic interpretation of the CJEU in the light of the Treaties and the European Charter of Fundamental Rights.[47]

## Consolidating European terminology: some examples

Limiting our investigation to consumer law, the common area of application of the DRC and the CESL, it has to be noted that they both insist on the same core terms listed in a specific article devoted to 'definitions'.[48] Moreover, only in a few cases do the texts deviate from the DCFR model.[49] Major innovations aim to adapt EU consumer legislation to changing markets in the digital environment,[50] the autonomous

[45] CESL, art. 4. See Micklitz and Reich, *The Commission Proposal*, n. 43 above, at p. 31.

[46] *Ibid.* recital 34.

[47] The CESL does not mention the need for compliance with EU fundamental rights as foreseen by the DCFR in art. I 1:102(2); Mak, 'Europe-building through Private Law', n. 23 above. It also does not include either the third paragraph of art. I 1: 102 which aims to promote uniformity of application, good faith and fair dealing and legal certainty. As to the pragmatic approach adopted by the Commission: C. Castronovo, 'L'utopia della codificazione europea e l'oscura realpolitik di Bruxelles dal DCFR alla proposta di regolamento di un diritto comune della vendita' (2011) *Europa e diritto privato* 857.

[48] The technique has been criticised as a 'burden for the reader'. Most definitions should be placed in the chapter in which they belong: O. Lando, 'Comments and Questions relating to the European Commission's Proposal for a Regulation on a Common European Sales Law' (2011) *ERPL* 722.

[49] Both DCR and CESL validate the definition of 'durable medium' referring to any support device, including 'paper, USB sticks, CD-ROMs, DVDs, memory cards or computers' hard disks as well as e-mails', able to store information personally addressed to the consumer or the trader: art. 2(10) and recital 23 DRC and art. 2(t) CESL. See art. 2(h) of Directive 2008/122/EC; art. 3(m) of Directive 2008/48/EC; art. 2(f) of Directive 2002/65/EC. See recital 23 DRC. The same wording, deviating from the DCFR, was advanced in the Proposal (art. 2(10)) and in its European Parliament amended version, as well as art. 2(9) of the Feasibility Study.

[50] Studies commissioned by the European Commission: Europe Economics, *Digital Content Services for Consumers: Assessment of Problems Experienced by Consumers* (2011) and

definition of 'digital content' marking out a new category of such contracts.[51] The Directive then distinguishes the applicable regime on the basis of the nature of its support. In doing so it introduces, besides goods and services, a third *genus*[52] constituted by digital content not supplied on a tangible medium.[53] In the other cases, as analysed below, the DRC and the CESL converge on existing terminological solutions derived from the debate on previous texts.

### *Definition and qualification of contract*

The notion of contract is one of the traditional examples noted by comparatists when they warn of misleading translations[54] since it is a core concept 'differently understood in each legal system'.[55] The complexity of the issue is demonstrated by the fact that no uniform definition can be found at the international level or in the *lex mercatoria*. The UNIDROIT Principles, as well as the Principles of European Contract Law (PECL), do not contain a general definition of contract. They only

University of Amsterdam (Prof. M.B.M. Loos), *Analysis of the Applicable Legal Frameworks and Suggestions for the Contours of a Model System of Consumer Protection in relation to Digital Content Contracts*, App. 9 'Output from the Consumer Survey'. Both available at http://ec.europa.eu/justice/newsroom/consumer-marketing/events/digital_conf_en.htm.

51 Digital content is 'data which are produced and supplied in digital form': see art. 2(11) and recital 19 DRC and art. 2(j) CESL. The wording recalls the version proposed in the Feasibility Study, art. 2(11). Compared to the DRC, the CESL adds the condition 'whether or not according to buyer's specification' as tailor-made products comprise an important part of the Internet market. This solution enables the application of the rules governing the sale of goods to digital content and provides the relevant adaptations or derogations: University of Amsterdam Study, n. 50 above, at p. 178.

In revising the DRC Proposal, the European Parliament suggested a new definition of goods including 'intangible item usable in a manner which can be equated with physical possession' (Amendment 61, art. 2(b)). In the opinion of the University of Amsterdam Study, the main advantage of this would have been the application of 'otherwise familiar legal concepts ... to new types of goods and services': University of Amsterdam Study, n. 50 above, at p. 172.

52 The University of Amsterdam Study, n. 50 above, warns about 'the difficulty of developing new legal concepts and thus entails the risk of legal uncertainty as to the meaning of these concepts' (p. 179). See the proposed definition (p. 11) and the proposal for art. IV.A.103 on digital content contracts (based on existing DCFR provisions).

53 DCR, recital 19.

54 R. Sacco, *Introduzione al diritto comparato* (Turin, 2003), p. 31. See also R. Sacco, 'Il contratto nella prospettiva comparatistica' (2001) *Europa e diritto privato* 479.

55 L. Miller, 'The Common Frame of Reference and the Feasibility of a Common Contract Law in Europe' (2007) *Bus Law Rev.* 385.

govern the conditions required for the existence of a contract (formation). This difficulty has not yet been overcome in EU law[56] and it has even been increased by its *pointilliste* limiting of the scope of application to specific contracts.[57] Only Directive 90/314/EC proposed a definition of the term 'contract', as 'the agreement linking the consumer to the organiser and/or retailer', reducing the contract to the agreement binding the consumer and the professional to be read in the context of the specific field of EU consumer law concerned.

Only the DCFR, aiming to regulate general contract law, proposed a model of definition[58] subsequently modified and incorporated into the Feasibility Study.[59] The experts, in fact, abandoned the DCFR version in order to leave out additional concepts such as 'juridical act' and 'legal relationship',[60] as well as any reference to the intention of the parties opting for a more precise and user-friendly definition (i.e., formulated in plain language).[61] Following the suggestion of the Expert Group, the CESL drafters referred to the contract as 'an agreement intended to give rise to obligations or other legal effects'.[62] Given that the DRC does not contain any analogous provision, if the draft version of the CESL were to be maintained in practice, it could constitute a very important realignment.

In fact, alongside this original definition, EU law seems to focus on the qualification of specific contracts, delimiting their proper scope of

[56] 'The use of the term "contract" in the *Acquis communautaire* and in the *Acquis International* reveals that the traditional terminological distinctions are still relevant': Fauvarque-Cosson and Mazeaud, *Materials for a Common Frame of Reference: Terminology, Guiding Principles, Model Rules*, n. 32 above, at p. 6.

[57] See e.g., Directive 2008/122/EC, art. 2.

[58] 'A contract is an agreement which is intended to give rise to a binding legal relationship or to have some other legal effect. It is a bilateral or multilateral juridical act.'

[59] Document published on 2 July 2010 by the Experts Group on a CFR in European Contract Law (Synthesis of the Second Meeting, 24 June 2010).

[60] They did not retain the reference to legal relationship, but the text reads: 'makes reference to the fact that the contract is an agreement which gives rise to obligations, which may also have other legal effect': see the CFR Group's report of 10 June 24 (Synthesis of the Experts Group's First Meeting, 21 May 2010).

[61] Feasibility Study of the Experts Group (3 May 2011). See also the previous CFR Group's report of 10 July 2002 (Synthesis of the Second Meeting, 24 June 2010).

[62] Article 2(a) CESL and art. 2(5) of the Feasibility Study. See DFCF, art. II 1:101(1). Drafters have thus preferred a 'narrow definition' the main element of which is the intention of the party taking on the obligation. An alternative solution would have been to 'move forward identifying the exchange which leads to reliance': Fauvarque-Cosson and Mazeaud, *Materials for a Common Frame of Reference: Terminology, Guiding Principles, Model Rules*, n. 32 above, at p. 3.

application on the basis of the dualistic distinction between contracts for the sale of goods and contracts for the supply of services.[63] According to article 2(k) of the CESL and article 2(5) of the DRC,[64] a contract for sale is characterised by two corresponding obligations which reflect the essence of the contract, consisting in the transfer of the ownership of goods and the payment of a price.[65] Meanwhile, service contracts are defined as a residual category[66] including 'any contract other than a sales contract under which the trader supplies or undertakes to supply a service to the consumer and the consumer pays or undertakes to pay the price thereof'.[67] Nevertheless, even this sharp distinction in the DRC does not adequately clarify the extent of the application of sale provisions to sales contracts having a service element.[68]

### *Consumer contracts*

Consumer contracts are not defined in the *acquis* but they can be qualified as such on the basis of their personal and material scope. Only the CESL makes this assumption explicit, proposing a tautological definition of consumer sales contracts as contracts for sale in which 'the seller is a trader and the buyer is a consumer'.[69] Meanwhile, with regard to the delimitation of the personal scope, it now seems accepted that the party contracting with the consumer is defined as the 'trader'. The CESL[70]

63 Even though this consideration seems to be overcome by the introduction of a regime of a *tertium genus* generated by those digital content contracts that are not supplied on a tangible medium.

64 The same wording was proposed in the Feasibility Study, art. 2(15).

65 The definition provided in the DCFR presents some slight differences. It includes the transfer of goods 'or other assets to the buyer, or to a third person, either immediately on conclusion of the contract or at some future time'. See DCFR, art. IVA 1:202.

66 DRC, art. 2(6).

67 The wording deviates from the DCFR. Under the Draft, the definition only includes the obligation of the service provider to supply a service to the client without mentioning payment.

68 C. Twigg-Flesner, *Fit for Purpose? The Proposals on Sales*, available at http://ssrn.com/abstract=1342702. Mixed contacts are explicitly excluded in CESL, art. 6.

69 CESL, art. 2(1). No analogous definition is provided in the DRC or in the DCFR.

70 Following the DCFR model, the Expert Group maintained the term 'business' (art. 2(1)) but this choice has been discarded in the final CESL version (art. 2(e)). In the DCFR 'business' means any natural or legal person, whether public or private, acting for purposes relating to the person's self-employed trade, work or profession, even if engaged in a non-profit activity (art. I 1:106(2)).

and the DRC,[71] as well as the more recent Directives,[72] define the term 'business' according to the Unfair Commercial Practices Directive.[73]

However, this terminological choice is unlikely to have any substantial effect but merely constitute a further clarification of the existing meaning,[74] which includes 'any natural or legal person who is acting for purposes relating to that person's trade, business, craft, or profession'. The major variation introduced in the DRC, and added to the DCFR, is the specification according to which public and private legal persons are included, a specification which has not been maintained in the CESL.[75] Moreover, only the Directive explicitly includes 'any other person acting in his name or on his behalf',[76] although the issue seems purely formalistic, as demonstrated by the fact that the expression 'business to consumer' (B2C) is still largely used to qualify consumer contracts rather than 'T2C'.

Similarly, the definition of 'consumer' has been finally confined to the narrow definition that has been consolidated in the existing *acquis*,[77] referring to any 'natural person who is acting for purposes which are outside his trade, business, craft or profession'.[78] First, such a full harmonised definition only concerns a 'natural person' according to the CJEU's interpretation.[79] Though the DRC allows Member States to extend the application of its provisions,[80] the uniform law of the CESL cannot be derogated from – a situation which could lead to important

[71] DRC, art. 2(2). [72] Directive 2008/122/EC, art. 2(e); Directive 2006/114/EC, art. 2(d).

[73] Directive 2005/29/EC, art. 2(b).

[74] According to the Commission Staff Working Document accompanying the Proposal for a Directive on Consumer Rights, the new term should improve the quality of legislation by tidying up legislation: see Annex 4, Table 1, p. 58.

[75] See Micklitz and Reich, *The Commission Proposal*, n. 43 above, at p. 12.

[76] The same reference in Directive 2008/122/EC.

[77] Directives 2008/122/EC, art. 2(f); 2005/29/EC, art. 2(a); 1999/44/EC, art. 1(a); 93/13/EC, art. 2(b); 90/314/EC, art. 2(4); 2000/31/EC, art. 2(e); 2008/48/EC, art. 3(a); 2002/65/EC, art. 2(d). However, Directive 2002/65/EC seems to allow a broader definition including 'non-profit organisations and persons making use of financial services' (recital 29). The CJEU has rendered a strict interpretation, see n. 79 below.

[78] DCR, art. 2(1); CESL, art. 2(f). The same wording was referred to in the Feasibility Study, art. 2(3). The most limited option suggested by the Commission in its consultation on the Green Paper has thus been adopted: M. Hesselink, 'Towards a Sharp Distinction between B2B and B2C? On Consumer, Commercial and General Contract Law after the Consumer Rights Directive' (2010) 18 *ERPL* 57, 69.

[79] C-541–2/99 *Cape Snc* v. *Idealservice Srl* [2001] ECR I-9049, para. 16. See also C-464/01 *Johann Gruber* v. *Bay Wa AG* [2005] ECR I-439.

[80] DRC, recital 13.

asymmetries,[81] as the DRC would not prevent Member States from protecting a larger category of persons.[82]

If we then consider the definition of the consumer's purposes, this rejects the broader notion proposed by the DCFR regulating dual purposes contracts,[83] which remain regulated according to the CJEU's approach in *Gruber*.[84] The choice is political.[85] The narrow definition endorses the stakeholders' preference expressed during the public consultation on the Green Paper,[86] but is strongly criticised by those who consider that no formal or material arguments justify such a restrictive protection.[87] We here support the position of those who consider that all different contractual relationships affected by asymmetries between the supplier and recipient could be more broadly described in the light of a more general policy of customer protection.[88]

In this sense, some propose that it might be easier to extend the notion of the consumer than to introduce a new category of 'business

[81] This definition could lead to the 'paradoxical result' that any form of extension 'to contracts involving a consumer interest in the broad sense as private users or customers would probably not be possible due to its preclusionary effects on national law': Micklitz and Reich, *The Commission Proposal*, n. 43 above, at p. 14.

[82] Already the case in several national provisions, *inter alia*, in Spain the definition of '*consumidor*' in art. 1.2 of Law of 19 July 1984, No. 26/1984 (Ley General para la Defensa de los consumidores y usuarios, LGDCU). Meanwhile, in France the extension of some consumer rules to subjects other than physical persons has been promoted: Cour de Cassation, Chambre civil I, 15 March 2005, no. 02–13285, *Bull.* 2005 I no. 135 p. 116. In the Netherlands the legislator included a new category covering those who are self-employed and that have no staff: Hesselink, 'Towards a Sharp Distinction between B2B and B2C?', n. 78 above, at 71.

[83] The DCFR inserted the adverb 'primarily' to include those acts that are mainly devoted to a personal purpose, introducing the definition proposed by the *Acquis* Group. See App. III, pp. 162–4. V. Roppo, 'From Consumer Contracts to Asymmetric Contracts: A Trend in European Contract Law?' (2009) *ERCL* 333.

[84] Recital 17 provides that 'where the contract is concluded for purposes partly within and partly outside the person's trade and the trade purpose is so limited as not to be predominant in the overall context of the contract, that person should also be considered as a consumer'. See *Gruber*, n. 79 above, para. 54; C-361/89 *Criminal Proceedings against Patrice Di Pinto* [1991] ECR I-1189, para. 16.

[85] H. Unberath and A. Johnston, 'The Double-headed Approach of the ECJ concerning Consumer Protection' (2007) *CMLRev.* 1237.

[86] Commission Staff Working Paper, *Report on the Outcome of the Public Consultation on the Green Paper on the Review of the Consumer Acquis* (13 October 2010), p. 5.

[87] Hesselink, 'Towards a Sharp Distinction between B2B and B2C?', n. 78 above, at 100.

[88] Roppo, 'From Consumer Contracts to Asymmetric Contracts', n. 83 above, at 304.

in need of protection' as provided for in the CESL.[89] Moreover, a broader notion would be more consistent with EU consumer policy because, if it is true that the Treaties do not contain any definition of 'the consumer', a constructive interpretation could be challenged on the basis of the Treaty of Lisbon and the EU Charter of Fundamental Rights which both impose a high level of consumer protection.[90]

### *Distance and off-premises contracts*

These two specific contracts are part of the core of the *acquis communautaire* as they represent the potentially major 'aggressive' techniques in consumer transactions in the digital era. Highlighting this common nature, the DCFR regulates the horizontal aspects related to information requirements under the same heading addressed to 'contracts with a consumer who is at a particular disadvantage'.[91] Similarly, in dealing with 'particular rights of withdrawal', the DCFR refers to a broader category of 'contracts negotiated away from business premises', including what is referred to in the DRC and CESL as 'distance and off-premises contracts'.[92] Once again, this definition includes distance contracts as well as off-premises contracts,[93] emphasising situations where 'the consumer's offer or acceptance was expressed away from the business premises'.[94]

However, this model has not been taken into consideration in the final version of the DRC nor in the CESL, abandoning any attempt to elaborate a general contract law: they are treated separately, as they represent

[89] Micklitz and Reich, *The Commission Proposal*, n. 43 above, at p. 15. The CESL covers contracts in which at least one of the contracting parties is an SME (art. 7(2)). It had already been argued that the exclusion of SMEs from the definition of consumer has led to 'social dumping': J.W. Rutgers, 'An Optional Instrument and Social Dumping Revisited' (2011) *ERCL* 350.

[90] Charter of Fundamental Rights of the European Union, Art. 38.

[91] DCFR, art. II 3:103. The notion includes: 'transactions that place the consumer at a significant information disadvantage because of the technical medium used ... the physical distance between business and consumer, or the nature of the transaction'. It should therefore be applied to distance contracts, entered into using 'direct and immediate time distance communication' (art. II 3:104) and to off-premises contracts as well as to 'other types of contracts the conclusion of which places the consumer at a particular disadvantage': T.Q. De Booys, C. Mak and M. Hesselink, *Comparison between the Model Rules of the Draft Common Frame of Reference and the European Commission's Proposal for a Consumer Rights Directive: How the CFR can Improve the Consumer Rights Directive*, p. 17, available at http://ssrn.com/abstract=1492660.

[92] DCFR, p. 38. [93] *Ibid.* art. II 5:201. [94] *Ibid.* art. II 5:201(3).

peculiar forms of contracts, but together when regulating specific aspects that they both share, such as rules on consumer information and the right of withdrawal.[95] Distance contracts are defined in the DRC as:

> any contract concluded between the trader and the consumer under an organised distance sales or service-provision scheme without the simultaneous physical presence of the trader and the consumer, with the exclusive use of one or more means of distance communication up to and including the time at which the contract is concluded.[96]

This definition insists on the absence of the 'simultaneous physical presence' and the use of 'exclusive means of distance communication',[97] reintroducing the condition under which the trader must be carrying on his activities pursuant to an organised distance sales or service-provision scheme.[98]

Convergence is also seen in the broader definition of off-premises contracts as 'any contract between the trader and the consumer',[99] concluded when parties are simultaneously and physically present in a place which is not the business premises of the trader[100] or immediately after the consumer was 'personally and individually addressed' in a place which is not the business premises of the trader.[101] This definition must be read together with the definition of 'business premises' in article 2(9)

95 Their common peculiarity has been even more evident since the DRC was reduced to an amendment to make them suitable in the evolving digital markets. See recitals 3, 4 and 5.

96 DRC, art. 2(5). See recital 20. Compared to the version in Directive 97/7/EC, this wording seems now accepted and confirmed also in the CESL, art. 2(p).

97 The formula adopted includes the definition of 'means of distant communication' that was previously provided separately: Directives 97/7/EC, art. 2(4), 2002/65/EC, art. 2(4).

98 See recitals 12, 13 of the original version of the DRC Proposal. This change had already been made in the European Parliament amendment (amended art. 2(6)) and it is now confirmed in the CESL (see art. 2(8) of the Feasibility Study). According to DRC, recital 13, Member States can extend its scope to contracts not concluded under an organised distance sales or service-provision scheme. The so called 'prosumer' supplying online products and services outside an organised distance sales or service-provision scheme seems to be excluded. The issue is particularly relevant in relation to e-commerce of digital content where these types of C2C contracts play a controversial role.

99 The definition of 'sale and service' (art. 2(8) of the DRC Proposal and art. 2(13) of the Feasibility Study) contracts has been omitted.

100 Article 2(8a) DRC; art. 2(qi) CESL. Referring to the trader, the latter expressly includes the natural person representing the trader (when it is a legal person), modifying the wording 'anyone acting in the name or on behalf of the business' proposed in art. 2(13) of the Feasibility Study. This condition is applicable also to offers made by the consumer in the same circumstances: art. 2(b).

101 The previous version merely referred to contracts 'negotiated away from business premises' (art. 2(8b) of the DRC Proposal). This expression aims to describe the

of the DRC and article 2(r) of the CESL, distinguishing immovable and movable retail premises, with the only requirement that the activity is carried out on a usual basis.[102] Finally, the difference between solicited and unsolicited visits is no longer relevant.[103]

## Conclusions

While we await the final version of the optional instrument on contract law, the DRC represents the only measure that seeks to introduce a specific 'European contract law terminology' related to consumer contracts. If we compare the definitions provided in the DRC, the consolidation of certain meanings can be highlighted: article 2 of the CRD constitutes, *de facto*, the first (though limited) core of established notions shared by the European institutions, the academic community and stakeholders. This consensus is supported by a convergence of the different versions that have been discussed in the European debate. However, the emerging common terminology found in both instruments does not always constitute a constructive evolution, as some choices are still quite far from representing a satisfying result. For example, looking at the definition of 'consumer', it is still confined to the narrowest meaning contained in the *acquis*, when it should be broadened to the idea of a 'customer' and contain a clearer characterisation of relevant purposes of transactions.

Meanwhile, the use of new legal concepts relating to 'digital content' have yet to be tested. Furthermore, more general considerations must be addressed for a coherent construction of a common European terminology. In order to truly improve the working of the market, the core of the established definitions should be expanded, covering a larger range of terms applicable to the entire *acquis*. The adoption of a common and shared linguistic strategy should be of the utmost importance if a coherent and clear contractual terminology is to be arrived at. Moreover, the common terminology has to be available in each official language.

conditions under which negotiations have been conducted. Such a variation had already been proposed in art. 2(13) of the Feasibility Study.

102 The reference to market stalls and fair stands (art. 2(9b) of the DRC Proposal) has been omitted and introduced in recital 22.

103 See art. 1 of Directive 85/577/EC. The limitation to unsolicited visits had already been eliminated in the DRC Proposal and in the Feasibility Study. The CESL extends this provision to the supplying of digital content or related services to the consumer (art. 2qiii).

In this process, the opportunity to refine the in-depth comparative analysis of existing contract law should not be wasted:[104] a common legal terminology which respects and promotes Europe's rich linguistic and cultural diversity must be forged.[105] This approach could have important effects on the legislative process.[106] While the elaboration of European rules should be preceded by a thorough and insightful analysis of the related legal concepts, and though this method has been promoted by the European institutions, the results are still not satisfactory. Moreover, using a comparative method that is suitable for analysing the feasibility of a proposed definition could avoid recurring disputes:[107] the critical notion of 'contract' is the emblematic example of a still misleading definition that it is not easily traceable to a single unified concept.

Finally, the development of a common European terminology could only be made possible by the hermeneutic role of the CJEU.[108] To promote such a European culture, a comprehensive comparative study of European legal systems needs to be promoted at University level.[109] Given these considerations, any artificial legislative exercise that does not correspond to the development of a *terminologie contractuelle commune* is liable to prove inadequate.[110]

[104] See Antoniolli, Fiorentini and Gordley, 'A Case-based Assessment of the Draft Common Frame of Reference', n. 32 above, at p. 358.

[105] M. Rosaria Ferrarese, 'Interpretazione e traduzione' in E. Ioriatti Ferrari (ed.), *Interpretazione e traduzione del diritto* (Padova, 2008), p. 35.

[106] Cf. X. Lagarde, 'Du bon usage de la terminologie contractuelle commune' 128 *LPA*, 29 June 2009, 11.

[107] See H. Muir Watt, 'La fonction subversive du droit comparé' (2000) *RIDC* 503.

[108] Pozzo, 'Multilinguismo, Terminologie giuridiche e problemi di armonizzazione del diritto privato europeo', n. 2 above, at 26; V. Jacometti, 'European Multilingualism between Minimum Harmonisation and "A-Technical" Terminology' (2009) 6 *Revista general de derecho público comparado* 4.

[109] Bussani, 'Faut-il se passer du common law (européen)?', n. 29 above, at 16; M. Hesselink, 'How to Opt into the Common European Sales Law? Brief Comments on the Commission's Proposal for a Regulation' (2012) *ERPL* 195.

[110] B. Pozzo, 'Harmonisation of European Contract Law and the Need of Creating a Common Terminology' (2003) 11(6) *ERPL* 754. See Ajani and Ebers, 'Introduction', n. 25 above, p. 1; S. Van Erp, 'Linguistic Diversity and a European Legal Discourse' (2003) 7 *EJCL*; J.-S. Bergé, 'Terminologie contractuelle commune et droit européen: les mots de la comparaison' (2008) *Revue des contrats* 1352.

8

# Private law discourse and scholarship in the wake of the Europeanisation of private law

OLHA CHEREDNYCHENKO

## Introduction

Private law has been traditionally conceived as that part of law which secures a sphere of positive freedom for private parties and provides a special legal framework which enables the parties to enjoy such freedom. To ensure that the exercise of the positive freedom is not subject to extensive government controls in the public interest, private law is constructed as a system of rights or entitlements such as freedom of contract or the enjoyment of private property. This idea of private law implies that private law discourse aims to dispense corrective justice between private parties, focusing on the criteria originating in the relationship between the parties and not on the attainment of external political, social or economic goals.[1] As such, private law reasoning is distinct from questions of policy and distributive justice which are inherent in public law discourse.[2] Even though particularly during the last half century or more private law discourse in many legal systems has to a greater or lesser extent been influenced by policy considerations following the rise of economic and social regulation,[3] the basic ethical-societal conception of private law as the law which should *primarily* focus

Associate Professor of European Private Law and Comparative Law at the University of Groningen, the Netherlands.

[1] On this, see F. Bydlinki, *System und Prinzipien des Privatrechts* (Springer, Vienna/ New York, 1996), p. 92 *et seq.*

[2] On the conventional characteristics of private law in more detail, see e.g., H. Collins, *Regulating Contracts* (Oxford University Press, 1999), p. 31 *et seq.*; O.O. Cherednychenko, *Fundamental Rights, Contract Law and the Protection of the Weaker Party: A Comparative Analysis of the Constitutionalisation of Contract Law, with Emphasis on Risky Financial Transactions* (Sellier, Munich, 2007), ch. 2.

[3] On this development, see Collins, *Regulating Contracts*, n. 2 above.

on the relationship between the two private parties has remained present.[4] Understanding private law in this way has also shaped the development of classical legal scholarship: legal scholars traditionally study law from the internal perspective, i.e., the perspective of a judge, and aim to secure legal integrity and doctrinal coherence.

The European Union challenges implicitly the traditional understanding of private law as it has evolved in national legal systems. It has been widely noted that the *acquis communautaire* in the field of private law aims to create the internal market and is therefore regulatory in nature.[5] Private law is viewed as an instrument for achieving the collective objectives of European integration. Alongside the central objective of establishing the European internal market, these objectives include, in particular, the protection of consumers, workers, small and medium-sized enterprises, the industry and the environment as well as non-discrimination policy. As Collins explains:

> [I]n its approach to the regulation of the internal market, the EU has never accepted the traditional distinction between public law regulation and private law. The question posed by the European legislator has been how to make the internal market function better. The resulting legislation chooses the regulatory technique that seems most appropriate to provide a solution to the perceived problem. From this perspective, the legislator's

[4] Cf. C.U. Schmid, 'The Thesis of the Instrumentalisation of Private Law by the EU in a Nutshell' in C. Joerges and T. Ralli (eds.), *European Constitutionalism without Private Law: Private Law without Democracy* (Joseph Beuys/Bono, Oslo, 2011), pp. 17, 21, who speaks in this context about the weak version of corrective justice which has remained present throughout the evolutionary path of private law. According to it, if one were to hypothetically ignore the regulatory dimension of a particular private law norm beyond the relationships between the two private parties, the application of the norm should lead to the outcome which respects the minimum requirements of justice between the parties. See also, Cherednychenko, *Fundamental Rights, Contract Law and the Protection of the Weaker Party*, n. 2 above, ch. 2, in particular, p. 49 *et seq.*

[5] See e.g., H.-W. Micklitz, 'The Concept of Competitive Contract Law' (2005) 23 *Penn State International Law Review* 549; C.U. Schmid, 'The Instrumentalist Conception of the Acquis Communautaire in Consumer Law and its Implications on a European Contract Law Code' (2005) 1 *European Review of Contract Law* 210; F. Cafaggi, 'Introduction' to F. Cafaggi (ed.), *The Institutional Framework of European Private Law* (Oxford University Press, 2006), p. 1; H. Collins, 'Governance Implications for the European Union of the Changing Character of Private Law' in F. Cafaggi and H. Muir-Watt (eds.), *Making of European Private Law: Governance Design* (Edward Elgar, Cheltenham/Northampton, 2009), p. 269; F. Caffaggi and H. Muir-Watt (eds.), *The Regulatory Function of European Private Law* (Edward Elgar, Cheltenham/Northampton, 2009); H.-W. Micklitz, 'The Visible Hand of European Regulatory Private Law: The Transformation of European Private Law from Autonomy to Functionalism in Competition and Regulation' (2009) 28 *Yearbook of European Law* 3.

> task is viewed as one of problem solving, not justice between the market participants, and certainly not one of securing legal integrity or doctrinal coherence.[6]

This contribution explores the implications of the ongoing process of the Europeanisation of private law for the traditional private law discourse in national legal systems and the role of private law scholarship. My argument, in a nutshell, is that the Europeanisation of private law reinforces the role of policy considerations related to the common good within a private law discourse, not only in areas that fall within the scope of EU law but also far beyond, further putting the traditional idea of private law under pressure; whilst public goals pursued by the European Union are often compatible with the traditional private law concerns of doing justice between the parties, at times the two may come into conflict with each other. In its turn, the tendency towards the instrumentalisation of private law presents new challenges for private law scholarship, strengthening the need for legal scholars to play a more proactive role in shaping (European) private law than they have played so far.

## (Excessive) instrumentalisation of private law by the European Union in the harmonised areas

Let us start our investigation by taking a closer look at the regulatory European private law and its impact on national laws in the areas of private law which have been harmonised by the European Union. Although European private law and national private laws are based on conceptually different ideas, the objectives pursued by the specific EU harmonisation measures in the field of private law are often compatible with the ethical-societal conception of private law.[7] Thus, for example, the idea of laying down minimum standards of consumer protection at EU level in order to redress the substantial imbalance of power between businesses and consumers does not contradict the traditional private law idea of respecting the minimum requirements of justice between the two private parties. All the more so, since many consumer protection standards contained in the EU consumer protection legislation build upon the standards developed within national legal systems by the private law

[6] H. Collins, 'The Hybrid Quality of European Private Law' in R. Brownsword, H.-W. Micklitz, L. Niglia and S. Weatherill (eds.), *The Foundations of European Private Law* (Hart Publishing, Oxford/Portland, 2011), p. 453.

[7] Cf. Schmid, 'The Thesis of the Instrumentalisation of Private Law', n. 4 above, at 23.

courts on the basis of open-ended private law norms, such as good faith and good morals. The Unfair Contract Terms Directive[8] is just one example. Protecting consumers through private law also serves the central objective of establishing the European internal market. It follows that national private laws, in which the EU consumer protection standards are implemented, may be instrumentalised for market integration purposes without compromising their ability to realise justice between the parties. The logic of market integration and the logic of traditional private law may thus mutually reinforce each other.

However, at times the instrumentalist conception of EU private law and the ethical-societal conception of national private laws may clash. As an example of the potentially excessive instrumentalisation of private law by the EU legislator, consider a general move away from minimum harmonisation towards full harmonisation in EU consumer law.[9] While minimum harmonisation measures allow Member States to maintain or adopt stricter rules than those contained therein, full harmonisation measures, as a rule, preclude Member States from so doing. The main explanation to this change in the European Union's approach lies in a modest degree of harmonisation which could be attained through the minimum harmonisation measures. In the European Commission's view, minimum harmonisation does not resolve the problem of legal fragmentation across the European Union, which is highly detrimental to cross-border trade.[10] What is needed is full harmonisation with regard to the legal issues that raise substantial barriers to trade for businesses and/or

8 Council Directive 93/13/EC of 5 April 1993 on unfair terms in consumer contracts [1993] OJ L95/29.

9 The policy shift from minimum harmonisation to full harmonisation was announced by the European Commission in the Communication on the Consumer Policy Strategy 2002–2006 of 7 May 2002, COM(2002) 208 final, pp. 12–13 and reinforced in the Communication on the EU Consumer Policy Strategy 2007–2013 of 13 March 2007, COM(2007)99 final, p. 7. Until 2002 the Product Liability Directive (85/374/EEC [1985] OJ L210/29) was the only Directive in the area of consumer law which was enacted on the basis of full harmonisation. Since 2002 several measures have been adopted on the basis of full harmonisation: Distance Marketing of Financial Services Directive (2002/65/EC [2002] OJ L271/16); Markets in Financial Instruments Directive (MiFID) (2004/39/EC [2004] OJ L145/1) and Directive implementing the MiFID (2006/73/EC, OJ L241/26); Unfair Commercial Practices Directive (2005/29/EC [2005] OJ L149/22); Payment Services Directive (2007/64/EC [2007] OJ L319/1); revised Timeshare Directive (2008/122/EC [2008] OJ L33/10); revised Consumer Credit Directive (2008/48/EC [2008] OJ L133/66); newly adopted Consumer Rights Directive (2011/83/EU [2011] OJ L304/64).

10 See e.g., Explanatory Memorandum to the Proposal for a Directive of the European Parliament and of the Council on Consumer Rights, COM(2008)614.

deter consumers from buying cross-border and are, therefore, most important for the establishment of the internal market.

Such an approach to law-making in the field of private law involves the risk of over-emphasising market integration over consumer protection. In its turn, 'downgrading' the consumer protection in the European Union[11] may result in neglecting the differences in economic, social and cultural needs of consumers across the European Union and, hence, the idea of justice between the market participants inherent in traditional private law discourse. In particular, it is questionable to what extent the full harmonisation strategy is suitable for the new EU Member States which have recently undergone the rapid transition from the communist command and control economies to market economies.[12] For instance, whilst the Product Liability Directive, as interpreted by the Court of Justice of the European Union (CJEU), seeks to achieve, in the matters regulated by it, full harmonisation in the area of civil liability on the part of producers in respect of damage caused by defective products,[13] one may doubt whether the exemption of liability claims for defective consumer products below €500 from the Directive's scope of application provided for in article 9(b) of the Directive appropriately addresses the needs of consumers in some new Member States.[14] While the threshold requirement of €500 makes sense in such old Member States as Germany and the Netherlands where consumers buy products far beyond this amount, the situation is different in such new Member States as Romania and Bulgaria where most consumers cannot afford to buy goods beyond this threshold on a regular basis. Therefore, what can be considered to be a minor material damage not worthy of protection in one Member State, cannot be considered as such in another Member State. As Member States, however, are not allowed to deviate from the threshold

[11] Cf. N. Reich, 'From Minimal to Full to "Half" Harmonisation' in J. Devenney and M. Kenny (eds.), *European Consumer Protection: Theory and Practice* (Cambridge University Press, 2012), pp. 3, 4.

[12] On this in more detail, see O.O. Cherednychenko, 'Securities Law', *Review of Central and East European Law*, Special Issue on Europeanisation of Private Law in Central and Eastern Europe Countries (CEECs): Preliminary Findings and Research Agenda (2013), forthcoming.

[13] See C-52/00 *Commission* v. *France* [2002] ECR I-3827, paras. 13–25; C-183/00 *María Victoria González Sánchez* v. *Medicina Asturiana SA* [2002] ECR I-3901, paras. 23–30; C-154/00 *Commission* v. *Greece* [2002] ECR I-3879, paras. 9–21.

[14] Cf. H.-W. Micklitz, *Review of Central and East European Law*, Special Issue on Europeanisation of Private Law in Central and Eastern Europe Countries (CEECs): Preliminary Findings and Research Agenda (2013), forthcoming.

requirement of €500 in their national laws and thus cannot introduce more consumer-friendly rules, the protective ambit of the Product Liability Directive in some countries is considerably reduced. This does not provide justice for many victims of defective products who, in the absence of more protective specific rules, have to bring action under the ordinary laws of contractual or non-contractual liability.

So far, the export of the Western type of EU private law to the new Member States has not been studied in the context of the economic, social and cultural needs of these countries.[15] The fully harmonised European private law may simply not suffice to deal with the economic, social and cultural realities of such countries. The new Member States may need more flexibility in the implementation of the EU standards within their national legal orders in order to be able to address specific issues that affect the consumer's position in these countries. Otherwise, the excessive pursuit of the public interest in the creation of the internal market through private law may jeopardise the ability of the latter to realise justice between the market participants in specific circumstances.

Similar concerns can also be raised with regard to the case law of the CJEU restricting the ability of the Member States to introduce or maintain consumer rights to information in their national laws beyond the information rights provided for in EU secondary law. In this context, the decision of the Court in the *Axa Royale* case,[16] which concerned the compatibility of the specific national information duty with EU law, in particular the Third Life Assurance Directive,[17] may serve as an illustration of the excessive instrumentalisation of private law by the CJEU. The Directive in question contains an extensive list of information to be communicated by the assurance undertaking to the policy-holder before the contract is concluded or during the term of the contract. Article 31(3) of the same Directive provides that the Member State may require assurance undertakings to furnish information in addition to that listed in the Directive 'only if it is necessary for a proper understanding by the policy-holder of the essential elements of the commitment'. The Belgian legislator exceeded the minimum information

[15] On this in more detail, see Cherednychenko, 'Securities Law', n. 12 above.

[16] C-386/00 *Axa Royale Belge SA* v. *Georges Ochoa Stratëgie Finance SPRL* [2002] ECR I-2209.

[17] Council Directive 92/96/EEC of 10 November 1992 on the coordination of laws, regulations and administrative provisions relating to direct life assurance and amending Directives 79/267/EEC and 90/619/EEC (Third Life Assurance Directive) [1992] OJ L360/1.

requirements provided for in the Directive by stipulating, *inter alia*, that a life assurance proposal or, in the absence of a proposal, a life assurance policy must inform a policy-holder that termination, reduction or surrender of an existing life assurance contract for the purpose of subscribing to another life assurance contract is generally detrimental to the policy-holder. The question referred to the CJEU in this case by the national court was whether Community law, and in particular the Third Life Assurance Directive, precludes such national legislation. The Court gave an affirmative answer to this question, reasoning that the information duty at issue was too general and vague and therefore inappropriate for the purposes of informing the policy-holder as to the choice to be made. The decisive argument of the Court, however, was that the information obligation in question was likely to dissuade the policy-holder from terminating an existing contract and, hence, it negatively affected the access of foreign insurers to the domestic market and the creation of the single assurance market.[18]

Although the duty to inform the policy-holder concerning the disadvantages resulting from the early termination of the existing contract may indeed produce such protectionist side-effects, such a duty is justified from the traditional private law perspective of ensuring justice between the market participants. In fact, it addresses the notorious problem that the premature termination of a life assurance policy is normally economically disadvantageous for the consumer. This is generally the case even if foreign insurance companies offer better insurance policies than national insurance companies. In view of the information asymmetry existing between life assurance companies and consumers holding life assurance policies, the information duty in question is essential for a proper understanding by the policy-holder of the essential elements of the life assurance contract, and thus for realising the objective which, ironically, has been explicitly mentioned in article 31(3) of the Third Life Assurance Directive as a legitimate justification for the imposition of additional information requirements at national level. Denying Member States the possibility to impose such a duty on insurance

[18] C-386/00 *Axa Royale Belge SA* v. *Georges Ochoa Stratëgie Finance SPRL* [2002] ECR I-2209, paras. 27–8. It is notable in this context that the information duty at issue in the *Axa Royale* case was laid down in the Belgian financial supervision legislation of a public law character. Considering the general formulation of the CJEU's ruling in this case and the fact that a public-private divide as such is not recognised in EU law, it can be assumed that not only public law but also private law legislation containing such a duty is incompatible with EU law for the above-mentioned reasons.

companies demonstrates the dominance of the internal market concerns over the contractual justice-based considerations in the CJEU's reasoning in the *Axa Royale* case. As a result, the private interest of the consumer to be informed about the real risk of high losses in case of premature termination of his or her life assurance policy is sacrificed for the realisation of the external public goal.[19]

## Spill-over effects of regulatory European private law in national private law

In addition to its direct impact on national private laws in the harmonised areas, regulatory European private law may also have spill-over effects in the general private law of the Member States outside the scope of EU law. As a result, formally unharmonised general private law may indirectly contribute to the attainment of the collective objectives of European integration. An important question which arises in this context is to what extent the spill-over effects of regulatory European private law are compatible with the justice-based logic of traditional private law. The interplay between general private law and the sector-specific contract-related rules under the Markets in Financial Instruments Directive (MiFID)[20] is particularly interesting in this respect and it will, therefore, guide our discussion.

The relationship between the investment service provider and its (potential) client was traditionally the exclusive domain of general private law, in particular contract law. More or less extensive duties of care and loyalty which should be observed by investment firms and credit institutions towards their clients have developed within private law systems across Europe. Thus, for example, already in 1993, the German Supreme Court in private law matters ruled that the recommended

[19] Cf. Schmid, 'The Thesis of the Instrumentalisation of Private Law', n. 4 above, at 28. The judgment of the CJEU in the *Axa Royale* case is in sharp contrast with the more consumer friendly line of case law concerning the interpretation of the EU consumer protection measures. See e.g., C-481/99 *Heininger* v. *Bayerische Hypo- und Vereinsbank AG* [2001] ECR I-9945; C-350/03 *Schulte* v. *Bausparkasse Badenia* [2005] ECR I-9215. In this context, see H. Unberath and A. Johnston, 'The Double-Headed Approach of the ECJ concerning Consumer Protection' (2007) 44 *Common Market Law Review* 1237.

[20] Directive 2004/39/EC of the European Parliament and of the Council of 21 April 2004 on markets in financial instruments amending Council Directives 85/611/EEC and 93/6EEC and Directive 2000/12/EC of the European Parliament and of the Council and repealing Council Directive 93/22/EEC [2004] OJ L145/1.

investment should be geared towards the personal circumstances of the client, and thus be suitable for that client (*'anlegergerechte' Beratung*).[21] Prior to providing investment advice, the bank should, therefore, obtain information concerning the client's knowledge and experience in the investment field relevant to the specific investment transactions he intends to enter into, and his investment objectives. In particular, advice has to be provided taking into account whether an intended investment transaction is aimed at making a certain investment or has a purely speculative character; if the bank does not have information concerning these facts about the client, it is obliged to obtain such information, so ruled the Supreme Court.

The leading role of private law in setting standards of care and loyalty in the relationship between investment service providers and their (potential) clients, however, has recently been put under pressure as a result of the regulation and supervision increasingly becoming relevant thereto. Being based on a public supervision and public enforcement model, the MiFID currently in force has accommodated many private law duties of care and loyalty within its ambit, transforming them into contract-related financial supervision rules of a regulatory nature governing the provision of investment services to their recipients at the precontractual and contractual stages, i.e., the so-called conduct of business rules.[22] The MiFID generally aims to bring about full harmonisation of these rules, allowing Member States to retain or impose requirements additional to those in this Directive only in exceptional cases.[23] Apart from the overall objective of market integration, the conduct of business regime under the MiFID has the twofold aim of ensuring a high level of

[21] BGH 6 July 1993, *BGHZ* 123, 126 = *NJW* 1993, 2433 (*Bond*).

[22] The provider who does not comply with these rules is subject to *administrative* sanctions which must be effective, proportionate and dissuasive (MiFID, art. 51). To ensure the effective administrative enforcement of the MiFID, Member States were required to establish *public* authorities (MiFID, art. 48(2)).

[23] See, in particular, art. 4 of the Directive implementing the MiFID (2006/73/EC): 'Member States may retain or impose requirements additional to those in Directive 2006/73/EC in exceptional cases where such requirements are objectively justified and proportionate so as to address specific risks to investor protection or to market integrity that are not adequately addressed by the Directive and provided that the specific risks addressed by the requirements are of particular importance in the circumstances of the market structure of that Member State.' Notwithstanding the 'exceptional' impact of the recent financial crisis, this provision was hardly used by the Member States to impose requirements additional to those in the MiFID and the Implementing Directive, to a large extent due to the difficulties involved in justifying such measures before the European Commission.

investor protection and the integrity and overall efficiency of the financial system. Imposing contract-related supervision rules upon investment service providers and ensuring their public enforcement are currently seen by the EU legislator as the primary means of achieving the said objectives. This trend has also been confirmed during the MiFID review. While the initial consultation document concerning the MiFID review contained the proposal of the European Commission to include the 'principle of civil liability' in the MiFID II, the proposal for the MiFID II is silent upon this issue.[24]

The core of the MiFID conduct of business regime is formed by the general duty of care and loyalty: any investment service provider must act honestly and fairly in the best interests of its (potential) clients.[25] This general duty is fleshed out in more specific rules of conduct, such as the duty to provide clear, fair and not misleading information, various disclosure obligations, in particular concerning the risks involved in a particular investment service or product and concerning the conflict of interests, and the duty to ensure 'best execution' of the client's order.[26] The MiFID conduct of business regime also contains the investment adviser's duty to know his client, which is similar to the above-mentioned private law duty established by the German Supreme Court in private law matters.[27]

As the extensive contract-related conduct of business rules contained in the MiFID were not written for and from the perspective of the *private law* relationship between an investment service provider and its (potential) client but predominantly from the perspective of their *public* enforcement via supervisory authorities,[28] it is not surprising that these rules were implemented by Member States not within the Civil Codes or consumer protection legislation but within the financial *supervision*

24 See European Commission, Directorate General Internal Market and Services, Public Consultation, Review of the Markets in Financial Instruments Directive (MiFD) p. 63, para. 7.2.6 (8 December 2010), available at http://ec.europa.eu/internal_market/consultations/docs/2010/mifid/consultation_paper_en.pdf (liability of firms providing services) and European Commission, Proposal for a Directive of the European Parliament and of the Council on markets in financial instruments repealing Directive 2004/39/EC of the European Parliament and of the Council (Recast), com(2011)656 final (20 October 2011) respectively.

25 MiFID, art. 19(1).

26 *Ibid.* arts. 18–24. The meaning of these provisions is further fleshed out in arts. 21, 22, 24, 26–50 of Directive 2006/73/EC implementing the MiFID.

27 MiFID, art. 19(4).

28 Cf. H.-W. Micklitz, 'Anlegerschutz – Analyse des EG-Rechts' in J. Keßler and H.-W. Micklitz (eds.), *Anlegerschutz in Deutschland, Schweiz, Großbritannien, USA und der Europäischen Gemeinschaft* (Nomos, Baden-Baden, 2004), pp. 267, 324.

legislation. As a result, the two-tier legal framework for the provision of investment services has emerged at national level, consisting of the unharmonised investor protection standards in general private law, on the one hand, and their harmonised counterparts in financial supervision legislation, on the other.[29]

At present, it seems to be undisputed that private law and the regulatory conduct of business standards do not exist in isolation from each other. Whilst general private law concepts had influenced the content of the conduct of business rules, the conduct of business rules have now been exercising a *radiating* effect (*Ausstrahlungsswirkung*) on the content of the private law concepts.[30] In German law, for example, the conduct of business rules contained in the Securities Trading Act (Wertpapierhandelsgesetz (WpHG)) 1994 specify the meaning of more general private law concepts, such as good faith (*Treu und Glauben*) contained in section 242 of the Civil Code, the commission agent's duty of loyalty (*Pflicht zur Interessenwahrung*) laid down in section 348 of the Commercial Code, or precontractual duties which can be based on section 311(2) of the Civil Code.[31] In Dutch law, the private law concepts, such as the service provider's general duty of care (*zorgplicht van een goed opdrachtnemer*) embodied in article 7:401 of the Civil Code serve as an umbrella under which the conduct of business rules laid down in or pursuant to the Financial Supervision Act (Wet financieel toezicht (Wft)) 2006 enter into private law.[32] Also in English law the conduct of business rules, which are now contained in the *Conduct of Business Sourcebook* (COB) enacted by

29 On this in more detail, see O.O. Cherednychenko, 'European Securities Regulation, Private Law and the Investment Firm-Client Relationship' (2008) 17 *European Review of Private Law* 925 and O.O. Cherednychenko, 'The Regulation of Retail Investment Services in the EU: Towards the Improvement of Investor Rights? (2010) 33 *Journal of Consumer Policy* 403, 418 *et seq.*

30 Cf. D. Busch, 'Why MiFID Matters to Private Law: The Example of MiFID's Impact on an Asset Manager's Civil Liability' (2012) 12 *Capital Markets Law Journal* 1, 7–8.

31 See e.g., BGH 11 November 2003, *Wertpapier-Mitteilungen* (2004), 24, 26; BGH 8 May 2001, 22 *Zeitschrift für Wirtschaftsrecht (ZIP)* (2001), 1580, 1581; BGH 5 October 1999, *BGHZ* 142, 345, 346. See also A. Fuchs, *Wertpapierhandelsgesetz (WpHG): Kommentar* (Beck, München, 2009), p. 1196, with further references.

32 See, in particular, the case law of the alternative dispute resolution boards in the field of financial services: the Dutch Securities Institute Complaints Board (Klachtencommissie DSI (KCD)) and the Appeal Commission of the Dutch Securities Institute (Commissie van Beroep (KHCB)), as well as their successor, the Financial Services Disputes Board (Geschillencommissie financiële dienstverlening) of the Financial Services Complaints Institute. See e.g. KHCB 30 July 2002, JOR 2002/165; KCD 30 July 2003, no. 107; KCD 16 December 2005, 05-282.

the Financial Services Authority (FSA),[33] have become highly influential in shaping the common law standards of care, in particular the scope of the duty of care in the tort of negligence.[34]

Such influence prevents private law from developing totally independently from supervision standards, and, through the accommodation of regulatory duties within its ambit, private law indirectly contributes to the attainment of the EU regulatory objectives. In fact, the effect of supervision standards in private law is possible, and also highly desirable from the point of view of legal certainty, because the twofold aim of the EU regulation – investor protection and strong financial markets – as such is not repugnant to it. After all, over the decades, private law courts of many EU legal systems have developed investor protection standards in individual cases decided under general private law, thus indirectly contributing to the adequate functioning of the financial markets. Therefore, the radiating effect of the supervision standards of investor protection on the interpretation and application of general private law concepts in individual cases may reinforce the ability of private law to realise justice between the parties.

However, it is not unthinkable that at times, the logic of the regulatory financial supervision standards aimed to address typical risk situations, and the logic of general private law concerned with doing justice between the parties, would clash in the circumstances of an individual case. Consider, for example, the recent *Levob*, *Dexia* and *Aegon* cases[35] which arose in the Netherlands following the large-scale 'mis-sellings' of investment schemes that allowed retail investors to purchase securities with borrowed money, also known as '*effectenlease*'. In these cases, the banks submitted that at the time the contract between them and their clients was concluded, the duty to know one's client when selling such investment products had not been included in the public law legislation then in

[33] The FSA has extensive statutory powers to make rules under the Financial Services and Markets Act (FSMA) 2000 (ss. 138–48).

[34] See e.g., *Lloyd Cheyham & Co. Ltd* v. *Eversheds* [1985] 2 Lloyd's Rep. PN 154; *Bankers Trust International PLC* v. *PT Dharmala Sakti Sejahtera* [1996] CLC 518; *Gorham and others* v. *British Telecommunications plc, Trustees of the BT Pension Scheme and Standard Life Assurance Company* [2000] 1 WLR 2129; *Brandeis (Brokers) Ltd* v. *Black and others* [2001] 2 All ER (Comm) 980; *Loosemore* v. *Financial Concepts (a Firm)* [2001] Lloyd's Rep. PN 235; *Seymour* v. *Caroline Ockwell & Co.* (2005) 39 PNLR 758.

[35] HR 5 June 2009, RvdW 2009, 684 (*Levob Bank NV* v. *B en GBD*); HR 5 June 2009, RvdW 2009, 683 (*De T* v. *Dexia Bank Nederland NV*); HR 5 June 2009, RvdW 2009, 685 (*Stichting Gedupeerden Spaarconstructie* v. *Aegon Bank NV*).

force, the Securities Transactions Supervision Decree (Besluit toezicht effectenverkeer) 1995 and the Further Regulations on Market Conduct Supervision of the Securities Trade (Nadere Regeling gedragstoezicht effectenverkeer) 1995 and 1999. The absence of such a duty in this financial supervision legislation was also in line with the Investment Services Directive (ISD)[36] then in force which preceded the MiFID and which, in contrast to the latter, contained only a few broadly formulated conduct of business rules based on the idea of minimum harmonisation. Hence, the banks argued, they could expect that by complying with the public law conduct of business rules, they had also been acting in conformity with their duty of care in private law. Accepting this argument in the cases in question would mean that the Dutch private law courts would not be able to impose the duty to know their clients on the banks in the circumstances of the individual case even if the considerations of justice between the parties would so require. In all three cases, however, the bank's line of reasoning was unequivocally rejected by the Dutch Supreme Court. The latter held that the private law duties of care can go further than the public law duties of care contained in the conduct of business rules. Accordingly, when determining the scope of the bank's special duty of care towards the client under general private law, the Court ruled that prior to the conclusion of the *effectenlease*-contract the banks were, *inter alia*, to obtain information concerning the client's financial situation and to assess the appropriateness of the financial product for the client in the light of this information.

The absence of the *ex ante* duty to know one's client when selling prepackaged investment products to consumers in the financial supervision legislation thus did not prevent the private law court deriving such a duty *ex post* from a general private law concept in the circumstances of the individual case. In reaching this conclusion, the Supreme Court was influenced by the opinion of the Advocate-General in the same cases who argued as follows:

> The argument of the banks referred to above does not take into consideration the fact that although when determining the scope of the bank's special duty of care, which follows from the requirements of good faith, the content of the public law legislation may be taken into account, it is untenable to claim that this private law duty of care may not go further than the conduct of business rules contained in the public law legislation.

[36] Council Directive 93/22/EEC of 10 May 1993 on investment services in the securities field [1993] OJ L141/27.

> Adopting such an approach would ignore the fact that the Netherlands has a system of *double* duties of care – the *public law* duties of care and the *private law* duties of care (primarily developed by the Supreme Court). The public law supervision legislation aims to safeguard a diligent, professional and honest conduct of business by an investment intermediary (and/or a credit provider) and, to this end, it contains further rules on the basis of which a supervisory authority can promote these goals. The requirements of good faith as well as that which can be imposed upon a good service provider are tailored to an *individual* case and may entail that a financial service provider is under a further-reaching duty of care than that following from the public law legislation in force at that time; this is so because the public law duty of care *influences* the private law duty of care but does not *determine* it.[37]

This line of reasoning acknowledges the need to take into account the regulatory financial supervision standards when interpreting and applying general private law concepts, but at the same time it clearly rejects the idea of denying general private law the possibility to go further than the policy-driven financial supervision standards in individual cases. The cases in which this standpoint was adopted also provide a good example of the situation where the exclusive reliance by the courts on the regulatory standards could compromise their ability to do justice between the banks and the consumers to whom highly risky and unsuitable *effectenlease*-products had been sold.

Yet, it remains to be seen whether general private law and private law courts will retain a certain degree of autonomy from the regulatory supervision standards and supervisory authorities in the wake of the *full* harmonisation of conduct of business rules under the MiFID. It is notable in this context that, following the adoption of the MiFID, some authors have argued that private law duties of care and loyalty have been superseded by the contract-related financial supervision rules under the MiFID, considering that the latter is a full harmonisation Directive.[38] According to this line of reasoning, as full harmonisation measures preclude Member States from maintaining or adopting stricter

[37] Opinion of the Advocate General of 13 February 2009 in *Levob Bank NV* v. *Ben en GBD*, *De T* v. *Dexia Bank Nederland NV*, and *Stichting Gedupeerden Spaarconstructie* v. *Aegon Bank NV*, n. 35 above, para. 3.21 (my translation and emphasis).

[38] See e.g., P.O. Mülbert, 'The Eclipse of Contract Law in the Investment Firm-Client Relationship: The Impact of the MiFID on the Law of Contract from a German Perspective' in G. Ferrarini and E. Wymeersch (eds.), *Investor Protection in Europe: Corporate Law Making, the MiFID and Beyond* (Oxford University Press, 2007), pp. 299, 318; Busch, 'Why MiFID Matters to Private Law', n. 30 above, at 10–11.

rules than those contained therein, Member States may not impose stricter requirements on investment firms than the MiFID, irrespective of whether such stricter requirements follow from private law or from financial supervision legislation.

The adoption of such an approach may lead to the excessive instrumentalisation of general private law for market integration purposes. Even though the MiFID contains a much more developed body of investor protection rules than its predecessor, the ISD, the risk of unfair outcomes in individual cases should not be underestimated, considering the untried nature of the regulatory standards and unpredictable changes in market behaviour. For example, adjusting a private law standard of care to a supervision standard could result in a situation where the bank would not be held liable for its failure *personally* to warn a particularly vulnerable non-professional investor about the risks involved in taking a certain extremely risky investment decision, as under article 19(3) of the full harmonisation MiFID, providing a warning in a *standardised* form would suffice. The exclusive application of the *ex ante* supervision standard of care may thus result in an unfair *ex post* outcome in the circumstances of the individual case. If judges, therefore, are to blindly follow contract-related supervision standards when adjudicating disputes between investment service providers and their clients, they may not be able to address problems arising in the provider-client relationship and, hence, to do justice between the parties in the circumstances of each individual case.

In the absence of the ruling from the CJEU on the issue of whether national private laws may deviate from the MiFID conduct of business rules, Member States may adopt different approaches to it. For example, the private law courts in France are not allowed to subject financial institutions to duties that go further than the applicable regulatory duties, which seem to include the standards implementing the MiFID; this outcome is explained by the principle of strict interpretation of financial rules which prohibits *contra legem* decisions (i.e., decisions that are stricter than the law).[39] By contrast, the German Higher Regional Court in Düsseldorf, for example, recently explicitly rejected the view that the private law courts may not impose stricter duties than the MiFID.[40] Hence, the extent of the

[39] D. Busch and D.A. DeMott (eds.), *Liability of Asset Managers* (Oxford University Press, 2012), para. 3.46.

[40] OLG Düsseldorf 16 Decmber 2010, WM 2011, 399, 400. See also BGH 27 September 2011, WM 2011, 2268, para. 47.

instrumentalisation of national private laws in the investment services field may vary across the European Union, depending on the approach adopted in a particular Member State to the relationship between general private law and the regulatory supervision standards of EU origin.

## General implications of an instrumentalist conception of European private law for private law discourse

As has been demonstrated in the previous sections, in pursuing the goals of regulating the internal market, European private law has entered into the territory of national private laws, not only in the harmonised areas but also in the areas closely related thereto, at times putting the ethical-societal conception of private law under considerable pressure. The ongoing Europeanisation of national private laws in the last two decades, however, may also have broader implications for traditional private law discourse reaching far beyond the immediate effects of the regulatory European private law. Even in areas not touched upon by EU law as yet, under the impact of the instrumentalist understanding of private law by the EU institutions, national courts are likely increasingly to consider policy considerations relating to the common good, such as political, social or economic goals, when resolving individual cases under general private law.

Although external public goals have traditionally been regarded as irrelevant for the relationship between the two private parties, taking such goals into account in individual disputes between the parties is not an entirely new phenomenon. In fact, such considerations have played a significant role in shaping private law rules. As has already been mentioned above, particularly during the last half century or more, private law discourse in many European legal systems has to a greater or lesser extent been influenced by policy considerations related to the interests of the community. An important role in triggering this change in legal reasoning has been played by the growing impact of social and economic regulation. As a consequence, in many legal systems, judges, to a greater or lesser extent, tend to reconcile the aim of doing justice in individual cases that cannot be resolved through the application of 'formal' rules with taking external policy objectives into account.[41] English courts in

[41] On this development see, in particular, Collins, *Regulating Contracts*, n. 2 above, Part 2 'The New Regulation'; Collins, 'Governance Implications for the European Union', n. 5 above, at 276 *et seq*.

particular are famous for openly discussing and balancing policy considerations in individual cases. At the same time, even though private law discourse has been influenced by instrumental considerations, reasoning in private law did not become the same as reasoning in the application of policy-oriented regulation. As Collins puts it, '[p]rivate law has become a synthesis that combines both its traditional concerns about corrective justice between individuals and instrumental ambitions about steering markets towards distributive justice'.[42]

A good illustration of the private law discourse in which traditional private law interplays with policy considerations is provided by the decision of the House of Lords in *Barclays' Bank plc.* v. *O'Brien*,[43] in which a wife, Mrs O'Brien, had charged the matrimonial home to secure her husband's business debt. Delivering the decision of the House of Lords in this case, Lord Browne-Wilkinson began by expressly recognising that such cases involve weighing competing policy considerations. According to him:

> [A]lthough the concept of the ignorant wife leaving all financial decisions to the husband is outmoded, the practice does not yet coincide with the ideal. In a substantial proportion of marriages it is still the husband who has the business experience and the wife is willing to follow his advice without bringing a truly independent mind and will to bear on financial decisions. The number of recent cases in this field shows that in practice many wives are still subjected to, and yield to, undue influence by their husbands. Such wives can reasonably look to the law for some protection when their husbands have abused the trust and confidence reposed in them.[44]

At the same time, however, Lord Browne-Wilkinson emphasised the importance of keeping a sense of balance in deciding what degree of protection should be afforded to the vulnerable. As he put it:

> It is easy to allow sympathy for the wife who is threatened with the loss of her home at the suit of a rich bank to obscure an important public interest, viz. the need to ensure that the wealth currently tied up in the matrimonial home does not become economically sterile. If the rights secured to wives by the law render vulnerable loans granted on the security of matrimonial homes, institutions will be unwilling to accept such security, thereby reducing the flow of loan capital to business enterprises. It is therefore

[42] *Ibid.* 278. Cf. Schmid, 'The Instrumentalist Conception', n. 5 above at 210, in particular, at 214 *et seq.*; Cherednychenko, *Fundamental Rights, Contract Law and the Protection of the Weaker Party*, n. 2 above, at p. 40 *et seq.*, in particular, p. 44.

[43] *Barclays' Bank plc.* v. *O'Brien* [1994] 1 AC 180.

[44] [1994] 1 AC 180, 188.

> essential that a law designed to protect the vulnerable does not render the matrimonial home unacceptable as security to financial institutions.[45]

In this way, their Lordships explicitly recognised that the need to protect the vulnerable must be counterbalanced against the need of the creditors to resort to security when extending finance, to ensure that the wealth invested in the matrimonial home is not rendered economically sterile. They considered that a fair balance between these competing interests of vulnerable sureties and creditors and an adequate resolution of disputes between the two could be achieved by applying the ordinary equitable doctrine of notice. The husband of Mrs O'Brien had misrepresented the effect of the charge to his wife. Because the bank knew that the principal debtor and the surety were in the kind of relationship in which misrepresentation, undue influence or duress was likely and it also knew that the transaction was not to the advantage of Mrs O'Brien, the bank was 'put on inquiry' as to the circumstances in which Mrs O'Brien had agreed to stand as a surety for the debt of her husband. Once put on inquiry, the bank had the duty to take reasonable steps necessary to bring home to Mrs O'Brien the risks she was running by standing as a surety and to advise her to take independent advice. As the bank failed to take such steps, it was fixed with constructive notice of misrepresentation made to Mrs O'Brien by her husband. Therefore, according to the House of Lords, Mrs O'Brien was entitled as against the bank to set aside the legal charge on the matrimonial home securing her husband's liability to the bank.[46]

The decision of the House of Lords in *Barclays' Bank plc.* v. *O'Brien* shows how, in the absence of any specific regulation of national or European origin in a particular field, public goals become integrated within the private law discourse in the course of the interpretation and application of general private law doctrines in an individual case. It is submitted that the rise of regulatory private law at EU level is likely to reinforce this type of legal reasoning in national legal systems, and lead private law courts across the European Union to become more obviously concerned with the external effects of their judgments in individual cases for the societies as a whole. Even in countries like France, where the discussion of the various arguments in favour of and against a certain outcome of the case is still largely hidden behind rules of a legal-technical nature, courts may become more willing to openly consider competing

[45] *Ibid.*

[46] The approach of the House of Lords in cases involving family sureties was further clarified in *Royal Bank of Scotland* v. *Etridge (No. 2)* [2001] All ER 449.

policy considerations involved in a particular individual case.[47] As a result, legal reasoning would increasingly become less formalistic.

The need to take the external dimension of private relationships into account has become increasingly obvious in the aftermath of the financial crisis.[48] We have seen how irresponsible lending in one country, for example, may not only hurt the vulnerable consumer who concluded the mortgage contract, but, when such transactions are concluded on a large scale, also have global effects on the well-functioning of the financial markets and economies at large. In the absence of specific regulation that would help to prevent such effects from occurring, general private law could potentially step in to do so, even though it may not be as effective as specific regulatory instruments.

Obviously, such an approach involves the danger of unrestrained instrumentalisation of private relationships, as considerations of justice between the parties to a particular dispute may clash with those that relate to broader community interests.[49] In fact, as has been shown in the previous sections, the risk of excessive instrumentalism is inherent in the Europeanisation of private law in view of the regulatory function of European private law. If private law discourse becomes dominated by the pursuance of public goals, and the considerations of justice between the parties become subordinate thereto, the court could decide a particular dispute on grounds that have nothing to do with the relationship between the parties to that dispute. It is important, therefore, that national private law courts do not ignore the relationship between private

[47] Cf. J.M. Smits, 'The Europeanisation of National Legal Systems: Some Consequences for Legal Thinking in Civil Law Countries' in M. Van Hoecke (ed.), *Epistemology and Methodology of Comparative Law* (Hart Publishing, Oxford, 2004), p. 229, s. 5.

[48] Cf., for example, S. Grundmann, 'On the Unity of Private Law from a Formal to a Substance-Based Concept of Private Law' (2010) 18 *European Review of Private Law* 1055, 1073 *et seq.*, P.B. Lurger, 'Consumer Protection and Social Justice' in C. Joerges and T. Ralli (eds.), *European Constitutionalism without Private Law: Private Law without Democracy* (Joseph Beuys/Bono, Oslo, 2011), p. 93, in particular, p. 106; B. Lurger, 'Old and New Insights for the Protection of Consumers in European Private Law in the Wake of the Global Economic Crisis' in R. Brownsword, H.-W. Micklitz, L. Niglia and S. Weatherill (eds.), *The Foundations of European Private Law* (Hart Publishing, Oxford/Portland, 2011), p. 89, in particular, p. 112. See also H. Collins, 'The Hybrid Quality of European Private Law' in R. Brownsword, H.-W. Micklitz, L. Niglia and S. Weatherill (eds.), *The Foundations of European Private Law* (Hart Publishing, Oxford/Portland, 2011), p. 453.

[49] Cf. H. Collins, *Utility and Rights in Common Law Reasoning: Rebalancing Private Law through Constitutionalization*, LSE Law, Society and Economy Working Papers 6/2007, pp. 12–13, available at www.lse.ac.uk/collections/law/wps/wps.htm.

parties in individual cases and tend to reconcile traditional private law concerns about dispensing justice between the parties with the pursuance of public goals.[50]

## Challenges for legal scholarship

As has been discussed above, the Europeanisation of private law reinforces the role of external policy considerations within a private law discourse and further puts the traditional idea of private law under pressure. The impact of regulatory European private law is not necessarily limited to areas directly or indirectly affected by EU law. The instrumentalist conception of European private law, which considers private law as an instrument for the achievement of specific public goals, in particular, the overriding objective of market integration, is likely to intensify the more policy-oriented private law discourse in national legal systems even in areas which have not been touched upon by the harmonisation measures as yet. What implications does this development have for the traditional academic approach to studying law that focuses on the systematisation of legal rules and finding coherence between them? To what extent is studying law solely from the internal perspective within the boundaries of a particular national legal system still justified in the wake of the Europeanisation of private law?

The question concerning the core of contemporary legal scholarship in itself is not new. Particularly in the last two decades, the traditional academic approach to studying law has come under fire from different sides of the academic spectrum. It goes beyond the scope of this contribution to provide an in-depth analysis of the reasons for criticism, as well as new perspectives on the tasks of modern legal scholarship and the appropriate methodology.[51] In the following, therefore, I will limit myself

[50] *Cf.*, for example, *ibid.* p. 13; A. Robertson, 'Constraints on Policy-based Reasoning in Private Law' in A. Robertson and T. Hang Wu (eds.), *The Goals of Private Law* (Hart Publishing, Oxford/Portland, 2009), p. 261, in particular, p. 272 *et seq.*; S. Waddams, *Principle and Policy in Contract Law* (Cambridge University Press, 2011), ch. 8.

[51] For interesting perspectives on these issues, see e.g., E.J. Weinrib, *The Idea of Private Law* (Harvard University Press, Cambridge, MA, 1995); R. Korobkin, *A Multi-disciplinary Approach to Legal Scholarship: Economics, Behavioural Economics, and Evolutionary Psychology*, UCLA School of Law Research Paper 01–5 (2001); R.A. Posner, 'Legal Scholarship Today' (2002) 115 *Harvard Law Review* 1314; J.B.M. Vranken, *Exploring the Jurist's Frame of Mind* (Kluwer, Deventer, 2006); C. McCrudden, 'Legal Research and Social Sciences' (2006) 122 *Law Quarterly Review* 632; M.W. Hesselink, 'A European

to a discussion of the implications of the growing role of policy considerations related to the common good in the wake of the ongoing Europeanisation process for legal scholarship in the field of private law. My argument is that this development poses three major challenges for the traditional academic approach to studying law.

In the first place, the tendency towards the instrumentalisation of private law urges legal scholarship to expand its focus beyond traditional academic boundaries and to play a more proactive role in shaping (European) private law. In addition to answering questions concerning the systematisation of legal rules and securing coherence between them, legal scholarship should play a greater role in answering normative questions of what the law *should* say on a particular issue, so that full weight is given to individual interests of the parties and at the same time public interests are served. Should extremely risky financial transactions, for instance, be totally prohibited or allowed on the condition that the bank took the steps necessary to ensure the informed consent of its client to enter into such transactions? Should discrimination within a private sphere be prohibited or allowed? And where should a private sphere stop and a public sphere begin? Such questions are different from questions of what positive EU law and/or national law says on a particular issue and whether the legal framework pertaining thereto is coherent. Answering the 'should'-type of questions requires that legal scholars become more actively involved in the debate on sensitive issues to be addressed by law, in particular those concerning the balance between public and private interests in the course of European market integration and beyond. In so doing, legal scholarship could provide arguments in favour of and against particular solutions and investigate whether these arguments fit into the existing doctrinal framework.[52] Such scholarly findings could subsequently guide legislators, courts and other actors when making (European) private law.

Legal Method? On European Private Law and Scientific Method' (2009) 15 *European Law Journal* 20; S. Hedley, 'Looking Outward or Looking Inward? Obligations Scholarship in the Early 21st Century' in A. Robertson and T. Hang Wu (eds.), *The Goals of Private Law* (Hart Publishing, Oxford/Portland, 2009), p. 193; J.M. Smits, 'Redefining Normative Legal Science: Towards an Argumentative Discipline' in F. Coomans, F. Grünfeld and M. Kamminga (eds.) *Methods of Human Rights Research* (Intersentia, Antwerpen/Oxford, 2009), p. 45; J.M. Smits, *The Mind and Method of the Legal Academic* (Edward Elgar, Cheltenham, 2012).

52 Cf. Smits, 'Redefining Normative Legal Science', n. 51 above, at 54.

Secondly, it goes without saying that this task of legal scholarship can only be accomplished if legal scholars are prepared to openly discuss various arguments in favour of or against a certain solution. In order to do so, it is important to distinguish between describing what the law says, on the one hand, and providing a normative view as to what the law should say, on the other. This distinction has not always been made in scholarly writings where normative views have often been presented as the interpretation of the existing principles or rules of private law. Moreover, as a result of the growing impact of fundamental rights on private law in the last two decades or more, the debate on age-old private law issues, like the extent to what the weaker contractual party must be protected, has occasionally moved from the level of private law to the level of fundamental rights, where substantive arguments in favour of or against a particular solution could easily be concealed under the cover of fundamental rights interpretation.[53] The tendency towards the instrumentalisation of private law, however, urges legal scholars to make their arguments more explicit and it is questionable to what extent resorting to broadly formulated fundamental rights, which usually protect the interests of both parties to a private law dispute, will be helpful in this respect.

Thirdly, in order to be able to play a more proactive role in shaping (European) private law with due regard to both public and private interests, legal scholarship cannot rely solely on studying national private law from an internal perspective. The Europeanisation of private law urges legal scholars to resort to internal and external comparative law methods. This implies taking into account the developments within public law when doing research into private law within one particular legal system (internal comparison), as well as looking beyond the borders of a particular legal system (external comparison). Furthermore, the growing role of policy considerations related to the common good within private law discourse goes hand-in-hand with the need to take on board insights from other fields of law and other disciplines. The Europeanisation of private law, therefore, reinforces the tendency

[53] On this, see e.g., Cherednychenko, *Fundamental Rights, Contract Law and the Protection of the Weaker Party*, n. 2 above, in particular, p. 549 *et seq.*; O.O. Cherednychenko, 'Subordinating Contract Law to Fundamental Rights: Towards a Major Breakthrough or towards Walking in Circles?' in S. Grundmann (ed.), *Constitutional Values and European Contract Law* (Kluwer Law International, Alphen aan den Rijn, 2008), p. 35; Smits, 'Redefining Normative Legal Science', n. 51 above, at 55 *et seq.*

towards more inter-disciplinary research which, to a greater or lesser extent, can already be observed in many European legal systems.[54] This does not mean, however, that private law should become exclusively guided by insights from other fields of law or other disciplines; such insights should first be internalised within private law with due regard to the existing doctrinal system of a particular jurisdiction. The difficulties confronting legal scholars in this respect mirror the complexity facing courts in reconciling the traditional private law concerns about justice between the parties with serving the public interest in an individual case.

## Conclusion

In its approach to the regulation of the internal market, the European Union has never accepted the traditional conception of private law as it has evolved in national legal systems. Whilst national private laws have been primarily concerned with justice between market participants rather than the pursuance of specific public goals, the European Union has viewed private law as an instrument for achieving the collective objectives of European integration. Although the logic of regulatory European private law and the logic of traditional private law may mutually reinforce each other, at times they may also clash. The process of the Europeanisation of national private laws is marked by tension between private interests and public goals. This tension is reflected not only in the areas of private law directly or indirectly affected by European regulatory private law, but also in those areas which have not been touched upon by the European Union as yet. The Europeanisation of private law reinforces the role of policy considerations related to the common good within private law discourse, prompting the instrumentalisation of private law even beyond the scope of EU law and thus further putting the traditional idea of private law under pressure. As a result, when resolving individual disputes private law

[54] In this context, a new scientific approach of 'contract governance' deserves particular mention which deals with the institutional framework of contractual relations on markets from an interdisciplinary perspective with a view to improving market functioning. On this, see e.g., F. Möslein, 'Contract Governance: A Draft Research Agenda' (2009) 5 *European Review of Contract Law* 248; P. Zumbansen, 'The Law of Society: Governance through Contract' (2007) 14 *Indiana Journal of Global Legal Studies* 191; P. Vincent-Jones, 'Contractual Governance: Institutional and Organizational Analysis' (2000) 20 *Oxford Journal of Legal Studies* 317.

courts increasingly face a difficult task of reconciling private interests with collective goods. The tendency towards the instrumentalisation of private law also presents new challenges for legal scholarship in the field of private law. It strengthens the need for legal scholars to play a more proactive role in shaping (European) private law by openly discussing what the law should say on a particular issue, in view of both the traditional concerns about justice between market participants and the broader policy considerations. Legal scholars are urged to look beyond the traditional sources of national private law and to take on board insights from other legal systems, other fields of law and other disciplines. An important challenge facing legal scholarship in this context is how to internalise external perspectives in private law, so as to avoid excessive instrumentalisation of private law discourse in the name of the common good and to find a proper balance between public and private interests.

# 9

## Contract codification and the English: some observations from the Indian Contract Act 1872

WARREN SWAIN

The comparative legal historian, Professor Van Caenegem, has argued that 'If common law stands for anything, it is absence of codes, and likewise civil law stands for codification'. He continues, 'through a variety of political circumstances the English mind has come to associate codes with all that is abhorrent'.[1] Perhaps the most extensive period of codification actually predated the birth of the common law, albeit that the Anglo-Saxon law codes cannot really be described as law codes in a modern sense.[2] The last fifty years has seen a lessening of hostility towards codification in England, in some circles at least.[3] Developments in mainland Europe may in the end have the final say.[4] The recent publication of the Draft Common Frame of Reference has raised the possibility of a Europe-wide Code of private law of one sort or another.[5] The exercise has been

Senior Lecturer in Law in the TC Beirne School of Law, University of Queensland, Australia.

[1] R.C. Van Caenegem, *Judges, Legislators and Professors* (Cambridge University Press, 1993), pp. 39, 49.

[2] The role of the law codes as an index of 'governing mentalities' is explored in the seminal, P. Wormald, *The Making of English Law: King Alfred to the Twelve Century*, vol. I, *Legislation and its Limits* (Blackwell, Oxford, 1999).

[3] Supporters of codification in England include judges and former judges: L. Scarman, *A Code of English Law?* (Hull University Press, 1966); *Codification and Judge-made Law* (Holdsworth Club, Birmingham, 1966); M. Arden, 'Time for an English Commercial Code?' (1997) 56 *Cambridge Law Journal* 516. For an overview of some of the debates, see E. Steiner, 'Codification in England: The Need to Move from an Ideological to a Functional Approach – A Bridge Too Far?' (2004) 25 *Statute Law Review* 209. For a note of caution which still merits attention thirty years on, see H.R. Hahlo, 'Here Lies the Common Law: Rest in Peace' (1967) 30 *Modern Law Review* 241.

[4] For a discussion of some of the background, see C. Twigg-Flesner, *The Europeanisation of Contract Law* (Routledge-Cavendish, Abingdon, 2008), ch. 5.

[5] The editors state that, 'It may be that at a later point in time the DCFR will be carried over at least in part into a CFR, but that is a question for others to decide'. See C. von Bar and E. Clive, *Principles, Definitions and Model Rules of European Private Law: Draft*

criticised,[6] not least because it raises difficult questions about compatibility with domestic law.[7] Formidable obstacles, political and practical, still have to be overcome before a European Code of private law can become a reality. Whether or not such a code is either desirable or possible is best left to those more qualified to judge.[8] The aims of this chapter are the rather more modest ones of seeking to add historical gloss on the business of the codification of private law from an English perspective.

## Codification and utopianism

In England, codification has always attracted its fair share of idealists. This may, in part, account for a failure of such projects to appeal to mainstream opinion. In Thomas More's *Utopia*, first published in 1516, there are no lawyers and the few laws that exist are codified:

> For, according to the Utopians, it's quite unjust for anyone to be bound by a legal code which is too long for an ordinary person to read through, or too difficult for him to understand.[9]

A century later, the Protestant radical, Gerrard Winstanley, took up the cause of codification.[10] Winstanley's views were unconventional; he also favoured

*Common Frame of Reference* (Oxford University Press, 2010), p. 3. There is no consensus about the precise effect and intention behind the DCFR. It has been suggested that it can be viewed as a non-legislative code, see N. Jansen and R. Zimmerman, 'A European Civil Code in All but Name: Discussing the Nature and Purpose of the Draft Common Frame of Reference' (2010) 69 *Cambridge Law Journal* 98. Simon Whittaker has argued that the dominant purpose of the DCFR 'is to provide the basis for the future codification of civil law to be used either as an optional instrument or as the basis for some future legislative codification', see S. Whittaker, 'A Framework of Principle for European Contract Law' (2009) 125 *Law Quarterly Review* 645.

6 H. Eidenmüller *et al.*, 'The Common Frame of Reference for European Private Law: Policy Choices and Codification Problems' (2008) 28 *Oxford Journal of Legal Studies* 659.

7 There are several fundamental inconsistencies between the DCFR and English contract law in philosophical and practical terms, see S. Whittaker, *The Draft Common Frame of Reference: An Assessment Commissioned by the Ministry of Justice, United Kingdom* (November 2008), available at http://webarchive.nationalarchives.gov.uk/±/http://www.justice.gov.uk/docs/eu-contract-law-common-frame-reference.pdf.

8 The literature on this subject is vast. For an introduction, see Twigg-Flesner, *Europeanisation*, n. 4 above, ch. 6. For an overview of some of the problems of codification more generally from an English perspective, see P.M. North, 'Problems of Codification in Common Law Systems' (1982) 46 *Rabels Zeitschrift* 490.

9 P. Turner (ed.), *Thomas More, Utopia* (Penguin, London, 1965), p. 106.

10 J. C. Davies, *Utopia and the Ideal Society: A Study in English Utopian Writing 1516–1700* (Cambridge University Press, 1983), ch. 7. For an account of Winstanley and the Levellers, see C. Hill, *The World Turned Upside Down* (Penguin, London, 1991), ch. 7.

the abolition of private property. For a brief period either side of the English Revolution, codification did begin to attract much wider support.[11] This could not be sustained and was soon crushed beneath the dominant strand of English legal thought which celebrated the common law.[12]

Sir William Blackstone's *Commentaries on the Laws of England* divided the law of England into '*lex non scripta*, the unwritten, or common law; and *lex scripta*, the written, or statute law'.[13] Blackstone's treatment of statute law was extremely brief, though not actually hostile.[14] Legislation, wrote Blackstone, 'may and frequently does, intervene to remove the doubt' where the common law was contradictory or unclear.[15] In the event of a conflict, 'the common law gives place to the statute'.[16] The relatively minor role legislation played at this time compared with a century later helps to explain the relative absence of statute law in the *Commentaries.*[17] Sitting in Blackstone's audience was a young man who would come to play a pivotal role in advancing the cause of codification. His name was Jeremy Bentham.

Writing in *A Comment on the Commentaries*,[18] a critique of Blackstone, Bentham argued that 'the Common law is but the shadow of statute law, although it came before it'.[19] Whilst the tradition in English legal writing was to venerate the common law, Bentham owed his notoriety to criticising it.[20] In Bentham's positivist version of a legal

[11] B. Shapiro, 'Codification of the Laws in Seventeenth Century England' (1974) *Wisconsin Law Review* 428. The debate about the merits of codification took place against the backdrop of a wider law reform movement, see D. Veall, *The Popular Movement for Law Reform* (Oxford University Press, 1970); B. Shapiro, 'Law Reform in Seventeenth Century England' (1975) 19 *American Journal of Legal History* 280.

[12] When statute was discussed it tended to be in the context of the debates about the need for a consolidation of existing statutes: D. Lieberman, *The Province of Legislation Determined: Legal Theory in Eighteenth-century Britain* (Cambridge University Press, 2002), ch. 9.

[13] W. Blackstone, *Commentaries on the Laws of England* (Clarendon Press, Oxford, 1765), vol. I, p. 63. The same division had earlier been used by Matthew Hale, see M. Hale, *The History of the Common Law of England* (C. Gray (ed.), University of Chicago Press, 1971), p. 3.

[14] H. G. Hanbury, 'Blackstone in Retrospect' (1950) 66 *Law Quarterly Review* 322.

[15] *Commentaries on the Laws of England* (Clarendon Press, Oxford, 1768), vol. III, p. 328.

[16] *Ibid.* vol. I, p. 89.

[17] S. Lambert, *Bills and Acts Legislative Procedure in Eighteenth Century England* (Cambridge University Press, 1971), p. 52.

[18] J. Bentham, *A Comment on the Commentaries* (J.H. Burns and H.L.A. Hart (eds.), Oxford University Press, 2008).

[19] *Ibid.* 119.

[20] For Bentham's critique, see G. Postema, *Bentham and the Common Law Tradition* (Oxford University Press, 1986), chs. 5–9; Lieberman, *Province*, n. 12 above, ch. 11.

system, law was a command issued by a sovereign.[21] Legislation, wrote Bentham, 'is the act of making Laws'.[22] The common law was not law at all. The 'dark chaos'[23] that it generated could only be rectified by legislation.

In the 1770s, Bentham began work on a digest of the common law and statute[24] with the intention of making the existing law better known. By the 1780s, he began to switch his attention to an even more ambitious project: the construction of a 'pannomion' or a complete body of law. The 'pannomion' would dominate the rest of his life.[25] Bentham associated codification with 'utility, notoriety, completeness, manifest reasonableness'.[26] He proposed a Code of civil law, penal and constitutional Codes, alongside Codes dealing with legal procedure and the legal system.[27] In the *Principles of a Civil Code*, Bentham argued that utility in the civil law could be maximised through subsistence, abundance, security and equality.[28] Bentham's *Principles* was never intended to be a complete substantive code. It was an opportunity to set out his basic ideas and some definitions.[29]

Bentham was only too well aware of the likely opposition that a code would face from what he called 'sinister interests'[30] in England. The greater legal certainty that he envisaged would flow from codification would benefit the public but not the lawyers:

> [S]ay that a lawyer has no interest in the uncertainty of the law, as well might you say, that a gunpowder maker has no interest in war, or a glazier in the breaking of windows.[31]

[21] For a discussion of Bentham's legal philosophy from a number of different perspectives, see H.L.A. Hart, *Essays on Bentham* (Oxford University Press, 1982).

[22] Lieberman, *Province*, n. 12 above, at pp. 222–3. [23] *Ibid.*, 198.

[24] For details of this project, see Lieberman, *Province*, n. 12 above, ch. 12; M. Lobban, *The Common Law and English Jurisprudence 1760–1850* (Oxford University Press, 1991), ch. 6.

[25] J. Dinwiddy, *Bentham* (Oxford University Press, 1989), ch. 4; P. Schofield, 'Jeremy Bentham: Legislator of the World' (1998) 51 *Current Legal Problems* 115.

[26] P. Schofield and J. Harris (eds.), *J. Bentham, 'Legislator of the World' Writings on Codification, Law and Education* (Oxford University Press, 1998), p. 168.

[27] The precise details changed over time, Dinwiddy, *Bentham*, n. 25 above, at p. 60.

[28] J. Bowring (ed.), *The Works of Jeremy Bentham* (William Tait, Edinburgh, 1859), vol. I, p. 302.

[29] Lobban, *Common Law*, n. 24 above, at p. 177.

[30] P. Schofield, *Utility and Democracy* (Oxford University Press, 2009), ch. 5.

[31] Schofield, 'Jeremy Bentham', n. 25 above, at 133.

Like More, Bentham hoped that with greater knowledge[32] and understanding of the law it would be possible for the lay man to conduct his own affairs without recourse to lawyers.[33]

Bentham was optimistic that governments in America, Russia, Spain, Portugal and Greece and elsewhere would take up his invitation to codify their laws. His optimism proved not to be justified.[34] Meanwhile in England, in the Spring of 1808, Bentham tried to persuade Samuel Romilly and Francis Horner to take up his cause in the House of Commons. Although sympathetic, they refused to do so because he had yet to produce a complete code.[35] In the 1820s, Bentham took up the cause of English codification with renewed enthusiasm by circulating his *Petition for Codification*.[36] His proposals were widely discussed in newspapers and periodicals.[37] This time he also found a willing advocate in Parliament in the person of Daniel O'Connell but, in the end, the result was just the same.[38]

By this time other English lawyers were beginning to take an interest in codification. Some, like the legal philosopher John Austin, were influenced by Bentham's writings.[39] He was not the only source of inspiration. James Humphreys, whose *Observations on the actual state of the English laws of Real Property with the Outlines of a Code* appeared in 1826, based his Code on the Napoleonic Code.[40] As Humphreys found, the mere use of the term 'code' could be relied upon to raise strong passions. Edward Sugden, the future Lord Chancellor, would even claim that 'a greater calamity could not befall the country than the adoption of the proposed code'.[41] A Real Property Commission began work in 1828 but the reform

[32] This was a reflection of Bentham's wider belief in the importance of informing the public. See D. Liberman, 'Economy and Polity in Bentham's Science of Legislation' in S. Collini *et al.* (eds.), *Economy, Polity and Society: British Intellectual History 1750–1950* (Cambridge University Press, 2000), pp. 107, 124–34.

[33] *Ibid.* 133–7.

[34] Schofield and Harris, *Legislator of the World*, n. 26 above, at pp. xii–xxxv.

[35] Schofield, *Utility*, n. 30 above, at p. 244.

[36] As well as his *Codification Proposal*, reproduced in Schofield and Harris, *Legislator of the World*, n. 26 above, at pp. 244–372 and dating from 1821–22.

[37] J.R. Dinwiddy, *Radicalism and Reform in Britain, 1780–1850* (Hambledon, London, 1992), p. 348.

[38] Schofield, *Utility*, n. 30 above, at pp. 319–20.

[39] W. L. Morison, *John Austin* (Austin, London, 1982), pp. 38–48.

[40] B. Rudden, 'A Code Too Soon. The 1826 Property Code of James Humphreys: English Rejection, American Reception, English Acceptance' in P. Wallington and R.M. Merkin, *Essays in Memory of F.H. Lawson* (Butterworths, London, 1986), pp. 101–16.

[41] *Ibid.* 103.

proposals fell a long way short of Humphrey's Code.[42] In criminal law it was much the same story. A Criminal Law Commission was set up in 1833 but, in the face of parliamentary and legal opposition, the final reforms were modest.[43] Two years before Bentham's own death in 1832, the Law Magazine had already announced that 'Codification ... has become a dead letter in England'.[44] This proved to be a rather pessimistic prediction even in England. But it was even more wrong in India, then the most important territory of the British Empire.

## Codification movement in India

Speaking in the House of Commons in 1833, Thomas Macaulay argued that, 'I believe that no country ever stood so much in need of a code of law as India, and I believe that there never was a country in which the want might be so easily supplied.'[45] The following March, Macaulay sailed for India in order to take up the post of Law Member of the Governor General's Council.[46] He was one of a number of influential Indian administrators who were sympathetic to at least some of Bentham's ideas.[47] The time was seen to be ripe for codification in India for other reasons as well. It can also be seen as part of the growing Anglicisation of Indian society,[48] also reflected by an ideological commitment to imposing English notions of the rule of law.[49] Further momentum was generated by complaints from lawyers and officials out in India of the impracticalities of the *status quo*.[50] All of these factors came together in the guise of the Indian Law Commission, which was

42 S. Anderson, 'Property' in W. Cornish *et al.* (eds.), *The Oxford History of the Laws of England*, vol. XII, *1820–1914: Private Law* (Oxford University Press, 2010), pp. 49–78.

43 L. Falmer, 'Reconstructing the English Codification Debate: The Criminal Law Commissioners, 1833–45' (2000) 18 *Law and History Review* 397; K. Smith, 'Criminal Law' in W. Cornish *et al.* (eds.), *The Oxford History of the Laws of England*, vol. XIII, *1820–1914: Fields of Development* (Oxford University Press, 2010), pp. 193–205.

44 (1830) 4 *Law Magazine* 244 cited by Smith, *ibid.* 192.

45 (1833) 19 HC Deb. 479, 531.

46 For his role in India, see J. Clive, *Macaulay: The Shaping of the Historian* (Harvard University Press, 1987), ch. 11. For Macaulay's political philosophy, see J. Hamburger, *Macaulay and the Whig Tradition* (University of Chicago Press, 1976).

47 E. Stokes, *The English Utilitarians and India* (Oxford University Press, 1959).

48 In D.A. Washbrook, 'India, 1818–1860' in A. Porter (ed.), *The Oxford History of the British Empire: The Nineteenth Century* (Oxford University Press, 1999), pp. 395, 415–19.

49 T. Metcalf, *Ideologies of the Raj* (Cambridge University Press, 1994), p. 37.

50 Whitley Stokes believed that the origins of the reform movement could be traced to correspondence in the 1820s between Sir Charles Metcalfe, a colonial governor,

appointed in 1833 and given a remit to implement a programme of codification. A Penal Code was quickly drafted. Macaulay also advocated reform of civil law by quoting an Indian judge of his acquaintance on the state of commercial law: 'He told me that it was a mere lottery. He knew how he should himself decide them. But he knew nothing more'.[51] Following Macaulay's return to England, the momentum for codification was lost for several decades. The Penal Code was not enacted until 1861.[52]

One of the greatest challenges facing the Commissioners was the fact that since the days of the East India Company, different bodies of law had, in theory at least, applied to different sections of the Indian population.[53] Edmund Burke regarded this as a matter of good governance:

> Where thirty millions are to be governed by a few thousand men, the government must be established by consent, and must be congenial to the feelings and to the habits of the people.[54]

Events in America, claimed Burke, were an example of a failure to heed this important lesson.[55] The Charters that created a Supreme Court in Calcutta and Recorders' Courts in Madras and Bombay, the other Presidency towns, decreed that Muslim and Hindu residents would continue to be governed by their own laws of contract.[56] In the absence of indigenous judges or barristers, native law officers provided opinions on points of Hindu and Muslim law. Some English observers were more doubtful about the status of native laws. Sir Francis Macnaghten claimed that in his experience he 'never knew or heard of an instance in which the Supreme Court was called upon in a case of contract, to decide by Hindu

and the judges of Bengal, see W. Stokes, *The Anglo-Indian Codes* (Oxford University Press, 1887), vol. I, p. x.

51 (1833) 19 HC Deb. 479, 532.

52 K.J.M. Smith, 'Macaulay's "Utilitarian" Indian Penal Code: An Illustration of the Accidental Function of Time, Place and Personalities in Law Making' in W.M. Gordon and T.D. Fergus, *Legal History in the Making* (Hambledon Press, London, 1991), pp. 145–64.

53 B.S. Cohn, *Colonialism and its Forms of Knowledge* (Princeton University Press, 1996), ch. 3; B.S. Cohn, 'From Indian Status to British Contract' (1961) 21 *Journal of Economic History* 613.

54 P.J. Marshall (ed.), *The Writings and Speeches of Edmund Burke: India: Madras and Bengal 1774–1785* (Oxford University Press, 2000), vol. V, p. 141, 27 June 1781.

55 *Ibid.*

56 (1781) 21 Geo. III c. 70 s. 17; (1797) 37 Geo. III c. 142 s. 13. For details on the operation of the courts see M.P. Jain, *Indian Legal History* (2nd edn, Tripthi, Bombay, 1966).

laws and usages'.[57] Writing in 1860, William Macpherson called the 'privilege, if it can be so called of little value' and continued that, 'English Law is generally found to supply just principles'.[58] A recent, detailed study of the case law supports these observations.[59] Native law played a sporadic role at best in contract disputes in the Charter courts. In cases of contracts between Europeans, the English common law, with some allowance for local conditions, applied.[60]

There was more scope for indigenous law outside the Charter courts.[61] Judges were often not legally trained. Henry Maine complained:

> The inferior judges, when they were applying some half-remembered legal rule learnt in boyhood, or culling a proposition of law from a half-understood English textbook, no doubt honestly thought in many cases that they were following the rule prescribed for them, to decide, 'by equity and good conscience' wherever no native law or usage was discoverable.[62]

The formula, 'equity and good conscience' allowed a good deal of flexibility.[63] In this respect these courts were not much different from the Courts of Conscience in England which proved to be so popular in low value contract litigation prior to the creation of the new County Courts in the 1840s.[64] In a minute produced in his capacity as the legal member of the Governor General's Council in 1867, Henry Maine[65]

[57] F. Macnaghten, *Considerations on the Hindoo Law, as is current in Bengal* (Serampore, 1824), p. 403.

[58] W. Macpherson, *Outlines of the Law of Contract as administered in the Courts of British India* (London, 1860).

[59] S. Tofaris, *A Historical Study of the Indian Contract Act 1872* (unpublished Ph.D, University of Cambridge, 2011), ch. 1.

[60] *Ibid.*

[61] For a discussion of these courts, see *Report of the Law Commissioners on the Judicial System of India* (1842).

[62] H. Maine, *Village-Communities in the East and West* (3rd edn, J. Murray, London, 1876), p. 299. For similar remarks by a Bengal barrister in 1868, see IOR/L/PJ/5/15 (Money).

[63] IOR/L/PJ/5/15 (Superintendent of Stamps, Fort St George).

[64] On the Courts of Conscience, see W. Holdsworth, *A History of English Law* (3rd edn, Methuen, London, 1922), vol. I, pp. 190–1; M. Finn, *The Character of Credit* (Cambridge University Press, 2003), ch. 5; W.H.D. Winder, 'The Courts of Requests' (1936) 52 *Law Quarterly Review* 369; H.W. Arthurs, 'Without the Law: Courts of Local and Special Jurisdiction in Nineteenth Century England' (1984) 5 *Journal of Legal History* 130, 132–7. For a contemporary account, see W. Hutton, *Courts of Requests: Their Nature, Utility and Powers Described* (Birmingham, 1787).

[65] For the life of Maine, see G. Feaver, *From Status to Contract: A Biography of Sir Henry Maine 1822–1888* (Longmans, London, 1969); R. Cocks, *Sir Henry Maine: A Study in Victorian Jurisprudence* (Cambridge University Press, 2004). On his role as Law Member,

argued that 'justice, equity and good conscience have of late years been much affected, as a fact, by the English law of contract'.[66] Macpherson claimed that judges, 'generally avoided any wide departure from its [the common law's] principles except in cases affected by some of the special features of oriental life and transactions'. These remarks may be true of the 1860s but in earlier decades a combination of indigenous law and common sense informed judgments rather more than the common law.[67] As time passed the role of indigenous law diminished even in these courts. Anglo-Indian writers from Sir William Jones onwards began to produce digests and other works on Hindu and Muslim law.[68] These heavily Anglicised versions came to be relied on by judges at the expense of the native law officers. These same men were often at pains to stress the similarities between the common law of contract and the indigenous laws.[69] Irrespective of the value of such comparisons, they expressed a mindset in which codification of contract became a realistic proposition.

## Codifying Indian contract law: the Second Report

The Third Indian Law Commission was appointed in 1861. Work which began on a report on contract law in 1864 was finished by 1866. Three of the six Commissioners were judges.[70] This group was headed by the Master of the Rolls, John Romilly, the son of Bentham's close friend Samuel Romilly.[71] Sir Edward Ryan, a former Chief Justice of India and

see G. Johnson, 'India and Henry Maine' in A. Diamond, *The Victorian Achievement of Sir Henry Maine* (Cambridge University Press, 1991), pp. 376–88.

66 'Statement of Objects and Reasons', 9 July 1867, *Copies of Papers Showing the Present Position of the Question of a Contract Law for India* (1867–68) [239] PP vol. xlix 86.

67 G. Rankin, *Background to Indian Law* (Cambridge University Press, 1946), p. 90.

68 For a useful general discussion, see Tofaris, *A Historical Study*, n. 59 above, at pp. 49–56. For Jones, see D. Ibbetson, 'Sir William Jones as a Comparative Lawyer' in A. Murray (ed.), *Sir William Jones 1746–94: A Commemoration* (Oxford University Press, 1998), pp. 17–42. These works included W. Jones, *Institutes of Hindu Law* (Calcutta, 1794); H. Colebrooke, *A Digest of Hindu Law on Contracts and Successions* (Calcutta, 1798); T. Strange, *Elements of Hindu Law* (London, 1825). On Colebrooke's work on India, see R. Rocher and L. Rocher, *The Making of Western Ideology* (Routledge, London, 2012), pp. 33–9.

69 Macnaghten, *Hindoo Law*, n. 57 above, at p. 403.

70 The Commission responsible for contract was appointed in 1864, when two members of the Third Commission appointed in 1861, Willes J and Sir William Earle, retired. See *Commissions and Appointments in India*, IOR/H/25.

71 J. A. Hamilton, rev. P. Polden, 'Romilly, John' in *Oxford Dictionary of National Biography* (Oxford University Press, 2004–13). Romilly was Master of the Rolls between 1851–73.

author of Ryan and Moody's Law Reports, was a long time supporter of codification.[72] The final judge, Sir William James, was Vice Chancellor of Chancery at the time and later a Lord Justice of Appeal. James had a special interest in India.[73] They were joined by Sir John Macleod, a civil servant who had been a member of the Indian Law Commission since its inception,[74] Robert Lowe, later Chancellor of the Exchequer and Home Secretary,[75] and John Henderson,[76] a barrister. The Secretary to the Commission, William Macpherson, was an expert on Indian contract law, having published his *Outlines of the Law of Contract as Administered in the Courts of British India*[77] a few years before.

In his Preface to his contract treatise of 1826, Joseph Chitty remarked that 'Perhaps no branch of the jurisprudence of the country has of late years been more subject of judicial inquiry and decision than the Law of Contracts'.[78] By the time of the Indian Law Commission Report, the law of contract in England had undergone several more decades of change. The most striking thing about these developments was the way in which the old learning which had attached to the forms of action fell away.[79] Contract law was increasingly seen as a unified body of doctrine within a clear substantive structure. Procedural changes, particularly the emasculation of the jury, played an important part in this process. In combination with changes in the way that contract actions were pleaded, these reforms helped to firm up the boundary between questions of law and

[72] Ryan was Chief Justice between 1833–43, see K. Prior, 'Ryan, Sir Edward' in *Oxford Dictionary of National Biography*, n. 71 above.

[73] He wrote a book on the history of India, *The British in India* (Macmillan, London, 1882), which was edited by his daughter Mary Schwabe. It was written between 1864 and 1869 and published posthumously.

[74] In a letter to his friend Thomas Ellis, Macaulay described Macleod, as 'the cleverest man that I have found in India by many degrees': T. Pinney (ed.), *The Letters of Thomas Babington Macaulay* (Cambridge University Press, 1976), vol. III, p. 201.

[75] J. Winter, *Robert Lowe* (University of Toronto Press, 1976).

[76] On his death Henderson was replaced by Sir Robert Lush, the judge, see J.A. Hamilton, rev. H. Mooney, 'Lush, Sir Robert' in *Oxford Dictionary of National Biography*, n. 71 above.

[77] (London: 1860).

[78] J. Chitty, *A Practical Treatise on the Law of Contracts not under Seal* (S. Sweet, London, 1826), p. iii.

[79] These developments are discussed at length in D. Ibbetson, *A Historical Introduction to the Law of Obligations* (Oxford University Press, 1999), ch. 12; A.W.B. Simpson, 'Innovation in Nineteenth Century Contract Law' (1975) 91 *Law Quarterly Review* 247; P. Hamburger, 'The Development of the Nineteenth-Century Consensus Theory of Contract' (1989) 7 *Law and History Review* 241; W. Swain, 'The Classical Model of Contract: the Product of a Revolution in Legal Thought?' (2010) 30 *Legal Studies* 513.

fact. Judges were left searching for definitions of law that could be presented to a jury. Much of the doctrine that emerged was not new in conception. It reflected earlier practice and the way that juries decided cases, but it did begin to take a clear substantive form. The doctrine of mistake is a particularly striking example.[80] Some existing doctrines, in particular consideration, remained resistant to reform. A growing body of legal literature played an increasingly significant role as legal writers began to present the law of contract in a systematic and principled manner.[81]

The nineteenth century jurist and contract scholar, Sir Frederick Pollock, would claim that the 1866 Report was 'an elementary statement of the effect of common law and equitable doctrine as understood about forty years ago'.[82] But as the Report's authors admitted, 'we have deemed it expedient to depart, more or less, from the English law in several particulars'.[83] It would have been difficult for the Commissioners to have ignored the common law altogether. The Commissioners were too steeped in its values. Several were leading lawyers. The common law was also well established in India. At the same time, the nature of their remit afforded them much more room for manoeuvre than they would have had, had they been drawing up a domestic code. Certain aspects of the proposed Code would prove to be controversial all the same. There were some major departures from the current common law and the process also raised questions about contract law, public policy and local conditions.

The Second Report is, in many respects, a surprising document. In some respects it runs counter to some of the received wisdom about the attitude of English lawyers both to codification and reform of the law of contract. Even where there are shared characteristics with English law, these sometimes take a slightly different form. The Third Commission

[80] For a detailed analysis, see C. MacMillan, *Mistakes in Contract Law* (Hart, Oxford, 2010), chs. 4–7.

[81] A.W.B. Simpson, 'The Rise and Fall of the Legal Treatise: Legal Principles and the Forms of Legal Literature' (1981) 48 *University of Chicago Law Review* 632. For the importance of principle, see S. Waddams, 'What *were* the Principles of Nineteenth-century Contract Law?' in A. Lewis, P. Brand and P. Mitchell (eds.), *Law in the City Proceedings of the Seventeenth British Legal History Conference, London, 2005* (Four Courts Press, Dublin, 2007), pp. 305–18.

[82] F. Pollock and D. Mulla, *The Indian Contract Act with a Commentary, Critical and Explanatory* (Oxford University Press, 1905), p. v.

[83] *Contract Law for India*, n. 66 above, at p. 3.

was prepared to borrow quite openly from civil law.[84] Indirect civilian influences were even more important. The French jurist, Robert-Joseph Pothier, whose *A Treatise on the Law of Obligations or Contracts*[85] appeared in a translation by Sir William Evans in 1806, was 'frequently referred to'[86] in England from the early nineteenth century by writers and judges.[87] Pothier's central notion, that a contract was formed by a meeting of wills began to be used to structure English contract law.[88] His influence was greatest when the common law was silent or incomplete. But even here, for example in the case of contractual mistake, 'English treatise writers did not accept Pothier's work . . . in its entirety: they were selective in their borrowing and they merged this with common law concerns, such as objectivity'.[89] Because the Third Commission enjoyed considerably more freedom than English textbook writers and judges, it was possible to take English developments a stage further.

In the draft Code, a contract was defined as 'an agreement between parties whereby a party engages to do a thing or engages not to do a thing'.[90] This closely mirrors the French Civil Code[91] and Pothier's treatise.[92] The description of contract as an agreement was hardly unfamiliar in England.[93] The difference lay in the way that in civilian sources this principle informed the way that the subject was structured. This was not true in England. Things were beginning to change here too, though the process was not well advanced until the 1870s. Section 10 of the Indian Contract Act is as explicit a statement of will theory as it is possible to find outside mainland Europe: 'All agreements are contracts if they are made by the free consent of parties competent to contract, for lawful consideration and with a lawful object, and are not hereby expressly declared to be void'. The Act goes on to define 'free consent'

84 For example, *Contract Law for India*, n. 66 above, p. 5.

85 W. Evans, *A Treatise on the Law of Obligations or Contracts by M. Pothier* (J. Butterworth, London, 1806).

86 (1807) 3 *Law Journal* 297, 301.

87 For some discussion of Pothier's influence on English judges, see B. Rudden, 'Pothier et la common law' in J. Monéger (ed.), *Robert-Joseph Pothier, d'hier à aujourd'hui* (Economica, Paris, 2001), pp. 91–101.

88 See the literature cited at n. 79 above.

89 MacMillan, *Mistakes*, n. 80 above, at p. 133.

90 Cl. 1.

91 Book 3, 3, 1 s. 1101.

92 Pothier, *Obligations*, n. 85 above, 1.1.1 s. 1.

93 Examples include a case in covenant in 1321, see H. Cam, *Year Books of Edward II* (Selden Society, London, 1969), p. 286; *Reniger* v. *Fogossa* (1550) Plo 1, 17, 75 ER 1; T.F.T. Plucknett and J.L. Barton (eds.), *St German's Doctor and Student* (Selden Society, London, 1974), p. 228.

before analysing coercion, undue influence, fraud and misrepresentation in terms of its absence. A few English writers, including Colebrooke and Jeremy, had already experimented with versions of this approach,[94] but the Act was largely ahead of its time. This sort of analysis only reached full fruition in Pollock's textbook of 1876.[95] So close was the Indian Contract Act to Pollock's own treatment of these subjects, that he added an appendix in his treatise containing the relevant provisions of the legislation.[96]

The Second Report was ahead of English law in other significant ways as well, particularly in its treatment of mistake. Clause 7 states that 'where both parties to an engagement by contract are under a mistake as to a matter of fact essential to the engagement, the engagement is void', and is pure Pothier.[97] That the Commission turned to Pothier was not a matter of chance. The Secretary to the Commission, William MacPherson, had specifically praised Pothier's analysis of mistake in his treatise.[98] A well defined doctrine of mistake had not yet emerged in England by the time the Report was published.[99] The first full length treatment of the subject in an English contract treatise, Stephen Leake's *The Elements of the Law of Contract*,[100] did not appear until the following year along with the first unequivocal judicial statement on the subject by Blackburn J in *Kennedy* v. *Panama, New Zealand and Australia Royal Mail Company*.[101]

The attitude of the Commission towards well-established doctrine was even more surprising, nowhere more so than its treatment of consideration. Consideration was based on the idea that contracts were founded on reciprocity. Since earliest times there had been some flexibility around the edges in terms of genuine reciprocity.[102] Over the years, these exceptions had grown.[103] Nevertheless, the core of the doctrine had remained intact. With the growing popularity of the will theory,

94 H. Colebrooke, *Treatise on Obligations and Contracts* (London, 1818); G. Jeremy, *A Treatise on the Equity Jurisdiction of the High Court of Chancery* (London, 1828).
95 F. Pollock, *Principles of Contract at Law and in Equity* (Stevens & Sons, London, 1876).
96 *Ibid.* 542–55.
97 Pothier, *Obligations*, n. 85 above, 1.1.3.1 ss. 17–18.
98 MacPherson, *Contract*, n. 58 above, at p. xi.
99 Before mistake emerged as a distinct doctrine, it was just one of a number of matters considered by the jury.
100 (Stevens, London, 1867). 101 (1867) LR 2 QB 580, 8 B & S 571.
102 Ibbetson, *Historical Introduction*, n. 79 above, at pp. 141–5.
103 For a discussion of the contours of consideration in the nineteenth century, see W. Swain, 'The Changing Nature of the Doctrine of Consideration, 1750–1850' (2005) 26

the continued existence of an additional requirement of consideration became difficult to square with the idea that the binding force of contracts was derived from the meeting of wills. By the mid-nineteenth century, consideration was a minimal threshold which could be crossed fairly easily when both parties intended to create a binding contract.[104] But at the same time, consideration was not completely devoid of content and remained a requirement for enforcing a contract in the absence of a deed in England. Having weighed up but rejected the possibility of abolishing the requirement of consideration altogether, the Commission proceeded to modify is application in ways that were unthinkable in England. Clause 10 removed the need for consideration when the agreement was in writing and the contract was registered. Minus the registration requirement, Lord Mansfield and Wilmot J had advocated something similar in the mid-eighteenth century[105] before their approach was quickly extinguished by *Rann* v. *Hughes*.[106] The importance of a second reform, the proposal that a promise to pay a pre-existing debt amounted to good consideration, would only become fully apparent nearly two decades later following *Foakes* v. *Beer*,[107] in which the House of Lords held that a promise to pay a pre-existing debt was not good consideration.[108] There are several other examples in the Second Report and the final legislation where the law in India diverged from England. The provisions on recovery of money paid or services rendered were more liberal at a time in England when liability for money had and received was tightly restrained.[109] The canonical interpretation of *Tweddle* v. *Atkinson*,[110] that only parties to a contract could bring a claim upon it, had yet to take hold in England and is not addressed.[111]

*Journal of Legal History* 46; M. Lobban, 'Contract' in Cornish *et al.*, *The Oxford History*, n. 42 above, at pp. 358–99.

104 For example in *Bainbridge* v. *Firmstone* (1838) 8 Ad & E 743.

105 In *Pillans* v. *Van Mierop* (1765) 3 Burr. 1663.

106 (1778) 4 Bro. PC 27, 7 TR 350, LI MS Misc. 130 f. 74. For an analysis, see Swain, 'Consideration', n. 103 above, at 49–53.

107 (1884) 9 App. Cas. 605.

108 M. Lobban, 'Foakes v. Beer' in C. Mitchell and P. Mitchell, *Landmark Cases in the Law of Contract* (Hart, Oxford, 2008), pp. 223–67.

109 W. Swain, 'Moses v. Macferlan' in C. Mitchell and P. Mitchell (eds.), *Landmark Cases in the Law of Restitution* (Hart, Oxford, 2006), pp. 19, 29–34. This was noted by a respondent to the Bill, IOR/L/PJ/5/15 (Pitt-Kennedy).

110 (1861) 1 B & S 393, 30 LJQB 265, 4 LT 468, 9 WR 781.

111 D. Ibbetson and W. Swain, 'Third Party Beneficiaries in English Law' in E. Schrage, *Ius quaesitum tertio* (Duncker & Humblot, Berlin, 2008), pp. 191, 210–13.

The Act did, though, abandon the traditional rule that consideration must move from the promisee.[112]

## Reaction to the Second Report and the Indian Contract Act 1872

Having been referred to a select committee, the draft Bill was circulated amongst lawyers and government officials in India. The reaction was neither wholly favourable nor consistent. One Indian judge argued that judges were left with too little discretion;[113] another that they were left with too much.[114] A few provisions attracted the majority of adverse comment. The decision of the Commission to omit an Indian equivalent of the Statute of Frauds was, wrote one respondent, likely to 'cause much baseless litigation'.[115] The proposal to abandon the distinction between penalty and liquidated damages clauses was even more contentious. In England, a liquidated damages clause was enforceable, a penalty was not. Making the distinction in practice was far from easy. Various approaches were tried. By around 1870, the earlier test for determining the character of a clause, supposedly based on intention of the parties, but which was in fact rather formulaic, had given way to an assessment of whether the stipulated sum was proportionate.[116] Abolishing the distinction simplified matters but a judge in the Bombay Small Causes Court thought it would 'afford greater facilities to the grasping money lender to impose upon the ignorant borrower'.[117] The measure was also described as a 'retrograde step',[118] one that caused 'grave apprehensions'[119] and 'regrettable'.[120] Another judge of the Small Causes Court put the opposite point of view when he argued that:

> The penalty of a contract is, in my opinion, always intended, in fact, as a device to ensure the punctual and exact performance of a contract; and whether it be in the nature of a punishment, or only by way of fixing

112 Ibbetson and Swain, 'Third Party Beneficiaries', n. 111 above, at 196–200. The third example in clause 10 can be read in this way. It might be argued that the draft was ambiguous even if the final Act was not, see Tofaris, *A Historical Study*, n. 59 above, at p. 160.

113 IOR/L/PJ/5/15 (Belli). 114 IOR/L/PJ/5/15 (West).

115 IOR/L/PJ/5/15 (Pitt-Kennedy). For other criticism, see IOR/L/PJ/5/15 (Cochrane)

116 Lobban, 'Contract', n. 103 above, at pp. 523–9.

117 IOR/L/PJ/5/15 (Canoba). For similar remarks, see IOR/L/PJ/5/15 (Deputy Commissioner, Delhi) who argued that 'the people of this country need to be protected against the results of their own rashness in entering into over-reaching contracts'.

118 IOR/L/PJ/5/15 (Coghlan). 119 IOR/L/PJ/5/15 (Turner).

120 IOR/L/PJ/5/15 (Ráo).

> definitely beforehand by mutual consent the amount of damage consequent on a breach appears to me to be wholly immaterial, so long as both parties with their eyes open have consented.[121]

The Act combined both approaches by allowing the parties to stipulate the level of damages in advance without needing to resort to the actual loss but restricting recovery to a proportionate amount.[122] The debate over two other clauses would have wider consequences. The proposal that a bona fide purchaser took good title even where the seller lacked title was contrary to the traditional common law rule of *nemo dat quod non habet*. Some of the respondents also thought that it would encourage theft of cattle.[123] In the original version of the Contract Bill, the Indian Law Commission had added a series of clauses introducing specific performance as a remedy in contract disputes.[124] The remedy was not to apply to agreements to cultivate land in a particular manner or to grow particular crops.[125] This limitation was inserted for a very particular reason. Tensions between the indigenous growers of indigo, the ryots, and European planters had caused problems, including civil unrest, for decades.[126] The ryots argued that they were being exploited by the planters; the planters that the ryots, having received advance payment, were refusing to perform their contracts. Henry Maine, as legal member of the Governor General's Council, produced a series of minutes on the subject.[127] His main objection that the proper place for specific performance was a code of procedure rather than of substance masked wider misgivings. John Lawrence, the Governor General, was in favour of the clauses but decided that it was expedient to omit them and refer the matter to the Secretary of State.[128] When he in turn referred the matter back to the Indian Law Commissioners, they stood by their original recommendations.[129]

At this point relations between the various interested parties began to deteriorate. A Select Committee of the Indian Legislature drew up their own draft Bill which reinstated the *nemo dat*

121 IOR/L/PJ/5/15 (Fagan).

122 H.S. Cunningham and H.H. Shepherd, *The Indian Contract Act of 1872* (3rd edn, Thacker, Calcutta, 1878), p. xlviii, s. 74. This approach was championed by one of the respondents, see IOR/L/PJ/5/15 (Cochrane).

123 IOR/L/PJ/5/15 (Fitzpatrick, Baden-Powell, Oliphant).

124 Cls. 51–5.

125 Cl. 52.

126 For an interesting account, see B. Kling, *The Blue Mutiny: The Indigo Disturbances in Bengal 1859–1862* (University of Pennsylvania Press, 1966).

127 *Contract Law for India*, n. 66 above, at pp. 86–9, 91–2, 94–5, 95–6, 97–8, 99–100.

128 *Ibid.* 92–3, 96, 101.

129 *Ibid.* 101–3.

rule.[130] The Duke of Argyll, the new Secretary of State for India, sided with the Indian Law Commission.[131] This left Maine in a difficult position. His defence of the Indian Legislature in a Minute of April 1868 stressed the need to take account of local conditions:

> I have striven to prevail on the Legislature to sanction the Commissioner's drafts with the minimum of change; and they will believe me when I say that, in making this effort, I have often had to contend against criticisms which were at least plausible, and to struggle with difficulties which however slightly they may be believed at home, are still real and substantial, and not in the less real and substantial because they assume a form somewhat unlike that which impede legislation in England.[132]

Both sides became increasingly intransigent. In the Spring of 1870, the Indian Government reiterated their support for the position adopted by the Select Committee on the *nemo dat* rule and stressed that it was not for the Secretary of State to impose a Bill in the teeth of objections of the Indian Legislature. In July of the same year, the Indian Law Commission resigned, complaining that despite much 'time and labour' their proposals had still not been implemented.[133] An Indian Office minute noted rather dryly that such delays were not unusual.[134] The Commissioners could not be persuaded to reconsider. Their final letter to the Secretary of State concluded rather bitterly:

> We must repeat that no information which has reached the Commissioners does in our opinion explain the inaction of the legislature to which we adverted in our former letter, and which we have been obliged to consider as systematic and persistent.[135]

In the meantime, Henry Maine had returned to England in order to take up the post of Corpus Professor of Jurisprudence at Oxford.[136] He was replaced by James Fitzjames Stephen.[137] Stephen admitted that whilst the

[130] Report of the Select Committee on the Bill to Define and Amend the Law Relating to Contracts (1868) IOR/L/PJ/5/15.

[131] Rankin, *Indian Law*, n. 67 above, at p. 84.

[132] H. Maine, *Minutes by the Honourable Sir HS Maine (1862–69)* (Government of India, Calcutta, 1890), p. 134.

[133] Cited by C. Ilbert, 'Indian Codification' (1889) 5 *Law Quarterly Review* 347, 351–2.

[134] IOR/L/PJ/5/438 (July 1870).

[135] Cited by Ilbert, 'Codification', n. 133 above, at 352.

[136] On Maine's departure and his part in securing Stephen's succession, see Feaver, *Status to Contract*, n. 65 above, at pp. 106–7.

[137] For Stephen's role in codification in India, see K.J.M. Smith, *James Fitzjames Stephen* (Cambridge University Press, 2002), pp. 126–32; C. Ilbert, 'Sir James Fitzjames Stephen as a Legislator' (1894) 10 *Law Quarterly Review* 222.

Law Commission remained in place 'there was the difficulty of altering their work to any considerable extent'. With their departure, the Secretary of State also conceded defeat and ordered the Indian Legislature to deal with the matter as they sought fit.[138]

Stephen was now free to make further amendments. Of all the contentious clauses in the original Bill, only those omitting the Statute of Frauds remained unscathed.[139] The impact of the reform of consideration was also reduced in the final Act. A written agreement that was registered was only binding where it was made 'on account of natural love and affection between the parties standing in near relation to each other',[140] or the exact opposite of Lord Mansfield's position in *Pillans* v. *Van Mierop*.[141] Stephen complained that the first part of the original Bill was 'arranged in a very obscure and confused manner'.[142] His changes to its structure and the addition of a new definitional section[143] did not meet with general approval. James Bryce complained that Stephen's 'capacity for the work of drafting was deemed not equal to his fondness for it'.[144] Pollock took exception to the definitional section which was described as 'in a wholly different style and not altogether in harmony with the body of the work'.[145] Stephen admitted that he had relied on David Dudley Field's New York Civil Code[146] when drafting the legislation, much to the displeasure of Pollock and others.[147]

138 Abstracts of the Proceedings of the Council of the Governor-General of India (1871), p. 757; IOR/V/9/11–12.

139 This was welcomed by some: F. Pollock and D. Mulla, *Indian Contract Act* (2nd edn, Oxford University Press, 1909), p. 377, described the Statute of Frauds as 'happily not in force in British India'.

140 Section 25(1).

141 (1765) 3 Burr. 1663. Lord Mansfield limited his exception to commercial parties. In the same case, Wilmot J had suggested a wider exception not limited to commercial parties where an agreement was in writing. The only evidence that this was ever supported is the unreported case of *Williamson* v. *Losh* (1774) noted in J. Chitty, *A Practical Treatise on Bills of Exchange* (5th edn, London, 1818), pp. 93–4.

142 IOR/L/PJ/5/438. 143 Section 2.

144 J. Bryce, *Studies in History and Jurisprudence* (Oxford University Press, 1901), p. 129.

145 Pollock and Mulla, *Indian Contract Act*, n. 139 above, at p. v.

146 Field may have influenced the direction of the legislation all the way back to the Law Commission's original Bill, see Ilbert, 'James Fitzjames Stephen', n. 137 above, at 223; IOR/L/PJ/5/15 (C.D. Field in 1868). Field was strongly influenced by civilian ideas, see D. Clark, 'The Civil Law Influence on David Dudley Field's Code of Civil Procedure' in M. Reimann, *The Reception of Continental Ideas in the Common Law World 1820–1920* (Duncker & Humblot, Berlin, 1993), pp. 63–87.

147 Ilbert, 'James Fitzjames Stephen', n. 137 above, at 223; Pollock and Mulla, *Indian Contract Act*, n. 139 above, at, pp. vii, 164.

## Codification: some lessons from the nineteenth century

The nineteenth century[148] was sandwiched between two major Civil Codes, the French Code Civile and the German Bürgerliches Gesetzbuch (BGB).[149] If English hostility to codification had, by the end of the century, not exactly been replaced by rousing enthusiasm, then, up to a point, it was more widely accepted. A series of major statutes dealing with large swathes of commercial law and covering bills of exchange, partnership, sale of goods and marine insurance were enacted in the decades around 1900.[150] With the exception of the Partnership Act, which was drafted by Frederick Pollock, these Acts were the creations of one man, Mackenzie Chalmers.[151] Chalmers would claim that the idea of codification was suggested to him by the Indian Codes.[152] He also had a strong ideological commitment to the exercise,[153] combined with a belief that codification gave businessmen greater certainty.[154] Commercial interests also played an important role particularly, but not exclusively, in relation to the Partnership Act.[155]

This legislation was not the work of cranks or even Benthamite zealots. Pollock and Chalmers were respected lawyers who had produced digests on partnership,[156] bills of exchange and insurance.[157] Chalmers' views on Bentham are unknown but Pollock was, at best, an 'ambivalent admirer'.[158] At least some mainstream lawyers, businessmen and

[148] From a very different historical perspective, see A. Kanning, 'The Emergence of a European Private Law: Lessons from 19th Century Germany' (2007) 27 *Oxford Journal of Legal Studies* 193.

[149] F. Wieacker, *A History of Private Law in Europe* (T. Weir (trans.), Oxford University Press, 2003), pp. 269–75, 371–86.

[150] Bills of Exchange Act 1882; Partnership Act 1890; Sale of Goods Act 1893; Marine Insurance Act 1906.

[151] S. Hedley, 'Sir Mackenzie Dalzell Chalmers' in *Oxford Dictionary of National Biography*, n. 71 above.

[152] M. Chalmers, 'Codification of Mercantile Law' (1903) 19 *Law Quarterly Review* 9, 11. From 1896 to 1899, Chalmers served as the Law Officer on the Governor General's Council.

[153] R.B. Ferguson, 'Legal Ideology and Commercial Interests: The Social Origins of the Commercial Law Codes' (1977) 4 *British Journal of Law and Society* 18.

[154] Chalmers, 'Codification', n. 152 above, at 14–15.

[155] Ferguson, 'Legal Ideology', n. 153 above, at 26–7. So too was the Bills of Exchange Act, see M. Chalmers, 'An Experiment in Codification' (1886) 2 *Law Quarterly Review* 125.

[156] F. Pollock, *A Digest of the Law of Partnership* (Stevens and Sons, London, 1877).

[157] M. Chalmers, *A Digest of the Law of Bills of Exchange, Promissory Notes and Cheques* (Stevens and Sons, London, 1878); M. Chalmers, *A Digest of the Law of Marine Insurance* (Clowes and Sons, London, 1901).

[158] Duxbury, *Pollock*, in Davies, n. 10 above, at p. 104.

politicians were prepared to come out in favour of legislation of this sort. But there were limits. This was not the sort of general code advocated by Bentham. Attempts to introduce a much wider mercantile code which would apply to both England and Scotland came to nothing.[159] Pollock praised the Indian Contract Act in the Preface to his contract treatise as 'the most instructive example of what can be done to consolidate and simplify English case-law'.[160] But the prospects of an English equivalent to the Indian Contract Act were just as remote as a mercantile code. A proposal to partially reform contract in statute the year after Pollock's death was scuppered by the Second World War.[161] A more extensive Contract Code produced in the 1970s by Harvey McGregor[162] fell victim to disagreements between the English and Scottish Law Commissions.[163] English contract law remains stoutly resistant to codification.

Writing the year after the Indian Contract Act came into force, Sheldon Amos warned of the dangers of those anxious to advance the cause of codification in England drawing too close an analogy with events in India.[164] His remarks remain valid today. A colonial territory, even one as important as India, does not sit in the same position as the modern day United Kingdom as a member of the European Union.[165] Nevertheless, the Indian Contract Act remains the best example that

[159] Lord Rodger, 'The Codification of Commercial Law in Victorian Britain' (1991) 80 *Proceedings of the British Academy* 149 reproduced in (1992) 108 *Law Quarterly Review* 570. For a contemporary account, see Anon., 'The Proposed Mercantile Code' (1885) 29 *Journal of Jurisprudence* 186.

[160] Pollock, *Contract*, n. 95 above, at p. viii.

[161] Law Revision Committee, *Sixth Interim Report (Statute of Frauds and the Doctrine of Consideration)* (Cmd 5449) (HMSO, London, 1937). For a contemporary account, see R.S. Chorley *et al.*, 'The Law Revision Committee's Sixth Interim Report' (1939) 1 *Modern Law Review* 97.

[162] H. McGregor, *Contract Code Drawn Up on behalf of the English Law Commission* (Giuffré Editore, Milan, 1993). The Code abolished the doctrine of consideration.

[163] H. MacQueen, 'Glory with Gloag or the Stake with Stair? T. B. Smith and the Scots Law of Contract' in E. Reid and D. Carey Miller, *A Mixed Legal System in Transition: T B Smith and the Progress of Scots Law* (Edinburgh University Press, 2005), pp. 138, 159–61. For accounts of these events from the English and Scots participants, see L.C.B. Gower, 'Reflections on Law Reform' (1973) 23 *University of Toronto Law Journal* 257, 264–5; T.B. Smith, 'Law Reform in a Mixed Civil Law and Common Law Jurisdiction' (1974–75) 35 *Louisiana Law Review* 927, 946–8.

[164] S. Amos, *An English Code, Its Difficulties and Modes of Overcoming Them* (Strahan, London, 1873), pp. 86–94.

[165] Though if one takes the word of the current President of the European Commission at face value the differences might not be as great as they might first appear, 'Barroso hails the European empire', *Daily Telegraph*, 11 July 2007.

English lawyers have of an attempt to codify the law of contract, as well as serving a warning of some of the problems that contract codification might bring in its wake.

The starkest lesson of the whole episode is captured in Amos' remarks that, 'No one who has practically tried his hand at the Codification of the English Law can be unaware of the extraordinary difficulties by which the task is beset'.[166] At the same time, the Indian Contract Act showed that an extensive code, as opposed to the more limited reforms of aspects of commercial law, was possible. It is a testament to those involved in the legislation at all stages that it still remains in force. It continues to attract admirers into the present day. The Jersey Law Commission has recently recommended using the Act as a template for developing its own Contract Code.[167] But the Act was only ever possible within its own terms. This was not codification in the grand manner envisaged by Bentham. It was not informed by 'utility, notoriety, completeness, manifest reasonableness'. This was not legislation from first principles. Such principles as there were came from the will theory but these were blended with the existing common law of contract then in force in India. There was no clean break with the past. Some doctrines like consideration which remained contrary to will theory were retained. Bentham's dream of a code that could be understood by the lay man would not be realised in India. P.K. Nambyar, an advocate of the High Court of Madras, remarked in 1879 that:

> The Indian Contract Act, surely requires schools for its explanation, and casuists (as Bentham puts it) to unravel its subtleties. It does not speak a language familiar to everybody. The Indian Contract Act is not distinguished from other books by its great simplicity and clearness. And so if Bentham were alive to see the Indian Contract Act, he would emphatically say, that the measure is an imperfect one.[168]

The Act did not reduce the need for judges. It was not exhaustive. There were too many problems of interpretation. These were resolved with reference to the English common law.[169] Other factors worked against a Benthamite Contract Code in India. There are always going

[166] Amos, *English Code*, n. 164 above, at p. 1.

[167] Jersey Law Commission, *Report on the Law of Contract* (Topic Report No. 10, 2004).

[168] P.K. Nambyar, *The Principles of the Indian Law of Contract* (Vyjayanti Press, Madras, 1897), p. 111.

[169] R.N. Gooderson, 'English Contract Problems in Indian Code and Case Law' (1958) 16 *Cambridge Law Journal* 67.

to be frictions when a remote body of experts, in this case the Indian Law Commission, attempt to impose a code on a local population without proper regard to local conditions. In a letter to his friend Grant Duff, Henry Maine, having criticised the Indian Law Commission as 'a perfectly irresponsible body' with little recent experience of India continued:

> I am greatly afraid that the law commissioners have formed a radically false notion of the India of the present day. I admit that . . . on the subject of the first Code, the Penal Code, there is much to countenance an impression that India is a field for the application of a diluted Benthamism . . . As to the Penal Code, nobody cares about criminal law except theorists and habitual criminals . . . a substantive Civil Law applying to everybody and cutting across every transaction of everyday life, is a very different matter.[170]

The principal objections to the proposed Indian Code were practical rather than based on doctrinal purity. But the process was not ideologically or politically neutral.[171] The pre-legislation system was presented as inefficient. At the same time, the differences between the indigenous laws and the common law were downplayed. This was not an accident. The fate of Dudley Field's Code demonstrated that without the political will no code, however well drafted, could hope to prosper.[172] The participants in the project were prepared to face the political realties by accepting that the legislation would have to take account of local conditions. They disagreed on the full extent of the compromise that was necessary. The fate of codification in India in the nineteenth century was not only determined by the political conditions in India and England. The role of large personalities such as Macaulay, Maine and Stephen in determining the speed and direction of codification was crucial.[173]

170 Reproduced in Feaver, *Status to Contract*, n. 65 above, at pp. 101–3.

171 For a discussion of the politics of codification more generally in the nineteenth century, see P. van den Berg, *The Politics of European Codification* (Europa Law Publishing, Groningen, 2007).

172 For an account of these events, see M. Reimann, 'The Historical School of Codification: Savigny, Carter and the Defeat of the New York Civil Code' (1989) 37 *American Journal of Comparative Law* 95.

173 The role of individuals in shaping the direction of legal change is not a fashionable one. No one now believes along with Thomas Carlyle that, 'For as I take it, Universal History, the history of what man has accomplished in this world, is at bottom the History of the Great Men who have worked here': *On Heroes, Hero-worship and the Heroic in History* (Ams Press, New York, 1969), p. 1. The power and influence wielded by the Law Member makes nineteenth century India a good illustration of the importance of individuals, albeit, individuals who are products of their own time and place.

There are obvious parallels between events in nineteenth century India and some of the debates over European codification and English contract law. Like their Ango-Indian counterparts, advocates of codification are keen to both downplay differences between legal systems and stress the practical value of codification.[174] The English law of contract has always been open to civilian influences[175] but in a piecemeal rather than wholesale manner. Major differences with other legal systems remain.[176] Practical or economic arguments favouring a unified code are not yet decisive one way or another.[177] In India, codification was driven by a belief both in the value of codes and the type of legal system that its drafters proposed to create. Here, the parallels may be particularly strong. European contract codification involves political choices.[178] The fact that academics are heavily involved in the process does not mean that the participants have no political agenda. The various bodies of scholars working on contract codification over the last few decades may have slightly different aims and methodologies but they do not start from a position of neutrality. Like the Indian Law Commission they share a belief in the value of codification.[179] Some individual academics are sceptical about the merits and practical difficulties of codification but there is, as yet, no group arguing against codification.[180] In India, the codification project was bound up in the ideology of the Raj in

[174] O. Lando, 'Liberal, Social and Ethical Justice in European Contract Law' (2006) 43 *Common Market Law Review* 817, 825: 'The national contract laws differ, but often more in the formulations and techniques than the results'.

[175] See the literature cited at n. 79 above.

[176] Perhaps the most intractable is the doctrine of good faith: G. Teubner, 'Legal Irritants: Good Faith in British Law or How Unifying Law Ends Up in New Divergences' (1998) 61 *Modern Law Review* 11.

[177] H. Wagner, 'Economic Analysis of Cross-border Legal Uncertainty' and J. Hage, 'Law, Economics and Uniform Contract Law: A Sceptical View' in J. Smits, *The Need for a European Contract Law: Empirical and Legal Perspectives* (Europa Law, Groningen, 2005), chs. 2–3; S. Vogenauer and S. Weatherill, 'The European Community's Competence to Pursue the Harmonisation of Contract Law: An Empirical Contribution to the Debate' in S. Vogenauer and S. Weatherill (eds.), *The Harmonisation of European Contract Law* (Hart, Oxford, 2006), pp. 105–48.

[178] M. Hesselink, 'The Politics of a European Civil Code' (2004) 10 *European Law Journal* 675.

[179] Some of the leading figures are clear on this point: O. Lando, 'Can Europe Build Unity of Civil Law while Respecting Diversity?' (2006) 2 *Europa e diritto private* 1. Von Bar is more circumspect but his aims are no less clear, C. von Bar, 'From Principles to Codification: Prospects for European Civil Law' (2002) 8 *Columbia Journal of European Law* 379.

[180] P. Legrand, 'Against a European Civil Code' (1997) 60 *Modern Law Review* 44.

its pomp.[181] Some modern scholars are just as unequivocal in their belief that civil codification provides an opportunity to impose a particular ideological vision on the citizens of Europe.[182] Whether the European Contract Code ever comes to fruition and the form that it will take remains to be seen. No one doubts that producing a code will not be easy. It is to be hoped that whatever the outcome, any code that is produced does not earn the epithet attached to the original Indian Contract Bill by one Bengal Barrister: 'a painful and cruel infliction'.[183]

[181] Which has been described as 'the late Victorian unified sub-continental British Raj, with its arrogant . . . elite bureaucracy', see B. Lenman, 'Britain and India' in H.T. Dickinson, *A Companion to Eighteenth Century Britain* (Blackwell, Oxford, 2002), p. 472. Any similarities with the current European Commission are purely coincidental.

[182] Study Group on Social Justice in European Private Law, 'Social Justice in European Contract Law: A Manifesto' (2004) 10 *European Law Journal* 653; H. Collins, *The European Civil Code: The Way Forward* (Cambridge University Press, 2008), ch. 9. This approach is at least transparent, but social justice is not inherently a cause worth promoting. For a powerful argument the other way, see the seminal F. Hayek, *Law Legislation and Liberty*, vol. 2, *The Mirage of Social Justice* (Chicago University Press, 1978), p. 97: 'the phrase social justice is not, as most people probably feel, an innocent expression of good will towards the less fortunate, but it has become a dishonest insinuation that one ought to agree to a demand of some special interest which they can give no reason for it'.

[183] The Barrister in question was J.B. Money, an Assistant Secretary in Bengal. He was writing in 1868, IOR L/PJ/5/15.

# 10

# Consequences of implementing EU legislation: an Estonian experience

IRENE KULL AND SANDER KÄRSON

## European private law as the basis for Estonia's private law

Nearly twenty years have passed since the Western legal tradition could be reinstated in Estonia. The start of this period from the perspective of legal reforms was formally marked by the decision of the Estonian Parliament in 1992 on the continuity of legislation.[1] In practice this could have led to a situation in which the laws which were in force prior to the occupation of Estonia by the Soviet Union would have once more become effective and the set of rules which regulated and determined our legal life in the beginning of the twentieth century would have seamlessly assumed the same role without any modification in the wake of the twenty-first century. But fortunately this was only a parliamentary policy decision and did not indicate a direction that was obligatory to follow. In practice, the recommendation to use old laws and draft legislation from the first period of Estonian independence to draft the new legislation on contract law was ignored.[2]

The timing of drafting new laws and regulations in Estonia was quite opportune due to the fact that it coincided with the movements and events which we can now refer to as the founding of European private law[3] as well as with the adoption of the new Dutch

Chair of Commercial Law and Intellectual Property Law, Faculty of Law, University of Tartu, Estonia; Ph.D student, Faculty of Law, University of Tartu, Estonia. This contribution is part of project ETF9301.

1 Riigikogu 1. detsembri 1992. a otsus seadusloome järjepidevusest (Decision of the Riigikogu (Estonian Parliament) of 1 December 1992 on the consistency of legislative drafting, RT 1992, 52, 651 (in Estonian).

2 I. Kull, 'Reform of Contract Law in Estonia: Influences of Harmonisation of European Private Law' (2008) 14 *Juridica International* 122.

3 A section of Part I of the Principles of European Contract Law (PECL) was published in 1995, which was revised in 2000 when Part I and Part II were published, and Part III was published in 2003. UNIDROIT Principles of International Commercial Contracts (UNIDROIT

Civil Code[4] and the final stage of the Law of Obligations reform in Germany.[5] Due to the length of the Soviet occupation and the substantial differences between the planned and market-based economy, the legal tradition had discontinued and there was a distinct lack of contentious social debate about what should be the fundamental principles of the new legal system. In addition, society was ready and willing to accept concepts and principles which originated from the 'West'.[6]

It was clear to the legal scholars in Estonia that the goal could not be the creation of an original private law for Estonia. This would have been rather unreasonable and impractical in today's legal environment of intensive harmonisation and unification.[7] However, there was still a need to choose a legal system and a legal family into which to anchor the Estonian legal system. The Estonian legal community had an historic opportunity to choose from among the Romanistic, Germanic, Nordic and common law 'families'.[8] After lengthy deliberation, the Germanic family of law was chosen as the basis of Estonian private law.

However, this did not mean that German law was simply copied in Estonia, but rather that guidance was taken from the characteristics of the private law of Germany, Switzerland, Austria and other countries belonging to the Germanic family of law.[9] Moreover, for example, the Law of Obligations Act (LOA),[10] which is the largest part of the Civil Code, was also based on the Civil Codes of the Netherlands, Quebec, Louisiana, etc., as well as the Principles of European Private Law (PECL), UNIDROIT Principles, CISG and the relevant private law *acquis communautaire.*[11] Largely the same can be said about

Principles) were first published in 1994 and the United Nations Convention on Contracts for the International Sale of Goods (CISG) had been in operation already for a decade.

4 Burgerlijk Wetboek, which was largely reformed in 1992.

5 Gesetz zur Modernisierung des Schuldrechts, adopted on 26 November 2001 and effective as of 1 January 2002. BGBl. I S. 3138 (in German).

6 For possible arguments related to the acceptance of the foreign law, see B. Markesinis and J. Fedtke, 'The Judge as Comparatist' (2005) 80 *Tulane Law Review* 11.

7 P. Varul, 'Legal Policy Decisions and Choices in the Creation of New Private Law in Estonia' (2000) 5 *Juridica International* 105.

8 It must be noted that legal scholars from Nordic countries were more than willing to help Estonia become a member of the Nordic family of law.

9 Varul, 'Legal Policy Decisions', n. 7 above, at 105.

10 Võlaõigusseadus, adopted on 26 September 2001 and in force as of 1 July 2002, RT I 2001, 81, 487, 4 February 2011, 2 (in Estonian).

11 P. Varul, I. Kull, V. Kõve and M. Käerdi, *Võlaõigusseadus. I, Üldosa (§§ 1–207). Kommenteeritud väljaanne* (Law of Obligations Act I, General Part (ss. 1–207) Commentary) (Juura, Tallinn, 2006), p. 2 (in Estonian).

the General Part of the Civil Code Act (GPCCA),[12] which forms the general part of the Estonian pandectic system of civil law.[13]

It is apparent from the aforesaid that the LOA and also the GPCCA can be regarded as the 'product' of a modern European private law, comprising the best features of European Civil Codes and the latest model rules.[14] The LOA and the newly revised GPCCA have been in force for more than eight years now, but despite the rather short period during which these Acts have served as applicable law for contracts and extra-contractual relations (e.g., tort, unjust enrichment, etc.), there is already a substantial amount of court practice on the LOA and GPCCA, allowing us to have a real-life insight into the functioning of some model rules which form a part of today's European private law. Furthermore, these contemporary pieces of legislation have been in force during a period of rapid socio-economic change in Estonia, which has given an opportunity to test the LOA and GPCCA against some extreme examples of the real-life situations that private law must confront and resolve. In the following two sections, we shall discuss some of the general issues which have arisen recently in the application of the LOA and GPCCA by the Civil Chamber of the Supreme Court of Estonia and which may also have some relevance to the Europeanisation of private law more generally.

[12] Tsiviilseadustiku üldosa seadus, adopted on 27 March 2002 and in force as of 1 July 2002. RT I 2002, 35, 216; 2010, 38, 231 (in Estonian).

[13] Varul, 'Legal Policy Decisions', n. 7 above, at 110.

[14] This view was strongly supported by Schlechtriem who has stated: 'the system of remedies for breach of an obligation in general and breach of contract in particular are not only compatible with the modern solutions to be found in the European Principles, in the UNIDROIT Principles and in the Convention on the International Sale of Goods, but also with modern reform projects such as the draft for a new law of obligations in Germany ... the structure of this concept of remedies of unjust enrichment is not only in line with the basic structures of the European law of unjust enrichment as revealed by comparative law research, but also very progressive and drafted with intimate knowledge of issues and policies ... the concept and structure of the new Estonian law of torts is very modern, well-drafted and adjusted to the European solutions to be expected in the near future ... And if the noble project of a European Civil Code should be successful, Estonian jurists who had to study the new Estonian Law of Obligations Act should have no problems in understanding the coming European law, for their domestic law is fully in conformity with the tendencies and basic structures of the European law to come or having arrived already in the form of Directives of the EC.' See P. Schlechtriem, 'The New Law of Obligations in Estonia and the Developments Towards Unification and Harmonisation of Law in Europe' (2001) 6 *Juridica International* 16.

## Conflict of principles and specific rules: a problematic legacy of Pandectist School or a ground for wider concerns?

Even though Estonia is a civil law country and belongs to the Germanic legal family, it is a common trend among practitioners, legal scholars and lower rank courts to rely on the judgments of the Supreme Court of Estonia in similar cases and refer to them as binding when interpreting the applicable law. Thus, the impact of the 'law of precedents' is not an unfamiliar notion to Estonian lawyers. By way of illustration, the Supreme Court established in three judgments[15] a rule in respect of applying the former wording of article 143 of the LOA on contracts of consumer surety. Yet even though article 143 of the LOA has now been changed,[16] the rule established by the Supreme Court is based on its previous wording, a precedent which is of great relevance to domestic law. We believe that the Estonian experience, set out below, can contribute to and inform the ongoing process of the Europeanisation of private law.

Article 143 in its first section provided a definition of a contract of consumer surety under which a consumer surety contract is a contract in which the surety is a consumer. The full meaning of a consumer surety is set out in the second section of article 143, which states that a contract of consumer surety is void if the maximum amount of money covered by the liability of the surety is not agreed upon. The aim of such a rule was to limit the liability of the consumer and to focus the consumer's attention on the sum s/he can be held liable for.[17] The former wording of the first section of article 143 was a legal transplant from article 7:857 of the Dutch Civil Code and the second section of Article 143 is a legal transplant from article 7:858 of the Dutch Civil Code, as well as article 493(1) of the Swiss Civil Code.[18] Based on the former wording of the first

[15] See the Supreme Court decisions of 23 March 2006 in Civil Case No. 3-2-1-8-06, of 5 November 2008 in Civil Case No. 3-2-1-89-08 and of 8 December 2009 in Civil Case No. 3-2-1-126-09.

[16] The new wording of the first section of art. 143 of the LOA provides that the rules regarding the contract of consumer surety are applicable if the surety is a natural person. The amendment of the law entered into force as of 5 April 2011 and it was initiated due to the reasons described above.

[17] Varul, Kull, Kõve and Käerdi, *Võlaõigusseadus. I, Üldosa*, n. 11 above, at p. 499, s. 143, commentary 3.

[18] *Ibid.* 499, s. 143, commentary 2. Under art. 493(1) of the Swiss Civil Code (Obligationenrecht) the liability must be limited in every instance and also the surety guarantee must meet certain form requirements if the amount of the guarantee is higher than 2000 Swiss francs. See text of the Swiss Civil Code, available at www.admin.ch/ch/d/sr/2/220.de.pdf (in German).

section of the article 143 of the LOA, the Supreme Court established that article 143 of the LOA must be interpreted in such a way that a contract of consumer surety is not concluded and a consumer guarantee effected where the surety guarantee is given for the benefit of a company in which the surety has a professional or economic interest by holding all or the majority of the shareholding in the company.

The period between 2002 and 2008 was a time of rapid economic growth in Estonia, which was mostly fuelled by foreign capital channelled into the economy through the banks and other financial institutions. Typical devices used by the banks to secure their interests in the repayment of loans were mortgages, but guarantees were often additionally demanded from the shareholders of the company, who usually also held the positions on the management board of the company. In many cases, the amounts which they secured by the guarantee were ten or even more times higher than the share capital paid into the limited liability company and often there was no maximum limit. Due to the surety guarantee given by the shareholders, the shareholders of the limited liability companies were liable to the creditors of the companies to a much higher extent than actually one would have expected from the fact they were using limited liability companies in order to conduct their business. The solution adopted by the Supreme Court met with a negative reaction among legal practitioners, scholars and the wider public.

One of the main arguments the attorneys relied upon while defending such shareholders in the courts was reference to article 143, claiming that the surety guarantee they had given was void due to the fact that the maximum amount of money covered by the liability of the surety had not been agreed upon. Prior to the previously referred to rulings of the Supreme Court, this seemed a reasonable argument, mainly due to the fact that otherwise the concept of the limited liability company would have been violated.[19] After the decisions of the Supreme Court, such an argument was no longer compelling.

One may argue that giving a surety guarantee is an expression of a free act of will and is consistent with the private autonomy which is the fundamental principle of private law in Europe. However, the practical experience of many such persons who became sureties was that they actually did not acknowledge the liabilities they were incurring by signing a surety contract and sometimes they did not even have a choice:

[19] This argument has been used at least once by the lower rank court, see the Supreme Court decision of 5 November 2008 in Civil Case No. 3-2-1-89-08.

signing a surety contract was one of the preconditions for granting the loan and in many cases receiving financing from the bank was the only way to keep the business going. Therefore, the interpretation of the former wording of article 143 of the LOA by the Supreme Court may have seemed quite unjust and not in line with the principle of shareholders' limited liability.

It appears from the merits of the judgments[20] that the Supreme Court made its decision mainly based on the definition of the consumer, which is provided in article 34 of the LOA. In legal literature, the definition of the consumer, as set out in the LOA, is solely based on the *acquis communautaire*.[21] Taking into account the well-established notion of the consumer in the consumer *acquis*, it is also clear that the Court did not have any other choice than to interpret article 143 as it did. One could say that the Supreme Court of Estonia followed the best traditions of the Pandectist School, to whom the law became merely a 'technical' process, a sort of mathematics obeying only the 'logical necessity' of abstract concepts and having nothing to do with practical reason, with social value judgements, or with ethical, religious, economic or policy considerations.[22] As mentioned above, Estonian law has its roots in the Germanic legal family, thus the activities of the Supreme Court were completely in line with the applicable dogmatic approach. This is despite the fact that the solution may violate the principle of limited liability of a shareholder in a limited liability company and is also contrary to the solution that the majority of the public would have considered just.[23]

In addition to being an interesting example of applying the law, which was the result of using the 'tools' of Swiss, Dutch and EU legislation in the Germanic legal family, the Supreme Court's reasoning described

[20] See n. 15 above.

[21] Varul, Kull, Kõve and Käerdi, *Võlaõigusseadus. I, Üldosa*, n. 11 above, at p. 122, s. 34, commentary 2.

[22] K. Zweigert and H. Kötz, *An Introduction to Comparative Law* (3rd edn, Clarendon Press, Oxford, 1998), p. 140.

[23] We admit that one should not forget the rule stated in art. 7:857 of the Dutch Civil Code, which states that the provisions of the section covering surety guarantees given by a natural person apply only to guarantees entered into by a natural person acting neither in the conduct of a profession or business, nor for the benefit of the normal exploitation of the business of a company limited by shares or a private company with limited liability of which he is a director and in which, alone or with his co-directors, he holds a majority of the shares. See H. Warendor *et al.* (transl.), *The Civil Code of the Netherlands* (Kluwer Law International, Alphen aan den Rijn, 2009), p. 898.

above may also lead to conclusions which have relevance to the further Europeanisation of private law.

First, it can be seen that rules of different origin and background, designed separately and embodying different purposes, may interact with each other and other norms in specific socio-economic circumstances and deliver results that do not provide the moral justification one could expect from the law. Thus, a combination of legal transplants requires careful deliberation and design in order to build a coherent legal system. We do not doubt that such deliberation occurs every time, for example, when new rules are designed by the European Union and when rules deriving from the private law *acquis* are implemented into the Members States' legal systems. We are highlighting that even if there is sector-specific rule-making at the EU level,[24] it is very useful to have a set of rules which is not based on the national legislation but which carries in itself something that can be called a 'common heritage' of European private law. Such rules and the discussion initiated by them[25] can be of great help in drafting legal rules or of assistance to the judiciary when making decisions. Furthermore, these rules could contribute to 'more just' solutions in the future and help to avoid results such as we have described. The last holds true especially with respect to those smaller countries which have rejoined the European legal culture recently, and thus have limited resources to be found in their own legal cultures to rely on. There is no evidence that the solution described above was intended by the legislator when drafting the initial wording of article 143 of the LOA – it was rather a result of the evolution of the law.

The second conclusion is that the different levels of economic and social development of countries within the European Union mean that sometimes a different approach is necessary. The features of the ultra-liberal Estonian economy and the relatively unrestricted application of the concept of freedom of contract in Estonia are not characteristics that describe the older EU Member States, which have been operating a market economy since the Second World War. Therefore, social behaviour in different countries under the same rules can vary to a great extent. In addition, even if the economic differences disappear, the cultural

[24] O. Lando, 'Have the PECL been a Success or a Failure?' (2009) 17(3) *ERPL* 370.

[25] There is already a vast literature available on the topic which we can refer to as European private law, see further N. Jansen and R. Zimmermann, 'A European Civil Code in All But Name: Discussing the Nature and Purposes of the Draft Common Frame of Reference' (2010) 69(1) *Cambridge LJ* 107.

differences still largely remain. This leads us to the possible conclusion that a uniform approach towards the applicable law in Europe may not be the future for European private law, or at least not in the near future.[26]

## Effect of the introduction of casuistic rules in the *acquis*

Another case deserving special attention is the example of the 'SMS loans'. During 2005, the first financial providers of 'SMS loans' services entered the credit market in Estonia. The concept of the product was as follows: the consumer credit contract was concluded and a small sum of credit (always below the threshold of €200) was withdrawn by the client by sending an SMS to the credit provider stating the name, personal identification code and also the bank account number to which the credit was to be transferred.[27] The problem with such credit products was, on the one hand, their popularity and, on the other hand, the high interest rates of such loans (the average annual interest was approximately 400 per cent). This led to the situation where many persons who had taken out 'SMS loans' were unable to fulfil their obligations and due to the high interest rate the obligation of the borrowers very often became quite burdensome. The tendency was that these people took additional 'SMS loans' in order to pay back their orginal debts and this was mainly due to the fact that the 'SMS loans' were easily available and people did not really acknowledge the risks which such loans entailed.

According to the established practice of the Supreme Court, the mere fact that a loan had a high interest rate was not sufficient grounds to regard the transaction as void.[28] Under the rule established by the Supreme Court, a high interest rate alone could not provide grounds to regard the transaction as contrary to good morals and thus void.[29] In addition, the Supreme Court had repeatedly stated that the court does

[26] The same view is shared by Lando: see Lando, 'Have the PECL been a Success', n. 24 above, at 375.

[27] It must be mentioned that as the amounts of loans which were given under such loan agreements were always below the threshold above which regulation of consumer credit contracts would have been applied to the contract, conclusion of contracts in the above-described manner was completely lawful. In addition, the system was later improved as the problem of taking SMS loans was becoming more apparent: the persons were obliged to conclude a framework agreement with the credit provider before the loan amount could be withdrawn, in order to allow for a proper identification of the person taking the loan.

[28] See the decisions of the Supreme Court of 24 April 2006 in Civil Case No. 3-2-1-21-06 and of 29 January 2007 in Civil Case No. 3-2-1-137-06.

[29] See decision of the Supreme Court of 29 January 2007 in Civil Case No. 3-2-1-137-06.

not have the authority to intervene in the free economic activities of the parties in the absence of a legal basis provided in law allowing assessment of whether the transaction is void or not.[30]

The roots of the problem lay in two articles of the GPCCA: namely, articles 97 and 86. Article 97 provided that the transaction can be cancelled if it was concluded under very unfavourable conditions to one party and the other party abused the other's extraordinary needs, inexperience, dependency or other similar circumstances. Article 86 provided that the contract as such is void if it is against good morals or public order. The Supreme Court stated many times in its rulings that, in the cases referred to above, the claimant should have invoked article 97 instead of article 86 in order to enable the court to invalidate the agreement under which the excessive interest rates were imposed.[31] However, the claimant was in most cases unable to do this because s/he could not sufficiently prove that abuse of his/her extraordinary needs, inexperience, dependency or other similar circumstances had taken place.[32]

As there was evident need for a solution, the legislator stepped in. Article 97 was annulled and article 86 was amended so that the article, which previously consisted of one section and one line, was supplemented by three long sections. The main purpose of the amendment was to make it easier for the borrowers to render a transaction void due to violation of good morals where, *inter alia*, the annual percentage rate imposed on a consumer exceeds, at the time of grant of the credit, the average annual percentage rate of consumer loans granted to private persons by a factor of more than three. The rule which had been adopted in some other countries was set out in court practice and written into the law in Estonia. Moreover, this was done in a very casuistic manner, which cannot be regarded as in harmony with the traditions of the Germanic legal family where rules, especially if these are stated in the general part of the Civil Code, must be as abstract as possible, in order to be applicable in every field of private law and in every possible situation of life today, tomorrow and in the future.

[30] The decisions of the Supreme Court of 22 October 2002 in Civil Case No. 3–2–1–108–02 and of 13 February 2008 in Civil Case No. 3–2–1–140–07.

[31] See decisions of the Supreme Court of 31 March 2004 in Civil Case No. 3–2–1–29–04 and of 29 January 2007 in Civil Case No. 3–2–1–137–06.

[32] *Tsiviilseadustiku üldosa seaduse ja võlaõigusseaduse muutmise seaduse seletuskiri. Eelnõu nr 365 SE* (Explanatory Memorandum to the Draft Act changing the General Part of the Civil Code Act and the Law of Obligations Act, Draft No. 365 SE), p. 2, available at www.riigikogu.ee/?page=en_vaade&op=ems&eid=420369&u=20101124234538 (in Estonian).

The amendment of the GPCCA was initiated by the Estonian Ministry of Justice and it is of course very difficult to determine, setting aside the political reasons, what exactly was the decisive pressure which caused the Ministry of Justice to draft the amendment of article 86 in the terms in which it was finally introduced in to the GPCCA. However, we would offer the following remarks in respect of this amendment.

As the issue described above is related to consumers, one must turn to the consumer *acquis* and the relevant types of legislation. Even without carrying out a profound analysis, it is clear that the casuistic style of drafting the rules provided in the Regulations and Directives is a distinctive feature of the consumer *acquis*. This is illustrated by one of the latest examples, namely, Directive 2008/48/EC and its article 5, which lists altogether nineteen different categories of information which the creditor has to provide to the consumer during the precontractual negotiations.[33] This style of legislation puts one in mind of the Das allgemeine Landrecht der preussischen Staate. We agree that in order to secure the uniform implementation of the consumer *acquis* in all twenty-seven EU Member States, the style is appropriate and must be taken as inevitable. However, one must be careful to ensure that such style does not become a part of everyday law-making, especially with regard to changes that affect the general private law rules. Despite the casuistic nature of the consumer *acquis*, there are still specific instances where general abstract rules, based on which the court can elaborate more specific rules, provide the best solution. This has apparently been forgotten by the Estonian legislator and we predict that article 86 of the GPCCA will quite soon lose its importance since it is oriented to solve a specific problem, which may disappear with the passage of time.

It is appropriate to refer to some positive examples of abstract rule-making in the field of European private law. For example, the Draft Common Frame of Reference (DCFR) is also influenced by abstract general rules, which reflect the general underlying principles of the DCFR. The authors of the DCFR have pointed out that it is based on four principles: freedom, security, justice and efficiency.[34] These

[33] Directive 2008/48/EC of 23 April 2008 on credit agreements for consumers and repealing Council Directive 87/102/EEC [2008] OJ L133 66.

[34] C. von Bar, H. Beale, E. Clive and H. Schulte-Nölke, 'The Underlying Principles of Freedom, Security, Justice and Efficiency' in C. von Bar *et al.* (eds.), *Principles, Definitions and Model Rules of European Private Law: Draft Common Frame of Reference* (DCFR) (Outline Edition) (Sellier, München, 2009), p. 60.

principles are embodied in general and abstract rules, for example, the principle of freedom of contract is stated, *inter alia*, in articles I 1:102(1), II 4:101 and IX 5:101 of the DCFR and none of these rules are casuistic in nature. In addition, the DCFR in article II 1:101(2) provides a concept of juridical acts, which is the best embodiment of the general rules and included, *inter alia*, due to the need for systematic generalisation.[35] Regard must also be had to the fact that the DCFR additionally contains rules which are in their nature more casuistic, but these are mainly connected with business-to-consumer relationships,[36] and it must be taken into account that neither a critical review of the consumer *acquis* nor a profound examination of its ramifications appear to have been carried out in the process of drafting the DCFR.[37] This is mind, we believe that there is strong basis to suggest that the amendment made to article 86 of the GPCCA by the Estonian legislator was a deviation from the mainstream endeavours of the European private law.

## Concluding remarks

The challenges that European private law faces are quite similar to the challenges facing the European Union: to create unity, while at the same time preserving the differences of the elements it comprises. There are many obstacles to a unified European private law and among them is the fact that many lawyers in Europe claim that their national law is part of the nation's cultural heritage.[38] However, much has been achieved already, especially in the field of contract law. In spite of 200 years of 'nationalisation', contract law is still more international in substance and character than any of the other traditional core areas of private law.[39] Good examples of these achievements, not solely in the field of contract law, are the Estonian LOA and GPCCA, which encapsulate the most recent ideas on what we can now call European private law.

Countries such as Estonia, which had an obligation to restore and thus also a possibility to renew their legal systems at the end of the twentieth

[35] A. Vaquer, 'Farewell to Windscheid? Legal Concepts Present and Absent from the Draft Common Frame of Reference (DCFR)' (2009) 17(4) *European Review of Private Law* 493.

[36] For example, see art. II 3:101(1) and compare it with art. II 3:102(2).

[37] H. Eidenmüller *et al.*, 'The Common Frame of Reference for European Private Law: Policy Choices and Codification Problems' (2008) 28(4) *Oxford Journal of Legal Studies* 696.

[38] Lando, 'Have the PECL been a Success', n. 24 above, at 373.

[39] R. Zimmermann, 'The Present State of European Private Law' (2009) 57(2) *American Journal of Comparative Law* 481.

century, and which took advantage of this opportunity, can be used as a testing ground for modern European private law. Even though the socio-economic situation of such countries is different from the countries in 'Old Europe', this should not be seen as something negative. On the contrary, in these 'new' countries the basic concepts are sometimes put to the test in extreme circumstances, as we showed above, and if the concepts then provide positive results they should be considered as legally approved. We admit that the examples described above do not reflect the principal problems of current European private law, but are rather implications of the side-effects of Europeanisation. However, these side-effects could well serve the purpose of determining the further development of European private law.

11

# The impact of Europe on Irish contract law

CLIONA KELLY

The relatively narrow scope of European Directives dealing with contract law means that Europe has had an impact on only a small portion of the existing *corpus* of Irish contract law; however, in this chapter it is argued that even in areas where mandatory European measures exist, failures in transposition and enforcement, as well as a lack of engagement by both the government and the courts, have reduced the impact of those measures in the Irish context. The main influence on Irish contract law continues to be the common law, particularly the English common law, and even when applying European instruments the inclination is to seek interpretative guidance from the United Kingdom. This trend of seeking solutions in the common law is also evidenced in the Irish approach to law reform; although more recently law reform proposals have given a salutary nod in the direction of the Common Frame of Reference and the civil law tradition, considerably more attention is given to reforms and developments in common law jurisdictions. Europe is mostly taken into account in the form of an acknowledgement that reforms may have to take European measures 'into account' or be delayed pending European developments such as the proposed Consumer Rights Directive.

Although certain improvements in the approach to the transposition and enforcement of European Directives have been witnessed in recent years, in particular improvements in the consolidation of existing legislation, an increased level of engagement with Directives which aim at maximum harmonisation and more creative use of enforcement techniques, Ireland still has a long way to go before it can be said to have assimilated European contract law. It is submitted that the major

Cardiff Law School. The author would like to thank Caterina Gardiner for her helpful comments on an earlier draft, and Robert Clark and Ray Bryne at the Irish Law Reform Commission for their helpful response to various queries.

objection to this 'segregation'[1] of European and domestic law is that it results in an incoherent regulatory regime which is reactive, minimalist and inconsistent with the Irish Government's acknowledgement that its role is to 'to provide a clear, consistent and predictable legal framework, to promote a pro-competitive environment in which electronic commerce can flourish, and to ensure adequate protection of public interest objectives such as ... prevention of fraud, consumer protection and public safety'.[2] However, if the European agenda moves towards a model based on regulatory competition, diversity and enhanced cooperation and dialogue, as advocated for example by Miller,[3] Ireland could find itself on familiar territory. Ireland has a strong tradition of comparative jurisprudence and scholarship, and inspiration is frequently drawn from outside its borders. Admittedly, the first port of call tends to be other common law jurisdictions, including non-European jurisdictions such as Canada, Australia and New Zealand, but it is submitted that this global outlook should be viewed as a strength rather than a weakness, and it may be an advantage to civil law jurisdictions seeking to examine the common law approach to look not only to solutions adopted in the United Kingdom but also to those adopted in Ireland.

## Is there an 'Irish' contract law? External influences on Irish contract law

Foreign laws have been imposed for centuries in Ireland, with it once having been described as the 'first great adventure of the common law'.[4] The relationship between the Irish and English legal systems has been turbulent since the initial reception of English laws into Ireland in the late twelfth and early thirteenth century,[5] but it cannot be denied

1 S. Whittacker 'A Framework of Principle for European Contract Law?' (2009) *Law Quarterly Review* 616, 625.

2 Government Action Plan, *New Connections, A Strategy to Realise the Potential of the Information Society* (2002), para. 2.1, quoting a Communiqué issued by the United States and Ireland on Electronic Commerce, 4 September 1998, available at www.taoiseach.gov.ie.

3 See L. Miller, *The Emergence of EU Contract Law: Exploring Europeanization* (Oxford University Press, 2011).

4 W.J. Johnston, 'The First Great Adventure of the Common Law' (1920) 36 *Law Quarterly Review* 9.

5 In 1172 Hugh de Lacy was appointed first Justiciar of Ireland and in 1204 King John directed Irish courts to apply the common law. For a good summary of the development of the Irish legal system, see R. Byrne and P. McCutcheon, with C. Bruton and G. Coffey,

that the English common law has been, and continues to be, a significant influence on Irish law generally[6] and Irish contract law in particular. On Independence, transitional provisions meant that more than 1,200 pre-Independence Acts which were in force in Ireland on 6 December 1922 were to remain in force in Ireland unless they were repealed by the Irish Parliament (Oireachtas) or declared unconstitutional.[7] As a result, key contract and commercial law statutes emanating from the Westminster Parliament in the late nineteenth or early twentieth century, including the Sale of Goods Act 1893, the Infants Relief Act 1874, the Apportionment Act 1870, the Partnership Act 1890, the Bills of Exchange Act 1882 and the Marine Insurance Act 1906 all still apply in Ireland, although some have been amended by subsequent legislation. Even since 1922, certain (although by no means all) legislative changes introduced in the UK have motivated similar legislative changes in Ireland, and some Irish legislation has been modelled upon earlier UK legislation.[8] In addition, English judicial decisions prior to 1922 are regarded as being of significant precedent value in Ireland, although the Irish courts are not bound to follow them.[9] Although English decisions post-1922 are of persuasive value in the same way as decisions from other common

*Byrne and McCutcheon on the Irish Legal System* (5th edn, Bloomsbury Professional, Dublin, 2009), pp. 27–63.

6 The absence of a written Constitution in the United Kingdom means that sometimes, particularly in cases involving constitutional rights or the separation of powers, 'more appropriate guidance' is found 'in the decisions of courts in other countries based upon a similar constitutional framework': *Irish Shell Ltd* v. *Elm Motors Ltd* [1984] IR 200, 227 per McCarthy J.

7 See art. 73 of the 1922 Constitution of the Irish Free State (Saorstát Eireann) and art. 50(1) Bunreacht na hÉireann 1937. The Statute Law Revision (pre-1922) Act 2005, the Statute Law Revision Act 2007 and the Statute Law Revision Act 2009 have resulted in the repeal of a significant number of public and private pre-Independence statutes, including some dating back as far as the thirteenth century, although more than 100 pre-Independence Acts (a full list of which is available in Sch. 1 to the 2007 Act) remain in force.

8 For example, the Sale and Goods and Supply of Services Act 1980 was enacted soon after the UK Sale of Goods Act 1979, and Part V of the Sale of Goods and Supply of Services Act 1980 is based on the UK Misrepresentation Act 1967.

9 There has, however, been some disagreement regarding how the Irish courts should treat pre-1922 decisions: compare the approach of McCarthy J in *Irish Shell Ltd* v. *Elm Motors Ltd* [1984] IR 200 and Gavan Duffy J in *Exham* v. *Beamish* [1939] IR 336 (both of whom stressed the independence of Irish courts from the pre-1922 jurisprudence) with the approach of Costello J in *Tromso Sparebank* v. *Beirne (No. 2)* [1989] ILRM 257 and *MMcC v. JMcC* [1994] 1 IR 293 (Irish courts should be reluctant to refuse to follow a firmly established principle in English law pre-1922).

law jurisdictions,[10] the links and similarities between the two legal systems, as well as factors such as the familiarity of the format and language of decisions, the accessibility of the decisions, and physical proximity have meant that Irish courts will make reference to decisions of the English courts much more frequently than to other jurisdictions such as Australia, Canada and New Zealand.[11]

Despite this, Irish contract law differs in a number of important respects from contract law in England and Wales. For example, while the English Court of Appeal has rejected any equitable jurisdiction to set aside a contract where it was induced by a common fundamental mistake,[12] the Irish courts have continued to apply equitable principles, unhindered by the difficulties with precedent that faced the English Court of Appeal.[13] The leading Irish Supreme Court decision on the question of whether an exclusion clause can exclude a fundamental breach[14] pre-dates the House of Lords' decision in *Photo Production*[15] and follows the 'rule of law' approach which the House of Lords rejected in that case. Judges in the Irish High Court have since cited the decision in *Photo Production* with approval,[16] but a Supreme Court decision would be necessary to keep the Irish law in line with English (or Australian[17] or Canadian[18]) law. There is a long line of distinctly Irish jurisprudence dealing with both the propriety of transactions where

[10] The lack of a system of binding precedent means that civil law cases will rarely, if ever, be relied upon by the Irish courts: see Byrne and McCutcheon, *Byrne and McCutcheon on the Irish Legal System*, n. 5 above, at p. 440.

[11] A study carried out in 1983 by Profs. Boyle and Greer showed that between 1921 and 1975, the Irish courts referred to English or Scottish cases in 50 per cent of reported cases. A study of Irish reported decisions by Byrne and McCutcheon in 1995 showed that this figure had reduced to 33 per cent, and a study in 2005 showed a further reduction to 28.9 per cent. This change appears to have been mostly attributable to an increase in references to 'home grown' Irish cases, although there is also an increase in references to the Court of the European Union (CJEU), as well as cases from the United States, Australia, Canada and New Zealand. See Byrne and McCutcheon, *Byrne and McCutcheon on the Irish Legal System*, n. 5 above, at pp. 437–9.

[12] *Great Peace Shipping Ltd* v. *Tsavliris (International) Ltd* [2002] 4 All ER 689.

[13] See *Intrum Justitia BV* v. *Legal and Trade Financial Services* [2005] IEHC 190; *O'Neill v Ryan* [1991] ILRM 672. See generally R. Clark, *Contract Law in Ireland* (6th edn, Thomson Round Hall, Dublin, 2008), pp. 289–94.

[14] *Clayton Love* v. *B&I Transport* (1970) 104 ILTR 157.

[15] *Photo Production Ltd* v. *Securicor Transport Ltd* [1980] 2 WLR 283.

[16] See e.g., *Western Meats Ltd* v. *National Ice and Cold Storage Co.* [1982] ILRM 101.

[17] *Nissho Iwai Australia* v. *Malaysian International Shipping* (1989) 86 ALR 375.

[18] *Beaufort Realities (1964) Inc.* v. *Belcourt Construction (Ottowa) Ltd* (1980) 116 DLR (3d) 193; *Hunter Engineer Co.* v. *Syncrude Canada Ltd* (1989) 57 DLR (4th) 321.

one party is likely to have unduly influenced the other[19] and the equitable jurisdiction to set aside unconscionable or improvident bargains.[20] With regard to the duty on banks to ensure that guarantors are not subject to undue influence, the decision in *Barclay's Bank* v. *O'Brien*[21] has been cited with approval by the Irish Supreme Court,[22] but there has been no Irish equivalent to the decision in *Etridge*[23] and it has been suggested that the Irish courts are likely to follow the broader equitable approach to the issue seen in Canada and Australia.[24] In addition, common law doctrines have been affected by the Irish Constitution, particularly in the area of employment law where, for example, terms have been implied into employment contracts so that they reflect constitutional rights such as the right to disassociation[25] or the right to fair procedures.[26] The constitutional protection of the institution of marriage has also had an effect on cohabitation agreements[27] and rendered uncertain the validity of pre-nuptial agreements in Ireland.[28] There are also several differences in the legislative framework governing contract law, with the legislature in the United Kingdom being considerably more active than the Irish Parliament. For example, Ireland does not have any legislation

[19] See e.g., *White* v. *Meade* (1840) 2 Ir Eq R 420; *Croker* v. *Croker* (1870) 4 ILTR 181; *McMackin* v. *Hibernian Bank* [1905] 1 IR 296; *Gregg* v. *Kidd* [1956] IR 183; *Carroll* v. *Carroll* [2000] 1 ILRM 210.

[20] See *Grealish* v. *Murphy* [1946] IR 35; *Carroll* v. *Caroll* [2000] 1 ILRM 210.

[21] [1993] 4 All ER 417.

[22] *Bank of Nova Scotia* v. *Hogan* [1997] 1 ILRM 407, although on the facts of the case there was no undue influence.

[23] *Royal Bank of Scotland plc.* v. *Etridge (No. 2)* [2001] 3 WLR 1021.

[24] R. Clark, *Contract Law in Ireland* (6th edn, Thomson Round Hall, Dublin, 2008), p. 385.

[25] *Meskill* v. *CIÉ* [1973] IR 121.

[26] *Glover* v. *BLN* [1973] IR 388; *Garvey* v. *Ireland* (1979) 113 ILTR 61; *Gunn* v. *Bord an Choláiste Náisiúnta Ealaíne is Deartha* [1990] 2 IR 168.

[27] *Ennis* v. *Butterly* [1997] 1 ILRM 28. This is similar to the English case of *Windeler* v. *Whitehall* [1990] 2 FLR 505. The Law Reform Commission has, however, suggested that *Ennis* v. *Butterly* does not render all aspects of cohabitation agreements invalid, and in fact has recommended that cohabitation agreements should be more commonly used: *Rights and Duties of Cohabitants* (Report LRC 82–2006), ch. 3. The Commission's Report resulted in the 'cohabitation' section (i.e., Part 15) of the Civil Partnership and Certain Rights and Obligations of Cohabitants Act 2010.

[28] In 2006, the Government Study Group on Pre-nuptial Agreements was of the opinion that prenuptial agreements were enforceable under the current law, but in the absence of any court decision to this effect the Group recommended an amendment to the Family Law (Divorce) Act 1996 to expressly provide for the recognition of prenuptial agreements: *Report of the Study Group on Pre-nuptial Agreements* (April 2007), p. 71. Contrast the position of the UK Supreme Court in *Radmacher (former Granatino)* v. *Granatino* [2010] UKSC 42.

specifically dealing with the fairness of exemption clauses;[29] nor has there been legislation to deal with the effects of frustration of contract[30] or to reform the rule of privity of contract.[31] In the case of the sale of goods, while Ireland inherited the Sale of Goods Act 1893 it has not been amended to the same extent as in the United Kingdom and differences exist, for example in relation to the rules on the passing of property in quasi-specific goods,[32] the retention of the 'market overt' rule[33] and the implied condition that goods be of 'satisfactory' (as opposed to 'merchantable') quality.[34] Finally, while Irish courts have traditionally turned to the English courts for inspiration when looking for solutions to legal problems, increased access to decisions from other common law jurisdictions through online databases such as that hosted by the World Legal Information institute[35] has opened up the variety of influences on Irish contract law.

These differences are highlighted not to downplay the impact of English law on Irish law, but rather to serve as a reminder that there is not simply one 'common' contract law which applies uniformly across the two islands – Irish contract law may have been significantly influenced by English contract law, but it remains a distinct entity. The distinction drawn between Irish and English common law in the

[29] There are certain specific statutory restrictions on exemption clauses; for example, ss.55 and 40 of the Sale of Goods and Supply of Services Act 1980 restrict contract terms which attempt to waive or vary the rights of the buyer under ss. 12, 13, 14 or 15 of the Sale of Goods Act 1893 (as amended) and under s. 39 of the Sale of Goods and Supply of Services Act 1980. Its scope is thus considerably more limited than that of the UK Unfair Contract Terms Act 1977.

[30] See the Law Reform (Frustrated Contracts) Act 1943 and the Frustrated Contracts Act (Northern Ireland) 1947.

[31] See the Contracts (Rights of Third Parties) Act 1999 which reformed the law on privity of contract and third party rights in England, Wales and Northern Ireland.

[32] In the United Kingdom, this is now governed by the Sale of Goods (Amendment) Act 1995.

[33] Section 22 of the Sale of Goods Act 1893 allows a *bona fide* purchaser to acquire good title to goods bought in a 'market overt' even if the seller does not have good title. This rule was abolished in England by the Sale of Goods (Amendment) Act 1994.

[34] In Ireland, s.14 of the Sale of Goods Acts 1893–1980 implies a condition that goods must be of 'merchantable' quality, while in the United Kingdom, s.14 of the Sale of Goods Act 1979, as amended by s.1 of the Sale and Supply of Goods Act 1994, implies a condition that goods must be of 'satisfactory' quality and lists aspects of what is meant by satisfactory quality. It is doubtful that in practice there is any real difference between the two provisions, but the retention of the term 'merchantable' in Ireland seems somewhat archaic and particularly unsuitable in a consumer context.

[35] See www.worldlii.org.

notes to the Draft Common Frame of Reference is thus welcome,[36] although arguably increased Irish input in the project would be necessary to ensure that differences between the two jurisdictions continue to be recognised.

## Impact of European Directives on Irish contract law

Given that other common law jurisdictions are of persuasive influence only, while European measures such as Directives and Regulations must be given effect in the domestic sphere, one would be forgiven for thinking that Europe should have a more significant impact on Irish contract law than developments in common law jurisdictions, particularly in recent years; however, the impact of European Directives on Irish contract law has been diluted by a number of factors, in particular the unsatisfactory transposition of Contract and Consumer Law Directives in Ireland and a lack of creativity (at least until recently) in the enforcement methods used to ensure compliance with the regulatory framework. The fragmented and limited nature of European reforms aiming at minimum harmonisation of areas which appear to be of little consequence in Ireland, either because there is already legislation governing the area (e.g., consumer sales) or because the area appears to be of little relevance in the Irish socio-economic context (e.g., commercial agents), contributes to the lack of political impetus to engage with Directives, to discuss the policy options presented by them, to consider alternative enforcement mechanisms, and to transpose the Directive by means of primary legislation after a proper period of public consultation and debate. In contrast, when European measures aim at maximum harmonisation two factors increase substantially the impact of the measures in Ireland: first, the obligation to ensure that Irish laws, including the common law, offer no more protection than that available under EU law means that the Irish government must carry out a full review of the existing law; and secondly, the fear that standards of consumer protection currently available in Ireland will be threatened and reduced by Europe increases the level of public and political engagement with the proposed measure.

[36] See e.g., Note 2 on the 'Effect of stipulation in favour of a third party' which notes the retention of the privity rule in Ireland: C. von Bar and E. Clive, *Prinipcles, Definitions and Model Rules of European Private Law: Draft Common Frame of Refrence* (DCFR) (Oxford University Press, 2010), vol. 1, art. II 9:301.

### *Transposition of Contract and Consumer Directives in Ireland*

European Directives in the area of contract and consumer law have primarily been transposed in Ireland by means of ministerial regulation rather than primary legislation, at least where the Directive aims at minimum harmonisation only and allows Member States to introduce or maintain higher levels of consumer protection.[37] Where this method of transposition is chosen, there is little or no parliamentary debate or oversight[38] and the Government is effectively choosing merely to implement the minimum standards required by the Directive rather than make a policy decision to introduce further consumer protection measures. The major concern is compliance with European obligations rather than any wider consideration as to the particular position of the Irish consumer – 'no more, but certainly no less' appears to be the overriding principle to be applied.[39] Donnelly and White have been rightly critical of this approach to the transposition of Consumer Directives in Ireland:

> This minimal approach seeks to ensure compliance with European law but it does not do justice for the Irish consumer. Indeed, it is arguable that such an approach evidences a lack of commitment to the particular position of the Irish, as opposed to the European, consumer. European legislation is a result of negotiation and comprise between the Commission, Member States and Parliament. With membership of the Community now standing at 25, it is not realistic to expect that the particular needs of the Irish consumer can be satisfied by a piece of European legislation alone. Irish consumers exist in a particular socio-economic environment. For instance ... the Irish consumer society was late to develop and there is not a strong consumer lobby established in Ireland. These and other factors can only be addressed by Irish policy makers and

[37] Some Directives which allow for minimum harmonisation have been implemented by means of legislation. For example, Council Directive 90/314/EEC of 13 June 1990 on package travel, package holidays and package tours was implemented by the Package Holidays and Travel Trade Act 1995.

[38] Section 4(1)(b) of the European Communities Act 1972, inserted by s.1 of the European Communities (Amendment) Act 1973, gives the Oireachtas the right to make a resolution annulling any such regulation within a year of its creation but this does not appear to have ever been utilised in this context.

[39] *R* v. *Special Adjudicator, ex parte Ullah* [2004] UKHL 26, para. 20, per Lord Bingham. In this context Lord Bingham was commenting on the duty of national courts to keep pace with the jurisprudence of the European Court of Human Rights. See now *Re P* [2008] UKHL 38 and for the Irish application of this principle see *McD* v. *L* [2009] IESC 81.

> legislators considering, beyond the European standard, what is best for the Irish consumer and how can this be achieved in an Irish context.[40]

Objections to the transposition of Directives are not limited to the reluctance to go beyond what is strictly required by the Directive; considerable difficulties are encountered even when Irish legislation already provides extra protection to consumers. When existing legislation overlaps with or deals with the same issues as the Directive, the trend has been to simply transpose the Directive in a statutory instrument and to allow both the primary legislation and the statutory instrument to co-exist without any attempt at consolidation. A good example of this is the Consumer Sales Directive,[41] which was given effect in Ireland by the European Communities (Certain Aspects of the Sale of Consumer Goods and Associated Guarantees) Regulations 2003.[42] This Directive overlapped considerably with the Sale of Goods Act 1893, as amended by the Sale of Goods and Supply of Services Act 1980.[43] In theory, consumers are not harmed by this method of transposition: the 2003 Regulations are stated to be 'in addition to, and not in substitution for, any other enactment relating to the sale of goods or the terms of contracts concluded with consumers', including the Sale of Goods Acts 1893–1980.[44] If the Sale of Goods Acts provide for a greater level of protection for a particular consumer, the consumer may opt to rely on it rather than the Regulations, and *vice versa*,[45] although consumers may not take an *à la carte* approach whereby they pick and choose their rights and remedies from the range on offer across the Acts and the Regulations. However, the co-existence of three separate sources of rights and remedies has great potential to cause confusion. This is a particularly unsatisfactory situation when the target beneficiaries of the rights are consumers who most likely will not wish to seek legal advice over

[40] M. Donnelly and F. White, 'Regulation and Consumer Protection: A Study of the Online Market' (2006) 13(1) *Dublin University Law Journal* 27, 29–30.

[41] Directive 99/44/EC of the European Parliament and of the Council of 25 May 1999 on certain aspects of the sale of consumer goods and associated guarantees.

[42] SI No. 11 of 2003.

[43] For a comparison of the Directive and the Sale of Goods Acts 1893–1980, see F. White, 'The EC Directive on Certain Aspects of Sale of Consumer Goods and Associated Guarantees: A Step Forward and Two Steps Back?' (2000) *Commercial Law Practitioner* 3; M. Ní Shuilleabháin, 'Directive 1999/44 on Certain Aspects of the Sale of Consumer Goods and Associated Guarantees: Improving the Rights of the Irish Consumer?' in M.C. Lucey and C. Keville (eds.), *Irish Perspectives on EC Law* (Thomson Round Hall, Dublin, 2003), pp. 173–97.

[44] Regulation 3(1).

[45] Regulation 3(3) and (4).

disputes involving relatively small, though not insignificant, amounts of money. The lack of clarity in the existing legislative framework is likely to hinder consumers' ability to obtain redress in the event of a dispute, whereas a consolidated piece of legislation could have bolstered consumer rights and potentially resulted in a type of Consumer Sales Charter. It is, of course, arguable that even a consolidated version of legislation would pose difficulties of interpretation for consumers, and that an intermediary organisation such as the National Consumer Agency (NCA) would have to provide a 'plain English guide' to consumers' rights in any event. However, the diffusion of consumer rights across several pieces of primary and secondary legislation would seem to have caused confusion even in organisations such as this. For example, an educational quiz on the website of the NCA tells us that consumers have no rights when buying from other consumers (or non-business sellers).[46] While it is true that the 2003 Regulations apply only where the seller is a non-consumer,[47] consumers *do* have rights in this context under the Sale of Goods Acts 1893–1980, or even under basic contract law principles, albeit more limited rights than those available when buying from a non-consumer.[48] It is difficult to see how consumers can be expected to discern their rights, and businesses their obligations, when the statutory body charged with, *inter alia*, the job of encouraging compliance with relevant consumer law statutes[49] can make such a mistake.

In the context of consumer sales, some of the confusion stems from the fact that the principal statute governing sales law is the pre-Independence Sale of Goods Act 1893. Although this was amended in 1980, this was not done to the same extent as in the United Kingdom and there was no

[46] The answer to Q.4 of the 'Clever Consumer' quiz includes the statement '[Y]ou have no rights as a consumer if the product is sold to you by an individual rather than a business'. The 'consumer section' of the website where the quiz is available is www.consumerconnect.ie. The 'business and media' part of the website is available at www.nca.ie.

[47] A 'seller' is defined in reg. 2(1) as 'any natural or legal person who, under a contract, sells consumer goods *in the course of his or her trade, business or profession*' (emphasis added).

[48] For example, although s.14 of the 1893 Act, which implies a condition that goods sold are of merchantable quality, only applies when goods are sold 'in the course of a business', there is no such precondition in the case of s.13, which implies a condition that goods sold by description should match that description and it is clear that s.13 applies even where goods are sold by a non-consumer: *Beale* v. *Taylor* [1967] 3 All ER 253. Similarly, s.13 of the 1980 Act contains an implied condition relating to the safety of motor vehicles which applies 'in every contract for the sale of a motor vehicle' except where the buyer is a motor dealer.

[49] Under s.8 of the Consumer Protection Act 2007.

attempt to consolidate the two Acts or to repeal or amend redundant or irrelevant sections of the 1893 Act. The resulting confusion can be anecdotally referenced by the number of law students who get confused between section 13 of the 1893 Act, as amended by section 10 of the 1980 Act, which deals with sales by description, and section 13 of the 1980 Act, which deals with the safety of motor vehicles. This difficulty was to a certain extent resolved by an administrative Restatement[50] of the Sale of Goods Act 1893 and Part II of the Sale of Goods and Supply of Services Act 1980; however, despite the fact that the Restatement was certified on 27 February 2003, just over a month after the 2003 Regulations were signed by the Minister for Enterprise, Trade and Employment, no attempt was made to include the Regulations in the Restatement, or to delay publication of the Restatement so as to allow for their inclusion. This is somewhat questionable given that the Restatement was part of a government programme of regulatory reforms which recognised the need to make 'legislation more coherent and easily accessible to those who need it' and to help businesses comply with the legal system.[51] One explanation for the omission is that initially Restatements included *textual* amendments only to an Act, and the Regulations did not in fact amend the 1893 Act. Functional responsibility for the preparation of Restatements has now been transferred from the Office of the Attorney General to the Law Reform Commission,[52] and the Commission's approach is to include both textual and non-textual amendments, as well as other relevant material.[53] In 2008 the Irish Law Reform Commission indicated that it would update and reissue this restatement at some point in the future, potentially taking into account the impact of the Consumer Rights Directive and the Report of the Sales Law Review Group.[54] In the interim, a 'pre-certified' version of both Acts, updated to 8 April 2010, is available on the Commission's website[55] and this version makes reference to the non-textual

[50] This was prepared by the Office of the Attorney General and certified by the Attorney General under the Statute Law (Restatement) Act 2002.

[51] Department of the Taoiseach, *Reducing Red Tape: An Action Programme of Regulatory Reform in Ireland* (1999), p. 6. See also the Government White Paper, *Regulating Better, a Government White Paper Setting out Six Principles of Better Regulation* (2004). Both are available at www.betterregulation.ie.

[52] Restatements must still, however, be certified by the Attorney General under the Statute Law (Restatement) Act 2002.

[53] Law Reform Commission, *Report on Statute Law Restatement* (LRC 91–2008), para. 1.19.

[54] *Ibid.* paras. 4.28–4.29.

[55] See www.lawreform.ie.

amendments introduced by both the 2003 Regulations and the European Communities (Unfair Terms in Consumer Contracts) (Amendment) Regulations 2000.[56] However, despite the significant progress made on consolidation and accessibility of legislation by bodies such as the Law Reform Commission, funding for these consolidation and restatement projects was severely restricted almost as soon as it has been made available, a move which has provoked criticism from, amongst others, the OECD.[57] The OECD has also commented on the limits of restatements as a solution to the problems posed by the current method of transposition of European measures – the constant addition of new regulations means that legislative restatements are 'in an endless race against time', a situation which necessitates an *ex ante* solution as well as an *ex post* solution.[58]

Regulatory compliance with European Consumer Directives is further hindered when the transposing regulations copy directly the wording of the Directive, meaning that the ambiguities inherent in the original wording of the Directive are reproduced in the transposing regulations without any attempt at clarification. For example, the Distance Selling Directive[59] contains a number of unclear requirements, including the requirement that the seller provide information relating to 'arrangements' for payment, delivery or performance, or the requirement that the seller provide information concerning the 'existence of the right to withdraw', yet the transposing regulations[60] simply reproduce these requirements without any interpretative assistance or guidance.[61] It has been argued that this lack of clarity has contributed to a lack of compliance with the Directive by traders in Ireland,[62] and it is furthermore inconsistent with the Government's acknowledgement that its role is to 'to provide a clear, consistent and predictable legal framework, to

56 SI No. 307 of 2000.

57 OECD in partnership with the European Commission, *Better Regulation in Europe: Ireland* (2010), pp. 24–5.

58 *Ibid.* 25.

59 Directive 97/7/EC of the European Parliament and of the Council of 20 May 1997 on the protection of consumers in respect of distance contracts.

60 European Communities (Protection of Consumers in respect of Contracts Made by Means of Distance Communication) Regulations 2001, SI No. 207 of 2001.

61 See M. Donnelly and F. White, 'The Distance Selling Directives: A Time for Review' (2005) 56(2) *Northern Ireland Law Quarterly* 200 and M. Donnelly and F. White, 'Regulation and Consumer Protection: A Study of the Online Market' (2006) 13(1) *Dublin University Law Journal* 27.

62 *Ibid.*

promote a pro-competitive environment in which electronic commerce can flourish, and to ensure adequate protection of public interest objectives such as ... prevention of fraud, consumer protection and public safety'.[63]

The lacklustre approach to the transposition of Directives has even resulted in a situation where no decision was made as to which option is to be followed when a Directive mandated that Member States choose between two alternative measures. The European Communities (Commercial Agents) Regulations 1994,[64] which transposed the Commercial Agents Directive,[65] not only failed to outline the rights and obligations of commercial agents and their principals in any detail[66] but also failed even to refer to whether upon termination of the agency agreement commercial agents will be entitled to compensation or to an indemnity under article 17 of the Directive. The Commission decided to open proceedings against Ireland for non-implementation of the Directive[67] and the omission was eventually remedied in the European Communities (Commercial Agents) Regulations 1997,[68] with the Government opting to choose the remedy of compensation under article 17(3) of the Directive.

The decision to choose compensation under article 17 of the Directive in itself raises questions as to the appropriateness of secondary legislation in this context – is this not something that should be decided by the Parliament (Oireachtas) after debate and public consultation,

[63] Government Act Plan, *New Connections, a Strategy to Realise the Potential of the Information Society* (2002), para. 2.1, quoting a communiqué issued by the United States and Ireland on Electronic Commerce, 4 September 1998, available at www.taoiseach.gov.ie.

[64] SI No. 33 of 1994.

[65] Council Directive 86/653/EC on the co-ordination of the laws of Member States relating to self-employed commercial agents. On the interpretation of the Commercial Agents Directive in Ireland, see C. Gardiner, 'The EC (Commercial Agents) Directive: Twenty Years after its Introduction, Divergent Approaches Still Emerge from Irish and U.K. Courts' (2007) *Journal of Business Law* 412.

[66] Regulation 2(3) simply provides that the Directive 'shall, subject to these Regulations, apply to the relations between commercial agents and their principals from 1 January 1994'. This essentially means that to understand the impact of the 1994 Regulations on the relationship between commercial agents and principals, one would have to look up the original Directive, a further inconvenience which can only reduce the chance of regulatory compliance.

[67] In addition, despite being given until 1 January 1994 to implement the Directive (as opposed to 1 January 1990, which applied to all other Member States except the United Kingdom and Italy), Ireland failed to do so until 21 February 1994. Regulation 2(3) provides that the Directive is to apply retroactively to relations between commercial agents and their principals from 1 January 1994.

[68] SI No.31 of 1997.

rather than by executive order? This is not only a matter of regulatory transparency and effectiveness, but also potentially a constitutional imperative. Article 15.2.1° of the Irish Constitution (Bunreacht na hÉireann) provides that the 'sole and exclusive power of making laws for the State' is vested in the Oireachtas and that 'no other legislative authority has power to make laws for the State'. However, this is mitigated by article 15.2.2°, which allows for the creation or recognition of subordinate legislatures. Hence, the Oireachtas can delegate some of its law-making functions to the executive, provided the delegation is within certain constitutional parameters.[69] The European Communities Act 1972 contains an example of such delegation. Section 2 of this Act provides that acts adopted by EU institutions shall become part of domestic law under the conditions laid down in the EU treaties and Section 3(1) states that a Minister of State 'may make regulations' to enable Section 2 'to have full effect'. In *Meagher* v. *Minister for Agriculture*[70] the Supreme Court upheld this regulation-making power as constitutional as it was 'necessitated by the obligations of membership of the European Union'.[71] Finlay CJ, giving the opinion of the Court, stated:

> The Court is satisfied that, having regard to the number of Community laws, acts done and measures adopted which either have to be facilitated in their direct application to the law of the State or have to be implemented by appropriate action into the law of the State, the obligation of membership would necessitate facilitating of these activities, in some instances, at least, and possibly in a great majority of instances, by the making of ministerial regulation rather than legislation of the Oireachtas.[72]

However, in deciding whether to implement a Directive by means of primary legislation or ministerial regulation, a distinction is drawn based on whether any matter of principle or policy is to be decided:

[69] See the test set out by O'Higgins CJ in *Cityview Press* v. *An Chomhairle Oiliúna* [1980] IR 381, 399.

[70] [1994] 1 IR 329

[71] Article 29.4.5° of Bunreacht na hÉireann stated: 'No provision of this Constitution invalidates laws enacted, acts done or measures adopted by the State *which are necessitated by the obligations of membership of the European Union or of the Communities*, or prevents laws enacted, acts done or measures adopted by the European Union or by the Communities or by institutions therefore from having the force of law in the State.' (emphasis added). This is now art. 29.4.6° and is amended to include reference to the entry into force of the Lisbon Treaty.

[72] [1994] 1 IR 329, 352.

> If the directive left to the national authority matters of principle or policy to be determined then the 'choice' of the Minister would require legislation by the Oireachtas. But where there is no case made that principles or policies have to be determined by the national authority, where the situation is that the principles and policies were determined in the directive, then legislation by a delegated form, by regulation, is a valid choice.[73]

It is arguable that the decision to choose compensation under article 17 of the Directive was a policy decision which should have been made by the Oireachtas. A similar criticism has been made in relation to the transposition of the Unfair Contract Terms Directive,[74] which was implemented in Ireland by statutory instrument,[75] with little parliamentary debate,[76] despite the fact that it is arguable that several policy decisions had to be made for this implementation. This is even more surprising given that the transposition of this Directive was delayed pending the decision in *Meagher*.[77] To date, however, no argument as to the constitutional validity of the transposition of a Consumer or Contract Directive by means of a statutory instrument appears to have been put before the courts. This is arguably because these Directives have not resulted in significant disputes or criminal prosecutions (unlike *Meagher*, which involved a criminal prosecution), and also a reflection of the principle that the courts deal with constitutional issues only where the dispute cannot otherwise be resolved.[78]

In *Meagher*, the Supreme Court recognised the need in the early 1970s to find *some* way of dealing with the influx of European laws into the domestic order. However, the use of ministerial regulation with little or no input from the Oireachtas or public consultation, combined

[73] [1994] 1 IR 329, 365 per Denham J.

[74] Council Directive 93/13/EC of 5 April 1993 on unfair terms in consumer contracts. See F. Murphy, 'The Unfair Contract Terms Regulations 1995: A Red Card for the State' (1995) 13 *Irish Law Times* 156.

[75] European Communities (Unfair Terms in Consumer Contracts) Regulations 1995, SI No. 27 of 1995, as amended by the European Communities (Unfair Terms in Consumer Contracts) (Amendment) Regulations 2000, SI No. 307 of 2000.

[76] The limited debate which did occur centred on the question of whether steps would be taken to implement the Directive on time: see *Dáil Éireann Debates*, vol. 432 No. 1 col. 171, 9 June 1993; *Dáil Éireann Debates*, vol. 434 No. 8 col. 1515–1517, 19 October 1993.

[77] R. Quinn, Minister for Enterprise Trade and Employment, *Dáil Éireann Debates* vol. 434 No. 8 col. 1516, 19 October 1993.

[78] See *M* v. *An Bord Uchtála* [1977] IR 287; *Carmody* v. *Minister for Justice, Equality and Law Reform and others* [2009] IESC 71.

with often ambiguous phrasing and a lack of consolidation of measures dealing with the same area, has reduced the impact of these measures. In recent years the focus has moved from a question of quantity ('how do we transpose X number of European measures within the given timeframe?')[79] to one of quality ('what is the best method of transposition for ensuring compliance'?). Some improvements in the Irish transposition of European measures generally have recently been highlighted by the OECD,[80] in particular the establishment of 'clear and formalised structures' for the management of EU Regulations,[81] including the creation of parliamentary committees with mandates relating to regulatory management,[82] guidelines to government departments on best practice in transposition,[83] and the increased efforts of the government to 'better inform parliament on negotiation and transposition'.[84] However, significant difficulties still remain, in particular the fact that secondary regulations are relatively unplanned (compared with primary legislation) and are not made publicly available in advance,[85] thus reducing the likelihood that they will be well drafted and publicised.

### *Compliance and enforcement mechanisms*

European Directives will often leave considerable flexibility to Member States regarding enforcement mechanisms and means of judicial and administrative redress, containing provisions along the lines of: 'Member States shall ensure that adequate and effective means exist to ensure compliance with this Directive in the interests of consumers'.[86] In Ireland, however, the opportunity to develop innovative enforcement mechanisms to encourage and secure compliance with the new regulatory framework was missed. Enforcement measures in transposing

[79] This is, of course, still an issue, although Ireland's transposition deficit in 2010 was under the 1 per cent target set by the European Commission: OECD in partnership with the European Commission, *Better Regulation in Europe: Ireland* (2010), p. 27.

[80] *Ibid.* [81] *Ibid.* 27.

[82] These include the Joint Oireachtas Committee on Economic Regulatory Affairs, the Joint Oireachtas Committee on EU Scrutiny and the Joint Oireachtas Committee on Enterprise, Trade and Employment.

[83] OECD in partnership with the European Commission, *Better Regulation in Europe: Ireland* (2010), p. 27.

[84] *Ibid.* 19. [85] *Ibid.* 21.

[86] Directive 97/7/EC of 20 May 1997 on the protection of consumers in respect of distance contracts, art. 11(1).

regulations consisted of traditional command-based mechanisms,[87] with heavy-handed criminal sanctions for failure to comply with the regulations. This is particularly noticeable in the transposition of the Distance Selling Directive: the Directive itself does not require criminal sanctions to be imposed on businesses which fail to comply with the Directive,[88] yet the transposing Irish regulations[89] make, *inter alia*, each of the following a criminal offence: failure to provide the 'prior information' required by article 4 of the Directive;[90] failure to provide the 'written confirmation' of this information;[91] failure to comply with the right of withdrawal in article 6;[92] failure to reimburse any sums paid by the consumer who exercises their right of withdrawal;[93] failure to deliver the goods within thirty days;[94] and failure to comply with a request by a consumer to cancel payment where fraudulent use has been made of a payment card.[95] The ambiguity inherent in the wording of the regulations (discussed above) would render questionable the criminal liability of any individual under these regulations, and there is conflict within the regulations as regards the civil effects of a failure to comply,[96] but a more fundamental objection to this enforcement mechanism is its ineffectiveness. Despite the fact that it would appear that not one single prosecution has been brought against a trader for failure to comply with the regulations, an empirical study of eighty Irish-based websites carried out by Fidelma White and Mary Donnelly at University College Cork revealed a significant degree of non-compliance with the regulations by web traders.[97] Donnelly and White posited that 'compliance difficulties arise partly because of a failure at transposition stage

[87] See B. Morgan and K. Yeung, *An Introduction to Law and Regulation, Text and Materials* (Cambridge University Press, 2007), pp. 80–5.

[88] Arguably, art. 9 of the Directive, which prohibits inertia selling, would call for criminal sanctions.

[89] European Communities (Protection of Consumers in respect of Contracts Made by Means of Distance Communication) Regulations 2001, SI No. 207 of 2001.

[90] Regulation 4(3). [91] Regulation 5(5). [92] Regulation 6(5).

[93] Regulations 7(3) and 8(8).

[94] Regulation 9(6) – certain exceptions apply where goods are unavailable.

[95] Regulation 10(3).

[96] For example, reg. 5 provides that the failure to confirm certain information in a durable medium means that the distance contract 'shall not be enforceable by the supplier against the consumer', while reg. 6 states that where a supplier has not complied with the requirements of reg. 5 the consumers' right of withdrawal is extended by 3 months (seemingly regardless of whether the information is supplied) *or* from the day on which those requirements are eventually complied with.

[97] Donnelly and White, 'Regulation and Consumer Protection', n. 40 above.

and beyond to engage properly with the provisions of the Directive and partly because of the failure to utilise appropriate and effective enforcement mechanisms'.[98]

There have been some positive developments in recent years, however. Partly as a result of a 2005 Report which highlighted considerable gaps in consumer protection in Ireland,[99] in 2007 the Office of the Director of Consumer Affairs was replaced with the National Consumer Agency (NCA), which was given a broad remit not only to *enforce* statutory provisions but to *encourage compliance* with statutory provisions.[100] The NCA has avoided taking on controversial or difficult cases through litigation or prosecutions,[101] and instead has opted for soft enforcement measures, involving negotiations, cooperation, compromise and education. This reflects the NCA's overall risk-based and consultative approach to its investigations. Certain sectors will come to its attention, either because of consumer complaints made to the NCA or because of issues highlighted in the media, and where possible it will make use of one of the many soft enforcement measures in its arsenal[102] rather than resorting to court proceedings.

A good example of the impact of the NCA on contracts is its work on unfair terms commonly found in gym club contracts. In 2007, the NCA carried out a review of the consumer contracts of a number of leading leisure and fitness gyms in Ireland. Several of these gyms agreed to cooperate with the NCA and a number of terms in gym contracts which the NCA considered unfair were voluntarily amended, including, for example, terms in which gyms had disclaimed liability for personal injury

[98] *Ibid.* 27.

[99] Consumer Strategy Group, *Make Consumers Count: A New Direction for Consumers* (2007).

[100] Consumer Protection Act 2007, s. 8. The Director of Consumer Affairs in fact had similar powers, but the fresh mandate given to the NCA has reinvigorated the efforts to encourage compliance.

[101] Prosecutions will still be taken for serious breaches, and have been, for example, against certain car dealers who were 'clocking' cars (i.e., giving false mileage on the odometer) and publicans who were watering down alcohol.

[102] These include prohibition orders (s.71), compliance orders (s.75), undertakings (s.73), fixed payment notices (s.85), consumer protection list (s.86) and various powers under pricing regulations. During the six-month period from August 2010 to January 2011, of the fifty-eight enforcements which were taken against businesses, twenty-three were compliance notices and thirty-five were fixed payment notices, and all related to misleading pricing or failure to display prices. Details of enforcement actions are published regularly on the 'consumer protection list' (i.e., 'name and shame' list) available at www.nca.ie.

caused to consumers on the premises, or in which the club had the right to withdraw part or all of the facilities of the club for undertaking maintenance work for an unlimited time without any form of compensation or refund. As well as working with individual gym chains, in 2008 the NCA worked with the sector's representative bodies to produce a set of guidelines for gym contracts, offering 'positive suggestions' for achieving compliance with the Unfair Contract Terms Regulations 1995 and the Distance Selling Regulations 2001, and outlining the basis on which the NCA was likely to take enforcement action. It also produced 'Seven Principles for the Fitness and Leisure Sector'. These non-binding principles were described as 'best practice for leisure clubs in the context of their contractual commitments to consumers'[103] and in some ways went beyond the strict legal requirements of the regulations.

While the approach taken by the National Consumer Agency has its advantages, it has meant that there is a lack of judicial discussion on how the regulations should be applied and interpreted. The guidelines produced by the NCA on gym contracts are not court sanctioned and thus the categorisation of a term as either fair or unfair by the NCA is open to challenge.[104] Even in the one case where a court order declaring certain terms unfair was obtained by the Director of Consumer Affairs (the precursor of the NCA) there was no judicial discussion of the regulations.[105] This case arose in the context of the Irish housing boom, when the Law Society of Ireland and the Construction Industry Federation became aware that a number of building agreements were departing from the standard agreement which had been negotiated by the two bodies and recommended to their members, and that potentially unfair terms were being inserted by solicitors acting for builders. The Director of Consumer Affairs instituted proceedings in the High Court seeking a declaration that fifteen sample terms were invalid under the 1995 Regulations. On 20 December 2001, Kearns J in the High Court

[103] National Consumer Agency Press Release, 30 October 2008. The press release and details of the guidelines and 'Seven Principles' are available at www.nca.ie.

[104] The National Consumer Agency's *Guidelines for Gyms and Fitness Clubs* (2008) thus state: '[T]he revised terms used in this guidance are not advanced as being definitively fair. The Agency cannot "clear" terms for the purposes of the Regulations. Only the courts can give a final ruling on what is definitively unfair in any circumstances.'

[105] *Re an Application pursuant to Regulation 8(1) of the Unfair Terms in Consumer Contracts 1995*, High Court, unreported, 5 December 2001 (hearing and judgment) and 20 December 2001 (order). For a good summary of the case see P. Dorgan, 'Safe as Houses?' (2002) *Law Society of Ireland Gazette* (January) 12.

declared all fifteen sample terms invalid, stating that that 'no person or body shall use or, if appropriate, continue to use in building contracts' any of the fifteen sample terms, or any term having a like effect, 'the said terms having been adjudged by the court to be unfair terms' under the Regulations. These terms included an 'entire agreement clause' which excluded liability of the builder for any warranty or representation made by the builder or their agent which was not contained in the written agreement; a term which gave the builder the right to resell the site in the event that the consumer failed to pay an instalment of the contract price within a certain time-frame but which, in addition, provided that 'any excess realised on the sale' was to belong to the builder rather than be returned to the consumer; a clause which gave the builder the right to terminate the agreement without reasonable cause while simultaneously demanding that the consumer pay a high level of compensation with a high interest rate for any outstanding sums; a term which gave the builder the right to modify or deviate from the plans even where such deviation is not minor; and a term which provided that the builder is not liable for any loss incurred 'as a result of any delay howsoever caused'.

In addition, Kearns J held that any schedule for interim payments would be invalid if the interim payment demanded by the builder exceeded the actual work done or the goods supplied by the builder at the time the payment was due or if the interim payment exceeded the percentages specified in the Irish Home Builders' Association Code of Practice.

No written reasons for the order were given, which is very disappointing given the potential impact of the case on construction contracts and the fact that it was the first judicial decision applying the Unfair Contract Terms Regulations 1995 in Ireland. The exact basis on which each of the fifteen terms, and the interim schedule for payments, were declared invalid is thus unclear, and any analysis as to the reasoning must be based on the submissions of the Director of Consumer Affairs[106] and the other interested parties. It is likely that the failure to give reasons was based on the fact that all the interested parties were in agreement as to the invalidity of the terms (although not, as discussed below, the validity of the use of interim payments schedules). In fact, judgment was given on the same day the application was made (5 December 2001) and the parties interested were asked to

[106] These were published on the website of the Director of Consumer Affairs, but would no longer appear to be available online.

agree and lodge a draft order, which was approved by the court on 20 December 2001. The seemingly minimal level of intervention of the court, while perhaps understandable given the level of agreement by the interested parties, certainly reduced the value of the case as a precedent. It is also potentially open to criticism on the basis that the granting of a court order prohibiting unfair contract terms on application of the Director of Consumer Affairs is not a mere formality, but is said to be 'at the discretion of the Court'[107] which 'shall take account of all the interests involved and in particular the public interest'.[108] The mere fact that the parties before the court all agree should not necessarily be the end of the matter – the absence of a *legitimus contraditor* in the court does not mean that the case did not have implications for the freedom to contract of third parties not in court. There is an argument that while the challenged terms did not necessarily reflect best practice or keep to the standard terms negotiated between the Law Society and the Construction Industry Federation, it does not necessarily follow that they are invalid under the 1995 Regulations. However, Irish courts by and large follow the traditional common law approach of adjudicating based on the arguments set out before them and this decision most likely reflects that stance.

It is nonetheless disappointing that the court failed to take the opportunity to engage with the substance of the regulations or to attempt to provide clarity on the subject. There was no discussion of the general test of unfairness in article 3(1) of the Directive, including the new concept of 'good faith', and no judicial analysis of the exemption in article 4(2) of the Directive.[109] This latter omission is particularly striking when it is considered that there is at least an argument that the interim payment schedule concerned 'the adequacy of the price and remuneration, as against the goods and services supplied'. This is not to say that the Irish courts should feel compelled to follow the stance of the UK Supreme Court on this issue,[110] but the complete absence of any discussion on whether and how the unfairness test should apply to matters relating to the contractual consideration is regrettable.

[107] Regulation 8(1). [108] Regulation 8(5).

[109] This is found in reg. 4, which states: 'A term shall not of itself be considered to be unfair by relation to the definition of the main subject matter of the contract or to the adequacy of the price and remuneration, as against the goods and services supplied, in so far as these terms are in plain, intelligible language.'

[110] *Office of Fair Trading* v. *Abbey National Plc* [2009] UKSC 6.

This case also raised the question of whether the implementation of the 1995 Regulations should be left to the Director of Consumer Affairs (now the National Consumer Agency) or whether other interested third parties such as the Law Society should have jurisdiction before the courts. This was an issue in the case as the Law Society had wished to obtain a complete ban on stage payments, but the Director of Consumer Affairs only applied for a restriction on stage payments and the Law Society did not have jurisdiction to bring an application seeking a full ban.[111] If the issue was a matter of controversy it seems somewhat unsatisfactory that it should be determined prior to the court proceedings by the Director of Consumer Affairs (through her refusal to apply for a complete ban), rather than leaving it to the court to interpret and apply the regulations. The 1995 Regulations were amended in 2000[112] to allow consumer organisations set up for the purpose of protecting consumer rights to seek a court order under regulation 8(1), but this still would not give the Law Society or other interested individual a right to bring an action in the public interest.[113] This can be contrasted with the Consumer Protection Act 2007, which provides in section 71 that *anyone* can apply to the Circuit Court or High Court for an order prohibiting a trader from committing or engaging in a prohibited act or practice.[114]

The lack of judicial analysis of European Directives, whether caused by a lack of cases being taken before the courts or a lack of judicial discussion within cases which are taken, inevitably results in reliance on case law and *dicta* from the United Kingdom. This is evident both in academic commentary on European Directives,[115] and in the few cases which have been taken. For example, in *Malcolm Marshall* v. *Capital Holdings Ltd t/a Sunworld*,[116] the High Court referred to two English

[111] For a criticism of the stance of the Director of Consumer Affairs, see Dorgan, 'Safe as Houses?', n. 105 above.

[112] By the European Communities (Unfair Terms in Consumer Contracts) (Amendment) Regulations 2000, SI No. 307 of 2000.

[113] See *Malcolm Marshall* v. *Capital Holdings Ltd t/a Sunworld*, High Court, unreported, 21 July 2006, per Murphy J, para.7.8.

[114] See N. Reilly, 'The Role of Traders in the Enforcement of the Unfair Commercial Practices Directive: A New Unfair Competition Law for Ireland?' (2009) 16(1) *Dublin University Law Journal* 100.

[115] See e.g., M. Donnelly, 'Loan Contracts and the Unfair Terms Regulations' (2010) 17(6) *Commercial Law Practitioner* 107 which, in the absence of any Irish cases on the topic, attempts to glean lessons from the United Kingdom on the application of the Unfair Contract Terms Regulations to loan contracts.

[116] *Malcolm Marshall* v. *Capital Holdings Ltd t/a Sunworld*, n. 113 above.

decisions concerning the validity of clauses in consumer contracts referring disputes to adjudication,[117] while avoiding discussing in any general manner the test of unfairness in the 1995 Regulations, including the concept of good faith. In *Scaife* v. *Falcon Leisure Group (Overseas) Ltd*,[118] the Supreme Court, charged with the job of interpreting the Package Holidays and Travel Trade Act 1995,[119] again made reference primarily to UK decisions on the Directive,[120] although it did also refer to an opinion of Advocate-General Tizzano.[121] This is not necessarily meant as a criticism of the results of these decisions but it is indicative of the Irish courts' continued reliance on English contract law decisions, even on matters of EU law, and can be contrasted with the more in-depth discussion and guidance offered by the courts in the United Kingdom.

### *Maximum harmonisation debate in Ireland*

European measures which aim at maximum harmonisation of the law have a greater impact in Ireland than those that aim at minimum harmonisation. The most direct or obvious reason for this is that maximum harmonisation requires the State to entirely revise the law so it is equivalent (insofar as is possible) to the European standards.[122] In addition, however, the threat to the *status quo* posed by maximum

[117] *Picardi* v. *Cuniburti* [2002] EWHC 2923 (TCC); *Bryen and Langley Ltd* v. *Boston* [2004] EWHC 2450 (TCC). In *Marshall*, the plaintiff objected to an arbitration clause in a holiday contract, which had been entered into on his behalf. However, while sub-paragraph (q) in the indicative list of unfair terms in the Schedule to the 1995 Regulations refers to a clause which requires a consumer to take disputes 'exclusively' to arbitration 'not covered by legal provisions', in this case the contract did not exclude other forms of litigation; nor was the arbitration not covered by legal provisions; nor was it carried out in such a manner that it would point to the arbitration being conducted other than by under provision of law. Murphy J also placed some weight on the fact that there was no proof of unfairness or lack of good faith in relation to the arbitration reference itself.

[118] [2007] IESC 57.

[119] This implemented Council Directive 90/314/EEC of 13 June 1990 on package travel, package holidays and package tours.

[120] These included *Hone* v. *Going Places Leisure Travel*, Court of Appeal, unreported, 13 June 2001; *Wong Mee Wan* v. *Kwan Kin Travel Services Ltd* [1996] 1 WLR 38 (a Privy Council case originating from Hong Kong); *Healy* v. *Cosmoair Plc* [2005] All ER 432. Reference was also made to the Irish pre-transposition case of *McKenna* v. *Best Travel Ltd* [1998] IR 57.

[121] Opinion of Advocate-General Tizzano in C-168/00 *Leitner* v. *TUI Deutschland GmbH & Co. KG*, Judgment of 12 March 2002.

[122] Thus, the Unfair Commercial Practices Directive (Directive 2005/29/EC), which called for maximum harmonisation of the laws relating to unfair business-to-consumer

harmonisation increases the level of political debate in the area of contract and consumer law in Ireland and in this way it has an impact beyond mere textual changes to the law. Although the scope of the Consumer Rights Directive has been greatly reduced since the original proposal, it has already had an impact on the Irish legal and political landscape by virtue of the debate and discussion it provoked. The threat that maximum harmonisation could impinge upon the standards of consumer protection in Ireland, particularly in the area of consumer sales, caused the proposal to be criticised by entities such as the Consumers' Association of Ireland[123] and significantly more time was given in Dáil debates to the proposal for the Directive than had been given to previous Consumer Directives.[124] The Sales Law Review Group, an expert group established by the Minister for Enterprise, Trade and Employment in November 2008, was established in part to 'examine the provisions of the proposed EU Directive on consumer contractual rights in the light of existing Irish consumer law and assess its implications for Irish consumer rights and law'[125] and its 2009 Position Paper was critical of the Directive.[126] In addition, prior to the Irish referendum on the Lisbon Treaty, Irish cinemas and television carried advertisements explaining how EU consumer safety standards were helping European citizens, and the then Commissioner for Consumer Affairs, Maglena Kuneva, attended a number of seminars in Ireland[127] and conducted an interview with the *Irish Times*.[128] This is not to imply that the level of engagement is as high as it could be – consumer issues still rarely featured in the Lisbon debate, Commissioner Kuneva's seminar in Galway was not well attended, some of the comments made during Dáil debates were remarkably ill-informed,[129] and an Oireachtas committee

commercial practices, was transposed by the Consumer Protection Act 2007 after a thorough review of the law.

[123] Consumer Association of Ireland, Submission to Oireachtas Committee on European Scrutiny, 2 December 2010.

[124] See e.g., *Dáil Éireann Debates*, vol. 172 No. 3 col. 445, 16 June 2010.

[125] Sales Law Review Group Terms of Reference, available at www.deti.ie/commerce/consumer/slrg.htm.

[126] Sales Law Review Group Position Paper on the Proposal for a Directive of the European Parliament and of the Council on Consumer Rights (May 2009).

[127] For example, at the European Commission Office, Dublin on 2 October 2008 and in Galway from 27–28 August 2009.

[128] P. Cullen, 'Up, up and away for consumers', *Irish Times*, 3 October 2008.

[129] Including a comment by W. Penrose TD that the Sale of Goods and Supply of Services Act 1980 was 'the real one': *Dáil Éireann Debates*, vol. 172 No. 3 col. 445, 16 June 2010.

discussing the proposal for the Consumer Rights Directive was attended by only two elected representatives.[130] Nor is it to imply that increased (forced?) engagement is a reason or justification for measures aiming at maximum harmonisation. It is merely an observation that the threat of maximum harmonisation appears to have the ability to cause at least some reaction in Ireland, and could be a platform for an increased level of discussion and debate regarding our policies on consumer protection. It will be interesting to see whether the impetus for discussion continues in light of the focus now on 'targeted' harmonisation of consumer law.

## Impact of Europe on Irish contract law reform

Contract law in Ireland is a neglected body of private law which is in serious need of revision and reform. Statutory provisions dealing with contract law dating as far back as 1695 remain in force[131] and the lack of any significant or systematic programme of contract law reform has meant that there are entire doctrinal areas where there is no contemporary legislative structure. The Irish Law Reform Commission has been relatively active in this area and has recommended reform of, for example, the doctrine of privity,[132] the capacity of minors,[133] limitation periods[134] and the availability of exemplary and punitive damages;[135] however, the level of implementation of these proposals is low, particularly when compared with other areas of law such as land law, where implementation rates are quite high. The lack of political interest in contract law reform may be understandable in a small jurisdiction, but

130 See P. Cullen, 'Consumer rights to be reduced in EU move', *Irish Times*, 3 December 2010.

131 Provisions of the Statute of Frauds 1695 dealing with formalities concerning guarantees and any agreement 'that is not to be formed within the space of one year from the making thereof' remain on the statute book. Its provisions regarding evidentiary requirements for the sale of goods are now to be found in s.4 of the Sale of Goods Act 1893 (which itself is out of date as it applies to sales of goods over £10, i.e., €12.70, a figure which is inappropriate in 2013) and recently the written requirements for the sale of an interest in land have been replaced by s.51 of the Land and Conveyancing Law Reform Act 2009.

132 Law Reform Commission, *Privity of Contract and Third Party Rights* (LRC 88–2008) recommended reform of the privity rule in Ireland. The author was the principal legal researcher for this Report. For a summary see C. Kelly, 'Privity of Contract: The Benefits of Reform' (2008) 1 *Judicial Studies Institute Journal* 145.

133 Law Reform Commission, *Report on Minor's Contracts* (LRC 15–1985).

134 Law Reform Commission, *Report on Statutes of Limitation: Claims in Contract and Tort in respect of Latent Damage (Other than Personal Injury)* (LRC 64–2001).

135 Law Reform Commission, *Report on Aggravated, Exemplary and Restitutionary Damages* (LRC 60–2000).

Ireland does not compare well even with similar sized jurisdictions such as New Zealand, where a genuinely innovative tradition of statute law reform of private law has been established.[136]

Change and debate at a European level has the potential to provide an opportunity to open up the contract law debate in Ireland, but more than that it has been argued that rather than simply reacting to European developments, Ireland should use the work being done at a European level to frame a 'proactive and coordinated' contract law agenda which aims at more than mere piecemeal reform.[137] The beginnings of such developments can be seen in the establishment of the Sales Law Review Group whose terms of reference included not only an examination of proposed EU measures affecting sales, but a wider mandate to recommend 'a scheme of legislation capable of providing a statutory sales law framework appropriate to modern-day conditions and needs'.[138] However, the European agenda cannot be ignored in works such as this, and the Group's work was to a certain extent delayed and restricted by European developments and flux in the area of consumer sales. In its position paper on the proposed Consumer Rights Directive, the Sales Law Review Group commented that it was 'somewhat surprising and disappointing' that in the drafting of the Directive there was little evidence of reliance on the Draft Common Frame of Reference.[139] However, in the Group's final recommendations, solutions to existing problems in Irish sales law were sought from other common law jurisdictions such as Australia and Canada, rather than European sources.[140] It would appear, therefore, that unless a European measure is mandatory, as opposed to being part of a wider 'tool-box' with an uncertain function, it will not form a dominant part of considerations in Irish law reform. A similar trend can be seen in reports of the Law Reform Commission, where consideration given to the civil law or

[136] See e.g., the Illegal Contracts Act 1970, Insurance Law Reform Act 1977, Contractual Mistakes Act 1977, Contractual Remedies Act 1979, Contracts (Privity) Act 1982.

[137] R. Clark, *The European Commission's Contract Law Project and Irish Law: More of an Opportunity than a Threat*, paper delivered to the Law Society of Ireland, (2004, paper on file with author).

[138] Sales Law Review Group Terms of Reference, available at www.deti.ie/commerce/consumer/slrg.htm.

[139] Sales Law Review Group Position Paper on the Proposal for a Directive of the European Parliament and of the Council on Consumer Rights (May 2009), pp. 3 and 9.

[140] Sales Law Review Group, *Report on the Legislation governing the Sale of Goods and Supply of Services* (The Stationery Office, Dublin, 2011).

the Draft Common Frame of Reference is brief when compared to the detailed analysis of solutions found in common law jurisdictions.[141]

## Conclusion

The Irish Government can be criticised for its failure, at least until recently, to transpose and enforce consumer and contract Directives in a way which bolsters consumer rights and encourages regulatory compliance within Ireland, rather than just meeting the state's minimum obligations under EU law. This is partly a result of a broader culture of political apathy regarding contract law issues, but it is also symptomatic of the general difficulties caused by a centralist, top-down approach to harmonisation with its emphasis on keeping up with European standards rather than necessarily on finding the best solution to any given problem. Moreover, the fact that Ireland and the United Kingdom have taken different approaches to the transposition of several European Directives shows that even where countries share common legal rules, so-called harmonisation may in itself cause further fragmentation. However, Irish contract law has been subject to external forces and influences for centuries, and Irish lawyers are well accustomed to looking to other jurisdictions for best practice, so it could well be that a European contract law agenda based on cooperation, dialogue and mutual learning could well be suited for Ireland, and that Ireland could prove a fruitful source of common law solutions for its European neighbours.

[141] See e.g., Law Reform Commission, *Privity of Contract and Third Party Rights* (LRC 88–2008), paras. 2.46–2.50, where the approach of different European legal systems to third party rights is discussed and reference is made to the work on the Draft Common Frame of Reference. However, there is significantly more discussion of developments in common law jurisdictions in both the Report and the Consultation Paper, *Privity of Contract: Third Party Rights* (LRC-CP 40–2006) and the final recommendations are modelled (albeit with some differences) on the Contracts (Rights of Third Parties) Act 1999 in England and Wales.

12

# The Europeanisation of insurance contract law: the insurer's duty to advise and its regulation in German and European law

PIOTR TERESZKIEWICZ

To sell insurance is to sell a story about a safe future.[1]

## Introduction

Insurance contracts can be distinguished by a number of specific features from other, more common types of contracts such as sale or rental contracts. First, as a classic contract of adhesion, insurance is a standard form contract drafted by the dominant party (insurance company), a repeat player, and adhered to by the policy-holder, who enters into few such agreements. By its very nature, modern insurance is a contract between a professional risk-manager and a usually unsophisticated policy-holder who has little insight into insurance matters. Secondly, a typical insured party views the insurance relationship to be one in which the company promises security and protection, rather than a detailed and obscure set of specifications and exclusions of cover.[2] This perception is nowadays strengthened through the presentation of insurance contracts by the insurance companies themselves in adverts portraying insurance as a guarantor of security and refuge from the dangers of the world. Such self-promotion on the part of the insurers is, however, difficult

Post-doctoral research fellow, University of Heidelberg, Institute of Legal History, Roman Law Section. This contribution has been written within the framework of a research project supported by the German Research Foundation (DFG).

[1] J. Benjamin, 'The Narratives of Financial Law' (2010) 30 *OJLS* 787, 789.

[2] For a thoughtful analysis of insurance as relational contract, see J. M. Feinman, 'The Insurance Relationship as Relational Contract and the "Fairly Debatable" Rule for First-Party Bad Faith' (2009) 46 *San Diego Law Review* 553.

to reconcile with the fact that the core of what the insurer sells and the policy-holder buys is found in the detailed terms of cover specified in the insurance policy.[3] Most importantly, the insurance policy is a highly complex document, comprising a number of sections devoted to such issues as the object of insurance, risks that are covered, exclusions from cover, limitations, conditions, and so on. The scope and size of policies may certainly vary depending on the type of insurance. It is common wisdom that consumers seldom read the policy documents, very often they do not understand them, and that the sales process may not facilitate or permit this. Thirdly, an insurance contract is characterised by the sequential performances of its parties. The insured party's essential obligation is to pay the premium, which is usually done at the time of contract formation. The insurer's essential obligation is to provide compensation for the insured party's loss, a performance which is only required later, if it all, for the risk insured against may never materialise. However, it is usually only at the point of loss that the policy-holder becomes aware of the limitations and exclusions from cover. It follows that the policy-holder's expectations pursuant to the insurers' self-promotion as guarantors of a safe future are in danger of not being fulfilled. To provide an example: a travel policy which features a picture of a skier on the front cover as well as beaches and cafés, may have an exclusion for winter sports, buried in the middle of a lengthy document.[4] Such an exclusion, if unnoticed at the time of contract formation, clearly does not match expectations of adequate cover induced by the way the policy has been presented.

The tension between the policy-holder's perception of insurance as a guarantee of security and the legal nature of insurance as a complex contract requiring sequential performance poses a serious challenge for the regulator. Product design, disclosure and advice rules appear to be the main tools for addressing this risk. Briefly turning to the product design issue, the idea that the law lays down a mandatory minimum extent of cover that should be offered in an insurance policy of a specific type is not universally recognised either in national laws or at EU level.[5] While the EC Directive on Unfair Terms in Consumer Contracts[6] applies to certain

[3] *Ibid.* 558.

[4] See P. Hinchliffe, 'Review of Principles of European Insurance Contract Law' (2008) 9 *ERA Forum* 167, 168.

[5] M. Clarke, *Policies and Perceptions of Insurance Law in the Twenty-First Century* (Oxford University Press, 2005), p. 265.

[6] Directive 93/13/EC of 5 April 1993 [1993] OJ L95/29.

terms in certain consumer contracts, the terms of insurance contracts are otherwise largely free from regulatory interference. In the process of creating the Single European Insurance Market, the Third Insurance Directive generally abolished the requirement that insurance contract terms should receive prior approval by a state supervisory agency.[7]

The lack of comprehensive rules governing design of insurance products or requiring product uniformity gives rise to a number of concerns. Insurance products accessible on the market are not standardised, which causes a deep and fundamental information asymmetry between the insurer and/or its agents in the distribution process and prospective policy-holders.[8] Insurance buyers face a marketplace with a variety of highly complex insurance products bearing the same or similar names but offering differing cover. This obviously increases the risk of the mis-selling of insurance and, consequently, of consumers being exposed to limitations and exclusions which are detrimental to their interests. It is rightly claimed that the information and advice needs of an average retail investor might be easier to specify and satisfy than those of buyers of some types of insurance.[9] For instance, to provide a comprehensive liability insurance cover or home contents' insurance, a broad and detailed profile of a prospective policy-holder must be specified, including, *inter alia*, his or her financial status, family situation, daily habits or even hobbies. Undoubtedly, establishing the concrete needs and demands of a prospective policy-holder has become a precondition of offering adequate insurance cover.

Consequently, a high degree of product deregulation in insurance law is a significant consideration supporting the case for imposing on the sellers of insurance duties to warn or advise about the scope of cover. The EU Directives in the field of insurance and consumer law have been concerned with imposing extensive precontractual provision of information and documentation.[10] Nevertheless, only the Insurance Mediation Directive

[7] Third Non-Life Insurance Directive 92/49/EEC of 18 June 1992 [1992] OJ L228/1; Life Assurance Consolidation Directive 2002/83/EC of 5 November 2002 [2002] OJ L345/1; generally see A. K. Schnyder, *Europäisches Banken- und Versicherungsrecht* (C.F. Müller, Heidelberg, 2005), p. 5.

[8] For an account of comparable issues as regards investment products see N. Moloney, *How to Protect Investors: Lessons from the EC and the UK* (Cambridge University Press, 2010).

[9] H. Dörner, 'Versicherungsrechtliche Informationspflichten' in E. Lorenz (ed.), *Karlsruher Forum 2000. Aufklärungspflichten* (Verlag Versicherungswirtschaft GmbH, Karlsruhe, 2001), pp. 39, 43.

[10] See art. 31 of the Third Non-Life Insurance Directive 92/49/EC and art. 36 of the Life Assurance Consolidation Directive 2002/83/EC.

(2002/92/EC, IMD), which deals with the duties of insurance intermediaries, lays down a more rigorous standard, setting rules about exploring the policy-holder's needs and referring to the advisory process in the sale of insurance. During a recent reform of insurance law, the German legislator generalised the IMD solutions, laying down a comprehensive regime on the duty to advise policy-holders. This chapter discusses the European and German regulatory approaches regarding the insurer's duty to advise a prospective policy-holder at the precontractual stage. A brief discussion of the IMD requirements precedes the analysis of German law, which is then followed by a look at the Principles of European Insurance Contract Law.

## Insurer's duty to advise

### *Directive 2002/92/EC on insurance mediation*

The Insurance Mediation Directive[11] (IMD) is a legal act of fundamental relevance for the European insurance contract law. As a minimum harmonisation Directive, the IMD aims at contributing both to the completion of the single market for financial services and to the enhancement of customer protection in this field.[12] Applying only to insurance intermediaries and not to insurers as such, the IMD takes a broad, functional approach, addressing various types of persons or institutions acting as intermediaries between insurers and policy-holders, such as agents and brokers.[13]

As far as its scope is concerned, the IMD deals with two major issues. First, it provides for regulatory requirements regarding the exercise of insurance intermediation in the internal market, such as the relevant professional standards for intermediaries. Secondly and most importantly, the IMD contains a number of provisions addressing the intermediary/policy-holder relationship.[14]

### *'Know your customer rule' under the Insurance Mediation Directive*

In addition to the limited disclosure and conflict of interest rules imposed by the IMD, article 12(3) provides for a more intensive duty to explore the potential policy-holder's needs. The provision reads as follows:

[11] Insurance Mediation Directive 2002/92/EC of 9 December 2002 [2003] OJ L9/3 (IMD).

[12] *Ibid.* Preamble, recitals 7 and 8.

[13] *Ibid.* Preamble, recital 9.

[14] Cf. D. Langer, J. Rosenow, 'Konsumentenschutz bei der Vermittlung von Versicherungsverträgen in der Schweiz und in Europa' in *Liber Amicorum Bernd Stauder* (Schultess, Bern, 2006), p. 195.

> Prior to the conclusion of any specific contract, the insurance intermediary shall at least specify, in particular on the basis of information provided by the customer, the demands and the needs of that customer as well as underlying reasons for any advice given to the customer on a given insurance product. These details shall be modulated according to the complexity of the insurance contract being proposed.

This provision imposes on an insurance intermediary a duty, on the one hand, to specify the demands and the needs of a prospective policyholder with a view to a specific contract, and, on the other hand, to specify underlying reasons for any advice the intermediary gives to a customer. This phrasing is rather broad and does not provide detailed guidance on the precise extent of the intermediary's duty. Nevertheless, the second sentence of article 12(3) IMD, namely, that details regarding the intermediary's duties 'shall be modulated according to the complexity of the insurance contract being proposed', can be regarded as guidance for national legislators as regards the criteria according to which the exact scope of intermediary's duties ought to be hammered out.

Moreover, article 12(3) IMD clearly obliges a prospective policyholder to cooperate with an intermediary by providing information on his coverage needs. In particular, this means that a prospective policyholder ought to communicate any unusual or non-standard wishes or needs to an intermediary, as otherwise they will not be reflected in the advice provided.

It may be worthwhile to turn to the specific issues which the IMD apparently leaves open and which may require a regulatory response at national level. First of all, it appears unclear whether article 12(3) IMD may be considered a legal basis of a duty to advise, since no guidance is provided as to the precise content of such a duty. Arguably, article 12(3) IMD imposes only a duty to specify reasons for the advice which is provided.[15] On this reading, there is no EU duty on intermediaries to advise clients, but only a duty to establish the client's needs and wishes as well as specifying reasons for the advice provided. Furthermore, it remains unclear whether an intermediary shall 'specify the demands and needs of a customer' in any case or only insofar as it is clearly recognisable to her that a customer is in need of advice, in particular given the complexity of the

[15] P. Reiff, *Versicherungsvermittlerrecht im Umbruch* (Hamburger Gesellschaftzur Förderung des Versicherungswesens mbH, Karlsruhe, 2006), p. 75; C. Armbrüster, *Aktuelle Rechtsfragen der Beratungspflichten von Versicherern und Vermittlern (§§ 6, 61 VVG)* (Verlag Versicherungswirtschaft GmbH, Karlsruhe, 2009), p. 2.

insurance product in question. What is more, the IMD does not oblige intermediaries to explore a policy-holder's personal situation and his/her expertise in insurance matters. Finally, the IMD apparently takes no position on a customer's right to waive advice, a feature which gave rise to controversy in the process of IMD implementation.[16]

Summing up, article 12(3) IMD cannot be taken to introduce a far-reaching duty to explore the needs of a prospective client.[17] Compared to the far more extensive MiFID[18] regime regarding investment products, the IMD appears to focus more on product than on a client's status or qualities.[19] Nonetheless, given that the IMD is a measure of 'minimum harmonisation', the manner in which article 12(3) IMD is drafted ('shall *at least* specify') allows Member States to extend the scope of such duties in the process of implementing this provision into national law.

### *Possible impact of Insurance Mediation Directive on the general conduct of insurance business*

Despite its apparently modest regulatory reach, a 'know your customer rule', as laid down in article 12(3) IMD, appears to have great relevance not only for the law regarding intermediaries, but also for the general conduct of the insurance business. While the IMD deals with a broad range of insurance intermediaries, it falls short of imposing parallel duties on insurers as such (article 2(3) IMD).[20] This makes it necessary to consider what legal implications the IMD may possibly have for the insurers' duties to provide advice. Should the protection afforded in article 12(3) IMD be dependent on the manner in which insurance products are bought? More specifically, should only insurance intermediaries be obliged to specify their prospective clients' needs and requirements and the reasons for the advice they provide? What about other distribution channels, in particular those clients dealing directly with insurers?

[16] See the discussion regarding the German Insurance Contract Act below.

[17] Moloney, *How to Protect Investors*, n. 8 above, at p. 254, calls this rule 'a quasi-know-your-client requirement'.

[18] Directive 2004/39/EC [2004] OJ L145/1 (MiFID) and Commission Directive 2006/73/EC [2006] OJ L241/26 (MiFID Level 2 Directive).

[19] For a comprehensive study of MiFID regulatory techniques, see Moloney, *How to Protect Investors*, n. 8 above, chs. 4, 5.

[20] See the IMD Preamble, recital 9.

Following enactment of the IMD, it has been claimed there is a strong case for a 'know your customer duty' to be applied to insurers as well.[21] On this interpretation, this rule should apply generally in the process of selling insurance. There are two major ways of extending this duty to insurers. First, it is arguable that provisions regarding intermediaries' duties could be applied *per analogiam* to direct insurers.[22] The *per analogiam* argument undoubtedly deserves attention. Nevertheless, it must be borne in mind that while intermediaries may provide advice about products accessible on a specific market, insurers as *sellers* generally advise on the scope of their products. This could definitely make analogous extensions of such duties to insurers debatable. Secondly, a less controversial manner of extending the 'know your customer' duty to insurers could consist of enacting specific provisions to this effect.[23]

The analysis of the recent German Insurance Contract Act, to which we now turn, provides a valuable illustration of the exact impact of the 'know your customer' duty, as provided by the IMD, on the general conduct of insurance business.

## Insurer's duty to advise in German law

A new German Insurance Contract Act[24] (VVG) was enacted on 23 November 2007 and entered into force on 1 January 2008, repealing the Insurance Contract Act of 1908. Designed as a comprehensive codification of the law relating to insurance contracts, the German Insurance Contract Act governs all types of insurance contract except for marine insurance and reinsurance (section 209 VVG). Furthermore, the VVG does not differentiate between commercial and consumer insurance contracts, but follows the lead given in EU law and divides insurance contracts into those covering 'mass risks', on the one hand, and those covering 'large risks', on the other hand.[25] Given that everyday insurance contracts, concluded by consumers or small and medium-sized businesses, are regarded as 'mass risk' insurance, the analysis deals with the provisions applicable to that category of contracts.

[21] H. Cousy, 'Les règles de conduit et le droit des assurances', in *Synthèses de droit bancaire et financier. Liber amicorum André Bruyneel* (Bruylant, Brussels, 2008), p. 505.

[22] *Ibid.* 505. [23] In favour of extending to insurers, *ibid.* 505.

[24] Versicherungsvertragsgesetz (VVG), Bundesgesetzblatt (BGBl) I, 2631. In English see a brief summary of the VVG's major provisions in K. Noussia, 'Reflections on the New German Insurance Contracts Law Contract' (2009) *JBL* 265.

[25] M. Wandt, *Versicherungsrecht* (Carl Heymann Verlag, Köln, 2010), p. 60.

The German Insurance Contract Act seeks to enhance the level of the policy-holder's protection, *inter alia*, by providing for more extensive and transparent information and advice delivered by the suppliers of insurance products.[26] The previous Insurance Contract Act of 1908 did not contain any provisions obliging insurers to advise prospective policy-holders, the law in this respect having been shaped by the courts' application of general rules of contract law.[27] In particular, the German jurisprudence required a consultancy agreement between the parties as a basis of an insurer's duty to advise. Furthermore, it remained unclear under what circumstances an insurer was obliged to warn or advise the prospective policy-holder about the scope of cover.[28] Yet another difficulty concerned the remedy for any breach of a duty to disclose or advise by an insurer, for this consisted in an insurance-specific judicial device of adjusting contract terms to reflect the policy-holder's expectations.[29]

As regards the German Insurance Contract Act's legislative history, it must be emphasised that the Insurance Mediation Directive profoundly influenced the legislative approach to precontractual duties in the marketing of insurance products. The rationale of the 'know your customer duty', as laid down in article 12(3) IMD, has been applied beyond the IMD's ambit to selling insurance through different channels. In what is perceived as an instance of 'Europeanisation of German insurance law', the VVG imposes a virtually identical scope of precontractual duties to advise clients on both insurers and insurance intermediaries.[30]

## Requirements of a duty to advise

Essential to our analysis is section 6 VVG which lays down the legal regime of insurers' precontractual duty to advise an insurance applicant in respect of insurance cover. The provision of fundamental importance

[26] See the legislative materials, Bundestagsdrucksache (BT-Drucks.) 16/3945, 59.

[27] See E.-M. Kieninger, 'Informations-, Aufklärungs- und Beratungspflichten beim Abschluß von Versicherungsverträgen' (1999) 199 *Archiv für die civilistische Praxis* 191.

[28] *Ibid.* 211, claims that the former rules did not guarantee adequate policy-holder protection.

[29] A so-called '*gewohnheitsrechtliche Erfüllungshaftung*', see E. Lorenz, 'Die "gewohnheitsrechtliche" Erfüllungshaftung des Versicherers im bisherigen und im zukünftigen Versicherungsvertragsrecht' in *Festschrift für Claus-Wilhelm Canaris* (C.H. Beck, München, 2007), vol. I, p. 757.

[30] See legislative materials BT-Drucks. 16/3945, 58. M. Ebers, 'Einleitung' in H-P. Schwintowski and C. Brömmelmeyer (eds.), *Praxiskommentar zum Versicherungsvertragsrecht* (Lexis Nexis Deutschland, Münster, 2008), p. 4, regards this as an instance of 'Europeanisation of German insurance law'.

is section 6(1) VVG which specifies the requirements and the scope of the insurer's precontractual duty to give advice. It may be useful to recite section 6(1) VVG in full:

> If the difficulty in assessing the insurance being offered or the policy-holder himself and his situation gives occasion thereto, the insurer must ask him about his wishes and needs and, also bearing in mind an appropriate relation between the time and effort spent in providing this advice and the insurance premiums to be paid by the policy-holder, the insurer shall advise the policy-holder and state reasons for each of the pieces of advice in respect of a particular insurance. He shall document this, taking into account the complexity of the contract of insurance being offered.[31]

As a significant exception, the duty to advise does not apply to distance contracts, as defined in sections 312b(1) and (2) German Civil Code.[32]

The full normative implications of section 6(1) VVG (a provision considered to be drafted in a highly complex manner) will only be established once the jurisprudence determines a number of key issues. Nevertheless, the prevailing view assumes that section 6(1) VVG does not provide for an unconditional (general) duty incumbent upon an insurer to explore and specify needs regarding insurance cover resulting from an applicant's situation and his or her requirements in any case.[33] Instead, section 6(1) VVG is interpreted as requiring a specific reason triggering the duty to advise.[34] Essentially, the insurer retains their original position of insurance seller, and the provisions of section 6(1) VVG should not turn him into an insurance advisor, unless specific circumstances arise.

It follows that the insurer's duty to advise depends on whether, taking into account the circumstances of a given case, there is a need for advice

31 The English translation of this provision comes (slightly adjusted) from the English translation of the entire German Insurance Contract Act, available at the German Insurance Association (GDV), www.gdv.de/Downloads/English/German_Insurance_Contract_Act_2008.pdf.

32 Distance contracts are contracts entered into between a business and a consumer solely by the use of means of distance communication as regulated in s. 312b(1) and (2) of the German Civil Code. The legislative materials justify the exclusion, claiming that a duty to advise could in practice not be fulfilled in distance contracting, BT-Drucks. 16/1935, 58. This exclusion is criticised, e.g. Ebers, in *Praxiskommentar*, § 6 Remark 54.

33 Wandt, *Versicherungsrecht*, n. 25 above, at p. 103, supports his position with an excerpt of legislative materials to that effect, cf. BT-Drucks. 16/1935, 24.

34 A so-called '*Anlassbezogene Beratung*', a concept developed by German courts and endorsed in German scholarship, see Ebers, 'Einleitung', n. 30 above, s. 6 Remark 3, with further references.

to be provided to the applicant.[35] In this respect, section 6(1) VVG specifies 'the difficulty in assessing the insurance being offered', 'the policy-holder himself or herself' or his or her 'situation' as the relevant criteria in evaluating whether a duty to advise should be triggered in a given case. While the wording of section 6(1) VVG may imply that these are the only criteria to be taken into account, the prevailing view tends to regard them as only illustrative, major examples.[36] It is submitted that a broad interpretation of these criteria will enable virtually all circumstances which may give rise to a duty to advise to be embraced.

As a necessary requirement, an applicant's need for advice must be recognisable to the insurer, which means no more than an 'objective' recognisability in a particular case. It is by no means clear, however, in the light of section 6(1) VVG, which of the parties to a future insurance contract should be charged with being proactive at the precontractual stage and to what extent: should the insurer actively explore the applicant's situation or is the applicant obliged to draw the insurer's attention to any of her particular needs?

A rule of thumb might set out that, on the one hand, insurers should be expected to spontaneously make enquiries resulting from the complex nature of their products, whilst, on the other hand, applicants should be held liable to spell out any atypical circumstances or features regarding them and their situation which may give rise to the need for advice on insurance cover.[37] This view appears alluring, as it corresponds to a balance of duties generally reflecting typical information asymmetries between parties to insurance contracts (policy-holder's knowledge of the risk to be insured against, on the one hand, and the insurer's expertise on products offered, on the other hand). In addition, this interpretation appears also in line with article 12(3) IMD which clearly obliges a prospective policy-holder to be proactive in making information available to an intermediary. Yet, given the complexity of modern insurance products and the limited comparability of market offers, reducing the information asymmetry between an insurer and a policy-holder as regards the product features appears difficult; even

[35] Wandt, *Versicherungsrecht*, n. 25 above, at p. 103.

[36] Major commentaries on VVG provide extensive guidance with regard to possible factors triggering the duty to advise, see e.g., P. Pohlmann, in D. Looschelders and P. Pohlmann, *VVG-Kommentar* (Carl Heymann Verlag, Köln 2010), s. 6, Remark 38 *et seq.*; Ebers, 'Einleitung', n. 30, s. 6, Remark 13 *et seq.*

[37] Pohlman, *ibid.*, s. 6 Remark 54.

extensive (and time-consuming) provision of information about the contract in question is unlikely to eliminate or substantially reduce this asymmetry. Therefore, the case for holding the insurer to a high degree of targeted inquiry intensifies proportionally to the extent to which the product is non-standardised, as the applicant is unlikely to be clear about the adverse effect of non-standard features on the cover expected.[38]

## Scope of a duty to advise

Imposing a duty to advise on insurers implies a normative decision about the specific content of that duty. According to German doctrine, an insurer is obliged to advise an applicant about features of specific insurance products which an applicant shows interest in. There is no doubt that a duty to advise is not satisfied by a mere provision of mandatory product information or a booklet on key features. By contrast, an insurer is obliged to make a specific recommendation as to an action which an applicant should take regarding his or her insurance needs.[39] Moreover, a view appears justified that an insurer's obligation does not consist primarily in warning the applicant about a specific lack of cover.[40] Limiting the insurer's obligation to some 'negative' advice (warning) appears contrary to the duty's rationale which is to assist an applicant in making a reasonable choice about insurance cover. Therefore, an insurer who cannot offer a product meeting the applicant's cover needs may be obliged to advise the applicant against buying his/her products.[41]

## Cost of advice provision

Arguably, the normative choices surrounding the intensity of insurers' duties need to take into account economic considerations. In providing precontractual advice, an insurer invests resources and it is by no means certain whether the insurer will receive any return on that investment, for a prospective applicant may eventually decide not to conclude a contract. There is also a cross-subsidisation concern: if an insurer does not charge

[38] Similarly Armbrüster, *Aktuelle Rechtsfragen*, n. 15 above, at p. 10, claiming an insurer bears the burden of exploring an applicant's needs at the precontractual stage.

[39] *Ibid.* 6.

[40] For such an interpretation see J. Grote and C. Schneider, 'VVG 2008: Das neue Versicherungsvertragsrecht' (2007) 62 *Betriebsberater* 2689, 2690.

[41] Convincingly: Armbrüster, *Aktuelle Rechtsfragen*, n. 15 above, at p. 8.

every customer individually for providing advice, but includes these costs in the insurance premiums, knowledgeable policy-holders are, in effect, forced to pay for a service they do not need or use, and subsidise providing advice to those who use it. The German legislator realised the controversies which imposing a duty to advise may cause. So as to address these concerns, section 6(1) VVG provides explicitly that 'in advising the applicant, the insurer is entitled to take into consideration an appropriate relation between the time and effort spent in providing advice and the insurance premiums to be paid by the future policy-holder'.

This provision has been met with criticism as apparently being contrary to the consumer protection objective of the German Insurance Contract Act.[42] While it is right that the provision's wording could be improved, the German legislator is generally correct to recognise that policy-holder protection comes at a price.[43] On the other hand, as explained above, an insurer can be clearly regarded as the 'cheapest cost avoider' with respect to transferring information about the content of insurance cover, for the insurer possesses a perfect knowledge about the products on offer. Therefore, it is necessary to elaborate a parallel interpretation of the 'appropriateness' requirement that will not weaken the core of the insurer's duty but will also provide an incentive for an insurer not to treat providing advice as a burden. According to a noteworthy interpretation, the 'appropriateness' test is fulfilled if an average applicant, in the place of a given customer, would be willing to pay a fee for being advised if the fee was charged separately from the insurance premiums due under a contract.[44] This account rightly emphasises the transparency of insurer's expenses as well as underlining that providing advice is a closely related but still a separate service on the part of the insurer. Furthermore, drawing on the presumed competence of an average policy-holder, this interpretation allows holding an insurer to higher standards of advice provision regarding the more complex types of

[42] See H. Dörner and A. Staudinger, 'Kritische Bemerkungen zum Referentenentwurf eines Gesetzes zur Reform des Versicherungsvertragsrechts' (2006) 60 *Wertpapiermitteilungen* 1710, 1711.

[43] In a related context of consumer's right of withdrawal under Directive 97/7/EC of 20 May 1997 on the protection of consumers in respect of distance contracts, Wagner has pointed out that, on his calculation, the extra cost imposed as a result of the Directive amounts to 2.80 euro per sale, cf. G. Wagner, 'Die soziale Frage und der gemeinsame Referenzrahmen' (2007) 15 *Zeitschfit für europäisches Privatrecht* 180, 207.

[44] Armbrüster, *Aktuelle Rechtsfragen*, n. 15 above, at p. 16.

insurance (e.g., life insurance), while also justifying not providing extensive advice where an insurer's quantum of advice costs would appear disproportionate given what is at stake for an applicant.[45]

Notwithstanding possible limitations resulting from the above interpretation, it is still possible to endorse the German doctrinal view that basic, necessary advice ought to be given regardless of the value of the insurance premiums in a given case. Moreover, where the policy-holder's understanding of insurance matters is poor, the criteria relating to the policy-holder's person or situation, as provided in section 6(1) VVG, may be relied upon to justify a duty to provide more extensive advice even as regards relatively simple products.[46]

## Waiving the right to advice

More controversially, section 6(3) VVG provides for an applicant's right to waive advice (including the insurer's duties of enquiry, advice and documentation), however, this can only be done by means of a written declaration in which an insurer explicitly indicates that such a waiver may have an unfavourable effect on the applicant's option for asserting a claim for damages against the insurer. This provision has been criticised for being inconsistent with the IMD (at least with regard to the strict scope of IMD application to intermediaries), since the latter does not provide for an explicit policy-holder's right to waive advice.[47] It is submitted that this provision may not guarantee a sufficient level of protection for cases where an insurance applicant does not realise that she does require assistance with choosing adequate cover.

## Remedy for a breach of a duty to advise

Undoubtedly, the intensity of policy-holder protection by means of precontractual advice depends largely on remedies which the law grants policy-holders if a duty to advise has been breached. In this respect, the VVG provides that an insurer who breaches the duty to advise, as set out in section 6(1) VVG, is liable to indemnify the policy-holder for any resulting loss or damage, unless the insurer is not responsible for the

45 Wandt, *Versicherungsrecht*, n. 25 above, at pp. 104–5.

46 Pohlmann, n. 36 above, § 6, Remark 12, referring to the legislative materials in BT-Drucks. 16/3945, 58.

47 Cf. Dörner and Staudinger, 'Kritische Bemerkungen', n. 42 above, at 1710, 1711.

breach (section 6(5) VVG). The wording of this provision clearly introduces a rebuttable presumption of the insurer's culpability, meaning that to avoid liability, it must be proven that no fault can be attributed to the insurer. Given that a duty to advise in the light of section 6(1) VVG is already breached when no advice has been provided, notwithstanding the insurer's recognition of a need for advice, it appears unlikely an insurer will be able to exculpate itself in such situations.[48] It follows that a policy-holder is obliged to prove there was a need for advice of which the insurer was aware, and it will then fall on the insurer to show that it has not been at fault in failing to detect the applicant's need for advice.[49]

Once a breach of a duty to advise has been established, an insurer is obliged to put a policy-holder in a position in which the latter would have found him/herself had the breach not been committed.[50] This may imply different forms of sanctions, among others, a retrospective termination of contract or adjusting of contract terms to what would have been accepted by a policy-holder had s/he been properly advised.

### Evaluation of the duty to advise under German law

Since the respective provisions have only been in force for a few years, it is impossible to provide a comprehensive evaluation of the duty to advise under The German Insurance Contract Act. Nevertheless, a number of comments regarding the statutory design of this duty appear justified. First, the exclusion of distance contracts from the duty to advise significantly reduces the Act's impact, as policy-holders nowadays increasingly turn to direct insurers selling online. Secondly, the requirement for a specific reason to trigger the duty to advise, as laid down in section 6(1) VVG, may undoubtedly be regarded as significantly different to the provisions of article 12(3) IMD. Thirdly, it is unclear whether the so-called '*anlassbezogene Beratung*' (occasion dependent advice), and the policy-holder's right to waive advice, are consistent

48 Cf. Pohlmann, n. 36 above, § 6, Remark 120.

49 *Ibid.*, s. 6, Remark 114, stressing the burden of proof would here be quite different were an insurer to be treated as an insurance advisor rather than a seller of insurance, however the latter being the case under German law.

50 German law recognises a rebuttable presumption that a policy-holder would have followed the insurer's advice, see C. Armbrüster in T. Langheid and M. Wandt (eds.), *Münchener Kommentar zum Versicherungsvertragsgesetz* (C.H. Beck, München, 2010), s. 6, Remark 319.

with the IMD.[51] Especially the latter right to waive advice could be viewed critically as fuelling over-reliance on the part of insurers to reduce their operations. Fourthly, it is submitted that the manner in which section 6(1) VVG has been drafted could imply that the German legislator wishes to protect insurers from excessive expectations on the part of potential applicants with respect to precontractual advice. On the other hand, it is possible that the fact of section 6 VVG having been drafted in the shadow of the IMD could enhance the practical impact of the duty to advise in Germany through a 'Europeanised' interpretation.[52] What appears crucial will be the precise interpretation of the 'appropriateness' requirement as a means by which to define the scope of insurer's duty to advise. This will be elaborated in the years to come, as the new rules are applied by the courts and the relevant supervisory bodies.

## Principles of European Insurance Contract Law

In order to provide a more complete account of the duty to advise in EU law, the extent to which the IMD and the German Insurance Contract Act influenced the position taken in the Principles of European Insurance Contract Law (PEICL)[53] should also be examined. The PEICL purport to be a 'Restatement of European Insurance Contract Law', modelled on American Restatements of the Law, in a manner which had previously been adopted by the Lando Commission on European Contract Law in the course of drafting its Principles of European Contract Law (PECL).[54] Most importantly, the PEICL have been drafted as a contribution to the Common Frame of Reference (CFR).

Providing general rules of insurance contract law, the PEICL encompass all types of insurance except reinsurance.[55] In their current shape, the PEICL form the 'general part' of insurance contract law, but the project's overall purpose is to provide the EU legislator with a model law designed to overcome the existing barriers to an integrated European insurance market. While partly based on the *acquis communautaire* in

[51] Ebers, in Praxiskommentar, s. 6, Remark 7, emphasising that recourse can be made to the CJEU.
[52] *Ibid.*, s. 6, Remark 7, expects such an evolution.
[53] J. Basedow *et al.*, *Principles of European Insurance Contract Law*, (Sellier, München, 2009), (PEICL).
[54] See Heiss in *ibid.* liii, with further references.
[55] *Ibid.* on the nature and the objectives of the PEICL.

insurance law, the PEICL do not transpose the IMD, as they do not deal with the professional duties of intermediaries at all. Yet, the IMD rules on precontractual duties toward prospective policy-holders remain relevant for the respective part of the PEICL, as discussed below.

## Duty to inform and advise under the PEICL

Section 2 of the PEICL is devoted to 'Insurer's pre-contractual duties'. To begin with, article 2:201 PEICL deals with the provision of precontractual documents by an insurer containing relevant information concerning the insurance contract. This rule, modelled on the Third Insurance Directives, appears to reflect a well-established duty under EU law.[56] Nonetheless, while article 2: 201 PEICL deals only with the process of transmitting specific information to a potential policy-holder, its design has far-reaching consequences for the position of a potential policy-holder as regards his/her familiarity with contract terms. It has been rightly pointed out that the content of article 2:201 PEICL suggests the potential policy-holder may not see all of the policy terms prior to the insurance cover commencing.[57] In this respect article 2:201(2) and (3) allow (exceptionally) for the possibility that the information required by article 2:201(1) is not provided to the policy-holder in advance of the conclusion of the contract. Furthermore, it is not entirely clear whether the significant features of the policy cover need to be included in the obligatory information.[58]

Thus, a concern about the limited availability of contract information to a policy-holder at the formation stage undoubtedly supports the case for an insurer's duty to warn, which has been dealt with in article 2:202 PEICL. It may be useful to recite paragraph (1) of article 2:202 in full:

> When concluding the contract, the insurer shall warn the applicant of any inconsistencies between the cover offered and the applicant's requirements of which the insurer is or ought to be aware, taking into consideration the circumstances and mode of contracting and, in particular, whether the applicant was assisted by an independent intermediary.

[56] See the Third Insurance Directives and the Directive on distance marketing of financial services (2002/65/EC); see Comment 1 to art. 2:201 PEICL.

[57] Hinchliffe, 'Review of Principles', n. 4 above, at 168.

[58] *Ibid.* 169. Article 2:201(1)(d) PEICL requires the provision of information about 'the subject matter of the insurance and the risks covered'. Admittedly, given this fairly general phrasing it is uncertain whether possible limitations and exclusions of cover need to be clearly communicated.

At first sight, article 2:202 PEICL appears to constitute a rather limited *duty to warn* the potential policy-holder about inconsistencies between the applicant's requirements and the cover offered. However, the treatment of the insurer's awareness of the inconsistencies regarding the insurance cover appears unclear. The first of the two alternatives, as mentioned in article 2:202 PEICL, namely, the case of the insurer having positive knowledge (without having made any specific enquiry) of an inconsistency between the applicant's requirements and the cover offered is rather straightforward. There is no doubt that an insurer is then under a duty to warn.

More complex is the second alternative set out in article 2:202 PEICL, namely, that an insurer *ought to* be aware of the inconsistency mentioned above. Providing that an insurer *ought to* be aware of the inconsistency implies that an insurer is under a duty to establish or specify the applicant's wishes and demands as regards the insurance cover. This first step corresponds to a 'know your client' duty, as analysed in the IMD. It has been claimed that the insurer's duty to explore the applicant's needs and wishes implies a duty to advise the latter about the insurer's products which may suit applicants' needs. On such a reading, one could claim that article 2:202 PEICL, though formally labelled 'a duty to warn', actually provides for a 'duty to advise'.[59]

The above interpretation does not appear entirely consistent with the exact wording of article 2:202 PEICL. According to this provision, however, in order to define the extent of the insurer's duty to warn or advise, the following factors must be 'taken into consideration': 'the circumstances and mode of contracting and, in particular, whether the applicant was assisted by an independent intermediary'. Two essential points need to be made in this regard.

First, the use of 'the circumstances and mode of contracting' as a criterion to define the duty to warn very clearly emphasises the open-ended character of article 2:202 PEICL. In this respect, the Drafters' Comments on article 2:202 PEICL provide an example of face to face precontractual negotiations between an applicant and an insurer as a typical situation where the duty to advise will be most extensive. In this respect the Comments make an explicit reference

59 See C. Armbrüster, 'Das Versicherungsrecht im Common Frame of Reference' (2008) 16 *Zeitschfit für europäisches Privatrecht* 775, 788, who claims that art. 2:202 PEICL obliges an insurer to make an enquiry about an applicant's specific demands as to insurance cover as well as advising her generally.

to article 12(3) IMD.[60] It may be then assumed that the insurer's duty under article 2:202 PEICL in such typical circumstances should correspond to the requirements made pursuant to article 12(3) IMD. Nevertheless, article 12(3) IMD does not provide definitive guidance on the extent of the duty to advise and leaves a number of issues unregulated. Furthermore, the PEICL, including the accompanying Comments, do not take a clear position on the extent of the duty to warn or advise with regard to distance contracts, the significance of which is nowadays rapidly growing.

Secondly, the Comments to article 2:202 PEICL make it clear that an insurer's duty to warn will arise only exceptionally, if an insurance applicant has been professionally advised by an independent intermediary.[61] This solution, which follows the position in German law, appears fully justified, given that an intermediary is subject to liability under the IMD for breaching his/her own duty to advise.

## Remedy for breach of duty to advise

While the requirements of a duty to warn under the PEICL are drafted in general terms, the remedies for breach of this duty have been dealt with in a more precise manner. Article 2:202(2) PEICL grants a policy-holder two remedies where an insurer breaches the duty to advise: first, the right to damages, and second, the right to terminate the contract. The PEICL provision on the policy-holder's right to claim damages for breach of a duty to warn by an insurer is very similar to the respective provision in German law that the insurer, where at fault, is liable for all possible losses resulting from its breach of duty to warn.

The policy-holder's right to terminate the contract, as provided for by the PEICL, merits attention, especially when compared to the position in German law. Except for the two months' period after learning about the insurer's breach, the PEICL do not appear to lay down any specific requirement of making use of this right to terminate. Neither the wording of article 2:202(2) PEICL nor the accompanying Comments support any restriction of the right to terminate. Instead, article 2:202(2) PEICL uses the connecting term 'and' to define the relationship between the two remedies. This means that the right to terminate the insurance contract could be invoked irrespective of whether the requirements of a

[60] PEICL, Article 2:202, Comment 4 PEICL. [61] *Ibid.* art. 2:202, Comment 4.

right to damages are fulfilled. As regards its effects upon the contractual relationship between the parties, the accompanying Comments provide that the termination of contract has no retroactive effects and works only for the future.[62] Generally, there is a plausible justification for the drafters' decision to provide for a right to terminate the contract. Once a breach of duty to warn becomes known to the policy-holder, he or she may not have enough confidence in the insurer's business integrity and may prefer the option of seeking insurance somewhere else in the market.

### Initial evaluation of the duty to advise under the PEICL

A straightforward conclusion regarding the way the PEICL deals with the insurer's duty to advise is difficult. To begin with, it must be emphasised that, in contrast to the technical and detailed provisions of EU Directives in consumer and insurance law, the PEICL are drafted 'with broad phrasing', as a codification of general norms of insurance contracts.[63] Following the PEICL's aim and scope, article 2:202 is drafted in a rather open manner, presumably in order to ensure its acceptability on the part of market actors and legislators across the European Union.[64]

Furthermore, it must be noted that the PEICL, more clearly than both the IMD and the German Insurance Contract Act, take into account the policy-holder's expectations resulting from the social perception of insurers in their function as guarantors. In this respect article 2:202 is rightly focused on establishing the duty to warn about possible inconsistencies between the 'presumed' cover (which may result from self-promotion on the part of the insurer) and the real cover offered. As far as remedies are concerned, the PEICL closely follows the German solution, offering a generally clear rule which facilitates claiming damages given the reversal of the burden of proof.

Finally, article 2:202 PEICL leaves a number of specific questions unanswered, in particular the issues pointed out regarding the IMD. Most importantly, as regards consumer contracts, this provision might be too general and needs to be made more specific by going beyond the general standard of 'the circumstances and mode of contracting'.

[62] *Ibid.* art. 2:202, Comment 9.

[63] Hinchliffe, 'Review of Principles', n. 4 above, at 171, emphasising also that the PEICL terminology does not appear to be closely related to that of the IMD.

[64] See H. Cousy, 'Le sectur des assurances sera-t-il "mifidise"?' (2009) *Bulletin des Assurances* 245, 253.

## Conclusions: toward a duty to advise in EU insurance law?

This chapter's objective has been to discuss the way in which an insurer's duty to explore a policy-holder's needs and provide advice is regulated in EU and German law. The discussion undoubtedly reveals the significant impact which the IMD has had on the recent German Insurance Contract Act, inspiring the imposition of an explicit duty to advise not only on intermediaries but also on insurers. This should be regarded as a noteworthy instance of Europeanisation of German insurance contract law. In this manner, despite the limited original scope of its application, the IMD has had a significant impact on the general conduct of business in the field of insurance and contributed to the Europeanisation process.

Providing an ambitious and comprehensive attempt at designing the duty to advise, the respective rules provided for under the German Insurance Contract Act present us with a number of complex legal issues which deserve our special attention. The Act's full implications, including the precise level of policy-holder protection and the impact on standards of conduct in the insurance sector, will be determined in the course of its application in the German courts and by the relevant supervisory bodies.

Turning to the duty to warn under the PEICL, it must be underscored that its design reflects to a significant extent the concepts of both the IMD and the German Insurance Contract Act. Nevertheless, given that the PEICL purport to be a 'Restatement of European Insurance Contract Law', their approach to a duty to advise is rather cautious in that they focus on a duty to warn and protect a policy-holder from a potential lack of cover. Nonetheless, the PEICL's use of broad phrasing should be noted, and the decision taken not to deal with a number of technical issues which would have allowed the PEICL to act as a basis for developing a more comprehensive regime for legislators, self-regulation schemes or the contracting parties themselves.

Undoubtedly, both the German Insurance Contract Act and the PEICL have the potential for inspiring national legislators, self-regulation in the insurance industry or the standard-setting function of the consumer associations. The broad phrasing used in both instruments, which appears immanent in the design of a duty to advise, dictates caution, but also leaves space for local regulators to tailor the design of the duty more specifically to local conditions. Clearly, there are matters meriting further attention. First of all, the extent to which a duty to advise takes into account the policy-holder's expectations resulting from the social perception of the insurers' role could be further refined. Furthermore, the design of a duty to warn or advise regarding distance contracting, not tackled in the instruments discussed, merits attention. Finally, a comprehensive regime of a duty to advise should also include criteria for judging the suitability of products in insurance law. The current discussion on the impact of the MiFID regime could provide a useful opportunity to inform further development of a duty to advise in insurance law.

# 13

# European contract law-making and development: lessons from the Unfair Contract Terms Directive's price term exemption

MICHAEL SCHILLIG

## Introduction

After ten years of intense debate on the future of European contract law[1] the European Commission recently issued the Proposal for a Regulation on a Common European Sales Law (CESL),[2] developed on the basis of the so-called Draft Common Frame of Reference (DCFR).[3] Under the Proposal, CESL constitutes an optional contract law regime, on an opt-in basis, available for cross-border contracts[4] between a trader and a consumer or a small or medium-sized enterprise.[5] The overall aim of the project is the reduction of transaction costs resulting from the applicability of different legal regimes and enhanced consumer

Dickson Poon School of Law, King's College London. This chapter draws on conclusions developed in M. Schillig, 'Directive 93/13 and the Price Term Exemption: A Comparative Analysis in the Light of the "Market for Lemons Rationale"' (2011) 60 *ICLQ* 933.

[1] Initiated at the beginning of the new millennium by Communication from the Commission to the Council and the European Parliament on European Contract Law, COM(2001)398 final; Communication from the Commission to the European Parliament and the Council on a More Coherent European Contract Law: An Action Plan, COM(2003)68 final; Communication from the Commission to the European Parliament and the Council on European Contract Law and the Revision of the *Acquis*: The Way Forward, COM(2004)651 final.

[2] European Commission, Proposal for a Regulation of the European Parliament and of the Council on a Common European Sales Law, COM(2011)635 final ('Draft Reg-CESL'). A further outcome of the review process is the recently adopted Consumer Rights Directive: Directive 20011/83/EU of the European Parliament and of the Council of 25 October 2011 on consumer rights, amending Council Directive 93/13/EEC and Directive 1999/44/EC of the European Parliament and of the Council and repealing Council Directive 85/577/EEC and Directive 97/7/EC of the European Parliament and of the Council [2011] OJ L304/64.

[3] C. von Bar *et al.* (eds.), *Principles, Definitions and Model Rules of European Private Law: Draft Common Frame of Reference* (DCFR) (Outline Edition) (Sellier, Munich, 2009).

[4] Art 4 Draft Reg-CESL, art. 4. [5] *Ibid.* art. 7.

confidence so that businesses and consumers can take full advantage of the internal market.[6]

Before embarking on a new and far-reaching venture in European contract law it is worth reflecting on past experiences in this area. For the time being, Directive 93/13/EC on unfair contract terms[7] (Unfair Contract Terms Directive) remains the most important and influential piece of European legislation in the heartland of contract law, and its 'price term exemption' vividly illustrates the fundamental difficulties of European contract law-making and development.

The 'price term exemption' is part of article 4(2):

> Assessment of the unfair nature of the term shall relate neither to the definition of the main subject matter of the contract nor to the adequacy of the price and remuneration, on the one hand, as against the services or goods supplies [*sic*] in exchange, on the other, in so far as these terms are in plain intelligible language.[8]

The efficacy of the fairness test at the heart of the protective regime hinges, to a large extent, on the delimitation of the scope of article 4(2).[9] The difficulties associated with this task have been recognised early on, albeit with a focus on the seller's or supplier's side of the bargain.[10] It was, however, the 'price or remuneration' side which has occupied national courts repeatedly.

At the level of European legislation, the Unfair Contract Terms Directive emerged as a compromise between two conflicting regulatory ideologies that obtained in the Commission and the Council, respectively: the consumer rights approach and the free markets and competition approach. No provision reflects the tension between both ideologies more clearly than article 4(2). This inherent conflict renders a coherent

[6] *Ibid.* art. 1.

[7] Council Directive 93/13/EC of 5 April 1993 on unfair terms in consumer contracts [1993] OJ L095 29. Article 32 of the Consumer Rights Directive merely inserts a new art. 8a requiring Member States to inform the Commission if they adopt stricter provisions pursuant to art. 8, in particular when the fairness test is extended to individually negotiated terms or to the adequacy of the price or remuneration.

[8] DCFR and CESL contain provisions to the same effect in DFCR, art. II 9:406 and CESL, art. 80(2) and (3), respectively.

[9] E. Macdonald, 'Mapping the Unfair Contract Terms Act 1977 and the Directive on Unfair Terms in Consumer Contracts' (1994) *Journal of Business Law* 441, 462.

[10] *Ibid.* 460; G. Howells and R. Brownsword, 'The Implementation of the EC Directive in Unfair Terms in Consumer Contracts: Some Unresolved Questions' (1995) *Journal of Business Law* 243, 247–52.

and consistent interpretation very difficult. A workable solution for the treatment of price terms may only be developed on the basis of a coherent and persuasive rationale that gives the Directive meaning and purpose. In recent years this rationale is emerging ever more clearly from the case law of the Court of Justice of the European Union (CJEU). When national courts are called upon to interpret European contract law in actual cases, often the picture that ensues is one of disharmony contrary to the internal market objective. As regards price terms, the case law of Germany's Federal Court of Justice (BGH) regarding banking related fees and charges appears to be very different from the solution adopted by the Supreme Court of the United Kingdom. Both approaches are inadequate. Only on the basis of a coherent rationale will national courts be able to ask the right questions in order to delineate the price term exemption. Ultimately, the task of interpreting article 4(2) must rest with the CJEU. Despite ample opportunity, the highest courts of Member States have so far not complied with their duty to refer to Luxembourg.

In the absence of a methodological and institutional framework that guarantees a uniform interpretation and application within the Union, merely providing a legislative text at European level may prove to be insufficient to overcome national differences in any meaningful way.

## Conflicting rationales of the Unfair Contract Terms Directive

When Directive 93/13/EC was drafted, the European Commission advocated a strict consumer rights approach. The first two proposals issued by the Commission were drafted with a view to subject every term in a consumer contract to a standard of fairness irrespective of whether it was individually negotiated or not. The Commission felt that it should be possible to assess the fairness of any contract or contract term and to invalidate it if it did not comply with the substantive standard of fairness protecting the economic interests of consumers provided for by the Directive.[11] Thus, consumers should be entitled to rights protecting

[11] European Commission, 'Amended Proposal for a Council Directive on Unfair Terms in Consumer Contracts, Explanatory Memorandum', (1992) 15 *Journal of Consumer Policy* 97, 98. In the amended Proposal of 1992 the standard of fairness for the assessment of individually negotiated terms was modified in order to better account for the principles of freedom of contract and *pacta sunt servanda* (Amended Proposal, art. 4).

their economic interests against business abusing its economic, social, psychological and intellectual superiority.[12]

This generated substantial criticism, in particular from Germany. According to Ulmer and Brandner,[13] subjecting any type of consumer contract, and in particular the equivalence of the relationship between the price and the goods or services, to fairness control would be 'anathema to the fundamental tenets of a free market economy'. They suggested to replace the inappropriate assessment of fairness with a market conform focus on improving transparency in respect of the principal obligations under the contract. This would help the market mechanism to prevent any imbalance between the parties' rights and obligations.[14]

This belief in the correcting effect of free markets and competition seems to have been prevalent in the Council of Ministers. Its Common Position of 22 September 1992 restricted the scope of the Directive to terms which have not been individually negotiated. As a compromise at the heart of the Directive, it also introduced article 4(2) and recital 19 in their final form in order to exclude 'anything resulting directly from contractual freedom of the parties (e.g. quality/price relationship)'.[15]

Thus, the Unfair Contract Terms Directive emerged as a compromise between a market-based approach necessary in order to justify the Directive in light of its legal basis,[16] and the consumer rights approach forcefully stated in recital 9. It has been submitted early on that the tension between these two conflicting rationales would make it difficult to coherently interpret and apply the Directive.[17] This is particularly true for article 4(2) at the heart of the compromise embodied in the Directive.

[12] H. Collins, 'Good Faith in European Contract Law' (1994) 14 *Oxford Journal of Legal Studies* 229, 236.

[13] H. Brandner and P. Ulmer, 'The Community Directive on Unfair Terms in Consumer Contracts: Some Critical Remarks on the Proposal Submitted by the EC Commission' (1991) 28 *CML Rev.* 647, 652–7.

[14] See further C.-W. Canaris, 'Wandlungen des Schuldvertragsrechts – Tendenzen zu seiner Materialisierung' (2000) 200 *Archiv für die civilistische Praxis* 273, 320–4.

[15] Council of the European Communities, 'Council Directive 92//EEC of 22 September 1992 on Unfair Terms in Consumer Contracts (Common Position)' 1992) 15 *Journal of Consumer Policy* 473, 485. The Council provides no further explanation for the amendment.

[16] Recitals 2, 5.

[17] E. Kapnopoulou, *Das Recht der mißbräuchlichen Klauseln in der Europäischen Union* (Mohr Siebeck, Tübingen, 1997), p. 75; *Director of Fair Trading* v. *First National Bank* [2002] 1 AC 498E, per Lord Steyn.

Moreover, neither approach can fully explain the case law of the CJEU on Directive 93/13/EC as it has developed over the last decade in the context of the internal market.

This case law is increasing rapidly.[18] Superficially, the Court appears to favour the consumer rights approach on the basis of the notion of an 'inequality of bargaining power'.[19] In a string of decisions, the CJEU has significantly strengthened the procedural and remedial aspects of the Directive. The power of a court to review a term of its own motion[20] and in disregard of national procedural restrictions,[21] as well as the

[18] Infringement proceedings: C-144/99 *Commission* v. *The Netherlands* [2001] ECR I-3541; C-372/99 *Commission* v. *Italy* [2002] ECR I-819; C-478/99 *Commission* v. *Sweden* [2002] ECR I-4147; C-70/30 *Commission* v. *Spain* [2004] ECR I-7999. Preliminary rulings: Joined Cases C-240 to C-244/98 *Océano Grupo Editorial SA* v. *Murciano Quintero* and *Salvat Editores SA* v. *Sánchez Alcón Prades and others* [2000] ECR I-4963; Joined Cases C-541/99 and 542/99 *Cape Snc* v. *Idelaservice Srl* and *Idealservice MN RE Sas* v. *OMAI Srl* [2001] ECR I-9049; C-473/00 *Cofidis SA* v. *Fredout* [2002] ECR I-10875; C-372/02 *Freiburger Kommunalbauten GmbH Baugesellschaft & Co. KG* v. *Hofstetter* [2004] ECR I-3403; C-302/04 *Ynos kft* v. *Varga* [2006] ECR I-371; C-168/05 *Mostaza Claro* v. *Centro Móvil Milenium SL* [2006] ECR I-10421; C-243/08 *Pannon GSM Zrt* v. *Erzsébet Sustikné Györfi* [2009] ECR I-4713; C-40/08 *Asturcom Telecomunicaciones SL* v. *Cristina Rodriguez Nogueira* [2009] ECR I-9579; C-484/08 *Caja de Ahorros de Piedad de Madrid* v. *Asociación de Usuarios de Servicios Bancarios (Ausbanc)* [2010] ECR I-4785; C-76/10 *Pohotovost' sro* v. *Korčkovská* [2010] ECR I-11557; C-137/08 *VB Pénzügyi Lizing Zrt* v. *Ferenc Schneider* [2009] ECR I-5347; C-453/10 *Pereničová and Perenič* v. *SOS finance spol. sro* (2012, nyr); C-472/10 *Nemzeti Fogyasztóvédelmi Hatóság* v. *Invitel Távközlési Zrt* (2012, nyr); C-618/10 *Banco Español de Crédito SA* v. *Calderón Camino* (2012, nyr).

[19] Joined Cases C-240 to C-244/98 *Océano Grupo Editorial SA* v. *Murciano Quintero* and *Salvat Editores SA* v. *Sánchez Alcón Prades and others* [2000] ECR I-4963, para. 25; C-243/08 *Pannon GSM Zrt.* v. *Erzsébet Sustikné Györfi* [2009] ECR I-4713, para. 22; C-40/08 *Asturcom Telecomunicaciones SL* v. *Cristina Rodriguez Nogueira* [2009] ECR I-9579, paras. 29–30; C-168/05 *Mostaza Claro* v. *Centro Móvil Milenium SL* [2006] ECR I-10421, paras. 36–8; C-40/08 *Asturcom Telecomunicaciones SL* v. *Cristina Rodriguez Nogueira* [2009] ECR I-9579, para. 51; C-484/08 *Caja de Ahorros de Piedad de Madrid* v. *Asociación de Usuarios de Servicios Bancarios (Ausbanc)* [2010] ECR I-4785, para. 27; C-76/10 *Pohotovost' sro* v. *Korčkovská* [2010] ECR I-11557, paras. 37, 38; C-453/10 *Pereničová and Perenič* v. *SOS finance spol. sro* (2012, nyr), paras. 27, 28.

[20] Joined Cases C-240 to C-244/98 *Océano Grupo Editorial SA* v. *Murciano Quintero* and *Salvat Editores SA* v. *Sánchez Alcón Prades and others* [2000] ECR I-4963, para. 26; C-243/08 *Pannon GSM Zrt.* v. *Erzsébet Sustikné Györfi* [2009] ECR I-4713, paras. 28, 32; C-168/05 *Mostaza Claro* v. *Centro Móvil Milenium SL* [2006] ECR I-10421, para. 30; C-40/08 *Asturcom Telecomunicaciones SL* v. *Cristina Rodriguez Nogueira* [2009] ECR I-9579, para. 59; C-472/10 *Nemzeti Fogyasztóvédelmi Hatóság* v. *Invitel Távközlési Zrt* (2012, nyr), para. 43.

[21] C-473/00 *Cofidis SA* v. *Fredout* [2002] ECR I-10875, para. 35; C-618/10 *Banco Español de Crédito SA* v. *Calderón Camino* (2012, nyr), para. 53.

extension of the collective procedure to merely recommended terms[22] and the further extension of the effect of such collective proceedings to all consumers who contracted with the respective seller or supplier,[23] enhances the effectiveness of the review procedure. By contrast, the Court has refused to provide any guidelines for even a minimum standard of substantive consumer protection.[24] If it was the purpose of the Directive to restore an effective balance between the rights and obligations of the parties distorted by an inequality of bargaining power, the Court's case law should provide at least an indication as to what an effective balance should look like. Pursuant to the rule in *Freiburger Kommunalbauten*, this is something the Court will not, and cannot, do.[25] Despite paying lip service to the consumer rights approach and the notion of 'inequality of bargaining power' this case law can be neither explained nor justified in light of this rationale.

The CJEU's case law can, however, readily be explained on the basis of the 'market for lemons' rationale.[26] According to this approach, the customer accepts the standard contract terms of his seller or supplier,

[22] C-372/99 *Commission* v. *Italy* [2002] ECR I-819, para. 15.

[23] C-472/10 *Nemzeti Fogyasztóvédelmi Hatóság* v. *Initel Távközlési Zrt* (2012, nyr), para. 38.

[24] Since *Freiburger Kommunalbauten*, the CJEU has repeatedly held that it may not rule on the application of the general criteria used by art. 3(1) to define the concept of 'unfair term' in respect of a particular term, C-372/02 *Freiburger Kommunalbauten GmbH Baugesellschaft & Co. KG* v. *Hofstetter* [2004] ECR I-3403, paras. 22–5; C-168/05 *Mostaza Claro* v. *Centro Móvil Milenium SL* [2006] ECR I-10421, para. 22; C-243/08 *Pannon GSM Zrt* v. *Erzsébet Sustikné Györfi* [2009] ECR I-4713, paras. 42–3. In *Océano*, the CJEU judged a term conferring exclusive jurisdiction on the court where the seller or supplier had its principal place of business to be unfair; Joined Cases C-240 to C-244/98 *Océano Grupo Editorial SA* v. *Murciano Quintero* and *Salvat Editores SA* v. *Sánchez Alcón Prades and others* [2000] ECR I-4963, paras. 22–4. However, Advocate-General Tizzano later stated that *Océano* represented 'a precedent that is most exceptional and is therefore not generally applicable'; AG Tizzano, Opinion in C-168/05 *Mostaza Claro* v. *Centro Móvil Milenium SL* [2006] ECR I-10421, para. 30. Thus, in *Pannon* the Court merely held that a similar term *may* be considered to be unfair, C-243/08 *Pannon GSM Zrt* v. *Erzsébet Sustikné Györfi* [2009] ECR I-4713, para. 44.

[25] In C-137/08 *VB Pénzügyi Lizing Zrt* v. *Ferenc Schneider* [2010] ECR I-5347, para. 44, the CJEU seemed to adopt a more activist approach. However, in C-453/10 *Pereničová and Perenič* v. *SOS finance spol. sro* (2012, nyr), para. 44 it returned to the traditional *Freiburger Kommunalbauten* formula. See further C-472/10, *Nemzeti Fogyasztóvédelmi Hatóság* v. *Initel Távközlési Zrt* (2012, nyr), para. 31.

[26] M. Schillig, 'Inequality of Bargaining Power versus Market for Lemons: Legal Paradigm Change and the Court of Justice's Jurisprudence on Directive 93/13 on Unfair Contract Terms' (2008) 33 *EL Rev.* 336; M. Schillig, 'Directive 93/13 and the Price Term Exemption: A Comparative Analysis in the Light of the "Market for Lemons Rationale"' (2011) 60 *ICLQ* 933.

not because of weakness in terms of knowledge and wealth,[27] but because it is not worth the effort to go through the small print and to fight for an alteration or to examine the offers of competitors in order to find more favourable terms. The customer will engage in searching and bargaining only up to the point at which the expected marginal benefits equal the marginal costs.[28] Where the probability of the respective risk materialising and/or the expected costs in that case are relatively low, the transaction costs resulting from negotiations and the search for better offers will often exceed the benefits. Moreover, because of unrealistic optimism and over-confidence, people tend to think that bad things are far less likely to happen to them than to others.[29] This further reduces the subjective net worth of a search effort. These considerations explain why the problem of standard contract terms cannot be solved on the basis of transparency alone, as advocated by Ulmer and Brander.

In this situation, sellers and suppliers use standard contract terms to shift certain risks they do not want to bear to their customers.[30] They do not have to be concerned about the loss of customers because these will be unaware of competing offers that would provide them with more favourable contract terms and a better price/quality ratio.[31] What ensues is Akerlof's 'market for lemons'[32] in respect of contract terms. Those sellers and suppliers who use low quality contract terms will gain an advantage. Others have no choice but to follow suit.[33] The result is a 'race to the bottom' towards, in the long run, contract terms which are the most disadvantageous for customers.[34] If the contract terms on offer do

[27] H. Kötz and A. Flessner, *European Contract Law* (Clarendon Press, Oxford, 1997), p. 139; W. Slawson, 'Standard Form Contracts and Democratic Control of Lawmaking Power' (1971) 84 *Harvard L Rev.* 529, 532.

[28] V. Goldberg, 'Institutional Change and the Quasi-Invisible Hand' (1974) 17 *Journal of Law and Economics* 461, 484.

[29] C. Jolls, C. Sunstein and R. Thaler, 'A Behavioural Approach to Law and Economics' (1998) 50 *Stanford L Rev.* 1471, 1524.

[30] Goldberg, 'Institutional Change and the Quasi-Invisible Hand', n. 28 above, at 484; Kötz and Flessner, *European Contract Law*, n. 27 above, at p. 138.

[31] See H.-B. Schäfer and C. Ott, *Lehrbuch der ökonomischen Analyse des Zivilrechts*, (4th edn, Springer, 2005), p. 515; Goldberg, 'Institutional Change and the Quasi-Invisible Hand', n. 28 above, at 485.

[32] G. Akerlof, 'The Market for "Lemons": Quality Uncertainty and the Market Mechanism' (1970) 84 *Quarterly Journal of Economics* 488, 495.

[33] Goldberg, 'Institutional Change and the Quasi-Invisible Hand', n. 28 above, at 486.

[34] Schäfer and Ott, *Lehrbuch der ökonomischen Analyse des Zivilrechts*, n. 31 above, at p. 515.

not comply with customer preferences, customers may leave the market and the market may disappear.[35]

In order to prevent this form of market failure it is necessary to provide for an effective control mechanism.[36] This requires an effective procedure guaranteeing that suspect terms will be subjected to review by an independent third party and will be disapplied or prohibited if found to be objectionable. In order to prevent the market from failing, it is sufficient to guarantee that the outcome of the review procedure is completely unpredictable to either of the contracting parties. Sellers and suppliers will be aware of the risk that their terms will be disapplied or prohibited if judged to be objectionable. Customers/consumers and the organisations representing their interests will equally be aware of the situation and will challenge only those terms that from their point of view are likely to be unjustifiable. Sellers and suppliers will realise that they will lose out if they go too far.[37] Their rational strategy will therefore be to provide unobjectionable terms. The formulation of a mandatory substantive standard of any specificity is unnecessary and not a matter for the control regime.[38]

This is not only consistent[39] with the CJEU's strengthening of the procedural and remedial aspects of the Directive, it neatly explains the Court's cautious approach in respect of the standard of fairness under

[35] M. Trebilcock and D. Dewees, 'Judicial Control of Standard Form Contracts' in P. Burrows and C. Veljanowski (eds.), *The Economic Approach to Law* (Butterworths, London, 1982), p. 108 *et seq.*

[36] See Kötz and Flessner, *European Contract Law*, n. 27 above, at p. 139.

[37] Consequently, a national provision that allows a court to revise the content of an unfair term is incompatible with Directive 93/13/EC. Such a power 'would contribute to eliminating the dissuasive effect on sellers or suppliers of the straightforward non-application to the consumer' of unfair terms, C-618/10 *Banco Español de Crédito SA* v. *Calderón Camino* (2012, nyr), para. 69.

[38] For a detailed analysis see Schillig, 'Inequality of Bargaining Power versus Market for Lemons', n. 26 above.

[39] No contrary argument can be derived form the CJEU's decision in C-484/08 *Caja de Ahorros de Piedad de Madrid* v. *Asociación de Usuarios de Servicios Bancarios (Ausbanc)* [2010] ECR I-4785. The Court held that Member States were not prevented from subjecting any contract term, including those falling within the ambit of art. 4(2), to an assessment of fairness. This seems to support the consumer rights approach. However, experience shows that minimum harmonisation tends to create new obstacles to free movement of goods and services, thus rendering the harmonisation effort futile from the outset. As a consequence, minimum harmonisation on the basis of the internal market competence must be deemed to be unlawful and provisions such as art. 8 should be interpreted in light of the EU Treaty; for details, cf. M. Schillig, *Konkretisierungskompetenz und Konkretisierungsmethoden im Europäischen Privatrecht* (DeGruyter, Berlin, 2009), pp. 58–62.

article 3 and the merely informative nature attributed to the provisions in the Annex.[40] Moreover, since Akerlof's 'market for lemons' is a specific form of market failure, any EU instrument which tackles this market failure can be justified much more easily on the basis of the internal market competence, at least when invoking the aim of enhancing cross-border economic activity.[41]

The 'market for lemons' rationale is also able to provide coherent and workable criteria for the definition and delineation of price terms.

## Price terms and the national courts

The difficulties of identifying price terms that fall within the ambit of article 4(2) are amply illustrated by the highly publicised litigation initiated by the OFT against seven high street banks and one building society[42] regarding terms which impose certain fees for unarranged overdrafts on bank customers. Under current accounts on a 'free-if-in-credit' basis[43] a bank will be able to use the customer's credit balance and pay an interest rate substantially lower than what it earns with the money. Where bank and customer arrange an overdraft facility in advance, the bank may charge a fee for making the facility available and will charge interest on the amount overdrawn. An 'unarranged overdraft' occurs where the bank honours a customer's payment instruction or request and the customer does not have sufficient funds in his account or a sufficient arranged overdraft facility to cover it.[44] In addition to charging interest on the overdraft, the bank may charge certain fees[45] in relation to the unarranged overdraft. The OFT brought a test case on whether the terms

[40] C-478/99 *Commission* v. *Sweden* [2002] ECR I-4147, paras. 20–2.

[41] As is done in recital 5.

[42] Abbey National plc, Barclays Bank plc, Clydesdale Bank plc, HSBC Bank plc, Lloyds Banking Group plc (including HBOS), Royal Bank of Scotland Group plc and Nationwide Building Society.

[43] These arrangements are described by Smith J in *OFT* v. *Abbey National plc and others* [2008] EWHC 875 (Comm), paras. 42–54.

[44] *OFT* v. *Abbey National plc and others* [2008] EWHC 875 (Comm), para. 55.

[45] The OFT identified, and the courts adopted, four basic categories of relevant charges: 'unpaid item charges', 'paid item charges', 'overdraft excess charges' and 'guaranteed paid item charges', *OFT* v. *Abbey National plc and others* [2008] EWHC 875 (Comm), para. 6; [2009] 2 WLR 1286, 1293A–F; [2009] UKSC 6, para. 24. According to an OFT Market Study (July 2008), banks earn over 30 per cent of their overall revenue from relevant charges; 23per cent of active accounts incurred at least one relevant charge in 2006, OFT, *Personal Current Accounts in the UK: An OFT Market Study* (July 2008), p. 5, available at www.oft.gov.uk/shared_oft/reports/financial_products/OFT1005.pdf.

imposing unarranged overdraft charges (the relevant terms) were exempt from an assessment of fairness under reg. 6(2) of the Unfair Terms in Consumer Contracts Regulations (UTCCR) 1999, SI 1999/2083, implementing article 4(2) in the United Kingdom.[46]

Since, as Lord Steyn has put it, in a broad sense all terms of the contract are related in some way to the price or remuneration[47] and because a multitude of different constellations are possible, further criteria are necessary in order to provide workable guidelines. The approaches adopted by the BGH in Germany and the Supreme Court of the United Kingdom in this respect differ and lead to conflicting results. To a greater or lesser extent, these approaches reflect either the consumer rights philosophy or the free market paradigm. Both are deficient and unsuitable as a basis for a coherent interpretation of article 4(2). By contrast, the 'market for lemons' rationale allows national courts and the CJEU[48] to ask the right questions.

### *BGH: exchange for goods or services*

According to the BGH's well settled case law, only those terms are exempt from assessment which describe the narrow area of mutual obligations in the sense that without these terms there cannot be a valid contract due to a lack of specification and determinability of its main content.[49] Conversely, terms that regulate the mutual obligations in deviation from statutory provisions or from the demands of good faith and good commercial practice, and could thus be substituted by default provisions, will be subject to assessment. Consequently, the BGH distinguishes between price terms that directly regulate the price or remuneration as the consumer's essential obligation and 'ancillary (price) terms'.[50] Although the latter may have an indirect impact on the price, in the absence of a valid agreement, they may be substituted by statutory default provisions. Statutory default provisions in that sense are not just

[46] The terms in question were challenged also in a large number of individual actions brought by individual customers. Those actions were for the most part stayed pending the outcome of the test case, see *OFT* v. *Abbey National plc and others* [2008] EWHC 875 (Comm), para. 2

[47] *Director of Fair Trading* v. *First National Bank* [2002] 1 AC 481, 499C–D per Lord Steyn.

[48] In C-472/10 *Nemzeti Fogyasztóvédelmi Hatóság* v. *Invitel Távközlési Zrt* (2012, nyr), para. 23, the CJEU has so far merely held that the price term exemption cannot apply to a term relating to a mechanism for amending the prices of the services provided to the consumer.

[49] BGHZ 100, 158, 174.

[50] BGH, 15 July 1997 – XI ZR 269/96 (1997) NJW 2752.

provisions that are codified, but also generally accepted legal principles and the essential rights and obligations of the parties as they follow from the nature of the respective contractual relationship. A seller or supplier may, according to general principles, claim a price or remuneration only for goods or services actually delivered or supplied on the basis of a contractual arrangement. A term which imposes a payment obligation that is not related to such an actual delivery or supply, but merely seeks to indemnify the seller or supplier for expenses that he incurred in discharging his own statutory obligations, is a term that deviates from statutory provisions and is therefore an ancillary term subject to assessment. Thus, the BGH assesses whether terms with an impact on price or remuneration do relate to an actual delivery or supply in exchange.[51] Thus, a term in a discount brokerage contract imposing a fee on the customer for transferring securities from one account to another was held to be an ancillary term subject to assessment as the transfer occurred in discharge of the customer's statutory claim to repossess securities which was to be effected by book entry.[52]

This may be contrasted with one of the leading cases where the BGH held that a term in a credit card contract providing for an additional fee where the card was used abroad was an exempt price term.[53] Qualifying the principles stated above, the court held that a term which imposes fees for additional services which are not part of the supplier's main obligations can be price terms if there are no statutory provisions dealing with the additional service. The normal services of the credit card provider were paid for with an annual basic charge. The additional fee for credit card use abroad was justified as consideration for an additional service for which no statutory default provisions existed. Similarly, terms imposing a charge for ATM transactions were held to be exempt price terms as the provision of ATMs amounted to a specific service provided by the bank for which no statutory default provisions existed.[54]

Reflecting the consumer rights notion ('value for money'), this approach subjects to control all those price related terms that impose a charge on the consumer merely incidentally and not in exchange for a (further) benefit bestowed on the consumer not already paid for by the actual price as part of the 'main subject matter of the contract'. The BGH's approach is an objective one that rests on, and depends upon, the

[51] *Ibid.* 2753. [52] BGH, 30 November 2004 – XI ZR 200/03 (2005) NJW 1275.

[53] BGH, 14 October 1997 – XI ZR 167/96 (1998) NJW 383.

[54] BGH, 7 April 1996 – XI ZR 217/95 (1996) NJW 2032.

applicable default provisions provided by statutes, general legal principles or the nature of the contract. The reference to codified default provisions and the demands of good faith render a uniform interpretation across the European Union almost impossible. The reference to the nature of the contract, in the absence of codified law, is obviously circular. Moreover, in a market economy committed to the principle of contractual freedom it is for the parties to decide which events may trigger payments and what are the composite elements of monetary consideration which may consist of separate payments to be paid for an overall package of services.[55] Also, in principle there is nothing wrong with passing on to the consumer costs generated by discharging the supplier's own statutory obligations.[56]

### *UK Supreme Court: 'monetary consideration'*

Under the former UTCCR 1994, reg. 3(2), the House of Lords discussed the definition of price terms in *Director of Fair Trading* v. *First National Bank*[57] in respect of a 'default term' which provided that interest would continue to accrue on the outstanding balance 'after as well as before' a consumer's payment obligation was reduced to judgment. Lord Bingham distinguished between terms, which express the 'substance of the bargain', and 'incidental terms' which surround them. In order not to frustrate the objective of consumer protection, reg. 3(2) was to be interpreted narrowly so as to cover only those terms 'falling squarely within it'.[58] Similarly, Lord Steyn argued for a 'restrictive interpretation' also in respect of the 'adequacy of price and remuneration'. As an ancillary or subsidiary 'default provision', dealing with secondary liability, the term in *First National Bank* was not exempt from assessment.[59]

Pursuant to the approach adopted by the majority[60] of the Supreme Court in *OFT* v. *Abbey National*, the purpose of the Regulations was

55 C.-W. Canaris, 'Wandlungen des Schuldvertragsrechts – Tendenzen zu seiner Materialisierung' (2000) 200 *Archiv für die civilistische Praxis* 273, 335–6.
56 M. Schillig, 'The Contribution of Law and Economics as a Method of Interpretation in European Private Law' (2009) 17 *ERPL* 853, 861.
57 [2002] 1 AC 481.
58 *Director of Fair Trading* v. *First National Bank* [2002] 1 AC 481, 491C–F per Lord Bingham.
59 *Ibid.* 499C–D per Lord Steyn.
60 Lady Hale and Lord Neuberger concurred with Lord Walker and Lord Mance, *OFT* v. *Abbey National plc and others* [2009] UKSC 6, para. 92 per Lady Hale; para. 119 per Lord Neuberger. By contrast, Lord Phillips adopted a different approach, but reached the same result as the majority; *ibid.* paras. 78–89 per Lord Phillips.

not consumer protection but consumer choice.[61] Based on the language of Directive and Regulations, the main subject matter of the contract may be goods or services. Where the goods consist of a multiplicity of items or the services are composite, there was no principled basis on which the court could decide that some services are more essential to the contract than others.[62] The services that banks offer to their current account customers were such a package of services. Deciding which prices are essential was equally difficult and reg. 6(2)(b) did not contain any indication that only an 'essential price or remuneration' was relevant. Any monetary price or remuneration payable under the contract would naturally fall within the language of reg. 6(2)(b).[63] Banking services to current account customers constituted a package, as did the consideration that moves from the customer to the bank.[64] Accepting Lord Steyn's and Lord Bingham's reasoning in *First National Bank*, Lord Walker reached the conclusion that the relevant terms did fall 'squarely' within reg. 6(2)(b). Whereas delivery of goods or peripheral extras may be regarded as ancillary for the purposes of reg. 6(2)(a), the charges for them, if payable under the same contract, are part of the price for the purposes of paragraph (b).[65] According to Lord Mance, article 4(2) and reg. 6(2) could loosely be described as being concerned with the assessment of 'core terms'. But that was on the basis that price and remuneration always fell within them.[66] The requirement of transparency being met, the consumer is assumed to be capable of reading the relevant terms and identifying whatever is objectively the price or remuneration under the contract.[67]

Applying these considerations to the relevant terms, Lord Walker held that the relevant charges were monetary consideration for the package of banking services.[68] While the incurring of relevant charges may well be something that customers would like to avoid, it was a clearly explained and a very important feature of the overall package.[69]

61 *Ibid.* para. 44 per Lord Walker; see also P. Davies, 'Case Comment: Bank Charges in the Supreme Court' (2010) 69 *CLJ* 21, 23.

62 *OFT* v. *Abbey National plc and others* [2009] UKSC 6, paras. 39, 40 per Lord Walker.

63 *Ibid.* para. 41 per Lord Walker; but not non-monetary obligations undertaken by the consumer.

64 *Ibid.* para. 42 per Lord Walker.

65 *Ibid.* para. 46 per Lord Walker.

66 *Ibid.* para. 112 per Lord Mance.

67 *Ibid.* para. 113 per Lord Mance.

68 *Ibid.* para. 47 per Lord Walker.

69 *Ibid.* para. 47 per Lord Walker; para. 88 per Lord Phillips.

This approach appears to be in line with the free market and competition rationale. As an eminent German writer puts it, in respect of the functioning of competition, it is irrelevant whether the price is contained in one term or dispersed across terms, as long as the consumer has at his disposal the necessary information to compare the terms of different suppliers and to decide on the basis of that comparison.[70] However, their Lordships fail to provide any criteria as to how to identify and differentiate the terms providing for 'monetary consideration' from other terms. Lord Walker's main point seems to be that the relevant charges are an important part of the bank's revenue structure. This argument is irrelevant from the point of view of the consumer rights approach, but it also has no bearing on the free market and competition rationale. Despite the banks' charging structure, market and competition may not function properly. There may be a monopoly with no choice for consumers at all. By contrast, Lord Mance's argument rests on the notion that a consumer, entering into a free-if-in-credit account, accepts the relevant charges, so long as they are transparent, as part of the bargain. But this is true for all transparent contractual terms, including clauses that exclude liability or 'default terms' of the *First National* variety. There is no justification why the former should be exempt from assessment and the latter should not. Overall, the Supreme Court's approach seems to be overly formalistic.[71] It neither considers nor reflects the reasons why standard contract terms are subjected to fairness review in the first place.[72] No persuasive criteria for the delineation of price terms are provided.

The Supreme Court's decision may be directly contrasted with BGH, 21 October 1997 – XI ZR 5/97. The issue was the fairness of terms in a current account contract that imposed charges where the bank refused to carry out a payment instruction (by standing order, direct debit, cheque or bank transfer) due to an insufficiency of funds in the respective account. These terms were held to be non-exempt ancillary terms. A service provider may charge only for services he actually provides to the customer on a contractual basis. Any price-related term that does not relate to an actual service, but seeks to indemnify the supplier for

[70] Canaris, 'Wandlungen des Schuldvertragsrechts', n. 55 above, at 330.

[71] Davies, 'Case Comment: Bank Charges in the Supreme Court', n. 61 above, at 22: 'more literal approach . . . than is perhaps desirable'.

[72] M. Chen-Wishart, 'Case Comment: Transparency and Fairness in Bank Charges' (2010) 126 *LQR* 157, 160–1.

expenses incurred for discharging his own statutory obligations or in pursuance of his own interests are terms deviating from statutory default provisions and, as ancillary terms, are subject to assessment. Where the bank rejects a payment instruction due to insufficient assets it does not provide a service to the customer but acts exclusively in its own interest.[73] In a later decision,[74] the BGH held, in respect of cases where a direct debit instruction is returned due to insufficient funds, that the customer has no obligation vis-à-vis his bank to maintain sufficient funds in order to carry out direct debits. In the case of direct debits, the payor's bank does not act upon an instruction coming from the payor; rather it receives an instruction from the payee's bank. Thus, only in its own interest and in the interest of the payee's bank does the payor's bank verify and decide whether to debit its customer's account or not.

Thus, in respect of 'unpaid item charges',[75] the outcome of the BGH's line of reasoning is clearly in conflict with the Supreme Court's decision. However, if faced with 'guaranteed paid item charges'[76] the BGH's conclusion should be the same as the Supreme Court's. In that case the bank, objectively, provides an additional service to its customer in exchange for an additional fee. The situation is comparable to fees for the use of a credit card abroad[77] or for ATM transactions.[78] The situation in respect of 'paid item charges'[79] and 'overdraft excess charges'[80] is more complex under the BGH's case law. Whether the bank provides a service in exchange for the charges depends on the reason for the overdraft. If it is due to a payment instruction coming from the consumer

73 BGH, 21 October 1997 – XI ZR 5/97 (1998) NJW 309, 310.

74 BGH, 8 October 2005 – XI ZR 154/04 (2005) NJW 1645.

75 An 'unpaid item charge' may be imposed where the customer gives an instruction or makes a request for payment that the bank declines to honour because the customer does not have sufficient funds in his account or a sufficient overdraft facility.

76 Some banks levy a 'guaranteed paid item charge' when they honour a payment instruction for which the customer does not have sufficient funds in accordance with a guarantee they have given third parties by way of a cheque guarantee card or under a guaranteed debit payment system.

77 BGH, 14 October 1997 – XI ZR 167/96 (1998) NJW 383.

78 BGH, 7 May 1996 – XI ZR 217/95 (1996) NJW 2032.

79 A 'paid item charge' may be incurred if the bank honours a relevant instruction and as a consequence the customer's account goes into debit or the debit balance exceeds the limit of an arranged overdraft.

80 An 'overdraft excess charge' may be levied where during a specified period, typically a day or a month, the account is/or goes into debit (or the debit balance exceeds the limit of an arranged overdraft).

the bank provides an additional service in exchange for a price. By contrast, if the overdraft is due to a direct debit, that is, the payment request comes from a third party, then the principles of BGH, 8 October 2005 – XI ZR 154/04, require to differentiate between the situation where the consumer owed the third party an amount equal to the payment carried out by the bank, and the situation where this is not the case. Only in the former situation does the bank provide an additional service to its customer. Consequently, where the respective terms do not distinguish between these situations they should be subject to fairness control in their entirety.[81] Thus, Supreme Court and BGH are on the same page only in respect of 'guaranteed paid item charges'. In all other cases their case law cannot be reconciled – a very unsatisfactory situation indeed.

### *Asking the right questions under the 'market for lemons' rationale*

When price terms are determined on the basis of the 'market for lemons' rationale, all terms in respect of which it can be established that the market fails in the manner described above are not (part of) the 'main subject matter of the contract' and should be subjected to fairness control. The decisive question therefore is whether the contract term at issue is exposed to market forces and free competition in such a way that consumers will take this term into account and factor it into their decision to enter into the contract. Only in that case may it be assumed that the market will ensure an adequate balance of the interests of the contracting parties, rendering judicial intervention unnecessary.[82] Consumers will be interested, first and foremost, only in those consequences of a contract that, foreseeably, will have an impact on their future dispositions. Consequences that are not of direct concern to the consumer, but may affect him only under certain (contingent) circumstances will usually not be worth the time and effort necessary for acquiring the requisite information, negotiating and searching for better offers. In respect of such terms, market and competition cannot unfold their correcting effect. This may be true, in particular, for terms that

[81] Article 5, Second sentence, prevents an interpretation of the term to the effect that it only applies where an additional service is rendered.

[82] L. Fastrich, *Richerliche Inhaltskontrolle im Privatrecht* (C.H. Beck, Munich, 1992), p. 265; M. Stoffels, 'Schranken der Inhaltskontrolle' (2001) *Juristen Zeitung* 843, 847.

impose payment obligations in exchange for services that, at the time of the contract, the consumer believes he will not call on.[83]

Here it must be emphasised, that the question is not whether a concrete consumer has factored the term into his decision to enter into a concrete contract, nor does it depend on whether an idealised consumer would have taken the term into account. Rather, the appropriate inquiry should be whether the market has produced non-competitive prices and contract terms; the focus should be on the competitive behaviour of markets, not on the decision-making patterns of individuals.[84] This is because the presence of at least some consumers in a market[85] who are informed and actively search for better prices and contract terms may create an external benefit for uninformed consumers.[86] If enough searchers exist and if it is too expensive for firms to discriminate against non-searchers,[87] firms have incentives to compete for the business of searchers and to offer the same terms to non-searchers.[88] As long as there is no reason to believe that consumers who search differ widely in their preferences from consumers who do not search, competition among firms for the business of searchers will generate prices and contract terms that are utility-maximising for non-searchers as well.[89] If the market behaves competitively in this manner, intervention cannot be justified.

Moreover, pursuant to article 4(2), a term will be exempt from assessment only to the extent that it is in 'plain intelligible language'. Obviously, terms that cannot be understood properly and that are not clear cannot be factored into a consumer's decision to enter into a contract. However, the question is not what is intelligible for some idealised, fictional consumer such as the average consumer who is

[83] *Ibid.* 848.

[84] A. Schwartz and L. Wilde, 'Intervening in Markets on the Basis of Imperfect Information: A Legal and Economic Analysis' (1979) 127 *University of Pennsylvania Law Review* 630, 631, 637.

[85] According to Schwartz and Wilde, a ratio of searchers to non-searchers of one-third or more would be sufficient; *ibid.* 653, 655.

[86] H. Beales, R. Craswell and S. Salop 'The Efficient Regulation of Consumer Information' (1981) 24 *J Law and Econ.* 491, 503.

[87] Firm discrimination among consumers will only occur in respect of individualised transactions where the firm representative spends a relatively large amount of time with the customer to get to know them; it will be too expensive as far as mass transactions are concerned, see Schwartz and Wilde, 'Intervening in Markets on the Basis of Imperfect Information', n. 84 above, at 662–5.

[88] *Ibid.* 638. [89] *Ibid.* 639.

reasonably well informed and reasonably circumspect. What matters is, for the reasons stated above, the competitive behaviour of the market in respect of the contract term in question. Thus, the criterion of 'plain and intelligible language' in article 4(2) is redundant and fully absorbed in the definition of 'main subject matter of the contract' on the basis of the 'market for lemons' rationale.

On the basis of this approach the right questions can be asked in order to determine whether the terms imposing charges for unarranged overdrafts are, as price terms, part of the 'main subject matter of the contract' and, thus, exempt from assessment under Directive 93/13/EC. The crucial question is whether customers in general are sensitive to these terms and factor them into their decision to contract when they enter into an account agreement with their bank; whether the market overall behaves competitively in respect of the relevant terms. This is an empirical question. The fact that relevant terms impose charges in contingent circumstances and that the relevant terms are not at the forefront of the banks' advertising may be an indicator that market and competition do not work well in this respect. The OFT's market study on personal current accounts in the United Kingdom found evidence of a lack of importance of unarranged overdraft charges to many consumers when they enter into a current account agreement. Only 5 per cent of the people surveyed felt that these charges were an important factor when they opened their main account. There was no significant difference between those who had incurred these charges in the last twelve months and those who had not. Moreover, internal bank documents suggested that banks knew that demand was not sensitive to relevant charges and that a bank could thus increase these charges without risking losing market share. Users of a price comparison site hardly ever looked at how much the relevant charges varied across banks. A study of banking in Northern Ireland also found that consumers did not consider relevant charges when choosing an account because they did not think they would apply to them.[90] This is precisely the form of market failure that the Unfair Contract Terms Directive seeks to prevent.

Ultimately, only the CJEU can guarantee the EU-wide uniform interpretation and application of the Directive by clarifying the meaning of the price term exemption under article 4(2). However, the

[90] OFT, *Personal Current Accounts in the UK*, n. 45 above, paras. 4.7–4.9.

preliminary ruling mechanism requires the cooperation of national courts. Unfortunately, to date the highest courts of Member States have not enlisted the Court's interpretative authority in respect of article 4(2), despite ample opportunity to do so.[91] Hopefully, when the time comes the CJEU will not shirk its responsibilities by relying on the outdated interpretation/application divide, and will ask the right questions on the basis of the 'market for lemons' approach.

## Conclusion

Whether Europe needs a unified contract law in the form of an optional instrument or otherwise is an open question and not the topic of this contribution. The lessons to be drawn from Directive 93/13/EC and the experience with its price term exemption are more limited. Where legal rules emerge as a compromise between conflicting philosophies and are not informed by a coherent underlying rationale, a uniform and consistent interpretation and application by national courts in different Member States and the CJEU will be extremely difficult. At least to some extent, this problem can and should be remedied during the drafting process by being clear about the aims and objectives of a certain rule and the means to achieve them. However, in order to make a real difference in practice more is required. It is in their application by national courts that these rules will generate their real-world impact on people's lives. In light of the different legal traditions within the Member States, uniformity of application can only be achieved if the law is based on a meaningful and coherent rationale that can inform the methods of legal reasoning and interpretation of national courts. Moreover, national courts must no longer decide in national isolation. Rather, what is required is a developed pan-European case law methodology where national courts take the decisions of the highest courts of other Member States into account by either following them or deviating on the basis of good reasons only. The *CILFIT* doctrine[92] carries the seed for such a development. This system must be completed by an institutional structure that guarantees the involvement of the CJEU as final interpretative authority. The preliminary ruling mechanism, in

[91] M. Schillig, 'Directive 93/13 and the Price Term Exemption: A Comparative Analysis in the Light of the "Market for Lemons Rationale"' (2011) 60 *ICLQ* 933, 961–2.

[92] 283/81 *CILFIT* [1982] ECR 3415.

its current form, is ineffective in guaranteeing the EU-wide uniform interpretation of European contract law and will have to be reformed, perhaps by granting parties a right to final appeal to the Court or a specialised panel on private law, at least where the issue is of general importance. In the absence of these prerequisites, uniformity of application will only be skin-deep and legal fragmentation will persist. The legislative efforts at European level will then not generate any measurable benefits.

14

# Enforcement or compensation? Damages actions in EU law after the Draft Common Frame of Reference

DOROTA LECZYKIEWICZ

## Introduction

This chapter looks at the potential impact of the Draft Common Frame of Reference (DCFR) on the EU legal institution of damages actions. Its purpose is to compare the nature and functions of damages actions as traditionally conceptualised by EU law and the approach to the corresponding legal institutions in the DCFR. For this purpose, the chapter discusses the existing law of damages actions in the European Union and the regime of non-contractual liability in the DCFR. The chapter explains that remedies in EU law have been dominated by the concern for devising an effective system of enforcement. The DCFR, on the other hand, is inspired to a great extent by ideas of corrective justice and compensation. At the deeper level, however, it hides many features which would enable the non-contractual liability regime in the DCFR to act as a mechanism of enforcement. The chapter argues that the two perspectives are in many respects incompatible.[1] A compensation-focused regime has the following features: (1) the existence of loss is a necessary condition of an award; (2) the award reflects the value of losses which have actually been proved; and (3) the award may be conditional on proving that the defendant acted negligently (was at fault), but the gravity of the defendant's misconduct

Leverhulme Trust Early Career Fellow, Faculty of Law and Trinity College, University of Oxford.

[1] See an elaboration of this claim with reference to competition law in W.H. van Boom, 'The Law of Damages and Competition Law: *Bien étonnés de se trouver ensemble?*' in R. Schulze (ed.), *Compensation of Private Losses: The Evolution of Torts in European Business Law* (Sellier, Munich, 2011), p. 165. One way of explaining the incompatibility between an enforcement-focused and a compensation-focused regime is by pointing to the prospective character of the former and the retrospective character of the latter.

does not affect the measure of damages. An enforcement-focused regime has the following features: (1) the existence of loss is not a necessary condition of liability; (2) the necessary condition of liability is a breach of a regulatory standard; (3) the award may exceed the value of losses which have actually been proved; (4) the gravity of the defendant's misconduct affects the measure of damages (directly or at least indirectly) and slight violation of a norm may be left unsanctioned; and (5) punitive damages are not excluded. The chapter argues that a damages actions regime based on the idea of enforcement is a more suitable approach for EU law in both the public and the private law context.

## Damages actions as an enforcement mechanism in EU law

In EU law, damages actions constitute a special mechanism for enforcing EU norms.[2] Their special character stems from the fact that since 1991 they do not constitute just one of the optional remedies which the Member States can choose to ensure effectiveness of an EU norm.[3] Instead, national courts are in certain situations obliged to make this remedy available to individuals, even if other enforcement mechanisms could ensure 'effective judicial protection' of EU rights.[4] Availability of the *Francovich* remedy *in casu* depends on conditions set out in EU law: an action has to be brought against a Member State for its failure to fulfil obligations stemming from EU law; the rule of law infringed by the Member State must be intended to confer rights on the claimant; the infringement of EU law must be sufficiently serious; and there has to be a direct causal link between the infringement and the damage sustained by the claimant.[5] These conditions can be divided into those which focus on the claimant (the existence of a right under EU law, the existence of damage) and those that focus on the defendant Member State (the existence of breach, sufficient seriousness of the breach, the causal link). This would suggest that the *Francovich* remedy

[2] Damages actions contribute to the regulatory effect of EU law. On the regulatory effect of tort liability, see P. Cane, 'Tort Law as Regulation' (2002) 31 *Common Law World Review* 305.

[3] 6/90 and 9/90 *Francovich* [1991] ECR 5357.

[4] Joined Cases C-46 and 48/03 *Brasserie du Pêcheur* [1996] ECR I-1029.

[5] Joined Cases C-46/93 and 48/93 *Brasserie du Pêcheur* [1996] ECR I-1029, para. 51; C-392/93 *British Telecommunications* [1996] ECR I-1631, para. 39; C-5/94 *Hedley Lomas* [1996] ECR I-6297, para. 25; Joined Cases C-178 to 179/94, 188–190/94 *Dillenkofer* [1996] ECR I-1531, para. 21; C-352/98 P *Bergaderm and Goupil* v. *Commission* [2000] ECR I-5291, paras. 41–4.

performs two functions, and given the fact that the remedy is that of damages the compensatory function might seem dominant. In reality, however, the way the Court of Justice of the European Union (CJEU) elaborated and used individual conditions of the *Francovich* liability largely confirms the view expressed by Harlow in 1995 that the primary function of the remedy is punitive.[6] Defendant-focused conditions of liability seem to play a much greater importance. Only one case before the CJEU failed because an individual could not show that he was granted a right by EU law.[7] Conversely, many cases were decided favourably for the Member States by the CJEU on the ground that the breach was not 'sufficiently serious'. These could be interpreted as policy decisions taken by the Court that in the event of moderate breach by the state it is not sensible to employ the complex machinery of the *Francovich* remedy.[8] Damage suffered by effectiveness of EU law and the prospective benefits of enforcing an EU norm were not in these cases, in the eyes of the Court, sufficiently significant. Damages actions are thus designed to act as a deterrent, contributing to better enforcement of obligations imposed on Member States. Compensation serves here as an encouragement for individuals to bring actions. Moreover, the CJEU, while not insisting on a punitive measure of damages, considers it acceptable in the context of the *Francovich* liability.[9]

## Damages actions against individuals

The *Francovich* remedy is restricted to actions against the Member States. In 2001, the CJEU decided *Courage*,[10] a case in which a tenant of a pub whose lease agreement included a 'beer tie' (the obligation to purchase beer exclusively from Courage, a co-owner of the pub in question) wished to rely on EU law to seek damages against the beer company as

[6] C. Harlow, 'Francovich and the Problem of the Disobedient State' (1995) 2 *European Law Journal* 199, but see T. Lock, 'Is Private Enforcement of EU Law through State Liability a Myth? An Assessment 20 Years after Francovich' (2012) 49 *Common Market Law Review* 1675. Punishment is an instrument of deterrence whose purpose is not only retribution but also to modify future behaviour.

[7] C-222/02 *Peter Paul* [2004] ECR I-9425.

[8] C-392/93 *British Telecommucations* [1996] ECR I-1631; Joined Cases C-283/94, C-291/94 and C-292/94 *Denkavit* [1996] ECR I-5063; C-319/96 *Brinkmann* [1998] ECR I-5255; C-224/01 *Köbler* [2003] ECR I-10239.

[9] Joined Cases C-46 and 48/03 *Brasserie du Pêcheur* [1996] ECR I-1029, para. 90.

[10] C-453/99 *Courage* v. *Crehan* [2001] ECR I-6297.

a counterclaim to their claim for unpaid deliveries. In English law the tenant's claim was barred by the defence of illegality and therefore a damages action was not available against the company who used anti-competitive practices. The CJEU held that 'a party to a contract liable to restrict or distort competition within the meaning of [Article 101 TFEU] can rely upon the breach of that provision to obtain relief from the other contracting party' and that the Treaty 'precludes a rule of national law under which a party to a contract liable to restrict or distort competition ... is barred from claiming damages for loss caused by performance of that contract on the sole ground that the claimant is a party to that contract'. This case showed that EU damages actions could be brought also against non-state actors, at least for the violation of Article 101 TFEU. Yet, the question of who had the right to damages under Article 101 TFEU remained open until the Court's judgment in *Manfredi*.[11] In this case, the Court was asked once again to interpret what is now Article 101 TFEU, this time to determine whether this provision entitled 'third parties who have a relevant legal interest to rely upon the invalidity of an agreement or practice prohibited by that Community provision and claim damages for the harm suffered where there is a causal relationship between the agreement or concerted practice and the harm'. On this occasion, the CJEU replied by holding that '[Article 101 TFEU] must be interpreted as meaning that any individual can rely upon the invalidity of an agreement or practice prohibited under that article and, where there is a causal relationship between the latter and the harm suffered, claim compensation for that harm'.

Similarly to the *Francovich* remedy, the *Courage* action is clearly perceived by the CJEU as a mechanism of enforcement of EU competition law.[12] Mere breach of Article 101 TFEU is the foundation of the claim. It seems unimportant for the Court that Article 101 TFEU in fact does not grant any rights to individuals (other competitors, consumers). The Court considered it sufficient that the provision had 'direct effect'. 'Any individual' may bring an action. The only condition of actionability

[11] Joined Cases C-255 and 298/04 *Manfredi* [2006] ECR I-6619.

[12] C-453/99 *Courage*, n. 10 above, para. 26; C-295 and 298/04 *Manfredi*, n. 11 above, para. 60. A.P. Komninos, 'Civil Antitrust Remedies between Community and National Law' in C. Barnard and O. Odudu (eds.), *The Outer Limits of European Union Law* (Hart Publishing, Oxford, 2009), p. 381. Cf. P. Nebbia, 'Damages Actions for the Infringement of EC Competition Law: Compensation or Deterrence?' (2008) 33 *European Law Review* 23; W.P.J. Wils, 'The Relationship between Public Antirust Enforcement and Private Actions for Damages' (2009) 32 *World Competition* 3.

(standing) is the existence of loss. Between the concern for ensuring corrective justice and the need to create an undistorted competitive EU market, the latter, forward-looking, concern seems of a far greater importance for the CJEU. In deciding whether the claimant bears significant responsibility for the distortion of competition, national courts should take account of such factors as 'the respective bargaining power and conduct of the two parties to the contract'. The court has to ascertain whether:

> the party who claims to have suffered loss through concluding a contract that is liable to restrict or distort competition found himself in a markedly weaker position than the other party, such as seriously to compromise or even eliminate his freedom to negotiate the terms of the contract and his capacity to avoid the loss or reduce its extent, in particular by availing himself in good time of all the legal remedies available to him.[13]

Most of these factors focus on the role of the claimant in creating a distortion to competition.[14] It follows that effectiveness of EU competition law is the primary concern. Even the very generous scope of damages demanded by EU law can be explained by the Court's concern for effective enforcement of Article 101 TFEU. As the Court itself held:

> it follows from the principle of effectiveness and the right of individuals to seek compensation for loss caused by a contract or by conduct liable to restrict or distort competition that injured persons must be able to seek compensation not only for actual loss (*damnum emergens*) but also for loss of profit (*lucrum cessans*) plus interest.[15]

That enforcement is the main rationale behind damages actions in EU competition law is also visible in two European Commission papers. The Green Paper explicitly located damages actions in the context of enforcement.[16] Due to some criticism, the Commission changed its

[13] C-453/99 *Courage*, n. 10 above, para. 33.

[14] See G. Monti, 'Anti Competitive Agreements: The Innocent Party's Right to Damages' (2002) 27 *European Law Review* 282, 285, who argues that 'an unqualified right to seek damages would frustrate the *effet utile* of Article [101(2) TEFEU]'.

[15] C-295 and 298/04 *Manfredi*, n. 11 above, para. 100.

[16] European Commission, *Green Paper on Damages Actions for Breach of the EC Antitrust Rules*, COM(2005)672 final, pp. 3 and 4: 'Damages actions for infringement of antitrust law serve several purposes, namely to compensate those who have suffered a loss as a consequence of anti-competitive behaviour and to ensure the full effectiveness of the antitrust rules of the Treaty by discouraging anti-competitive behaviour, thus contributing significantly to the maintenance of effective competition in the Community (deterrence). By being able effectively to bring a damages claim, individual firms or consumers

vocabulary (but not the approach) in the White Paper.[17] We read in the White Paper that:

> [e]ffective remedies for private parties also increase the likelihood that a greater number of illegal restrictions of competition will be detected and that the infringers will be held liable. Improving compensatory justice would therefore inherently also produce beneficial effects in terms of deterrence of future infringements and greater compliance with EC antitrust rules. Safeguarding undistorted competition is an integral part of the internal market and important for implementing the Lisbon strategy.[18]

The White Paper advocates the use of a presumption of fault for those who violated EU competition law, the only defence in that regard being an excusable error.[19] The White Paper also allows the passing-on defence, which would suggest that the primary concern is indeed fair compensation. However, indirect purchasers should, according to the Commission, be able to rely on the rebuttable presumption that the illegal overcharge was passed on to them in its entirety.[20] This, on the other hand, strongly suggests that disgorgement of profits is of primary concern, which reveals the particular focus of the Commission on deterrence.[21]

It is only in competition law that EU law possesses its own institution of damages actions against private parties. In other areas of EU law such actions are regulated primarily by the laws of the Member States, which makes it more difficult to determine their function as a matter of the EU legal order. Where complemented by public enforcement mechanisms, damages actions can be entrusted with the single function of providing compensation. Even there, however, EU law requires that the level of compensation, once damages are chosen by national law as the

in Europe are brought closer to competition rules and will be more actively involved in enforcement of the rules' (footnotes omitted).

17 European Commission, *White Paper on Damages Actions for Breach of the EU Antitrust Rules*, COM(2008)165 final, p. 2: 'Any citizen or business who suffers harm as a result of a breach of EC antitrust rules (Articles 81 and 82 of the EC Treaty) must be able to claim reparation from the party who caused the damage. This right of victims to compensation is guaranteed by Community law, as the European Court of Justice recalled in 2001 and 2006' (footnotes omitted).

18 *Ibid.* 3 (footnotes omitted). 19 *Ibid.* 7. 20 *Ibid.* 8.

21 The European Commission prepared two versions of the proposal for a Council Directive on rules governing actions for damages for infringements of Article 101 and Article 102 of the TFEU, one in March 2009 and the other in June 2009. The proposal was withdrawn by the Commission in October 2009 and is not publicly available. The Commission Work Programme 2012 foresees a new legislative proposal on actions for damages for breaches of antitrust law.

appropriate remedy for the protection of an EU right, complies with the requirement of dissuasiveness,[22] at the same time expecting national courts to abide by the principle of full compensation.[23] An interesting solution is adopted in intellectual property law, where EU law enjoys a centralised regulation of enforcement without total harmonisation of substantive law. The Directive on the enforcement of intellectual property rights includes a provision which obliges the Member States 'to ensure that the competent judicial authorities, on application of the injured party, order the infringer who is knowingly, or with reasonable grounds to know, engaged in an infringing activity, to pay the rightholder damages appropriate to the actual prejudice suffered by him/her as a result of the infringement'.[24] The Directive even goes so far as to prescribe the conditions of liability and the manner in which damages should be calculated.[25] Rules included in the Directive point to the compensatory and occasionally restitutionary nature of damages actions in intellectual property cases. However, even here we can observe the influence of enforcement-focused thinking. According to article 13(2), absence of (reasonably imputed) knowledge may justify the imposition of a modest sanction in the form of the recovery of profits or pre-established damages which will not reflect the full value of the loss. Only violations committed consciously can be deterred, so where the defendant was not aware of the fact that he was violating the claimant's intellectual property right the Directive sees it as appropriate to reduce the measure of damages.

[22] C-271/91 *Marshall* [1993] ECR I-4367, para. 24; C-460/06 *Paquay* [2007] ECR I-8511, para. 49.

[23] 14/83 *Von Colson* [1984] ECR 1891, para. 23; C-271/91 *Marshall* [1993] ECR I-4367, para. 33; C-180/95 *Draehmpaehl* [1997] ECR I-2195, para. 37.

[24] Directive 2004/48/EC of the European Parliament and of the Council of 29 April 2004 on the enforcement of intellectual property rights, art. 13(1) [2004] OJ L195/16.

[25] Article 13(1): 'Member States shall ensure that the competent judicial authorities, on application of the injured party, order the infringer who knowingly, or with reasonable grounds to know, engaged in an infringing activity, to pay the rightholder damages appropriate to the actual prejudice suffered by him/her as a result of the infringement. When the judicial authorities set the damages: (a) they shall take into account all appropriate aspects, such as the negative economic consequences, including lost profits, which the injured party has suffered, any unfair profits made by the infringer and, in appropriate cases, elements other than economic factors, such as the moral prejudice caused to the rightholder by the infringement; or (b) as an alternative to (a), they may, in appropriate cases, set the damages as a lump sum on the basis of elements such as at least the amount of royalties or fees which would have been due if the infringer had requested authorisation to use the intellectual property right in question.'

In contrast, discrimination law in the field of employment and supply of goods and provision of services is to a great extent harmonised, but until recently the Equal Treatment Directives, while demanding effective sanctions, did not prescribe any particular type of remedy.[26] Damages actions were not a method of enforcement explicitly prescribed by EU law. Currently, most Equal Treatment Directives still require the Member States to enact effective, proportionate and dissuasive sanctions and indicate that they merely 'may' comprise compensation paid to the victim of discrimination.[27] The Directive on equal treatment of men and women in the access and supply of goods and services and the Directive establishing a general framework for equal treatment in employment and occupation, on the other hand, explicitly require the availability of 'compensation'.[28] Provisions which prescribe damages actions as a matter of EU law appear in sections entitled 'Defence of rights', rather than 'Penalties'. This would suggest that the EU legislator treats damages in equal treatment cases as compensatory, rather than punitive. However, even in the current decentralised system, EU law specifies that liability for acts of discrimination should not be restricted by the condition of fault.[29] This can be interpreted as a strengthening of the compensatory function of damages actions at the expense of their regulatory benefits, but can be also seen as inspired by incentive and deterrence arguments. The employer has the opportunity to increase standards in the workplace and the fact that he may be liable regardless of fault acts as an incentive to devise remuneration and promotion policies which do not discriminate directly or indirectly against the protected group. Moreover, 'damage' suffered by the victim of discrimination is often perceived as non-material and its quantification based largely on the gravity of the defendant's conduct, further suggesting that it is in fact quite difficult to speak of the purely compensatory nature of

[26] J. Kenner, *EU Employment Law: From Rome to Amsterdam and Beyond* (Oxford, Hart Publishing, 2003), pp. 429–66; C. Barnard, *EC Employment Law* (3rd edn, Oxford University Press, 2006), pp. 375–9.

[27] See e.g., art. 15 of Council Directive 2000/43/EC of 29 June 2000 implementing the principle of equal treatment between persons irrespective of racial or ethnic origin [2000] OJ L180/22.

[28] Article 8 of Directive 2004/113/EC on equal treatment of men and women in the access and supply of goods and services [2004] OJ L373/37; art. 18 of Directive 2006/54/EC of the European Parliament and of the Council of 5 July 2006 on the implementation of the principle of equal opportunities and equal treatment of men and women in matters of employment and occupation (recast) [2006] OJ L204/23.

[29] C-177/88 *Dekker* [1990] ECR I-3941, paras. 24–6.

discrimination damages. Effectiveness of equal treatment measures is often put in doubt because they do not guarantee the procedural rights of non-governmental organisations or state agencies specialising in promoting equality.[30] If these claimants could bring damages actions the remedy would lose even further its compensatory nature.

Another area where there exists a considerable body of substantive rules, but where availability of damages actions is regulated independently by the Member States is environmental law.[31] The Environmental Liability Directive[32] envisages liability of the polluter but only towards the competent national authority which incurred costs by preventing and remedying environmental damage.[33] Thus, as such the Directive cannot form the basis of damages actions of a private litigant against a private polluter. Breach of regulatory Environmental Directives is unlikely to give rise to liability of a private party either. Quite apart from the problem of horizontal effect, Environmental Directives have been held by the CJEU not to grant rights to individuals, or have been considered insufficiently precise and unconditional.[34] It follows that applicability in national courts of EU Environmental Directives in actions for damages depends on national implementation of these measures and the content of national tort laws. If damages actions emerge in EU law in this

[30] See N. Reich, 'The Impact of the Non-discrimination Principle on Private Autonomy in EU Law' in D. Leczykiewicz and S. Weatherill (eds.), *The Involvement of EU Law in Private Law Relationships* (Hart Publishing, Oxford, 2013), ch. 11.

[31] For details, see M. Lee, *EU Environmental Law* (Oxford, Hart Publising, 2005), ch. 1.

[32] Directive 2004/35/CE of the European Parliament and of the Council of 21 April 2004 on environmental liability with regard to the prevention and remedying of environmental damage [2004] OJ L143/56.

[33] Article 8(2) of the Directive: 'the competent authority shall recover, *inter alia*, via security over property or other appropriate guarantees from the operator who has caused the damage or the imminent threat of damage, the costs it has incurred in relation to the preventive or remedial actions taken under this Directive'.

[34] See 380/87 *Enichem Base* [1989] ECR 2491, para. 23; C-236/92 *Coitati di Coordinamento per la Difesa della Cava* [1994] ECR I-483, para. 15; C-240/09 *Lesoochranárske zoskupenie VLK*, judgment of 8 March 2011, para. 45. But compare C-201/02 *Wells* [2004] ECR I-723, para. 61; Joined Cases C-165/09 to C-167/09 *Stichting Natuur en Milieu*, judgment of 26 May 2011, para. 100; C-213/03 *Pecheurs de l'Etang de Berre* [2004] ECR I-7357, para. 47. On the enforcement of EU environmental law in national courts, see M. Hedemann-Robinson, *Enforcement of European Union Environmental Law: Legal Issues and Challenges* (Routledge-Cavendish, 2006), chs 6 and 7; J. van Zeben, 'The Untapped Potential of Horizontal Private Enforcement within European Environmental Law' (2010) 22 *Georgetown International Environmental Law Review* 241; C. Glinski and P. Rott, 'Waste Incineration: Legal Protection in European Environmental Law' (2000) 12 *Journal of Environmental Law* 129, 142–3.

context the enforcement rationale will have to be dominant. Environmental damage is rarely individual. The cases often involve difficult questions of causation and it is also often the case that legal systems depart from standard rules of private law to ensure that substantive duties of polluters are not emptied of content.[35] Tort law is acting here as a mechanism of enforcement.

A middle ground is occupied by EU free movement law. On the one hand, damages actions brought against the Member States in cases involving violation of free movement provisions were the natural habitat of the *Francovich* remedy.[36] On the other hand, in horizontal cases free movement law did not progress beyond recognising that certain internal market freedoms may create obligations also for non-state actors. It remains unclear whether as a matter of EU law private parties could be made liable for a breach of free movement law.[37] Arguments in favour point to the need to ensure effectiveness of these provisions in a situation where individual conduct can neutralise the effects of actions of the European Union and of the Member States to create an integrated market. On the other hand, imposition of an obligation to compensate the claimant in full seems a disproportionate response in a situation where private parties 'violated' free movement law by exercising autonomy guaranteed for them by national law, and often in pursuance of interests otherwise protected by national law. Enforcement should be directed at those who actually bear the responsibility for bringing about a state of affairs incompatible with EU law. Only clearer articulation of situations in which private parties should be made liable for breach of free movement law would enable the CJEU to extend the *Courage*

[35] *Fairchild* v. *Glenhaven Funeral Services Ltd* [2002] UKHL 22, [2003] 1 AC 32, paras. 62 and 69.

[36] See e.g., Joined Cases C-46/93 and 48/93 *Brasserie du Pêcheur* [1996] ECR I-1029; C-5/94 *Hedley Lomas* [1996] ECR I-6297.

[37] In cases concerning the horizontal application of free movement provisions, the CJEU, despite demanding the applicability of these provisions against private actors, refrained from specifying the precise legal consequences flowing from the applicant's reliance upon the free movement provision against a non-state actor. See 36/74 *Walrave and Koch* [1974] ECR 1405; C-415/83 *Bosman* [1995] ECR I-4921; C-281/98 *Angonese* [2000] ECR I-4139; C-438/05 *Viking Line* [2007] ECR I-10779; C-341/05 *Laval* [2007] ECR I-11767. Therefore the ruling of the Swedish court in the *Laval* litigation, in which that court claimed that damages liability of a private party for breach of EU free movement law was a recognised principle of EU law (!) should be regarded as highly controversial. U. Bernitz and N. Reich, 'Case No. A 268/04, The Labour Court, Sweden (Arbetsdomstolen) Judgment No. 89/09 of 2 December 2009, Laval un Partneri Ltd v. Svenska Bygggnadsarbetareförbundet et al.' (2011) 48 *Common Market Law Review* 603.

remedy into the internal market freedoms. The institution of damages actions organised around the compensatory rationale is less likely to incorporate such concerns into its conceptual structure.

What follows from this analysis is that it is the enforcement-focused nature of damages actions in EU law which may explain why in this field Member States continue to retain such broad powers. In the same way that EU law's involvement in contract law often creates a schism within national private law, Europeanisation of law of non-contractual liability would lead to its reorientation from a focus on right vindication and compensation to a focus on enforcement. It is only where it remains within the competence of the Member States to choose the type of a remedy that national preferences as to what function this remedy should have alongside or above enforcement can be articulated and protected.

## Damages actions under the DCFR: compensation or enforcement?

The Draft Common Frame of Reference, while overtly not intended to supersede the EU law of remedies, due to its breadth and the wording of its individual provisions encroaches upon this terrain. This encroachment is, however, restricted to actions pending between private parties. Article I 1:101[38] provides that the DCFR is not intended to be used in relation to 'rights and obligations of a public law nature'. Article VI 7:103 located within the Book on non-contractual liability stipulates that this Book 'does not govern the liability of a person or body arising from the exercise or omission to exercise public law functions'. As a result, non-contractual liability of EU institutions is clearly not covered by the DCFR. The *Francovich* liability is probably also excluded from the substantive scope covered by the DCFR. The authors of the commentary to the DCFR explain that article VI 7:103 excludes any liability 'under public law',[39] which according to them means the 'liability of the State and its institutions as well as the personal liability of its office holders for the exercise or the failure to exercise sovereign power in breach of duty'.[40] As a result, the area of EU law particularly influenced by the enforcement

[38] The numbering of DCFR articles is taken from the Outline Edition (Sellier, Munich, 2009).

[39] C. von Bar and E. Clive, *Principles, Definitions and Model Rules of European Private Law: Draft Common Frame of Reference* (Full Edition) (Oxford University Press, 2010), vol. 4, p. 3086 (DCFR).

[40] *Ibid.* 3822.

rationale is left out from the scope of the DCFR. This in principle should mean that the non-contractual liability regime in the DCFR is organised according to different rationales.

Damages actions appear in the DCFR as an available remedy in three contexts: contractual liability, non-contractual liability and unjustified enrichment.[41] Book VI of the DCFR sets out the rules of non-contractual liability for damage caused to another. It adopts a model founded on many individual bases of liability by providing for distinct factual situations in which 'damage' is to be regarded as 'legally relevant' (articles VI 2:201–2:211) and therefore recoverable.[42] They include 'personal injury', 'loss suffered by third persons as a result of another's personal injury or death', 'infringement of dignity, liberty and privacy', 'loss upon communication of incorrect information about another', 'loss upon breach of confidence', 'loss upon infringement of property or lawful possession', 'loss upon reliance on incorrect advice or information', 'loss upon unlawful impairment of business', 'burdens incurred by the state upon environmental impairment', 'loss upon fraudulent misrepresentation', and 'loss upon inducement of non-performance of obligation'.

Placing the condition of 'legally relevant damage' at the centre of the non-contractual liability regime suggests that compensation is its primary function. Moreover, article VI 2:101 provides that 'legally relevant damage' may result from 'a violation of a right otherwise conferred by the law' or from 'a violation of an interest worthy of legal protection'. Categories of recoverable damage are thus not strictly fixed or closed in the DCFR, which is characteristic of systems motivated by the compensatory function.[43] On the other hand, however, it remains the case that mere existence of damage (an ability of the claimant to adduce evidence that they are (financially) worse off) is not enough to satisfy this condition of liability. Moreover, there is no specific indication how

[41] For more on remedies in the DCFR and their relation to the existing EU law of remedies, see D. Leczykiewicz '"Where Angels Fear to Tread": The EU Law of Remedies and Codification of European Private Law' (2012) 8 *European Review of Contract Law* 47.

[42] P. Larrouche, '*Legally Relevant Damage' and A Priori Limits to Non-contractual Liability in the DCFR*, TILEC Discussion Paper No. 2008–045, (2008).

[43] The DCFR provides no list of rights or interests whose violation makes the resulting damage 'legally relevant'. Therefore, it leaves it to judges to determine liability in the light of the particular facts of cases. Judicial discretion is limited by para. (2) of art. VI 2:101, which provides that in these situations loss or injury constitutes legally relevant damage only if it would be fair and reasonable for there to be a right to reparation.

the existence of damage/loss should be established, which suggests that it could be inferred. This is confirmed by article VI 6:204 of the DCFR, which prescribes that '[i]njury as such is to be compensated independent of compensation for economic or non-economic loss'. This indicates that compensation could be awarded independently from the proof of damage. Those who did not in fact suffer any loss could bring an action, inevitably turning the DCFR regime into an enforcement mechanism.[44]

Causation is a condition of liability which is important for both compensation-focused and enforcement-focused regimes. The difference lies in the type of causation which is demanded under each regime. In the compensation-focused regime, it is the causation of damage which is required, while in the enforcement-focused regime the most important is the authorship of the breach. The DCFR uses a mixed approach (article VI 4:101). Damage is causally linked to the defendant's conduct not only when it is 'to be regarded as a consequence of that person's conduct' but also when it is to be regarded as a consequence of 'the source of danger for which that person is responsible'. This means that the claimant does not have to prove that but for the defendant's conduct the same harm would not have happened. This elevates negligence to the status of a more important condition of liability.[45] 'Negligence' in the DCFR is defined in article VI 3:102(a) and (b) as including both breach of the particular standard of care provided by a statutory provision, whose purpose is the protection of the injured person from the damage suffered, as well as breach of a standard of a reasonably careful person. Thus, it is possible to show that the defendant

[44] The concept of 'injury' is not defined in the DCFR. 'Loss', on the other hand, is defined in the Annex in the following way: '"Loss" includes economic and non-economic loss. "Economic loss" includes loss of income or profit, burdens incurred and a reduction in the value of property. "Non-economic loss" includes pain and suffering and impairment of the quality of life' (arts. III 3:701(3) and VI 2:101(4)). Thus, in the framework envisaged by the DCFR 'injury' can exist, and has to be 'compensated', also in the absence of any 'loss'.

[45] Causation of 'legally relevant damage' leads to non-contractual liability if it was intentional or arises from the defendant's negligence. The defendant can also be liable without intention or negligence if the DCFR makes him 'accountable' by an express provision to that effect in Chapter 3 of Book VI of the DCFR. According to this Chapter, the defendant can be liable, *inter alia*, for damage caused by a defective product if he is a producer, importer, and in certain situations, a supplier of the defective product (art. VI 3:204). The defendant can also be liable without intention or negligence for damage caused by dangerous substances or emissions, if he is a keeper of such substance or an 'operator of an installation' and if he keeps the substance or operates the installation for purposes related to the defendant's trade, business or profession (art. VI 3:206).

acted negligently without showing that his conduct was unreasonable. Breach of a statutory standard of care is sufficient to establish negligence. This means that the DCFR non-contractual liability regime could be used as an enforcement mechanism, but on the condition that the requirement of the protective function is interpreted loosely. The DCFR would here interact directly with regulatory EU law.

Another feature of the non-contractual liability regime in the DCFR which is typical of an enforcement-focused approach to damages actions is article VI 6:202, according to which '[w]here it is fair and reasonable to do so, a person may be relieved of liability to compensate, either wholly or in part, if, where the damage is not caused intentionally, liability in full would be disproportionate to the accountability of the person causing the damage or the extent of the damage or the means to prevent it'. It follows that the DCFR allows a reduction of liability to ensure proportionality of sanction. It also envisages disgorgement damages. Article VI 6:101(4) states that '[a]s an alternative ... but only where this is reasonable, reparation may take the form of recovery from the person accountable for the causation of the legally relevant damage of any advantage obtained by the latter in connection with causing the damage'. It should be noted, however, that the DCFR does not allow further aggravation of liability in order better to achieve a deterrent effect. Absence of this latter possibility strongly suggests that the drafters of the DCFR were unable to break away completely from the compensation perspective and intended to incorporate only some elements of the regulatory (enforcement-focused) approach.

Let us now look more closely at specific areas of EU law, where enforcement would normally be the more natural concern, and how they were dealt with in the DCFR. *Courage* and *Manfredi* are reflected in article VI 2:208. This provision provides in paragraph (1) that 'loss caused to a person as a result of an unlawful impairment of that person's exercise of a profession or conduct of a trade is legally relevant damage'. Paragraph (2) deems 'loss caused to a consumer as a result of unfair competition' to be 'legally relevant damage' but only if EU or national law so provides. The first section covers anti-competitive behaviour only where exercise of profession or conduct of a trade is impaired or, for a consumer, if EU/national law so provides. This is interesting because it shows that it was difficult for the authors of the DCFR to allow straightforward compensation in the case of breach of competition law. Damage is an obvious and indispensable element, but the claimant also has to meet additional criteria. It is also possible that article VI 2:208(1) would not include all acts currently prohibited under Articles 101 and 102 TFEU.[46] This does not close the door to damages actions for victims of breaches of these two Treaty provisions which fall outside the scope of article VI 2:208. Given the fact that the direct effect of Articles 101 and 102 TFEU is sufficient to establish that these provisions grant rights, litigants should not find it cumbersome to establish that they also have a 'protective function'.

As for the EU law of equal treatment, the drafters of the DCFR divided it into two separate bodies of rules. Discriminatory acts committed by employers are outside the scope of the DCFR because employment relationships are left out altogether.[47] Discrimination which is regulated by the DCFR covers contracts whose object is to provide access to, or supply of, goods, other assets and services which are available to the public (article II 2:101). It follows that the DCFR does not cover such cases as *Marshall*,[48] but would be applicable to the facts of the CJEU's recent decision on equal treatment with respect to the calculation of insurance premiums and benefits.[49] As for remedies which are made available in the event of discrimination, they include both contractual and non-contractual remedies (article II 2:104(1)). This would entail that damage arising from discrimination is per se 'legally relevant damage'. Special provision regulates the measure of damages in discrimination cases. Article II 2:104(2) states that '[a]ny remedy granted [in cases of discrimination] should be proportionate to the injury or anticipated injury; the dissuasive effect of remedies may be taken into account'. The enforcement rationale of EU discrimination law could not in the end be avoided.

The DCFR overtly does not deal with remedies for violation of intellectual property rights. However, Book VI seems nevertheless to apply to damages actions brought in such cases. A trademark or a patent right should undoubtedly be seen as 'a right otherwise conferred by law' for the purpose of the general definition of 'legally relevant damage' (article VI 2:101). Alternatively, intellectual property rights could be seen as 'property' for the purpose of article VI 2:206, which deems loss

[46] G. Wagner, 'The Law of Torts in the DCFR' in G. Wagner (ed.), *The Common Frame of Reference: A View from Law and Economics* (Sellier, Munich, 2009), p. 225.

[47] Article VI 7:103 states that Book VI does not govern liability of employers to employees arising in the course of employment and of trade unions and employers' associations arising in the course of an industrial dispute.

[48] 152/84 *Marshall* [1986] ECR 723.

[49] C-236/09 *Test-Achats*, judgment of 1 March 2011.

upon infringement of property 'legally relevant damage'.[50] Yet, the conditions of the DCFR differ from those envisaged by the Enforcement Directive.[51] Under the DCFR, liability in damages is subjected to the requirement of intention or negligence, while the Enforcement Directive requires damages to be available when the infringer had 'reasonable grounds to know that he was engaging in an infringing activity'.[52] It would be challenging to reconcile both standards of liability. Either statutory provisions offering protection to intellectual property owners would have to be regarded as providing for 'the particular standard of care whose purpose is the protection of the person suffering the damage from that damage', and whose breach would then amount to 'negligence' (article VI. 3:102), or negligence would have to be established by showing that the infringer should have known that he was engaging in an infringing activity, rather than by reference to the quality of the defendant's conduct leading to the violation of the right.

## Harmonisation of non-contractual liability

Views diverge as to whether effectiveness of EU law requires a harmonised regime of non-contractual liability. It has been fashionable to talk about the 'enforcement deficit' in the European Union,[53] which is to be alleviated by EU law laying down the principles of public and private liability. The discussions sometimes failed to differentiate between two distinct problems: (1) that concerning the applicability of a given norm to the particular horizontal situation; and (2) that concerning the availability of a private action, such as, for example, a damages action, as a matter of EU right.[54] Horizontal non-applicability of a particular EU norm does not necessarily entail gaps in enforcement. The question of against whom the norm should be enforced comes first. A compensation focus may let

[50] Wagner, 'The Law of Torts in the DCFR', n. 46 above, at 225.

[51] See n. 24 above. [52] Enforcement Directive, art. 13(1).

[53] A.P. Tash, 'Remedies for European Community Law Claims in Member States Courts: Towards a European Standard' (1993) 31 *Columbia Journal of Transnational Law* 377; D. Curtin and K. Mortelmans, 'Application and Enforcement of Community Law by the Member States: Actors in Search of a Third Generation Script' in D. Curtin and T. Heukles (eds.), *Institutional Dynamic of European Integration* (Martinus Nijhoff Publishers, Dordrecht/Boston/London, 1994), vol. II, p. 423; R. Caranta, 'Judicial Protection Against Member States: A New Jus Commune Takes Shape' (1995) 32 *Common Market Law Review* 703.

[54] See e.g., G. Betlem, 'Torts, a European *Ius Commune* and the Private Enforcement of Community Law' (2005) 64 *Cambridge Law Journal* 126.

us overlook the issue of appropriate attribution of responsibility. Paradoxically, enforcement-focused regimes are here more restrictive because the question about the limits of effectiveness of standards they enforce forms part of their conceptual set-up. As I have explained elsewhere,[55] the DCFR does not address the question of how it would be ensured that EU measures which currently do not apply in private law relationships would remain inapplicable therein, and how the availability of damages actions as a remedy for breach of an EU norm by an individual would be restricted only to cases where the imposition of liability in damages is justified. As a result, damages actions could become available for breach of EU free movement or environmental law, even where the relevant provisions would not possess direct effect. It is precisely because the DCFR is such an easy source of damages actions that it would fail as a method of enforcement.

Probably, the best example here are EU rules on the quality of products, their technical standards, packaging, as well as EU rules on marketing, advertising and the commercial practices in general. Some of these rules are enacted as Regulations, for example, Regulations on the common organisation of the market in fruit and vegetables.[56] These Regulations were relied upon by two private companies, Muñoz and Fruticola, against another private company, Frumar, and its parent company Redbridge in a civil action before the Chancery Division of the High Court of England and Wales.[57] While the possibility to rely on the Regulations by the claimant was denied by the High Court, the CJEU, having received a reference from the Court of Appeal of England and Wales, deemed the Regulations applicable in an action between competitors and held, moreover, that it had to be possible to enforce the EU rules on quality standards 'by means of civil proceedings instituted by a trader against a competitor'.[58] The particular remedy sought by Muñoz and Fruiticola was an injunction against the marketing of grapes under an unlawful name. For this reason, the judgment did not have direct implications for damages actions, which are 'civil proceedings' but were not specifically prescribed by the Court's ruling in

[55] D. Leczykiewicz '"Where Angels Fear to Tread": The EU Law of Remedies and Codification of European Private Law' (2012) 8 *European Review of Contract Law* 47.

[56] Council Regulation (EC) 1035/72 of the Council of 18 May 1972 and Council Regulation (EC) 2200/96 of 28 October 1996 on the common organisation of the market in fruit and vegetables [1972] OJ English Spec. Edn II, p. 437, and [1996] OJ L297/1, respectively.

[57] *Muñoz* v. *Frumar* [1999] 3 CMLR 684.

[58] C-253/00 *Muñoz* [2002] ECR I-7289, para. 30.

*Muñoz* as the appropriate cause of civil action. However, the DCFR could provide the missing step between making EU Regulations necessarily enforceable by means of civil actions and creating a civil action (an action for damages), which would be available for a breach of any EU Regulation. Given the fact that the CJEU has already held in *Muñoz* that all Regulations are directly applicable in civil actions and that individuals may rely on them without the need to show that they satisfy some special conditions, national judges would be inclined to take a very lax approach to restrictions imposed by articles VI 2:101 (legally relevant damage) and VI 3:102 (negligence) of the DCFR, opening the floodgates to damages actions against private parties. Such an undiscriminating approach is unlikely to make damages actions an effective instrument of enforcement; there is a great danger of overkill and negative externalities.

Another example can be taken from the law of free movement. The market access approach used by the CJEU to regulate the boundaries of EU free movement law leads to a situation where national consumer and employee protection laws constitute potential barriers to trade caught by the relevant provisions of the Treaty. As *Laval* and *Viking* showed, an exercise by employees of the right to strike may interfere with free movement of services and freedom of establishment.[59] The concept on which EU law relies to resolve such conflicts is that of proportionality. Yet, there is an argument to be made that the balance between two interests protected by EU law should be located in different places depending on the type of remedy sought; or, if the location of the balance is to be similar for all types of sanctions and remedies, it is the conditions and severity of these sanctions which have to be adjusted to ensure that both interests are treated proportionately. The system of liability based entirely on the idea of ensuring full compensation to the victim will not enable judges to take such nuances into account. For example, an individual's conduct may constitute a disproportionate intrusion of an interest protected by a social right, but it would be a disproportionate response to such an infringement to hold the defendant liable to the full extent of damage.[60] The principle of full compensation cannot be

[59] C-438/05 *Viking Line* [2007] ECR I-10779; C-341/05 *Laval* [2007] ECR I-11767.

[60] For more about proportionality in damages liability of a private party in EU law, see D. Leczykiewicz, 'The Constitutional Dimension of Private Law Liability Rules in the EU' in D. Leczykiewicz and S. Weatherill (eds.), *The Involvement of EU Law in Private Law Relationships* (Hart Publishing, Oxford, 2013), pp. 199–222.

departed from in a system whose primary function is providing compensation, but it can be modified in a system which focuses on enforcement, where effective deterrence is more important than restoration.

## Enforcement or compensation?

EU law so far has used damages actions as an enforcement mechanism. Such an approach has received criticism; individuals were treated instrumentally, as private enforcers of EU law, who were granted a right to compensation as an incentive to bring judicial proceedings in the context of which particular breaches of EU law would be brought to light. Yet, this approach to damages actions has benefits. The focus on enforcement enables the EU legislator and the CJEU to select situations in which it is necessary and justifiable to employ the institution of damages actions to ensure the effectiveness of an EU norm. It enables conditions of liability to be devised which are adequate for a system focused on enforcement. In a system dominated by the compensatory function it would be impossible to allow punitive damages[61] or apply the principle of proportionality in determining the level of damages. Equally, leniency programmes are difficult to fit in, and so is the right of action on the part of non-governmental organisations. The EU law of non-contractual liability has to fit into the current enforcement-focused framework, rather than the alien structure of a non-contractual liability regime based predominantly on ideas of corrective justice.[62] It is for this reason that designing a general regime of liability in damages which would replace both national regimes of non-contractual liability, as well as the existing EU law of remedies, seems a misguided endeavour.

[61] See F. Marcos and A. Sanchez Graells, 'Towards a European Tort Law? Damages Actions for Breach of the EC Antitrust Rules: Harmonizing Tort Law through the Back Door?' (2008) *European Review of Private Law* 469, 477.

[62] Cf. C. Hodges, 'Competition Enforcement, Regulation and Civil Justice: What is the Case?' (2006) 43 *Common Market Law Review* 1381.

15

# Consumer complaints and alternative dispute resolution: harmonisation of the European ADR system

IMMACULADA BARRAL-VIÑALS

## Introduction

This chapter tries to show how harmonisation in the field of consumer law, which is part of contract law, will not be achieved unless we also start to work on the harmonisation of EU enforcement legislation, specifically regarding individual redress by means of alternative dispute resolution (ADR) systems. In fact, the choice made by the European Commission's Directorate General for Health and Consumer Policy (DG SANCO) about the development of ADR systems has created a heterogeneous context throughout Europe. This diversity means that the application of the same or at least equivalent pieces of legislation, i.e., harmonisation legislation, can lead to very different results depending on the ADR system used, at least in terms of how accessible the system is to the parties. Therefore, we propose a measure of ADR harmonisation as a way of enhancing the effective protection of consumers in Europe.

In this context, the aim of the chapter is to examine the Catalan system in the framework of the Spanish one, and to analyse the consumer mediation system in particular. We chose this specific ADR system because the Catalan Ministry of Justice recently launched a wide-ranging research project on this subject, which ended in October 2010 with the publication of a White Paper on Mediation in Catalonia.[1] The White Paper analyses mediation in consumer law in depth.

University of Barcelona.

[1] The White Paper set up by a Catalan Government Agreement on 7th, November 2008 and results: P. Casanovas, E. Lauroba and J. Magre (eds.), *Libro Blanco de la mediación en Cataluña* (Huygens, Barcelona, 2010). Complete study available at

The results of the White Paper show a complete picture of this ADR system, disclosing the scale of consumers' complaints and revealing some important trends. In particular, the research highlights the strengths and weaknesses of the system. The White Paper gathered data on mediation and describes the process in terms of costs, efficiency and accessibility. It is the first time that data of this kind has been collected in Catalonia. The results clearly highlight some issues that lead us to reconsider the diversity of the ADR system in Europe.

## Choice for individual redress in consumer complaints through ADR: harmonisation of the enforcement system

The harmonisation process in the fields of the consumer *acquis* and the Draft Common Frame of Reference (DCFR) attempts to provide the same or at least the equivalent contracting conditions throughout Europe. This goal of legislative harmonisation is very interesting as a process. However, of itself it is not enough to obtain either the effective protection of consumers throughout Europe or the real development of the single market, which the European Union has been working towards for a long time. Therefore, the individual redress mechanisms and especially the ADR systems that exist throughout Europe need to be part of the harmonisation process. The European Union has been developing a high level project in this direction, especially from 2009 onwards,[2] but in November 2011 an important step was taken when the European Union approved a Proposal for a Directive on Consumer ADR (Proposed ADR Directive)[3] which aims to offer a standard level of consumer protection throughout Europe. If the Directive is definitively approved,

www.llibreblancmediacio.com/ (an English version of the Recommendations and Conclusions is available now; the complete English version will be available shortly).

2 Commission Communication of 2 July 2009 on the enforcement of the consumer *acquis* (COM(2009)330 final). Issue also taken into account in the Commission's Communication on Europe 2020, COM(2010)2020 final (Brussels, 3 March 2010), stating at 21: 'A strategy for smart, sustainable and inclusive growth. The Commission will propose action to tackle bottlenecks in the single market by, among others: Adapting EU and national legislation to the digital era so as to promote the circulation of content with a high level of trust for consumers and companies. This requires updating rules on liability, warranties, delivery and dispute resolution . . . Making it easier and less costly for businesses and consumers to enforce contracts and to recognise court judgments and documents in other EU countries.'

3 Proposal for a Directive of the European Parliament and of the Council on Alternative Dispute Resolution for Consumer Disputes and amending Regulation (EC) 2006/2004 and Directive 2009/22/EC, COM(2011)793 final, 2011/0373 (COD).

a first and crucial step to the harmonisation of the enforcement system will have been taken. In this way, the choice of individual redress in consumer complaints through the mechanism of ADR will definitively be enhanced.

In the field of consumer law, the view of the European Commission is thus clear: enforcement is understood as an effective system of individual redress. For this reason, one area that the Commission has worked on is the development of tools to simplify the claims' process. Redress tools should be developed for consumers should they need to make a claim, since only fast, simple, inexpensive methods will persuade them to take the risk of seeking redress when a business fails to carry out its contractual promises or carries them out unsatisfactorily.[4]

Therefore, any alternative dispute resolution system that is used to deal with consumer complaints is considered to be a basic instrument for generating confidence in what is known as *consumer access to justice*. ADR systems have played a key role in enforcement for consumers across the European Union. This situation stems from the actions initiated by the Green Paper on consumer access to justice in the internal market in 1993,[5] which sought to design a regulatory framework in which mechanisms to ensure the effectiveness of consumer protection could be generated. The 1993 Green Paper observed the proliferation of various kinds of ADR for consumer complaints in EU Member States aimed at meeting the demand for faster and cheaper redress processes than the court system. This development was considered desirable and, consequently, the European Union has prioritised and promoted the adoption of ADR in the field of consumer complaints.[6] This is evident in the Commission Communication of 4 April 2001,[7] which states that

[4] This question has been referred to repeatedly in documents on e-commerce since the first e-Europe plan in 2002. Most recently, *Report on Cross-border E-commerce in the EU*, SEC (2009)283 final (March 2009), compiled by the Commission Working Group. This reports that 21 per cent of individuals do not use the Internet for shopping because they are worried about problems in the way complaints may be handled or failures on the part of businesses. See ec.europa.eu/consumers/strategy/docs/com_staff_wp2009_en.pdf.

[5] COM(93)576 final, p. 76.

[6] For the different systems in EU countries see Study Centre for Consumer Law, Centre for European Economic Law, Katholieke Universiteit Leuven, Belgium, *An Analysis and Evaluation of Alternative Means of Consumer Redress other than Redress through Ordinary Judicial Proceedings, Final Report* (2007). See ec.europa.eu/consumers/redress/reports_studies/comparative_report_en.pdf.

[7] Commission Recommendation of 4 April 2001 on the principles for out-of-court bodies involved in the consensual resolution of consumer disputes [2001] OJ L109 56–61.

ADR for consumer complaints appears to be the best alternative for consumers' individual requests and an element that is needed to ensure the realisation of their rights.

Therefore, the first step was to create a specific legal system, which stemmed from two resolutions. The first resolution was Commission Recommendation 98/257/EC on the principles applicable to the bodies responsible for out-of-court settlement of consumer disputes.[8] This Recommendation only regulated ADR systems that involve the intervention of a third party who proposes or imposes a solution. The second resolution was Commission Recommendation 2001/310/EC of 4 April on the principles for out-of-court bodies involved in the consensual resolution of consumer disputes (2001 Recommendation),[9] which applies to all those procedures which, no matter what they are called, attempt to resolve a dispute by bringing the parties together to convince them to find a solution by common consent (article 1). In the scope of application of this Recommendation, mediation should certainly be referred to as a specific method of ADR.

Therefore, ADR methods for dealing with consumer complaints are bound by a specific legal system. This system predates the general civil mediation regulations within the European Union, but is based on the same principles. In fact, Point 9 of the Preamble to Directive 2008/52/EC on certain aspects of civil and commercial matters indicated that this area is outside its scope of application, along with other practices which are not considered to be mediation. In this case, however, it is simply stated that 'consumer complaint systems' are excluded, i.e., any conflict resolution mechanism, whether or not it involves mediation, is excluded if it is used in the area of consumer complaints.

In accordance with this idea, all consumer complaints are excluded as they have their own general ADR system laid out in the two abovementioned sets of Community Recommendations. That is why the Proposed ADR Directive aims to offer a standard level of consumer protection throughout the European Union by means of developing a network of ADR entities that share common principles and are able to work together to resolve disputes. This represents the first attempt to harmonise the ADR system.

[8] Commission Recommendation 98/257/EC of 30 March 1998 on the principles applicable to the bodies responsible for out-of-court settlement of consumer disputes [1998] OJ L115 31–4.

[9] Recommendation, n. 7 above, at 56–61.

### Diversity of ADR systems across Europe: the search for standards

The choice of ADR is made without considering the promotion of any one ADR system in particular. The above-mentioned legal framework is broad enough to admit almost any ADR system and does not focus on the type of process but on the main principles: confidentiality, transparency, impartiality and fairness. These characteristics are thought to set down a minimum standard for consumers to gain access to 'alternative' justice.

Consequently, each country has developed its own system, which is why a wide range of ADR is currently used throughout the European Union. It is not yet clear whether this heterogeneity is a problem or not. Nevertheless, it definitely has two main consequences: first, it makes the system inconsistent in cases of cross-border transactions and can make cross-border claims rather unfruitful; and, secondly, it makes it difficult to establish an equivalent standard of individual redress in consumer resolution in the European Union and can render individual redress impossible. Thus, to ensure effective consumer access to justice, some additional general standards are needed in consumer ADR to improve accessibility and efficiency. In this sense, the Proposed ADR Directive does not impose a unique model of ADR, it only recognises any ADR that complies with a set of principles: impartiality, transparency, effectiveness and fairness in the terms described by the Proposal. Additionally, the proposals cover arbitration, mediation, conciliation and complaint boards' processes.[10] Only direct negotiation between the parties and systems depending on the trader are out of its scope of application.[11] Nevertheless, this proposed text offers many items subject to national choice, for instance, the binding dimension of the resolution.

That is why we will try to go a step beyond heterogeneity, to focus on the study of a specific system and a description of the choices that are involved in its implementation within the EU legal framework. In doing so we have used the *Civic Consulting Study on the Use of ADR in the European Union, Final Report* (October 2009).[12] This study identifies all of the ADR systems

[10] The proposed ADR Directive states in art. 2: 'this Directive shall apply to procedures for the out-of-court resolution of contractual disputes arising from the sale of goods or provision of services by a trader established in the Union to a consumer resident in the Union through the intervention of a dispute resolution entity which proposes or imposes a solution or brings the parties together with the aim of facilitating an amicable solution, hereinafter "ADR procedures"'.

[11] See Preamble, para. 12 and art. 2 of this Proposal.

[12] Civic Consulting, *Final Report to DG SANCO: Study on the Use of Alternative Dispute Resolution in the EU* (2009), available at ec.europa.eu/consumers/redress_cons/adr_study.pdf.

that are used in EU countries, showing that 750 ADR systems are suitable for business to consumer (B2C) disputes; however, the Commission has only been notified of around 462 (60 per cent) of these. The purpose of this study is to find the common ground that exists in ADR systems. Three crucial factors have been identified in this regard: whether the solution is binding for one or both parties; whether the system is general or sector-specific; and finally, the main problems detected: a lack of consumer ADR knowledge and companies' lack of interest in adopting the system. Analysis of these factors can tell us whether a specific ADR system could serve as a general option or not.

For this reason, we have chosen the Catalan mediation system for consumer complaints. We present the conclusions of a recent study of the Catalan mediation system that was supported by the Catalan Ministry of Justice, the White Paper on Mediation in Catalonia. We examine the special case of consumer mediation. First, to provide the context, we analyse the trends in ADR for Spanish consumers. Then, we describe the White Paper's conclusions, evaluating the strengths and weaknesses of the Catalan ADR system, which we will describe by way of a conclusion in the final section.

## Arbitration and mediation in consumers' complaints in Spain: key aspects of the legal framework

In Spanish legislation, the implementation of ADR for consumers' complaints predates European instruments (Recommendations 1998 and 2001). The Spanish system was introduced in General Act 22/1984 of 19 July 1984 for the Protection of Consumers and Users, which led to the creation of a dispute resolution system with decisions being 'final and binding on both parties'.[13] As Maluquer de Motes points out,[14] this precept falls within article 51 of the Spanish Constitution, which calls for 'effective procedures' for the protection of consumers that safeguard their health, safety and economic rights. Finally, Regulation 636/1993, adopting the arbitration system in consumers' affairs, ratifies this and opts for a system of institutional arbitration in a process that offers

[13] Replaced by Royal Legislative Decree 1/2007 of 16 November 2007, adopting the reformulated text of the General Act for Protection of Consumers and Users and other related regulations (BOE no. 287, 30 November, 287). See arts. 57 and 58.

[14] C.J. Maluquer de Motes Bernet, comment on Article 1 in Guilarte Gutiérrez, (ed.), *Comentarios prácticos a la Ley de arbitraje* (Lex Nova, Valladolid, 2004), p. 56.

consecutive phases of mediation and arbitration.[15] Thus, mediation is a matter of choice.

Since then, the Catalan Institute for Consumer Protection, which is now the Catalan Agency for Consumer Protection,[16] has developed a mediation system that should be used before an arbitration process is started. The regional government stresses the use of ADR based on the autonomy of the parties who can reach an agreement (mediation), before going on to a process in which a third party imposes a solution (arbitration). In a mediation process, an independent third party attempts to lead the conflicting parties to reach an agreement which is suitable for both of them, on a win-win basis.

This issue is even more evident in the most recent legislation, Regulation 231/2008 of 15 February 2008 regulating the consumer arbitration system (*Sistema Arbitral de Consumo*). In this text, mediation is seen as the first phase in the process (articles 37 and 38). However, this phase has sufficient conceptual independence, and can be used to reach an agreement between the two parties. Therefore, since 2008, the system has brought together both single party and third party ADR systems.[17]

The Catalan Consumer Code (CCCat)[18] goes even further within this legal framework: mediation is regulated in articles 132.2 and 132.3 as an independent ADR system that is used before going to arbitration. Its special features are defined: it is a voluntary process in which mediators, in an impartial and confidential way, help the parties to reach a binding solution. Therefore, the White Paper examined the specific application of these categories. This chapter will now analyse the consequences of the

[15] On consequences of a consumer arbitration system organised by the state, see C.J. Maluquer de Motes, 'El arbitraje de consumo como instrumento de calidad al servicio del consumidor y del empresario' in C.E. Florensa Tomas (ed.), *El arbitraje de consumo* (Tirant Monografías, Valencia, 2004).

[16] See Law 9/2004 of 24 December 2004, creating the Catalan Consumer Agency (Agència Catalana del Consum), DOGC no. 4291, 30 December 2004.

[17] About the Spanish mediation system in respect of consumers' complaints, see M. Blanco Carrasco, 'La alternativa de la mediación en conflictos de consumo: presente y futuro' (2009) 42 *Anuario jurídico y económico escurialense* 129; M. Blanco Carrasco, *Mediación y consumidores* (Instituto nacional de Consumo, Madrid, 2005); M.J. Cazorla González, 'La mediación de consumo en el arbitraje institucional' in Universitat Oberta de Catalunya (UOC), Internet Interdisciplinary Institute (IN3), *2009 Workshop Internacional sobre ADR/ODRs. Construyendo puentes: marco jurídico y principios* (15 September 2009), available at www.uoc.edu/symposia/adr/.

[18] See Law 22/2010 of 20 July 2010, adopting the Catalan Consumer Code *(Codi de consum de Catalunya).*

choice made in terms of creating a European standard for consumer redress through ADR.

## Catalan White Paper on Mediation and mediation in consumer complaints

In many of the Autonomous Communities, consumer protection is a federal responsibility, and Catalonia already had an arbitration and mediation system, which had existed since the 1990s. Therefore, in 2009, the Catalan Government launched an ambitious project that aimed to provide an overview of mediation in Catalonia, directed by Casanovas, Lauroba and Magre.[19] The study included a working group on mediation in consumer disputes that this author coordinated. Data was collected from all the bodies that offer consumer mediation services, which are either funded by the government or private enterprises.[20] This wide-ranging research project ended in October 2010 with the publication of the White Paper on Mediation in Catalonia. Mediation in consumer law is widely analysed in Chapter 5 'Mediation in consumer complaints'.[21]

In this contribution, we will focus on the Catalan system and particularly on consumer mediation services, using some of the White Paper's results. In a quantitative approach, the White Paper collected data from the mediation services that existed in Catalonia in 2008. This data included basic statistics on the mediation processes that were carried out in 2008, as well as relevant data about the mediators, parties and the mediation process. Regarding the qualitative data involved, open interviews were carried out with a selected group of mediators. We use their answers in relation to some relevant findings.

### *Some figures: active mediation services and mediation processes*

In 2008, eighty-five active mediation services were identified in Catalonia. These services covered both internal and cross-border mediation and institutional and private services. We collected data from all of these services.

[19] The White Paper process, set up by a Catalan Government Agreement of 7 November 2008, was based on foundation work: Obra social de La caixa.

[20] Complete study available at www.llibreblancmediacio.com.

[21] I. Barral-Viñals and J. Suquet Capdevila, 'La mediación en el ámbito del consumo' in Casanovas, Lauroba and Magre, *Libro Blanco de la mediación en Cataluña*, n. 1 above, at p. 301 ff.

Three levels of public bodies are involved in mediation: Consumer Arbitration Boards[22] (operating at federal and municipal level); the offices of public information for consumers (municipal consumer offices); and the county offices of public information for consumers.[23]

Regarding arbitration boards, there is a federal board, the Consumer Arbitration Board of Catalonia, and nine municipal boards. A total of sixty-one municipal offices of consumer information (OMIC) were identified, five of which have a different name but carry out the same task. Finally, the county offices of consumer information (OCIC) are assigned to the county councils.

As for private mediation, we collected data from the most representative consumer associations.[24] The following were consulted: Organització de Consumidors i Usuaris de Catalunya (Organisation of Consumers and Users of Catalonia, OCUC); Unió de Consumidors de Catalunya (Consumers' Union of Catalonia, UCC); Associació de Consumidors de la Provincia de Barcelona (Consumers' Association of the Province of Barcelona, ACPB); Coordinadora d'Usuaris de la Sanitat, CUS, Salut, Consum i Alimentació (Coordinator of Users of Health and Food); Federació Unió Cívica de Consumidors i Mestresses de Casa de Catalunya (Federation Civic Union of Consumers and Housewives of Catalonia, UNAE); and Associació d'impositors de Bancs i Caixes d'Estalvis de Catalunya (Association for the Defence of Consumers of Financial Products, ADICAE). Finally, the European Consumer Service of the Catalan Consumer Agency was identified as the entity in charge of cross-border mediation. (See Table 15.1.)

The results on mediation in consumer law were surprising.[25] Mediation in consumer law in Catalonia is characterised by an abundance of mediators (113), distributed throughout the territory fairly uniformly. There is a greater concentration in the metropolitan area of

[22] In Catalan, *Juntes Arbitrals de Consum.*

[23] We use 'county' as an aproximate translation for 'comarcal', pursuant to White Paper terminology, in the translation of the Conclusions and Recommendations, p. 13. See www.llibreblancmediacio.com.

[24] See arts. 37 to 39 of Royal Legislative Decree 1/2007 of 16 November 2007, adopting the reformulated text of the General Act for Protection of Consumers and Users and other related regulations (BOE no. 287, 30 November 2007) (TRLGDCU). See also Decree 23/1998 of the Catalan Government of 4 February 1998 (DOGC no. 2575, 10 February 1998) which sets out the profile of the more representative consumers' associations in Catalonia.

[25] See Chapter 5 of Barral-Viñals and Suquet Capdevila, 'La mediación en el ámbito del consumo', n. 21 above, at p. 130 ff.

Table 15.1 *Active mediation system*

| Kind of mediation service | Frequency | % |
|---|---|---|
| Catalan Agency for Consumer Protection (CACP)* | 5 | 5.88 |
| European Consumer Service (CACP) | 1 | 1.18 |
| County Consumer Services | 23 | 27.06 |
| Municipal Consumer Services | 42 | 49.41 |
| Consumer Arbitration Boards ** | 8 | 9.41 |
| Consumers Associations | 5 | 5.88 |
| Others | 1 | 1.18 |
| Total | 85 | 100 |

*Refers to the Catalan Consumer Arbitration Board
**Apart from the Catalan Consumer Arbitration Board
*Source:* White Paper on Mediation in Catalonia.

Table 15.2 *Mediations carried out in 2008*

| | Data source | | | | Total |
|---|---|---|---|---|---|
| | Cons. Assoc | Eur. Serv | CACP | Local Entities Survey* | |
| Eur. Serv. | | 972 | | | 972 |
| CACP | | | 7,440 | | 7,440 |
| Associations | 1,719 | | | | 1,719 |
| Local | | | | 12,987 | 12,987 |
| County | | | 3,596 | 821 | 4,417 |
| Consumer Arb. boards | | | | 3,186 | 3,186 |
| Others | | | | 34 | 34 |
| Total | 1,719 | 972 | 11,036 | 17,028 | 30,755 |

*Special survey on local entities conducted for the White Paper.
*Source:* White Paper on Mediation in Catalonia.

Barcelona. Their work is important, as 30,755 mediations were carried out in 2008 (see Table 15.2).

Mediation ended with an agreement in 50 per cent of the cases, although rates varied widely depending on the sector. However, very few disputes ended in administrative sanctions, except in some sectors such as electronic commerce or the carriage of passengers. We will not analyse these figures in detail here. In this survey, we now turn to analysing the trends in the system and their practical consequences.[26]

### *Mediation as a voluntary and binding process*

Mediation is legally defined as a voluntary ADR (Recommendation 2001, article 5 LMADP,[27] article 132.2.1 CCCat). Therefore, submission is voluntary for both enterprises and consumers. As a result, participation in a mediation process cannot be imposed. However, the legal framework allows enterprises to adhere to the public system of mediation and arbitration prior to a specific conflict. Consequently, firms are linked to the consumer arbitration system. The agreement to start a mediation process is defined once a consumer presents a claim against a firm (article 25 Regulation 231/2008). Nevertheless, this very well-established principle can present a practical problem in terms of awareness of the system among consumers and enterprises.

The 2001 Recommendation states that transparency is a key principle of mediation (as well as article 7 of the Proposed ADR Directive). This principle applies to mediation processes that are underway in two respects. First, it applies to information about the mediation process itself and the beginning of the process.[28] Secondly, it applies to the development of the specific processes that the parties have started. Both of these characteristics are related to the transparency principle. Compliance with this principle includes providing basic information on institutional mediation activity. The conclusion seems to be that, for

[26] *Ibid.* 313.

[27] There is a Catalan Act regarding mediation in private law matters: Law 15/2009 of 22 July 2009, DOGC no. 5432 of 30 July 2009 (LMADP). See E. Lauroba, 'Introducción: La apuesta del legislador catalán: de la mediación familiar a la mediación en el ámbito privado' in E. Lauroba, I. Barral and I. Viola (eds.), *Materiales jurídicos del Libro Blanco de la mediación en Cataluña* (Generalitat de Catalunya, Centre d'estudis jurídics i formació especialitzada, Barcelona, 2011), pp. 21 ff.

[28] Recommendation 2001/310/EC states that an essential element of mediation is the provision of information to consumers before the process starts, due to the inherent imbalance in B2B contracts. Consumers need to know the exact legal framework of a claim. This provision is the result of the fact that consumer rights are waived (art. 10 TRLGCU). Therefore, for a mediation agreement to be valid, this information must have been provided. This element may also affect the execution of an agreement. Due to the imbalance inherent in consumer relations, it is understood that the consumer needs to know the legal framework, while it is assumed that the firm already has this knowledge or has sufficient resources to find it out, such as internal legal services and lawyers.

mediation to be effective, mechanisms need to be established to ensure transparency. Hence, mediation should be promoted as an independent ADR method that can increase consumer confidence and add value for enterprises.

Consumer mediation is a one-way process, as only consumers can commence the complaint procedure. Indeed, consumer mediation has two main limitations: it only resolves a consumer's dispute with a business; and only the consumer can initiate the arbitration process (articles 33.1 and 34.1 Regulation 231/2008) and consequently, the mediation process. However, mediators and experts agree[29] that if businesses could begin the mediation process, their interest in it would increase. Bearing in mind that it is a voluntary process, the consumer might then more easily contact the company and let them know their position on the dispute. We should therefore explore the possibility of enterprises commencing the mediation process. The Proposed ADR Directive clearly goes in that direction and offers the traders the possibility of starting ADR (Preamble, para. 7).

A second main feature is that the agreement reached in a mediation process is binding for both parties (article 6 LMADP, article 132.3 CCCat). Regulation 231/2008, which governs arbitration systems, states that arbitration is binding, but says nothing about the mediation process. As discussed above, this is because the Regulation admits the mediation process as a possible ADR in consumer disputes, but does not regulate it. Therefore, the binding character of mediation must be found in the special regulation of this type of ADR (LMADP, CCCat), which applies to any mediation process. This feature makes the ADR system fairly consistent. Thus, on an initial view, mediation is a real alternative to the courts.[30]

Nevertheless, some problems can arise when one of the parties does not want to fulfil a mediation agreement. In this situation, a new dispute begins and the parties should be encouraged to start a further mediation process to find a new solution. However, as long as mediation is a voluntary process, the new mediation can only be of use when both parties agree to it. In other cases, as Viola states, a binding process must be supported by an enforcement/administrative system that allows the parties to request compliance with the agreement. In the Spanish case, enforcement is currently a matter for the courts and mediation agreements need to fulfil some formal requirements (a public document),

[29] Barral-Viñals and Suquet Capdevila, n. 21 above, at pp. 333 and 334.

[30] As the conclusions of the White Paper show, this statement is only true in a general sense.

which they normally do not have. Therefore, in practice, non-compliance with a mediation agreement leads to the start of an arbitration process, because it is easier to take an arbitration agreement to the courts to ensure its enforcement.[31] Hence, binding agreements are one of the strengths of the system, because the parties can rely on them. However, they do not solve the enforcement problem.

### *A matter of choice: institutional, free of charge and general mediation system*

#### Institutional mediation

In the Spanish system, mediation in consumers' affairs is carried out primarily from an institutional perspective. The consumer arbitration system, which offers consumers a tool with which to solve disputes, is a public service. As shown in Table 15.2, the mediation system mainly relies on *institutional mediation* (94.41 per cent of all mediation processes) for both internal and cross-border disputes. The private mediation services offered by consumers' associations only account for 5.59 per cent of the total.

This fact is very relevant, particularly when considering that mediation is offered as a public service and is free. Nevertheless, this institutional organisation has some interesting consequences for the everyday mediation process. An important White Paper finding is related to the expectations of the parties before they start a mediation process. Although the principles of impartiality and neutrality are very well-established, as EU and Spanish legislation dictates, both consumers and firms perceive that there is *no neutrality*. This certainly affects the development of the mediation process. The mediation system must clearly react to these perceptions, which really show a lack of knowledge or even a misunderstanding of this kind of ADR. Mediation is based on helping parties to reach a consensus solution to their dispute; such work is undermined if both parties consider that the system is incapable of offering an equitable solution.

This is a weak point in the mediation system. As it is an institutional ADR system, consumers think that the mediator should have 'favourable neutrality' towards them. However, as a result, enterprises perceive

[31] See I. Viola Demestre, 'La forma de la mediación y sus acuerdos (espeical referencia a al Ley 15/2009, de 22 de julio, sobre mediación en el ámbito privado)' in Lauroba *et al.*, n. 27 above, at p. 408 ff.

that they receive 'unfavourable neutrality'. Indeed, the mediator first has to convince the parties that he/she is a neutral and impartial party whose aim is to help them to reach a solution to the conflict. In the end, the parties must be persuaded to be flexible and willing to yield to mediation and find a satisfactory agreement for both of them.

Consumers tend to have a perception of favourable neutrality, because public consumer services have the primary goal of defending their interests. This consumer perception of favourable neutrality builds expectations that are too high and hinders agreement. As a result, consumers are rarely ready to accept the win-win basis that is required in mediation.

However, this misunderstanding of neutrality can be minimised if consumers are aware of the legal framework that applies to their cases. This empowerment helps them to consider the fairness of their complaint and the possibility of reaching a good agreement. For this reason, prior information about the legal framework is essential to ensure that consumers reach agreements that can meet their expectations. Hence, Recommendation 2001 (B.1,e) specifies transparency in mediation organisations and a need to inform the parties about the legal framework, as does article 7 of the Proposed ADR Directive. Nevertheless, mediators cannot provide this information, because it could affect their neutrality. The best solution should be the introduction of independent (online?) information systems. This problem can also occur in private mediation, when consumer associations try to mediate in their members' disputes.

The above-mentioned perceived lack of neutrality also discourages enterprises from using mediation. In this case, the problem is an inverse misrepresentation of neutrality, as firms tend to perceive the 'unfavourable neutrality' of institutional mediation services. The main consequence of this is that firms are reluctant to start mediation. This perception also leads to passivity, which increases the duration of the process. Companies tend to accept this kind of institutional mediation only with great suspicion. It is difficult to say whether they agree with the results because of the mediation process or because they simply want to avoid sanctions and coercive administrative power. Thus, we can say that the perception of unfavourable neutrality is not related to high expectations that hinder the agreement, as in the case of consumers, but to distrust towards the institutional mediation process, which reduces the willingness for active participation.

A possible solution would be to create a *trust label* for enterprises that accept mediation processes in cases of consumer complaint. The utility of such a label seems to be clear, as in 30 per cent of mediated disputes that did not result in an agreement the enterprises did not want to go on to an arbitration process.[32] Therefore, despite the perception of unfavourable neutrality, the mediation process has an added value for companies. A trust label would generate confidence in consumers and would distinguish enterprises in terms of their fairness.

### *Free of charge, small claims and 'alternative' systems*

The fact that the institutional system is the main mediation service is linked to an important aspect: it is *free of charge*, neither consumers nor enterprises have to pay for this service. The costs of mediation are met by the government department that offers the service. However, each party must pay the costs of gathering evidence at their request. Such costs may be redistributed in the subsequent arbitration process if the arbitration body considers that one side has acted recklessly or in bad faith (article 45 Regulation 231/2008). The costs of institutional mediation as a public service are high and unavoidable. However, in the current financial situation, new funding sources need to be explored. This system may now be too expensive and, for that reason, the introduction of lower fees should be considered to prevent undue claims.

The fact that mediation is free leads to a general awareness that small claims should be resolved through this truly alternative system. In fact, in consumer law, mediation is always understood as an 'alternative' dispute resolution system. Moreover, the Regulation specifies that in an arbitration process, the same facts cannot have been presented before any other judicial body or arbitration board. Hence, mediation as a phase of the arbitration process always acts as an alternative dispute resolution system to court processes.

Another factor which has a considerable impact is that consumers are not usually interested in going to court to resolve disputes if they involve small claims. The 2004 Eurobarometer survey on public access to justice stated that only 18 per cent of the surveyed population would go to court for claims between €500 and €100, while 11 per cent would go to court for claims between €200 and €100. However, even in these groups, 54 per cent stated that they would not go to court if the investment was too

[32] Barral-Viñals and Suquet Capdevila, n. 21 above, at pp. 331, 351 and 361.

high in relation to the purchase price.[33] This perception has been endorsed by interviews with mediators: the amounts involved in mediations range from cents to thousands of euros.

This is not the only view of small claims. In the United Kingdom, a Small Claims Mediation Service was set up in 2008. Intra-judicial mediation is voluntary when parties go to court for cases valued at less than £5,000. This system is producing good results (73 per cent of mediations are resolved by agreement). Nevertheless, the context is different, since the cost of a legal claim in this area is £25 when legal representation is not needed, so mediation is not an alternative.[34]

However, this solution is perhaps not so different from the Spanish context. Article 750 of the Spanish Procedural Code provides the opportunity to go to trial without representation for disputes that involve less than €1,200. This path does not overlap in case of disputes of little value. However, in some cases, it can be an interesting system for the consumer, instead of mediation and arbitration. It is also an option when mediation has been unsuccessful. Therefore, we should explore the relationship between mediation of consumer complaints and lawsuits and assess to what extent an intra-judicial system of mediation could be linked to the current system of mediation in consumer law.[35]

Bearing this question in mind, the Spanish Royal-Decree 5/2012 on Civil and Commercial Mediation[36] provides online mediation for claims of less than €600 (article 24). This provision will be mandatory, provided that the parties have access to the system. It supported the same idea as Additional Disposition 4a, which envisages the creation of an application for simplified electronic mediation for mass-claims with no dispute on legal grounds.

Therefore, we detected a tendency to accommodate claims of little economic value. Catalonia clearly chooses the path of ADR and mediation, but we cannot ignore the existence of other systems that provide access to the courts.

[33] Special Eurobarometer, *European Union Citizens and Access to Justice* (2004), pp. 28, 32 ff, available at ec.europa.eu/consumers/redress/reports_studies/eurobarometer_11-04_en.pdf.

[34] J. Tagg, 'The Small Claims Mediation Service in England and Wales' in *Materials of the Premières Assises Internationales de la Médiation Judiciaire. La médiation, langage universel de reglèment des conflits* (Paris, 2009).

[35] In addition, there has recently been an effort to allow these types of claims at European level. The small claims court case has been established in Europe to simplify, streamline and reduce legal costs for claims that amount to no more than €2,000.

[36] See Royal Decree-Law 5/2012 of 5 March 2012, Mediation in Civil and Commercial Matters.

### *General system in specific sectors*

The institutional mediation system in Catalonia and Spain is general. In other words, any complaint can be mediated provided that there is a consumer law relationship. Consequently, prior to admitting a claim, the governmental body should examine whether the dispute is a consumer law dispute. We find two items to support this. The first involves the concept of the consumer (article 3 TRLGDCU): a person (even a legal entity) acting in a purpose outside of his/her trade. The second is the concept of a consumer law relationship in the CCCat, article 111–2-m:

> Any relationship between, on the one hand, employers, professionals or public administration as a provider of goods and services and, on the other, the consumers. This includes information regarding the offer, promotion, advertising, marketing, use, sale and supply of goods and services, and the obligations that arise therefrom.

Nevertheless, this wide concept can include a great variety of sectors. The only limitation is found in article 2 Regulation 231/2008, which excludes some aspects such as personal injuries, death or criminal causes.

Despite the general system, disputes mainly occur in specific sectors: telephone/Internet shopping, carriage of passengers (air tickets, delays and loss of baggage), and supplies (gas, electricity and water). Sixty-eight per cent of the total mediations take place in these sectors. Forty per cent of these mediations involve the telephone/Internet sector. This figure is much higher than the percentages for the other two most problematic sectors. Except in the shopping sector, which is more varied, the other problematic sectors are dominated by large companies in a quasi-oligopoly that have a clear position of dominance over the consumer (see Table 15.3).

Most of the disputes that are mediated are related to *mass contracting*, which means that goods and services are offered to all potential consumers in an undifferentiated way. In terms of mediation, this results in a clear similarity between the disputes that often reflects the normal business practices in the different sectors. Thus, there is similarity in the motives and intentions: telephony, airlines and supplies tend to produce a series of basic types of dispute that are repeated. In addition, such services generate virtually identical points of dispute on specific problems. The repetition in the relationship means that a mediation process can become a benchmark for a company.

Table 15.3 *Mediation by sectors*

| | CACP | | Local Entities Survey | | Eur. Serv | | Total General | |
|---|---|---|---|---|---|---|---|---|
| Sector | Freq. | % | Freq. | % | Freq. | % | Freq | % |
| Hotels | 92 | 1.4 | 46 | 0.4 | 82 | 8.4 | 220 | 1.0 |
| Laundry | 49 | 0.8 | 64 | 0.6 | 0 | 0.0 | 113 | 1.0 |
| Others | 287 | 4.4 | 20 | 0.2 | 19 | 2.0 | 326 | 2.0 |
| Travel agencies | 303 | 4.6 | 62 | 0.6 | 13 | 1.3 | 378 | 2.0 |
| Electronic commerce | 202 | 3.1 | 63 | 0.6 | 67 | 6.9 | 332 | 2.0 |
| Transportation | 109 | 1.7 | 126 | 1.2 | 35 | 3.6 | 270 | 2.0 |
| Vehicles | 248 | 3.8 | 118 | 1.1 | 51 | 5.2 | 417 | 2.0 |
| Services | 277 | 4.2 | 286 | 2.8 | 59 | 6.1 | 622 | 3.0 |
| Financial services | 214 | 3.3 | 325 | 3.1 | 1 | 0.1 | 540 | 3.0 |
| Electric devices | 259 | 4.0 | 671 | 6.5 | 21 | 2.2 | 951 | 5.0 |
| Housing | 169 | 2.6 | 705 | 6.8 | 10 | 1.0 | 884 | 5.0 |
| Professionals services | 592 | 9.1 | 251 | 2.4 | 0 | 0.0 | 843 | 5.0 |
| Commodities | 523 | 8.0 | 853 | 8.2 | 0 | 0.0 | 1,376 | 8.0 |
| Carriage of passengers | 766 | 11.7 | 242 | 2.3 | 613 | 63.1 | 1,621 | 9.0 |
| Commerce of goods | 1,037 | 15.9 | 844 | 8.2 | 1 | 0.1 | 1,882 | 11.0 |
| Telephone/ Internet | 1,399 | 21.4 | 5,668 | 54.8 | 0 | 0.0 | 7,067 | 40.0 |
| Total | 6,526 | 100 | 10,344 | 100 | 972 | 100 | 17,842 | 100 |

*Source:* White Paper on Mediation in Catalonia.

In addition to the fact that most mediation occurs in a few sectors, most claims are made in relation to a small number of companies. In the four Spanish sectors mentioned above, most of the claims are made against fewer than ten companies. Hence, in practice, the general system works as a sector-based system: 70 per cent of mediations are carried out in relation to specific sectors, in particular network industries (gas, electricity and water supply services) and telecommunications, which are the most mediated sectors in Spain.

### *Overlap: 'financial services' and circuitous actions*

Finally, we will refer to a very interesting finding in this study in relation to financial services. Here there is an overlap in the general mediation system in the case of financial services, in which other ADR methods are implemented legally. The main problem is that different bodies can 'solve' the problem, so circuitous actions can arise. In fact, it is noteworthy that the legal framework of financial services creates circuitous actions. Therefore, it is difficult to channel an agreement between the parties in mediation processes. Indeed, Law 44/2002 of 22 November 2002 on Reforming the Financial System (articles 29 and 30)[37] states that credit institutions may have an ombudsman to receive, analyse and respond to complaints about financial services. The above-mentioned law also organises the customer services of these entities, which act, if possible, as specialised management offices to process and resolve customer requests. These offices are usually used prior to appealing to the ombudsman.

The ombudsmen are not mediators. As the White Paper has highlighted,[38] this system is not a third party system, as the commissioner or the ombudsman is appointed by the company and forms part of its structure, except when a single commissioner is appointed for a group of companies. However, such commissioners cannot be qualified as 'third parties', despite the prestige that they may have as professionals.

Table 15.3 shows that we found a significant percentage of complaints about financial products (214 in CACP, and 325 in local entities, in a total of 540). Agreements were reached through mediation on issues such as credit cards. In this case, the mediators indicated that they received consumer complaints and conveyed them to the company, which usually answered by referring the question to their customer services or to commissioners and ombudsmen. Thus, the mediator usually only played a limited role as an intermediary, channelling the answers. Consequently, in this case, there is an *overlapping system of ADR* from the point of view of consumers, which ends in a circuitous action. If the customer services, the ombudsman or the commissioner do not resolve a conflict, or the resolution goes against the bank or financial institution, the company is unlikely subsequently to accept institutional mediation. It will consider

[37] BOE no. 281, 23 November 2002.

[38] I. Barral, E. Lauroba, A. Marín, C. Martí, J.M. Tamarit, A. Vidal and I. Viola, 'El concepto jurídico de mediación' in P. Casanovas, L. Díaz. J. Magre and M. Poblet (eds.), *Materiales del Libro Blanco de la Mediación en Cataluña* (Generalitat de Catalunya, Centre d'Estudis Jurídics i Formació Especialitzada, Barcelona, 2009), p. 181 ff.

that the conflict has already been through its own binding systems of dispute resolution.[39] In our opinion this process is very similar to mediation. However, contact with a bank's ombudsman, who is potentially a neutral body, never has this characteristic.

Therefore, a general system is a valid answer because it is easier to promote and can be easier for consumers to understand. Nevertheless, the White Paper clearly shows us the limits of a general system that is focused on four main sectors and that can generate circuitous actions in some specific sectors, such as financial services.

## Concluding remarks

The ADR methods that are used in consumer disputes throughout Europe vary considerably, a situation that does not help cross-border mediation. Therefore, we propose ADR harmonisation as a way of achieving a more effective protection of consumers in Europe.

The Catalan Ministry of Justice launched a wide-ranging research project that ended in October 2010 with the publication of the White Paper on Mediation in Catalonia, in which mediation in consumers' disputes was widely analysed. The results of this White Paper illustrate the main features of this type of ADR, and the main consequences of the legal and practical choices. These results can be useful in the search for ADR standards that would increase the efficiency of mediation systems more generally.

The mediation system that was analysed is a voluntary process that leads to a binding solution. The system is general, institutional and free of charge. In addition to these main characteristics, the following points may help us to devise a general approach to ADR systems:

- A voluntary and binding process is a good choice, if we can offer good administrative mechanisms in case of unwillingness to meet the terms of the agreement.
- Similarly, an institutionalised system of ADR is a good option in terms of policy, but can become too expensive for the government. Perhaps a low fee should be considered in order to prevent undue claims. Other pathways should be explored for small claims.
- Consumer disputes typically involve small amounts and are usually settled outside the courts. Nevertheless, mediation as part of a court

[39] I. Barral-Viñals and Suqvet Capdevila, n. 21 above, at p. 326 ff.

process should be explored when consumers wish to bring an action against a company. Moreover, ADR and the court system are not comparable in situations in which consumers would not go to court but would use the mediation system. In this case, mediation processes have to be added to court disputes.

- Consumers tend to perceive that institutional ADR systems have 'favourable neutrality', but this means that enterprises perceive that there is 'unfavourable neutrality'. This is a weakness of the system, which can lead to it failing. In the case of consumers, prior information about the legal framework of the complaint can be very useful to empower them and encourage consumers to see the mediator as a real third party. From the companies' point of view, the creation of a trust label would increase confidence in mediation schemes.
- The White Paper clearly shows us the limits of a general system of ADR for consumers. For example, mediation mainly takes place in four main sectors and can generate circuitous actions in some specific sectors, such as financial services. Nevertheless, a general system is a valid solution because it is easier to promote and may be easier for consumers to understand.

# 16

## Conclusions: the transformation of European private law

JAMES DEVENNEY AND MEL B. KENNY

The intervention of EU law in national legal systems has led to the emergence of a 'wildly unsystematic'[1] body of secondary law and an unstable emergent 'Europeanised' private law[2] in which 'vertical' EU secondary law combines unevenly with divergent national transpositions and judicial interpretations.[3] Historically, this instability strengthened the case for further legislative intervention notwithstanding that the elaboration of a single *ius commune*[4] would require Treaty revision.[5] Yet functionalism, rather than a coherent, systemic approach, was the dominant characteristic of the body of law which emerged.[6] Indeed, initially, it was envisaged that EC law would simply erode national private law, a process dubbed 'negative integration',[7] and subsequent re-regulation under Articles 94 and 95 EC (now 115

[1] S. Weatherill, 'The Consumer Rights Directive: How and Why a Quest for "Coherence" has (Largely) Failed' (2012) 49 *CML Rev.* 1279, 1280.

[2] See generally, M. Kenny, 'Options between Legislative Intervention and Judicial Collaboration: Improving the Effectiveness and Coherence of EU Law?' (2012) 63 *NILQ* 435; R. Brownsword, H.-W. Micklitz, L. Niglia and S. Weatherill (eds.), *The Foundations of European Private Law* (Hart, Oxford, 2012).

[3] See C. Twigg-Flesner, '"Good-Bye Harmonisation by Directives, Hello Cross-border Only Regulation?" A Way Forward for EU Consumer Contract Law' (2011) *ERCL* 235.

[4] C. von Bar, 'From Principles to Codification: Prospects for European Private Law' (2002) 8 *Colum. J Eur. L* 379; O. Lando, 'Does the European Union Need a Civil Code' (2003) *RIW* 1.

[5] S. Weatherill, 'Why Object to the Harmonisation of Private Law by the EC?' (2004) 12 *ERPL* 636.

[6] N. Reich, 'A Common Frame of Reference (CFR): Ghost or Host for Integration?' (2006) 24 *Wis. Int'l Law J* 425.

[7] W. Sauter, 'The Economic Constitution of the EU' (1998) 4 *Colum. J Eur. L* 27; N. Reich, 'Europe's Economic Constitution, or: A New Look at Keck' (1999) *OJLS* 337.

and 114 TFEU).[8] However, outside the field of Europeanisation, national laws continued to apply and national legal demarcations within the Law of Obligations and its often complex relationship with the Law of Property held their diverse validities. To this backdrop the case for consolidation, or even codification, appears vital. Indeed, the prize of a European Civil Code, just as the introduction of a common currency, reinforces the functionalism at the heart of the European project.

Predictably, a plurality of reform proposals aimed at both substantive legislative intervention and procedural judicial realignment and collaboration followed:

- legislative intervention in the name of 'greater coherence':[9] initiatives variously advocating a shift to 'maximum' harmonisation;[10] a fully-fledged EU Civil Code pursuant to the Draft Common Frame of Reference (DCFR) initiative;[11] and/or an optional 'Common European Sales Law' (CESL) applicable to cross-border transactions;[12]
- judicial realignment: involving such steps as abandoning the CJEU's interpretative monopoly under the reference mechanism of Article 267 TFEU;[13] and/or allowing private parties a right of appeal to the CJEU on questions of interpretation;[14]
- deeper judicial collaboration, in recognition of a 'coordinate legal order', between national and supranational courts.[15]

Drilling down into the legislative process of 'Europeanising' private law, and set against a backdrop of a European Union in turmoil, a

[8] N. Reich, 'Economic Law, Consumer Interests and EU Integration' in H.-W. Micklitz *et al.* (eds.), *Understanding EU Consumer Law* (Intersentia, Antwerp, 2009), pp. 30–7.

[9] European Commission, *Action Plan on a More Coherent European Contract Law*, COM (2003)68 final.

[10] Consumer Policy Strategy 2002–2006, COM(2002)208 final [2002] OJ C137/2; Consumer Policy Strategy 2007–2013: Empowering Consumers, Enhancing their Welfare, Effectively Protecting them, COM(2007)99 final.

[11] C. von Bar and E. Clive, *Principles, Definitions and Model Rules of European Private Law: Draft Common Frame of Reference* (Oxford University Press, 2010).

[12] Introduction of the Optional Instrument, the Common European Sales Law, 11 October 2011, available at http://ec.europa.eu/justice/newsroom/news/20111011_en.htm.

[13] Per AG Villalón in C-173/09 *Elchinov* v. *Natsionalna zdravnoosiguritelna kasa*, judgment of 5 October 2010, casenote: A.P. van der Mei (2011) 48 *CML Rev.* 1297.

[14] M. Schillig, 'Inequality of Bargaining Power versus Market for Lemons: Legal Paradigm Change and the Court of Justice's Jurisprudence on Directive 93/13 on Unfair Contract Terms' (2008) 33 *EL Rev.* 336.

[15] C.F. Sabel and O. Gerstenberg, 'Constitutionalizing an Overlapping Consensus: The ECJ and the Emergence of a Coordinate Constitutional Legal Order' (2010) 16 *ELJ* 511.

number of specific and sometimes inconsistent initiatives have emerged: the work on the consolidation of the consumer acquis; the tapering of the Consumer Rights Directive; the magnitude of the Draft Common Frame of Reference; the European Commission's appointment of an Expert Group on a Common Frame of Reference in the Area of European Contract Law; the Commission's incendiary *Green Paper on Policy Options for Progress towards a European Contract Law for Consumers and Businesses*; the controversial proposal for an optional Common European Sales Law; and ongoing debate on the Grand Design of a European Civil Code.

So what of the future direction for European private law? This book addresses this question from a variety of perspectives: a comparative perspective (Waddams, Giliker, Amato), the law and economics standpoint (Halson and Campbell), a law and language approach (Perfumi) and the historical view (Swain). Additionally, the work engages with the substance of what has been addressed within the DCFR/CESL initiative (Kenny and Devenney), the alteration of private law discourse (Cherednychenko) as well as the debate on the (necessary) outer limits and exclusions from this transformation (Sparkes). The work also addresses the more specific and challenging effects at national level within both the new accession states (Kull and Kärson) and the common law community (Kelly). Equally, specific substantive questions have been raised in the context of the impact of Europeanisation on the insurance contract (Tereszkiewicz) and on the assessment of unfair terms in consumer contracts (Schillig). Finally, the work addresses broader issues relating to how or if the role of damages in the enforcement of EU law, on the one hand, and as an aspect of a compensatory regime for non-contractual liability, on the other, can be combined (Leczykiewicz) and, notwithstanding substantive consumer law harmonisation, the importance, role and characteristics of an EU ADR mechanism (Barral-Viñals).

In his contribution, 'The Draft Common Frame of Reference in relation to English contract law', Stephen Waddams drew some important conclusions on the DCFR exercise from a comparative lawyer's perspective. Waddams questions both the extent to which the DCFR accurately represents the law of the various civilian jurisdictions, and the extent to which it will ever be put to official or practical use, publicly or privately; a scepticism arguably subsequently borne out in the drafting process leading to the 2011 Directive on Consumer Rights. Waddams sees the DCFR extending well into general private law, allowing a more holistic approach to comparative questions – questions which frequently straddle multiple fields of law. But to Waddams the most important aspect of the DCFR exercise lies in its potential to enhance the quality of comparative analysis and debate more generally; in particular, Waddams anticipates that resort to the DCFR will work against the adoption of over-generalised conclusions about the law in civilian systems.

In Chapter 2, 'The Draft Common Frame of Reference and European contract law: moving from the "academic" to the "political"', Paula Giliker traces the evolution of the DCFR and its relationship to the CESL, the CESL being characterised as the 'future instrument' of European contract law. Giliker focuses, in particular, on precontractual liability to tease out the differences between the regimes and the way in which the CESL represents a more pragmatic response: the CESL confining itself, *inter alia*, to a non-excludable 'general principle' that each party has a duty to act in accordance with good faith and fair dealing. While not preventing the DCFR from being an important *point of reference* in the debate over contractual liability, the CESL thus emerges as a more autonomous instrument, distinct from the previous proposals for harmonised principles of European contract law.

Similarly, Cristina Amato in Chapter 3, 'the Europeanisation of contract law and the role of comparative law: the case of the Directive on Consumer Rights' adopts a comparative perspective to assess the potential improvement the DCFR could bring to bear on the legislative process. 'Bad law' in the European Union, Amato argues, results largely from an insufficiently rigorous review of legislative proposals. Moreover, Amato notes that only through the adoption of a more cautious methodology can 'targeted full harmonisation' be successful in circumventing both the regulatory 'race to the bottom' and the production of dangerous 'legal irritants'. Amato concludes by making the point that the time has come for EU institutions to think about their goals with greater precision, if a competitive tool-box is to emerge from the process.

In our chapter 'the private law dimension to the "State of the Union": (D)CFR/CESL initiatives and the Europeanisation of private law', we argue that the DCFR and CESL initiatives threaten disproportionate legislative intervention where much more circumspect steps respecting the established consumer *acquis* and the pre-existing conflicts framework may have been more appropriate. While reform needs to be more targeted to ensure that a genuine twenty-eighth regime is available to consumers in cross-border constellations, the (D)CFR/CESL initiaitve(s) go well beyond this brief and threaten, in fact, a competing rather than a purely opt-in regime which may lead to further legal fragmentation.

The suspicion must be that the proposals do more than simply assemble a tool-box, but prepare for a fragmentation out of which a broader exercise and further measures of consolidation can emerge.

In Chapter 5, 'european contract law: how to exclude land?', Peter Sparkes looks to the scope of the Europeanisation initiative in private law, criticising the legislative drafting of the DCFR and arguing that a new approach is required, one which furnishes a much more rigorous land exclusion – an exclusion which should extend to cover the law of property in movables. In Sparkes' view, only with such an exclusion would it be possible to address the sensitive issue of whether civil law can be separated between property and obligation in a manner that works for both civilian and common law systems. Given UK hostility, Sparkes predicts that any Frame of Reference which might emerge from this process may be 'Common' only within the boundaries of civilian, and not common law, assumptions.

Meanwhile, Roger Halson and Dave Campbell, from a law and economics perspective, focus on the economic argument for a European contract law, challenging the evidential basis for the proposition that differences in substantive law are a source of extensive problems between contracting parties in the European Union. Furthermore, Halson and Campbell observe that those involved in the initiative seem to perceive no need to prove the economic advantages of harmonisation because of the overarching functionalist argument, namely, that harmonisation is the inevitable corollary of membership of the European Union and its commitment to the single market. In particular, Halson and Campbell target the formulation of EU policy in this regard, attacking the European Commission's 'selective invocation of congenial evidence in support of a predetermined agenda'. Even further, to Halson and Campbell, the DCFR/CESL initiatives raise serious questions about any further extension of EU competences.

Similarly sceptically, Chiara Perfumi in Chapter 7 analyses the DCFR/CESL from a contract law terminology perspective. Perfumi argues that, to truly improve the operation of the single market, the core of the established definitions should gradually be expanded, to cover a larger range of terms applicable to the entire *acquis*. To this end, according to Perfumi, nothing less than a common and shared linguistic strategy is required. Inevitably, such an approach would have a significant impact on the legislative process. Fundamentally, to Perfumi, rather than the short-term promotion of 'artificial legislative exercise(s)', a comprehensive comparative study of European legal systems should be promoted to effectively advance any eventual consolidation measures.

Olha Cherdnychenko in Chapter 8, 'private law discourse and scholarship in the wake of the Europeanisation of private law', argues that the European Union has never shared the traditional conception of private law as it has evolved in national systems; national private law being primarily concerned with justice between market participants, the European Union viewing private law as an instrument for achieving the collective objectives of EU integration. As Cherednychenko notes, though these different conceptions may reinforce each other, they may also clash, the process of Europeanisation being marked by a profound tension between private interests and public goals, even in areas as yet untouched by EU policy encroachment, yet instrumentalised in the process of Europeanisation. Increasingly therefore, private law courts face the difficult task of reconciling private interests with collective goods. In this context, in Cherednychenko's view, it falls to legal scholars to do more to shape the emergence of Europeanised private law by elaborating what the law should say on particular issues both as regards concerns about justice between market participants but also as regards the broader policy considerations. Cherednychenko identifies an important overarching challenge as being how to avoid the over-instrumentalisation of private law discourse and to strike the right balance between public and private interests.

Meanwhile, in Chapter 9, Warren Swain draws illuminating parallels between the DCFR/CESL process and the Indian contract codification in the late nineteenth century. Swain notes that there are obvious parallels between the Indian Contract Act 1872 and the process of private law 'Europeanisation'. In Swain's view, like their Anglo-Indian counterparts, advocates of EU codification are keen both to downplay the differences between legal systems and to emphasise the practical value of codification. A particular symmetry lies in the fact that, while in India codification was driven by a profound belief in the value of codes and the type of legal system which was being promoted, European contract consolidation involves similarly 'political' choices. As Swain notes, the advocates of EU consolidation do not start from a position of neutrality. Similarly, in India, codification was bound up in the ideology of the Raj in its pomp. Swain concludes with the hope that any emergent European Contract Code does not deserve the description 'a painful and cruel infliction', applied to its Indian predecessor almost 150 years earlier.

Irene Kull and Sander Kärson look at developments from an Estonian perspective. The authors make the broader point that the challenges facing European private law are similar to the more general challenge facing the European Union: to create unity, while preserving the special differences of its constituent Member States. Kull and Kärson analyse the many obstacles to the creation of a unified European private law, yet draw consolation in the fact that contract law is still more international in substance than any of the other traditional core areas of private law. The authors go on to argue that countries such as Estonia, which had to renew its legal system in the very recent past, can be used as a testing ground for the elaboration of modern European private law.

In Chapter 11, Cliona Kelly, deals with the impact of Europeanisation on Irish contract law and draws some important conclusions from the DCFR/CESL process. Kelly observes that Irish contract law was, even before the DCFR/CESL initiatives, a neglected body of private law which was in need of comprehensive revision. Kelly notes that statutory contract law provisions dating back to 1695 remained in force in Ireland, and the lack of systematic law reform meant that there are whole areas of law where there is no contemporary legislative structure. The Irish Law Reform Commission has recommended, *inter alia*, reform of the doctrine of privity, the capacity of minors, limitation periods and the availability of exemplary and punitive damages, but the implementation of these proposals has been minimal. Change at EU level may therefore provide an opportunity to unlock the Irish contract law debate. Kelly argues that the beginnings of such developments can perhaps be made out in the establishment of the Sales Law Review Group (SLRG); yet these, arguably, only pay lipservice to the EU initiatives, meanwhile *solutions* to problems in Irish sales law were found in other common law jurisdictions, such as Australia and Canada.

Piotr Tereszkiewicz analyses, in Chapter 12, 'the Europeanisation of insurance contract law: the insurer's duty to advise and its regulation in German and European law'. To Tereskiewicz, this survey reveals the significant impact which the Insurance Mediation Directive 2002/92/EC (IMD) has had on the German Insurance Contract Act, inspiring the imposition of a duty to advise on intermediaries and insurers themselves, an instance of Europeanisation of German insurance contract law. Moreover, the IMD and German Insurance Contract Act have subsequently shaped the duty to warn now contained in the Principles of European Insurance Contract Law (PEICL). Tereskiewicz argues that both the German Insurance Contract Act and the PEICL could inspire national legislators, self-regulation in the insurance industry itself or the standard-setting function of the consumer associations. Clearly, as Tereskiewicz acknowledges, there are matters meriting further attention in this context, principally whether any comprehensive regime of advisory duties should also include criteria for judging the suitability of the insurance products themselves. Tereskiewicz concludes by arguing that the current discussion on the impact of the Markets in Financial Instruments Directive 2004/39/EC (MiFID) regime could supply a useful, additional framework by which to elaborate advisory duties.

Meanwhile, in Chapter 13, Michael Schillig deals with the lessons to be drawn from the treatment of the price exemption under the Unfair Contract Terms Directive 93/13/EC. Here, Schillig argues that, where legal rules emerge as a compromise between conflicting philosophies and are not informed by a coherent underlying rationale, a uniform and consistent interpretation and application by different national courts and the CJEU will be extremely difficult. For Schillig, more is required than a simple improvement in the drafting process; he argues that it is in their *application* by national courts that EU rules generate their practical impact. In light of the different national legal traditions, uniformity of application can only be achieved if the law is based on a meaningful and coherent rationale that can inform the methods of reasoning and interpretation in the national courts. Schillig goes on to maintain that national courts should actively seek the relevant EU dimension to the particular dispute at hand, adopting what he dubs a 'pan-European case-law methodology'. Moreover, such an approach needs to be complemented with an institutional structure which guarantees the place of the CJEU as the final interpretative authority. In this regard, Schillig argues for radical reform of the preliminary ruling mechanism, supplemented with a right to a final CJEU appeal or to a specialised CJEU panel on private law. Schillig concludes that without such steps legal fragmentation will persist and legislative intervention would fail.

Dorota Leczykiewicz analyses the potential impact of the consolidation initiative on enforcement in general and actions for damages in particular, critically asking whether a general regime of liability in damages could straddle both the national regime of non-contractual liability and the EU law damages regime. The nature and functions of damages actions as traditionally conceptualised in EU law, and the approach to the corresponding legal institutions in the DCFR are thus contrasted. Leczykiewicz explains that legal remedies in the European Union have been aimed exclusively at the effective enforcement of EU law, while the non-contractual liability regime is inspired by ideas of corrective justice and compensation. These two perspectives are seen to be, in many respects, incompatible. For example, in a system dominated by the compensatory perspectives, concepts of punitive damages, leniency, non-governmental action and proportionality could be allowed to play an important role in determining the level of damages. Leczykiewicz concludes that the EU law of non-contractual liability has to fit into the current enforcement-focused framework of EU law; that designing a general regime of liability to replace both national regimes of non-contractual liability, as well as the existing system of remedies in EU law, is a quixotic exercise.

Meanwhile, Immaculada Barral-Viñals, in a chapter complementing Leczykiewicz's focus on enforcement questions, looks to the issue of harmonisation of the European alternative dispute resolution (ADR) system, elaborating the point that harmonisation in EU consumer law is meaningless without a parallel harmonisation of EU enforcement legislation, specifically on individual redress by means of an EU ADR mechanism. In part, such a mechanism is required because of the diversity of consumer ADR mechanisms operating in the EU Member States, a diversity which renders cross-border mediation difficult. Barral-Viñals bases her insights on work undertaken on the White Paper on Mediation in Catalonia, in which mediation in consumers' disputes was widely analysed. The results of this initiative are analysed to produce a checklist of ADR standards that would increase the efficiency of mediation systems. Barral-Viñals suggests the following key features of a successful ADR mechanism: first, it takes the form of a voluntary and binding process; secondly, an institutionalised, low-fee system of ADR recommends itself; thirdly, mediation has to be carefully aligned to court processes; fourthly, information to both parties in consumer disputes is required to prevent misconceptions as to the impartiality of the process; fifthly, there are clear advantages of a generalised system in terms of application and transparency.

EU legislative intervention has thus far provided an unstable foundation for the shifting sands of the internal market. Indeed, this volume has sought to challenge some of the key assumptions underpinning the case for ever greater harmonisation. Nevertheless, calls for enhanced effectiveness and greater coherence abound and this collection has questioned the proposition that greater coherence would be the product of further measures of a *purely* traditional legislative response. Instead, a much more diverse response is required which, for example, is sensitive to linguistic, social, cultural and economic differences; a more innovative multidimensional response which, *inter alia*, recognises the complex, dynamic and often competing legal regimes and infrastructures throughout the European Union. More specifically, the sometimes chimerical quality of EU law exists for a number of important reasons: the polycontextual nature of legal doctrine across the European Union, subsidiarity and the need for the respect of national identities. As Weatherill perceptively notes '(c)oherent EU law comes at a cost: incoherent national law.'[16] EU law in this light requires something more than the responsorial Psalm of orthodox functionalism, requiring in its place discretion, competition, margins of appreciation *and* incompleteness; and this, not least, to accommodate the instability of CJEU judicial policy. In this regard, a critical review of what sort of internal market is being created and how far it is appropriate to surrender national regulatory autonomy is needed.[17]

In terms of policy development, the way events have conspired to support the introduction of a CESL and, by implication, the wider cause of codification, most recently exemplified in the European Law Institute's lobbying on the need to significantly upgrade the CESL, is sobering, especially so as a handful of practical steps might otherwise obviate the need for intervention. Again the initiative(s) seem result-oriented, with the European Commission at pains to obscure the true scale of the proposals: just as the DCFR extended well into private law, the proposed Common European Sales Law extends well into broad areas of general contract law. Such initiatives, to the extent that they would, with a new category of 'opt-in consumer law', drive further fragmentation between purely domestic and Europeanised private law, would ultimately serve as a stalking horse for further legislative intervention. Moreover, given that extension of the EU regime into broad areas of private law would entail the uncertain application of liability rules between private parties *inter se* and further reduce the margins of discretion and the field of application of national law, such intervention would produce further demarcational instability at the nexus of EU and national constitutional and private law. The danger of such policy development is clear with, once again, pragmatism and method being subverted by the imperative of the European Grand Design. Equally troubling, however, is the domestic policy context; for example, the delusional position in the United Kingdom where the branches of governance appear caught between the allure of exiting the European Union and the countervailing false perception of the essentially elective status of EU obligations.

16 Weatherill, 'The Consumer Rights Directive: How and Why a Quest for "Coherence" has (Largely) Failed', n. 1 above, at 1315.

17 *Ibid*. 1279.

# INDEX